Citizen Politics

Citizen Politics

Public Opinion and Political Parties in Advanced Industrial Democracies

THIRD EDITION

Russell J. Dalton
University of California, Irvine

CHATHAM HOUSE PUBLISHERS
SEVEN BRIDGES PRESS, LLC
NEW YORK · LONDON

Seven Bridges Press
135 Fifth Avenue, 9th Floor
New York, NY 10010-7101

Publisher: Ted L. Bolen
Managing Editor: Katharine Miller
Production Services: Linda B. Pawelchak
Composition: Lori Clinton
Cover design: Stefan Killen Design
Printing and Binding: Victor Graphics, Inc.

Library of Congress Cataloging-in-Publication Data

Dalton, Russell J.
 Citizen Politics : public opinion and political parties in advanced industrial democracies
 / Russell J. Dalton. 3rd ed.
   p. cm.
 Includes bibliographical references and index.
 ISBN 1-889119-32-6
 1. Political parties. 2. Political participation. 3. Democracy. 4. Public opinion. 5.
Comparative government I. Title.

 JF2011 .D34 2002
 323'.042—dc21   2001055967

Manufactured in the United States of America
10 9 8 7 6 5 4 3 2 1

To my three sons,
Penn, Mac, and Snickers

Contents

Tables and Figures

Tables

Figures

Preface

WHEN I BEGAN the first edition of this book in the early 1980s, many political scientists expressed open reservations about the viability of modern democracy. President Carter had lamented that "the gap between our citizens and our government had never been so wide," and prognostications about the future crisis of democracy were commonplace.

Against this background, the first edition of *Citizen Politics* argued that democracy was alive and well—if one looked at its citizens. The citizens of advanced industrial democracies believed in the democratic creed and wanted their governments to meet these expectations. The first edition presented evidence that contemporary publics were becoming more active in the political process, more likely to participate in elite-challenging activities, more likely to vote on issues and other policy criteria, and more demanding of their representatives. If democracy was in crisis, it was a crisis of institutions and not the spirit of democracy or its participants.

This contrarian argument in support of democracy was by overtaken events. The opening of the Berlin Wall, the collapse of the Soviet empire, and the global spread of democracy in the 1990s created a new euphoria for the democratic process. Even those who proclaimed the limits of democracy a few years earlier suddenly trumpeted a new wave of democratization. Suddenly it seemed that everyone was claiming that democracy represented the end of history.

One might join the new parade, but I am skeptical of fads, even those that reinforce my own views. My approach to academic trends follows Will Rogers's view of politics. He said that politics was a little like keeping your balance on board a ship. When the ship leaned left, you should lean right; when the ship leaned right, you should lean left. Thus, in revising this edition of *Citizen Politics,* I have highlighted the strengths of the democratic processes but also have examined the problems we must confront if democracy is to meet today's challenges.

Before we simply celebrate the inevitability of democracy, we should realize that advanced industrial societies are experiencing profound changes in the nature of the democratic process. New issue interests, new styles of participation, the inclusion of new groups, and new expectations for democracy are transforming the process. These changes in citizen politics create new opportunities to expand the democratic process, as well as new risks. Democracies must respond to these challenges if democratization is to continue. Indeed, I would argue that the ability to adapt is what gives democracy its strength.

This book was written in 2000 and early 2001, and it has gone to press a few months after the horrible terrorist attacks of 11 September 2001. At least in the short run, the terrorist attacks encouraged Americans to express their pride in their nation, and all Westerners reflected on the benefits of the democratic process and our freedoms. Politicians and media analysts also ceased the normal wrangling that typifies democratic politics. This was an event that can change how democracies function, although it is too soon to discern the likely direction of change. One hopes that the results will strengthen the democratic process.

This book introduces students to the knowledge we have gained about citizen political behavior, the questions that still remain, and the implications of these findings. The analyses focus on citizen politics in four nations: the United States, Great Britain, Germany, and France. In addition, this new edition expands the comparative coverage to examine these four nations in a larger cross-national context. Students of comparative politics can examine the rich variety of public opinion in different democracies. Even those interested in only a single nation can benefit from comparisons that highlight the similarities and dissimilarities across nations.

I hope this book will be of value to several audiences, but it was primarily written for classroom use in courses on comparative political parties, public opinion, and European politics. The first half of the book (chapters 1–6) introduces the principles of public opinion and the broad contours of citizen action and citizen beliefs. The second half of the book (and of the school term) could combine the chapters on party alignments (7–11) with other texts on political parties. The book concludes with a discussion of citizen attitudes toward democratic institutions and the political process.

A new feature is the addition of a data supplement from the 1996 International Social Survey Program study of the role of government. These data are used throughout the book, and a subset of items is available to instructors using this text. The list of variables is described in appendix B. I find that computer-based research projects on public opinion both enrich the subject matter of the course for students and provide them with a firsthand opportunity to understand the process of public opinion research.

At the graduate level, the book provides a useful core text for courses on West European politics or comparative political behavior. I summarize the existing knowledge in the field, as well as introduce the controversies that at present divide researchers. I hope the instructor will find that the materials facilitate discussion of the readings from primary research materials. Even senior scholars might find familiar data interpreted in new and thought-provoking ways.

Acknowledgments

AS IN THE first edition, this research has benefited from the advice and criticisms of my colleagues, as well as students who have used this text. More than my own efforts, this book reflects the insights I have gained from working with other scholars. I am forever indebted to Kendall Baker and Kai Hildebrandt for their collaboration on *Germany Transformed*. Many of the themes we first explored in that book appear in more comparative terms in these pages. I was also fortunate to work with an exceptional group of scholars on the *Political Action* project. This project shaped my understanding of political participation. More important, many of these individuals have become career-long colleagues and friends: Samuel Barnes, Max Kaase, Hans-Dieter Klingemann, and M. Kent Jennings. Most recently, Marty Wattenberg and I collaborated on an edited study of party change, *Parties without Partisans*, and I have borrowed shamelessly from the ideas in that book and have benefited from Marty's advice.

During the writing of this book, many others helped with advice, survey data, or moral support. Paul Abramson, Paul Beck, Scott Flanagan, Dieter Fuchs, Manfred Kuechler, Michael Lewis-Beck, Mary MacIntosh, Robert Rohrschneider, and Martin Wattenberg commented on the manuscript throughout the various editions. An equal debt is due to the students at the University of California, Irvine, who have used this book and shared their reactions. Several chapters were revised in the Strawberry Fields Clubhouse in Irvine, where social capital is constantly being created.

I also want to acknowledge a special debt to Ronald Inglehart. Ron was my mentor at the University of Michigan, and his provocative views about citizen politics have deeply influenced my own thinking. He has developed the World Values Survey as a true treasure-house for social science research, and many of the analyses in this book are based on World Values Survey data. I have constantly admired Ron's enthusiasm for social research and his creativity as a scholar. In innumerable ways, I am in his debt.

I would like to thank Michele Budz for her care in compiling the index.

This book has a bold objective: to provide an overview of the nature of citizen politics in advanced industrial democracies. The task is clearly beyond the means of any one individual, but with a little help from these friends, the resulting product can begin to outline the political changes, and political choices, that today face the citizenry in advanced industrial democracies.

CHAPTER 1
Introduction

THIS IS A book about people—as citizens, voters, protesters, campaign workers, community activists, party members, and political spectators, they are the driving force of the democratic process. We all watched in awe as the force of "people power" opened the Berlin Wall, led the Velvet Revolution in Czechoslovakia, brought democracy back to the Philippines, and created a democratization wave on a global scale. For the established democracies, the spectacle of an American party convention, the intensity of a French farmers' protest, the community spirit of a New England town meeting, or the dedication of an English environmental group creates an equally impressive image of the democratic process. Granting power to the people, even if that process is incomplete, is a radical development. Even with the recent spread of democratization, barely half of the world's nations have real democratic institutions and procedures.

The recent democratic transitions in Eastern Europe, Asia, and South Africa remind us how precious, and how fragile, democracy can be. These events are also a reminder of the importance of the public in sustaining the democratic process once it is established. Although it is intriguing to look at these new democracies and their people (and we will at times), our inquiry focuses on citizen politics in the established democracies of the West. These established democracies provide a model of success that might be relevant for the new democracies. Also, the process of democratization is open-ended, and we shall argue that democratization and the expansion of citizen influence is a continuing process even for the established democracies.

As the democratization wave swept across the world in the 1990s, there was a temporary euphoria about the democratic process among Western publics. But soon, new concerns emerged about the potential political problems facing these nations. Some scholars argue that social and civic engagement is weakening, which threatens the vitality of the democratic process. Others point to growing popular skepticism about the politicians, parties, and political institutions that are the essential elements of the democratic process. Ironically, democracy's success in winning the Cold War is accompanied by new doubts about the democratic process.

This book presents a populist view of the democratic process, emphasizing the attitudes and behaviors of the average citizen. The analyses are therefore incomplete; we do not study the role of elites, interest groups, and other political actors. I do not presume that the public is all-knowing or all-powerful. Indeed, there are many examples of the public's ignorance or error on policy issues (as there are examples of elite errors). There are also many instances in which policymakers disregard the public's preferences. The democratic process, like all human activities, is imperfect, but its strength lies in the premise that people are the best judges of their own destiny. The success of democracy is largely measured by the public's participation in the process, the respect for citizen rights, and the responsiveness of the system to popular demands. As Adlai Stevenson once said, in a democracy the people get the kind of government they deserve (for better or worse).

Before proceeding, I want to acknowledge the complexity of the topic we are studying. It is difficult to make simple generalizations about public opinion and political behavior because the public is not homogeneous. There is not a single public. The public in any nation consists of millions of individuals, each with his or her own view of the world and the citizen's role in politics. Some people are liberal, some moderate, some conservative; others are socialist, reactionary, communist, or none of the above. Opinions are often divided on contemporary political issues—this is why the issues are controversial and require a political decision. Some people favor strict environmental laws; some see environmental standards as excessive. Some favor international trade; some are skeptical of its claimed benefits. The study of public opinion underscores the diversity of the public.

People also differ in the attention they devote to politics and the experiences they bring to the political process. Although a few individuals are full-time political activists, most people have modest political interests and ambitions. On some issues, a broad spectrum of society may become involved; other issues are greeted with apathy. The public's views generally define the acceptable bounds of politics, within which political elites resolve the remaining controversies. When elites exceed these bounds, or when the issues immediately affect people's lives, the potential for political action is great. The difficulty is to understand and predict which course of action the public will take.

In short, as social scientists we deal with the most complex problem of nature: to understand and predict human behavior. Yet this is not a hopeless task. The development of scientific public opinion surveys provides a valuable tool for researchers. With a sample of a few thousand precisely selected individuals, one can make reliable statements about the distribution of attitudes and opinions (Weisberg, Krosnick, and Bowen 1996). Not only can we observe behavior, but with the survey interview we can inquire into the motivations and expectations that guide behavior. Furthermore, a survey can be divided into subgroups to examine the diversity in individual opinions.

Readers will find that this book relies heavily on public opinion surveys. I do not claim that all we know about the public is found in the statistics and percentages of public opinion surveys. Some of the most insightful writings about political behavior are qualitative studies of the topic. And yet, even insightful political analysts can make contradictory claims about the public. The value of the empirical method is that it provides a specific reference standard against which we can measure contrasting descriptions of the electorate. Surveys enable people to describe politics and their political actions in their own words, and thus survey research offers a tremendously valuable research tool for social scientists.

Drawing on an extensive collection of opinion surveys, this book examines the nature of public opinion in several advanced industrial democracies.[1] I describe how individuals view politics, how they participate in the process, what opinions they hold, and how they choose their leaders through competitive elections. These findings should further our understanding of citizen politics and thereby the working of the political process in contemporary democracies.

THE COMPARATIVE STUDY OF PUBLIC OPINION

This book is an explicitly comparative study, exploring public opinion and political behavior in several democracies. Our goal is to strike a balance between attention to national detail and the general characteristics of citizens that transcend national boundaries.

There are several advantages to the comparative study of political behavior in Western democracies. A common historical and cultural tradition unites Europe and North America. Although these nations differ in the specifics of their government and party systems, they share broad similarities in the functioning of the democratic process and the role of the citizen in the process. A comparative approach thus provides a basis for studying those aspects of political behavior that should be valid across nations. General theories of why people participate in democratic politics should apply to citizens regardless of their nationality. Theories to explain party preferences should hold for Americans and Europeans if they represent basic features of human nature. And yet, most of the major studies of public opinion focus on only one nation.

In most instances, we expect to find similar patterns of behavior in different democracies. If our theories do not function similarly across nations, however, then we have learned something new and important. Science often progresses by finding exceptions to general theory, which necessitate further theoretical work. The same applies to social science.

Comparative analysis also allows us to examine the effects of political structures on citizen political behavior. For example, does the nature of a nation's electoral system affect the public's voting behavior? Or does the structure of political institutions affect the patterns of political participation? Each nation produces a "natural experiment" in which general theories of political behavior can be tested in a different political context.

Finally, even if we are interested only in a single nation, comparative research is still valuable. An old Hebrew riddle expresses this idea: "*Question:* Who first discovered water? *Answer:* I don't know, but it wasn't a fish." By immersing oneself in a single environment, the characteristics of the environment are unobtrusive and unnoticed. It is difficult to understand what is unique and distinctive about American political behavior, for example, by studying only American politics. Indeed, many students of American politics may be surprised to learn that the United States is often the atypical case in cross-national comparisons. American public opinion and political processes are unique in many ways, but we understand this only by rising above the waters.

THE CHOICE OF NATIONS

To balance our needs for comparison and attention to national differences, this study focuses on citizen politics in four nations: the United States, Great Britain, the Federal Republic of Germany (FRG), and France.[2] I based the choice of these nations on several criteria: By most standards, these are the major powers among the Western democracies. Their population, size, economy, military strength, and political influence earn them leadership positions in international circles. The actions of any of these nations can have significant consequences for all the others.

These nations also were chosen because they highlight many of the significant variations in the structure of democratic politics. Table 1.1 summarizes some of the most important differences. For example, Great Britain is a pure parliamentary system of government. The popularly elected House of Commons selects the prime minister to head the executive branch. This produces a fusion of legislative and executive power, because the same party and the same group of elites direct both branches of government. American government has a contrasting presidential system, with extensive checks and balances to maintain a separation of legislative and executive power. French politics functions within a modified presidential system; the president is directly elected by the public and so too is the National Assembly that selects the premier to head the administration of government. Germany has a parliamentary system, with the popularly elected Bundestag selecting the chancellor as head of the executive branch. The German system, however, also contains a strong federal structure and a separation of powers that is uncommon for a parliamentary government. Excellent analyses of these contrasting institutional forms and their implications for the nature of democratic politics are found in the research of Arend Lijphart (1999).

Electoral systems are equally diverse. Britain and the United States select the members of the national legislature from single-member districts, and a plurality is sufficient for election. Germany uses a hybrid system for Bundestag elections; half the deputies are elected from single-member districts and half are selected from party lists. The French electoral system is based on deputies winning a majority in single-member districts, with a second ballot (*tour*) if no

Table 1.1 A Comparison of Political Systems

	United States	Great Britain	Germany	France
Population (in millions)	276.5	59.5	82.8	59.3
Gross domestic product/capita	$33,900	$21,800	$22,700	$23,300
Political regime established	1789	Seventeenth century	1949	1958
State form	Republic	Constitutional monarchy	Republic	Republic
Government structure	Presidential	Parliamentary	Modified parliamentary	Modified presidential
Chief executive	President	Prime minister	Chancellor	President
Method of selection	Direct election	Elected by Parliament	Elected by Parliament	Direct election
Legislature	Bicameral	Bicameral	Bicameral	Bicameral
Lower house	House of Representatives	House of Commons	Bundestag	National Assembly
Upper house	Senate	House of Lords	Bundesrat	Senate
Power of upper house	Equal	Subordinate	Equal on state issues	Subordinate
Electoral system				
Lower house	Single-member districts	Single-member districts	PR and single-member districts	Single-member districts
Upper house	Statewide elections	Inheritance and appointment	Appointed by states	Appointed by communes
Major parties	Democrats	Labour	Democratic Socialists (PDS)	Communists
	Republicans	Liberal Democrats	Greens	Socialists
		Conservatives	Social Democrats	Ecologists
			Free Democrats	UDF
			Christian Democrats/ Christian Social Union (CDU/CSU)	Gaullist (RPR)
				National Front

candidate receives a majority on the first ballot. Rein Taagepera and Matthew Shugart (1989) and G. Bingham Powell (2000) have presented excellent studies of how such institutional arrangements can affect electoral outcomes.

The party systems in these four nations are also varied. Party competition in the United States is usually limited to the Democratic and Republican parties. Both are broad "catchall" parties that combine diverse political groups into weakly structured electoral coalitions. In contrast, most European political parties are hierarchically organized and firmly controlled by the party leadership. Candidates are elected primarily because of their party label and not because of their personal attributes; in the legislature most party members vote as a bloc. Party options are also more diverse in Europe. British voters can select from at least three major party groups; Germans have five major parties in the Bundestag. French party politics is synonymous with diversity and political polarization. Jacques Fauvet described French politics in the following terms:

> France contains two fundamental temperaments—that of the left and right; three principal tendencies, if one adds the center; six spiritual families; ten parties, large or small, traversed by multiple currents; fourteen parliamentary groups without much discipline; and forty million opinions. (Ehrmann and Schain 1992, 231)

Although Fauvet was describing French politics in the late 1950s, much of his description still applies today. France, a nation of "perpetual political effervescence," provides the spice of comparative politics.

The contrasts across nations take on an added dimension as a consequence of German unification. Western Germans have developed the characteristics of a stable, advanced industrial democracy; the former East Germany, like most of the rest of Eastern Europe, is just beginning this process. Democracy is a new experience for eastern Germans, and understanding of the democratic process and commitment to democratic norms are uncertain. By including western-eastern comparisons into our analysis of Germany, we can better understand what is distinctive about public opinion in an established democracy, as well as the prospects for democratization in the East. Furthermore, when possible, we broaden the scope of our cross-national comparisons to place our four nations in the context of other advanced industrial democracies.

A NEW STYLE OF CITIZEN POLITICS

The reader will quickly realize that this volume emphasizes the changing nature of citizen political behavior. I maintain that these changes derive from the socioeconomic transformation of the four nations under study over the past fifty years. Western democracies are developing a set of characteristics that collectively represent a new form of *advanced industrial* or *postindustrial* society (Bell 1973; Inglehart 1977, 1990).

The most dramatic changes involve economic conditions. An unprecedented expansion of economic well-being occurred in the second half of the twentieth century. The economies of Western Europe and North America grew at phenomenal rates in the post–World War II decades. For example, analysts describe the astonishing expansion of the West German economy as the *Wirtschaftswunder* (Economic Miracle). Income levels in our four nations are two to four times greater than at any time in prewar history. By almost any economic standard, the four nations of this study rank among the most affluent nations of the world.

With increasing affluence has come a restructuring of the labor force. The size of the agricultural workforce has decreased dramatically in most Western nations, and industrial employment has remained stable or declined. There also has been a marked shift in the labor force to the service sector. In addition, because of the expansion of national and local governments, public employment now constitutes a significant share of the labor force. All four of the core nations in this volume have passed Daniel Bell's (1973) threshold for postindustrialism: half of the labor force employed in the service or governmental sector.

Advanced industrialism is associated not only with changes in the relative size of the three principal employment sectors but also with changes in the context of the workplace and the residential neighborhood. The continuing decline of rural populations and the expanding size of metropolitan centers stimulate changes in life expectations and lifestyles. Urbanization means a growing separation of the home from the workplace, a greater diversity of occupations and interests, an expanded range of career opportunities, and more geographic and social mobility. With these trends come changes in the forms of social organization and interaction. Communal forms of organization are replaced by voluntary associations, which in turn become less institutionalized and more spontaneous in organization. Communities are becoming less bounded, individuals are involved in increasingly complex and competing social networks that divide their loyalties, and institutional ties are becoming more fluid.

Educational opportunities also expanded rapidly over the past several decades. European governments historically restricted university education to a privileged few; the vast majority received minimal education (often only four years). In the late 1930s the proportion of university students among 20–24-year-olds was only 1 percent in England, 1 percent in Germany, and 3 percent in France. Access to education expanded following World War II. Minimal education standards were increased, and university enrollments skyrocketed. By 1997 about half of college-age European youth and more than three-quarters of American youth were enrolled in some form of tertiary schooling (World Bank 2000). This expansion of educational opportunities has fundamentally changed the educational composition of contemporary mass publics.

These increases in education have been accompanied by parallel increases in information resources. The growth of the electronic media, especially television, is exceptional. Access to other information sources, such as books and magazines, has increased. Even more revolutionary is the growth of electronic information processing: computers, the Internet, and related technologies. Information is no longer a scarce commodity. The contemporary information problem is how to adapt to life in cyberspace, managing an ever-growing volume of sophisticated knowledge.

Western democracies also changed the extent of the government's involvement in society. Two world wars and the Great Depression expanded the government's role in economic and social activities. Western publics now hold the government responsible for protecting and managing society. Governments increased their control over their national economy, and government programs became the guarantor of social needs. Many European societies developed the characteristics of a welfare state, in which an extensive network of generous social programs protects the individual against economic or medical hardship. Unemployment, illness, and similar problems still cause hardships, but the consequences under the welfare state are less dire than during earlier periods. People in advanced industrial societies enjoy both a high level of affluence and relative security.

Despite these trends, the publics in Europe, North America, and Japan are concerned about whether or not this developmental trend can continue. Everywhere, it seems, there has been a retrenchment in governmental social programs. Increased international interdependence has created new competitive economic strains within these nations. Elation about the end of the Cold War and the democratization of Eastern Europe has been tempered by worries about growing nationalism, ethnic conflict, and the financial burdens that modernization will require. In some established democracies, there are real worries that economic problems will revive reactionary political groups.

Admittedly the miraculous economic growth rates of the previous decades can seem like distant history. And yet the transformation of Western democracies is more than simply the politics of affluence. Changes in the occupational and social structure are continuing, and with them an alteration in life conditions and lifestyles. Expanded educational opportunities represent an enduring trait of modern societies. The information revolution is continuing; in fact, it is growing at an amazing rate. Advanced industrial societies are still dramatically different from their pre-1950s predecessors.

This book maintains that one result of these social changes is the development of a new style of citizen politics. One thing you quickly learn about political science is that serious researchers can reach different conclusions based on similar evidence. This book's basic premise of political change has been questioned by many others. In reviewing European public opinion trends, for example, Dieter Fuchs and Hans-Dieter Klingemann conclude: "The hypotheses we tested are based on the premise that a fundamental change had taken place in the relationship between citizens and the state, provoking a challenge to representative democracy . . . the postulated fundamental change in the citizens' relationship with the state largely did *not* occur" (1995, 429). Others have claimed that the evidence of increasing electoral change is a myth (Mair 1993). Begin your reading with this skepticism, and then see if the evidence supports it.

Our premise is that as the socioeconomic characteristics of these nations have changed, so too have the characteristics of the public. More educational opportunities mean a growth in political skills and resources, producing the most sophisticated publics in the history of democracies. Changing economic conditions redefine citizens' issue interests. The weakening of social networks and institutional loyalties is associated with the decline of traditional political alignments and voting patterns.

The elements of this new style of citizen politics are not always, or necessarily, linked together. Some elements may be transitory; others may be coincidental. Nevertheless, several traits coexist for the present, defining a new pattern of citizen political behavior. The goal of this volume is to systematically describe this new pattern of political thought and action.

One area of change affects the public's involvement in politics (chapters 2–4). Greater public participation in economic and political decision making is an important social goal. This development is closely tied to the spread of protests, citizen action groups, and unconventional political participation, but it involves more. Citizens are less likely to be passive subjects and are more likely to demand a say in the decisions affecting their lives. The new style of citizen politics includes a more active participation in the democratic process.

Another broad area of change involves the values and attitudes of the public (chapters 5–6). Industrial societies aimed at providing affluence and economic security. The success of advanced industrialism fulfills many basic economic needs for a sizable sector of society. Thus, concerns are shifting to new political goals (Inglehart 1990, 1997). Several of these new issues are common to advanced industrial democracies: social equality, environmental protection, the dangers of nuclear energy, sexual equality, and human rights. In some instances, historical conditions focus these general concerns on specific national problems, for example, racial equality in the United States, regional conflicts in Britain, or center-periphery differences in France. Many of these issues are now loosely integrated into an alternative political agenda that is another element of the new style of citizen politics.

Partisan politics is also changing (chapters 7–11). Until recently, comparative party research emphasized the stability of democratic party systems. This situation has changed in the past two decades. Stable party alignments are weakening, producing increased fragmentation and volatility in most Western party systems. Declining class differences in voting behavior reflect the general erosion in the social bases of voting. Studies in most of these nations document a decline in the public's identification with political parties and growing disenchantment with parties in general. In another work (Dalton and Wattenberg 2000), we describe these patterns as the *dealignment* of contemporary party systems.

These trends are at least partially the result of the addition of new issues to the political agenda and the difficulties the established parties have had in responding to these issues. New parties have arisen across the face of Europe—ranging from green parties on the New Left to New Right parties at the opposite end of the political spectrum—and new political movements seek access to the Democratic and Republican Parties in the United States. Increased party volatility is also caused by the changing characteristics of contemporary publics. Unsophisticated voters once relied on social-group cues and partisan cues to make their political decisions. Because of the dramatic spread of education and information sources, more people now can deal with the complexities of politics and make their own political decisions. Consequently, issues are becoming a more important basis of voting behavior as the influence of traditional group and party allegiances wanes. The new style of citizen politics includes a more issue-oriented and candidate-oriented public.

Finally, public orientations toward government represent a new paradox for democracy (chapter 12). New issues have been added to the agenda, the democratic process has become more inclusive, and the government has generally improved the quality of life—but at the same time people have become more critical of government. The conflict over new issues and new participation patterns may be a partial explanation of these trends. In addition, emerging value priorities that stress individualism and political participation produce skepticism of elite-controlled hierarchical organizations (such as bureaucracies, political parties, and large interest groups).

The development of this new style of citizen politics creates new strains for the political systems of advanced industrial democracies. Protests, social movements, partisan volatility, and political skepticism are disrupting the traditional political order. Adjustment to new issue concerns and new patterns of citizen participation may be a difficult process. More people now take democratic ideals seriously, and they expect political systems to live up to these ideals. I believe that democracy is not an end state but an evolutionary process. Thus, the new style of citizen politics is a sign of vitality and an opportunity for these societies to make further progress toward these democratic goals.

NOTES

1. Most of the data in this volume come from the Inter-university Consortium for Political and Social Research at the University of Michigan, Ann Arbor (www.icpsr.umich.edu). Additional data were made available by the Zentralarchiv für empirische Sozialforschung, University of Cologne, Germany, and the ESRC Archive, University of Essex, England. See appendix A for additional information on the major data sources. Neither these archives nor the original collectors of the data bear responsibility for the analyses presented here.

2. For a brief review of these nations, see Almond, Dalton, and Powell (2002). More detailed national studies are found in Budge et al. (1998) for Britain, Conradt (2001) for Germany, and Safran (1998) for France.

PART ONE

Politics and the Public

CHAPTER 2

The Nature of Mass Beliefs

ANY DISCUSSION OF citizen politics is ultimately based on assumptions about the political abilities of the electorate—the public's level of knowledge, understanding, and interest in political matters. For voters to make meaningful decisions, they must understand the options on which they are deciding. Citizens also need sufficient knowledge of the workings of the political system if they intend to influence and control the actions of their representatives. In short, for citizen politics to be purposeful, the electorate must have at least a basic level of political skills.

Examining the sophistication of voters also improves our understanding of the public opinion data presented in this book. With what depth of knowledge and conviction are opinions held? Do survey responses represent reasoned assessments of the issues or the snap judgments of individuals faced by an interviewer on their doorstep? It is common to see the public labeled as uninformed (especially when public opinion conflicts with the speaker's own views). Conversely, the electorate cannot be wiser than when it supports one's own position. Can we judge the merits of either position based on the empirical evidence from public opinion surveys?

Debates about the political abilities of the public remain one of the major controversies in political behavior research. This controversy involves normative assumptions about what level of sophistication is required for democracies to fulfill their political ideals, as well as differences in evaluating the empirical evidence.

THE SUPERCITIZEN

Political theorists have long maintained that democracy was workable only when the public had a high degree of political information and sophistication. John Stuart Mill, John Locke, Alexis de Tocqueville, and other writers saw these public traits as requirements for a successful democratic system. Most theorists further claimed that the citizenry should support the political system and share a deep commitment to democratic ideals such as pluralism, free expression, and minority rights (see chapter 12). Otherwise, an uninformed and unsophisticated electorate might be manipulated by misguided or unscrupulous elites. In a sense, these theorists posited a supercitizen model: The public must be a paragon of civic virtue for democracy to survive.

INTERNET RESOURCE

Visit the "Virtual Library on Democracy" for links to various sources on public opinion, political parties, and democracy:

www.democ.uci.edu/resource.htm

This ideal of the democratic supercitizen was often illustrated by examples from American politics.[1] A popular lore grew up about the sophistication of Americans. Tocqueville (1966) praised the social and community involvement of Americans when he described the United States in the nineteenth century. Voters in early America supposedly yearned for the stimulating political debates of election campaigns and flocked to political rallies in great numbers. New England town hall meetings became a legendary example of the American political spirit. Even on the frontier, it was claimed, conversations around the general store's cracker barrel displayed a deep interest in political matters.

Although these democratic norms were initially of European origins, history painted a less positive picture of the citizenry in many European nations. The right to vote came much later to most Europeans, often delayed until the beginning of the twentieth century. The aristocratic institutions and deferential traditions of British politics limited public participation beyond the act of voting and severely restricted the size of the eligible electorate. In France, the excesses of the French Revolution raised doubts about the principle of mass participation. In addition, the instability of the political system supposedly produced a sense of *incivism*, and people avoided political discussions and political involvement.

Germany presented the most graphic example of what might follow when democratic norms are lacking among the public. Authoritarian governments ruled during the Wilhelmine Empire (1871–1918), and people were taught to be seen and not heard. The democratic Weimar Republic (1919–33) was but a brief and turbulent interlude in Germany's nondemocratic history. The frailties of popular democratic norms during the Weimar Republic contributed to the system's demise and the rise of Hitler's Third Reich. A strong democratic culture eventually developed in the postwar Federal Republic of Germany. However, these historical experiences strengthened the belief that a sophisticated, involved, and democratic public is a requirement for democracy to succeed.

THE UNSOPHISTICATED CITIZEN

The start of scientific public opinion surveying in the 1950s and 1960s provided the first opportunity to move beyond the insights of political theorists and social commentators. We could finally test the lofty images of the democratic citizen against reality. The public itself was directly consulted.

In contrast to the classic images of democratic theory, early surveys painted an unflattering picture of the American public. Political sophistication was far short of the supercitizen model. For most people, political interest and involvement barely extended beyond casting an occasional vote in national or local elections. Furthermore, Americans apparently brought little understanding to their participation in politics. It was not clear that people based their voting decisions on rational evaluations of candidates and their issue positions. Instead, voting was conditioned by group loyalties and personalistic considerations. The seminal work in the area succinctly summarized the findings:

> Our data reveal that certain requirements commonly assumed for the successful operation of democracy are not met by the behavior of the "average" citizen. . . . Many vote without real involvement in the election. . . . The citizen is not highly informed on the details of the campaign. . . . In any rigorous or narrow sense the voters are not highly rational. (Berelson, Lazarsfeld, and McPhee 1954, 307–10)

The landmark study *The American Voter* substantiated these early findings (Campbell et al. 1960). Angus Campbell and his colleagues documented a lack of ideological understanding by the American electorate. In an influential essay on mass belief systems, Philip Converse (1964) spelled out the criteria for measuring political sophistication. As modeled in figure 2.1, Converse maintained there should be a basic *structure* at the core of individual political beliefs. An ideological framework such as liberalism/conservatism presumably provides this structure, at least at the highest level of sophistication. In addition, Converse held there should be *constraint* between individual issue positions. Constraint is measured by the strength of the linkage between specific issue positions and core beliefs and by the interrelationship among issues. A person who is liberal on one issue is expected to be liberal on others. Furthermore, opinions on one issue should be ideologically (or at least logically) consistent with other beliefs. Finally, Converse said that issue opinions should be relatively *stable* over time so that voters held beliefs that consistently guided their behavior. The overall result should be a tightly structured system of beliefs like that depicted in figure 2.1.

In testing this model, Converse found that Americans appeared deficient on most of these criteria. First, public opinion apparently lacked a general ideological structure. Most individuals did not judge political phenomena in ideological terms, such as liberalism/conservatism or capitalism/socialism. Converse reckoned that barely a tenth of the American public used ideological concepts to structure their belief system. Second, there was seemingly only a weak relationship between issues that we presume are connected. For example, voters who believed taxes

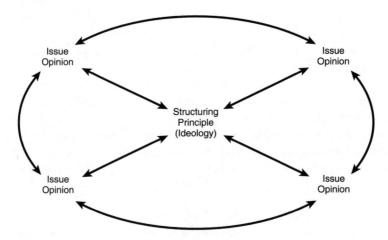

Figure 2.1   Model of a Structured Belief System

were too high nevertheless favored increases in spending for many specific government programs. Third, issue beliefs were not very stable over time. An analysis of the same group of individuals interviewed across three elections found that the opinions of many people seemed to vary capriciously. The lack of structure, constraint, and stability led Converse to conclude that public opinion researchers are often studying "nonattitudes" (Converse 1970). On numerous issues of long-standing political concern, many voters apparently lack informed opinions or any opinions. *The American Voter* concluded that the electorate

> is almost completely unable to judge the rationality of government actions; knowing little of the particular policies and what has led to them, the mass electorate is not able either to appraise its goals or the appropriateness of the means chosen to secure these goals. (Campbell et al. 1960, 543)

This research was soon followed by a series of surveys showing that many people could not name their elected representatives, were unfamiliar with the institutions of government, and did not understand the mechanics of the political process. Moreover, more recent research argues that little has changed in the last generation (Delli Carpini and Keeter 1996). The image of the American voter had fallen to a new low.

This image of the unsophisticated citizen also seemed to apply to Western Europeans. Once one moved beyond election turnout, political involvement in Europe was frequently lower than in the United States. Converse and Dupeux (1962) found that political interest was lower in France than in the United States, despite the tumultuous nature of the French party system. French voters also lacked well-formed opinions on the pressing issues of the day (Converse and Pierce 1986, chap. 7). Similar evidence emerged from surveys of the British public (Butler and Stokes 1969). For instance, 60 percent of Britons did not recognize the terms *Left* and *Right* as they applied to politics. There were again the telltale signs of nonattitudes—weak linkages between opinions on related issues and excessive opinion instability over time.

Other research raised doubts about the public's commitment to political tolerance and other values underlying the democratic process. The general public displayed support for democratic ideals in the abstract, but not when applied to real movements and political groups, such as communists, Nazis, atheists, and political nonconformists (Prothro and Grigg 1960; McClosky 1964; McClosky and Brill 1983). Again, the empirical reality apparently fell short of the democratic ideal.

ELITIST THEORY OF DEMOCRACY

Having found that most citizens fail to meet the requirements of classic democratic theory, political scientists faced a paradox. Most individuals are not "good" democratic citizens, and yet democracies such as the United States and Great Britain have existed for generations. Gradually, an *elitist theory of democracy* developed as scholars tried to interpret these survey findings in a positive light (Berelson, Lazarsfeld, and McPhee 1954, 313–23; Almond and Verba 1963, chap. 15). The new theory contended that democratic politics might prove unworkable if every person is active on every issue at all times. Images of the centrifugal forces destroying the Weimar Republic were fresh in many minds, generating concerns about the possible effects of excessive participation. These scholars suggested that the model citizen "is not the active citizen; he is the potentially active citizen" (Almond and Verba 1963, 347), and they argued that people must believe that they can influence the government and must be willing to make an effort if the issue is sufficiently important. Few will realize this potential, however. This balance between action and potential presumably assured that political elites had enough freedom to make necessary decisions, while keeping the public interest in mind.

Another element of this elitist theory stresses the heterogeneity of the public: "Some people are and should be highly interested in politics, but not everyone is or needs to be" (Berelson, Lazarsfeld, and McPhee 1954, 315). From this perspective, the responsiveness of the political system is assured by a small core of active citizens and political elites, leaving the rest of the public blissfully uninformed and uninvolved. This mix between involved and indifferent voters reportedly assures the stability and flexibility of democratic systems.

The elitist theory of democracy is drawn from the realities of political life— or at least from the hard evidence of survey research. It is, however, a very undemocratic theory of democracy. The theory maintains that "the democratic citizen . . . must be active, yet passive; involved, yet not too involved; influential, yet deferential" (Almond and Verba 1963, 478–79). The values and goals of democracy were at least partially obscured by a mountain of survey data.

Accepting this new creed, some analysts used this evidence to justify an extreme elitist model of the democratic process (Dye and Ziegler 1970; Crozier, Huntington, and Watanuki 1975; Huntington 1981). These critics of the public implied that citizen activism is undemocratic and politically destabilizing. Thomas Dye and Harmon Ziegler bluntly claimed:

> The survival of democracy depends upon the commitment of elites to democratic ideals rather than upon broad support for democracy by the masses. Political apathy and nonparticipation among the masses contribute to the survival of democracy. Fortunately for democracy, the antidemocratic masses are generally more apathetic than elites. (1970, 328)

If a supportive and quiescent public ensures a smoothly functioning political system, then it is virtually the duty of the individual to remain uninvolved. When the public began to challenge political elites during the turbulent 1960s and 1970s, these political scientists cautioned that democracy required a public of followers who would not question political elites too extensively. They argued that too much democracy could threaten the democratic process.

Despite these claims, I believe that the elitist theory overlooks the complexities of the democratic process and takes an unsophisticated view of the evidence. For instance, this theory ignores the inconsistencies that exist among political elites. Members of the U.S. Congress routinely endorse formal budget limits and then act to circumvent these same limits in the next piece of legislation. In one vote they endorse strict measures to limit crime; in the next they refuse to ban assault weapons.[2] Such inconsistencies in elite behavior are treated as examples of the complexity of politics; for the public these same patterns are signs of their lack of sophistication. In addition, the elitist critique of the public's abilities has been challenged on both normative and empirical grounds in recent years.[3] The picture of the public's abilities is not nearly as bleak as that painted by the elitist theory of democracy. As our scientific knowledge has increased, so too has our image of the electorate and its abilities.

POLITICAL SOPHISTICATION RECONSIDERED

Our challenge to conventional descriptions of an unsophisticated electorate is based on several points. Profound social and political changes in the advanced industrial democracies have increased the public's political abilities. In addition, research has enriched our understanding of how voters actually think about political matters. Each point deserves detailed attention.[4]

A Process of Cognitive Mobilization

The characteristics of the public in advanced industrial democracies dramatically improved during the second half of the twentieth century. The public's political skills and resources—traits such as education, media exposure, and political awareness—are vastly expanded since the 1950s. These trends contributed to a growth in the public's overall level of political sophistication through what is described as a process of *cognitive mobilization* (Inglehart 1990; Dalton 1984). Cognitive mobilization involves two separate developments. First, the cost of acquiring information about politics has decreased. Second, the public's ability to process political information has increased. Cognitive mobilization thus means that more citizens now have the political resources and skills that prepare them to deal with the complexities of politics and reach their own political decisions.

The public's access to political information has increased in many ways. The average citizen once might have suffered from a lack of information. In the past, one could read newspapers or magazines, but this is a time-consuming task, especially for an electorate with limited education. Particularly in Europe, the printed press is of uneven quality, and many mass newspapers are little more than scandal sheets. Today, however, there is a nearly unlimited supply and variety of political news, but one can easily forget that this is a relatively new development.

The expansion of the mass media, especially television, is the clearest example of this change. In the early 1950s television was still a novelty to most Americans and a luxury to most Europeans. Only half of American homes had a television set in the early 1950s, as did less than 10 percent in Britain and France, and less than 5 percent in West Germany. The expansion of television ownership over the next two decades was closely paralleled by the public's increasing reliance on television as a source of political information (figure 2.2). In the 1952 American election, 51 percent of the electorate used television news as an information source. By 1960 this figure had risen to a plateau of about 90 percent. In 1961 only 50 percent of the West German public depended on television for political information; by 1974 the Germans also reached the 90 percent plateau. The trends from Britain and France present a similar pattern.

As television viewership increased, so also did the amount of political information provided by the medium. The now-standard American nightly half-hour national network news program began only in 1963. Since then, technology and viewer interest have increased the television programming devoted to news and political affairs. Today, news reporting is instantaneous and occurs on a worldwide scale. Most Americans have access to news on a twenty-four-hour-a-day basis; CNN, C-SPAN, and other cable channels create a rich media environment.

Government-supervised national networks in Europe devote even more time to news, politics, and current events than U.S. networks. Political information accounts for about a third of all public network programming in France and Germany and about a quarter in Britain. Moreover, new information technolo-

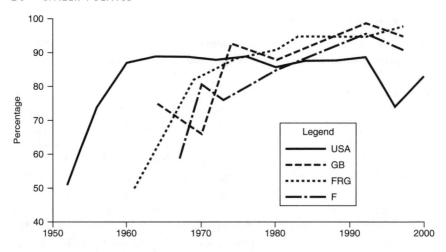

Figure 2.2   The Growth of Television as a Source of Political Information

Sources: United States, 1952–2000: American National Election Studies; *Great Britain*, 1963–74: British Election Studies, 1980–97: Eurobarometer 15, 37, and 47; *Germany*, 1961–69: German Election Studies, 1980–92: Eurobarometer 15, 37, and 47; *France*, 1965–74: Gallup (1976b), 1980–92: Eurobarometer 15, 37, and 47.

gies and the competition from new private channels are transforming the media environment in Europe. Most European households can receive cable channels ranging from the government networks to CNN or BBC World News to a host of private channels. Governmental restrictions on television have gradually weakened, expanding the media's political role. For example, before the 1964 election, the British government prohibited the BBC from carrying election news during the campaign period. Now television coverage is a central part of British campaigns, as well as German and French elections (Semetko et al. 1991; Semetko and Schoenbach 1994).

As a result of these trends, television is now the primary information source for Western publics (table 2.1). People uniformly cite television as the most frequently used source of political information.[5] The high ranking for television does not mean that other media are not used. Opinion surveys routinely find that large majorities of the public regularly watch television, read newspapers and magazines, and hear news on the radio. Electorates thus have access to an array of media sources that would have been unimaginable a generation ago. These increases in the quantity and quality of political information provided by the media should improve public awareness of political affairs.

Political scientists are divided on whether the expansion of television as a news source is a boon or a curse for the democratic process. Some scholars argue that the media tend to trivialize information, emphasizing entertainment and

Table 2.1   Most Important Source of Political Information (in percentages)

	United States 1992	Britain 1989	France 1989	West Germany 1989
Television	69	53	44	56
Newspapers	43	30	24	37
Personal discussion	6	19	15	26
Radio	16	12	13	20
Other	4	5	7	18
Total	138	119	103	157

Sources: United States, Stanley and Niemi (2000, 173); *other nations*, Eurobarometer 31A (June 1989).

Notes: Responses in the surveys total more than 100 percent because multiple answers were possible.

drama over substance, and creating a negative climate of opinion (e.g., Patterson 1993; Swanson and Mancini 1996). These concerns are well-founded, because television does have limits. At the same time, however, television can create a greater understanding of politics by allowing us all to watch legislative deliberations, to see candidates as they campaign, and to experience history firsthand. Watching an important parliamentary debate on television or watching the presidential inauguration live gives citizens a direct contact to their government and a better understanding of how democracy works. Television has great positive and negative potential, and the objective of democratic polities should be to maximize the benefits.

In addition to the media, we should realize that a lot of politically relevant information is available from our daily life experiences (Fiorina 1990; Popkin 1991). Governments now exercise a large role in society, and their performance of this role is important political information. For instance, contemporary governments can strongly influence economic conditions. Thus, the performance of the economy is a meaningful measure of how to judge the incumbents. Similarly, government runs most schools, sets health standards, administers family and social programs, protects the environment, and provides for our transportation needs. When a commuter notes that highways are deteriorating (or being improved) or parents note improvements (or deterioration) in their child's school, these are significant political facts. Political information is virtually unavoidable.

The expansion of political information provides an opportunity to the citizenry, but this information might seem like a cacophony unless the public can process and evaluate the information. Thus, it is important that the public's political skills also increase.

The most visible change in political skills involves educational levels. Advanced industrial societies require a more educated and technically sophisticated electorate, and modern affluence has provided the funding for an expanded educational system (see chapter 1). University enrollments grew dramatically during the latter half of the twentieth century. By the 1990s graduate degrees were almost as common as bachelor degrees were in mid-century. These trends have steadily raised the educational level of contemporary electorates. For instance, almost half of the 1948 American electorate had a primary education or less, and only a tenth had some college education. By 2000 the portion of the electorate with some college education outnumbered voters with only primary education by a ten-to-one ratio, and those with some college education made up almost two-thirds of the electorate. Parallel changes are transforming European publics. In postwar West Germany, for example, the number of citizens with only primary schooling exceeded those with a secondary school diploma (*Mittlere Reife*) by about five to one. Today, the number of better-educated Germans is twice as large as the lesser educated.

There is not a direct one-to-one relationship between years of schooling and political sophistication. Nevertheless, the evidence from survey research broadly shows that education is linked to a citizen's level of political knowledge, interest, and sophistication (Nie, Junn, and Stehlik-Barry 1996). Paul Sniderman, Richard Brody, and Philip Tetlock (1991) present persuasive evidence that educational levels are related to the modes of political decision making that citizens use. Samuel Popkin (1991, 36) suggests that rising educational levels increase the breadth of citizens' political interests, even if they do not raise overall levels of institutional knowledge or issue constraint by the same amount. Thus, better-educated individuals come closer to the classic model of ideological citizens and are more knowledgeable in their behavior. A doubling of the public's educational level may not double the level of political sophistication, but some increase should occur. Contemporary electorates are clearly the most educated in the long history of democracies, and this should contribute toward making a more sophisticated electorate and a new style of citizen politics.

Converse (1972, 1990) maintained that political attention is an even more important indicator of the public's political skills. Reflecting and reinforcing the general development of cognitive mobilization, interest in politics and government affairs has increased in most Western democracies. Figure 2.3 tracks political interest over time.[6] Interest in specific elections may vary from campaign to campaign, but these data suggest a trend of increasing politicization. Political interest has grown most steadily in the Federal Republic of Germany, partially for the reasons cited previously and partially because of the nation's resocialization to democracy. Yet there are similar trends of expanding interest in Britain and France. Americans' interest in campaigns has varied over time with little secular trend. Most Western democracies, however, display a pattern of generally increasing political

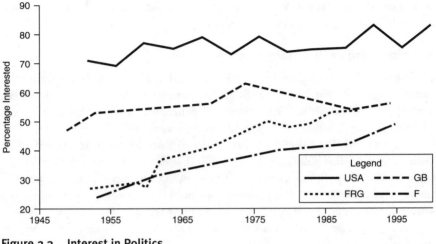

Figure 2.3   Interest in Politics

Sources: United States, 1952–2000: American National Election Studies; *Great Britain,* 1949–53: Gallup (1976a), 1963–79: British Election Studies, 1989: Eurobarometer 31A, 1994: Eurobarometer 41.1; *Germany,* 1952–90: Noelle-Neumann and Köcher (1993, 617–18); *France,* 1953 and 1978: Charlot (1980), 1962: Gallup (1976b), 1978–95: French Election Studies.

interest (Dalton and Wattenberg 2000, chap. 3). In sum, the trend of increasing political interest in advanced industrial democracies is unmistakable.

This debate on the sophistication of mass publics is not finished. For instance, Michael Delli Carpini and Scott Keeter (1996) claim that political information is limited and not increasing among Americans. In contrast, Morris Fiorina (1990, 335) makes the provocative argument that the more surprising fact is that citizens have as much information as they do, since the acquisition of political knowledge cannot be justified by narrow rationalist calculations of the value of that knowledge in influencing governmental policy. In part, it is a debate about expectations—what do we expect of citizens in democracies—and it is a debate over empirical evidence—what levels of political sophistication do voters actually possess.[7] When both factors are intermixed, it is easy to yield contrasting conclusions with the same empirical evidence.

I think the best evidence will come from the actual impact of cognitive mobilization on various aspects of citizen politics. More people seem to be shedding their reliance on social-group and partisan cues as a basis of voting (see chapters 8 and 9). The present level of issue voting is generally higher than during earlier periods (see chapter 10). Cognitive mobilization also expands political participation to include more demanding forms of political activity. We examine many of these specific trends more closely in the following chapters, and we will argue that the stereotype of an unsophisticated voter is clearly much less applicable today than during the 1950s.

Sophistication versus Satisficing

It probably was inevitable that early empirical studies would reach negative conclusions about the public's political sophistication. Analysts judged citizens against the lofty ideals of classic democratic theory, and reality fell short of the theoretical ideals. When this occurred, analysts stressed the shortfall.

I agree that the rational citizen cannot realistically keep informed on all political issues—few political elites or political scientists attempt this task. To the surprise of some political science professors, politics is only one part of people's lives. Because of the pressing demands of family and career, people can devote only a limited amount of time to politics. For instance, when the 1995 World Values Survey asked Americans what was very important in their lives, politics came at the end of the list:

- Family (95 percent)
- Friends (69 percent)
- Religion (58 percent)
- Work (53 percent)
- Leisure (42 percent)
- Politics (18 percent)

Citing such evidence, the elitist theorists argue that many (or most) citizens are overwhelmed and become political dropouts, and democracy is better for it.

We need a more balanced view of the topic, stripping away the idealized standards of classic democratic theory and the rationalizations of elitist democratic theory—looking instead at politics from the perspective of the voter. People are making political decisions on a regular basis, whether they involve a voting decision, donating funds to a political group, or participating in a political discussion. Rather than asking if citizens meet the expectations of democratic theorists, we should recognize that people are making these political choices and ask how these choices are actually made.

Following politics is demanding, but politics still has important effects on one's life. Most citizens thus do not drop out. Instead, they find a means of balancing the costs and benefits of political activity. One way of managing is through the use of "shortcuts" to simplify politics or manage the complexities of politics. Popkin writes that "the use of information shortcuts is . . . an inescapable fact of life, and will occur no matter how educated we are, how much information we have, and how much thinking we do" (1991, 218). In other words, we should think of how people make satisfactory or satisficing decisions, instead of holding the public up to the ideals of democratic theory.

The political science literature identifies three potential methods that citizens can use as information shortcuts. One approach suggests that people have specialized interests. Instead of following all issues, citizens concentrate their attention on a few topics of direct personal relevance or interest. The total electorate thus is divided into several partially overlapping *issue publics* (Converse 1964). Simply expressing an opinion is not enough to be a member of an issue public, since many people will state an opinion to an interviewer even if they have given little thought to the topic. An issue public implies that citizens have devoted prior attention to the issue and have firm beliefs. Many farmers, for example, closely monitor government agricultural policy but pay scant attention to urban renewal programs. Parents with school-age children may display considerable interest in educational policy, whereas the elderly are interested in Social Security. The largest issue publics generally exist for topics of broad concern, such as economic policy, taxes, and basic social programs. At the other extreme, only a few voters regularly follow issues of foreign aid, agriculture, or international trade. Very few citizens are interested in every issue, but most citizens are members of at least one issue public. To paraphrase Will Rogers, everybody is sophisticated, only on different subjects.

The concept of issue publics influences how we think about political sophistication. When citizens are allowed to define politics according to their own interests, a surprising level of political sophistication often appears. Robert Lane's conversations with a group of working-class men found coherent individual systems of political beliefs that sharply conflict with the findings of survey research (Lane 1962). David RePass (1971) documented a high level of rational issue voting when citizens identified their own issue interests. Opinion stability also is higher among members of the relevant issue public (Converse 1964; Schuman and Presser 1981, chap. 9; Feldman 1989). Thus, low issue constraint and stability in public opinion surveys do not mean the electorate is unsophisticated; the alternative explanation is that not all citizens are interested in all issues.

Some political scientists view issue publics as a negative aspect of mass opinion because a proliferation of distinct issue groups works against policymaking based on a broad, coherent ideological framework. Such criticism may be overstated, however. If citizens limit their issue interests, this does not mean that they fail to judge these issues using a broad political framework. Different clusters of issue interests still may emanate from a common underlying set of values. In addition, Lane (1973, 1962) pointed out the potential negative consequences of an overly structured belief system, for example, dogmatism and intolerance. In a slightly different context, Robert Dahl (1971) restated the Madisonian principle that the existence of many competing political groups, with overlapping and crosscutting memberships and shifting political alignments, is an essential characteristic of pluralist democracy. In some instances, therefore, issue publics may be a positive feature of citizen politics.

A second model of satisficing behavior generalizes the idea of issue publics into a broader framework of "schema theory" (Conover and Feldman 1984; Peffley and Hurwitz 1985). Instead of viewing belief systems as interconnecting a diverse range of political attitudes, as originally proposed by Converse, schema theorists maintain there is a *vertical structure* (or network) of beliefs within specific political domains as illustrated in figure 2.4. A broad organizing structure is linked to general political orientations; specific issue opinions are derived from one or more of these general orientations. For instance, attitudes toward governmental programs assisting minorities might reflect both orientations toward the role of government and attitudes toward minorities (Sniderman, Brody, and Tetlock 1991). At the same time, even if opinions on specific issues are strongly linked to broader political orientations, the relationships between specific issue opinions can be weak because issues might not be directly linked together. Thus, this model lacks the direct linkage between opinions on different issues as posited in *The American Voter* model (see figure 2.1, p. 16).

Furthermore, the specific political attitudes included within a schema, and the structures used to organize information, might vary across individuals. Some voters' beliefs will include only one part of the structure of figure 2.4, such as the issues on the left of the figure. For other people, their schematic structure might include another subset of issues and general orientations. Thus, the literature on schema theory tries to identify specific cognitive structures (or schema) that are relevant for subsets of issues, such as a foreign policy schema, a racial schema, or a schema for judging political candidates.[8]

In short, a complex belief system might exist within an issue public, linking issue positions to a structuring principle such as Left/Right position—even

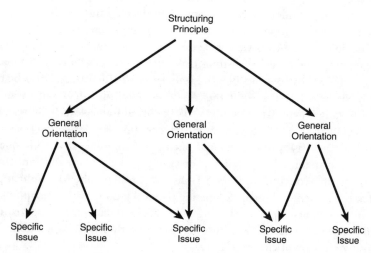

Figure 2.4   A Hierarchical Model of Beliefs

if schema are not linked across issue publics. Such belief structures provide voters with a method of managing information and making political judgments. Thus, even if citizens are not sophisticated on all political topics, they may have logical and structured beliefs within specific domains that enable them to manage political decision making.

A third model of satisficing involves the use of reference standards to simplify decisions. Instead of having to develop a complex schema, people can use political cues, or *heuristics*, to orient themselves to politics (Lupia and McCubbins 1998; Sniderman, Brody, and Tetlock 1991; Ferejohn and Kuklinski 1990). The cue provides a shortcut to collecting and processing information; one relies on the political directions of the cue-giver.

Social groups are one common source of political cues. Many policy issues can be cast as conflicts between class, religious, ethnic, or other social groupings. Membership in a social group, either formally or through psychological ties, can act as a guidepost in dealing with policy questions. French steelworkers, for example, might prefer nationalizing industry because the labor union suggests it will benefit workers like themselves. An avowed Bavarian Catholic may follow the pastor's advice to support governmental aid for religious schools. These voters might not explain their policy preferences with sophisticated ideological arguments or reference to specific legislative proposals, but on the whole they still are making reasonable political choices.

Early voting studies emphasized social groups as a source of voting cues. Paul Lazarsfeld and his colleagues (1948) constructed an *index of political predisposition* based on social class, religion, and rural/urban residence that was a potent predictor of voting behavior. The highly stratified nature of Western European societies produced even stronger group cues, and thus large group differences in European voting patterns (see chapter 8). As a result, when the French steelworker sees that other people in the same social class and with the same secular orientation favor a leftist party, the worker may also support a leftist party because it represents people like him (and presumably his interests).

Studies of ideological sophistication find that group references are a common basis of party evaluation (Converse 1964; Klingemann 1979). For many less educated citizens, group references may reflect political orientations that they have difficulty explaining in the terminology that would classify them as sophisticated ideologues. When social conflicts are salient, and the parties take clear positions on these conflicts, then social characteristics can provide effective cues for orienting oneself to politics.

An even more powerful source of political cues is partisanship. Many citizens develop a psychological bond to a specific political party that may persist through an entire lifetime (see chapter 9). This *party identification* sometimes is based on emotional and nonrational criteria, such as inheritance of parental partisanship, and may serve as a surrogate for social-group cues. As a standing sum of the individual's political history, partisanship provides a useful guide to political behavior.

The usefulness of social-group cues is limited to topics directly related to group interests, but party identification has broader applications. Parties are central participants in democratic politics, so most political phenomena can be judged within a partisan framework. Party attachments obviously can simplify voting choices, since most elections involve a choice between parties. In Western Europe, where parties act as cohesive units, party voting is an effective and efficient method of decision making. The heterogeneity of American parties lessens the policy value of party voting, but the complexity of American elections makes party a valuable voting cue when one must decide on a long list of federal, state, and local candidates. Partisanship is also an important force in shaping evaluations of political leaders and new political issues. If voters are unsure about an issue, party cues can suggest where their interests lie. An issue supported by one's party is more likely to benefit the individual, whereas the policies of the opposition are suspect. In sum, because of its ability to make sense of distant, complicated, and often arcane political phenomena, party identification frequently is viewed as the central thread connecting the citizen and the political process.

Left/Right (or liberal/conservative) orientations are another potential source of political cues. Most voters do not express sophisticated ideological views, but they still can locate themselves within a broad ideological family, or *tendance* (Fuchs and Klingemann 1989; Westholm and Niemi 1992; Jacoby 1991). A Left/Right orientation provides a reference structure for evaluating political objects. When an individual complains that a candidate is too liberal, or another is too conservative, this is a shortcut to learning about the candidates' views and evaluating them on this basis.

In most nations, partisanship and ideological orientations exist side by side and have reinforcing effects. But Left/Right orientations hold special importance in political systems in which party cues are weak or fluid, for example, in France. The French party system is notoriously volatile, which undercuts the continuity and value of partisanship. Ideological tendance thus plays a larger role in guiding the political behavior of the French and can bring some order to an ever-changing political landscape (Fleury and Lewis-Beck 1993; Michelat 1993).

Table 2.2 summarizes the diverse criteria that people use in making political judgments. People in several nations were asked to describe the good and bad points of two major political parties in their nation. Only a small percentage actively employ ideological concepts in judging the parties. This does not mean, however, that the remaining individuals are devoid of political judgments. About 40 percent of the American, British, and German electorates evaluated the parties according to social-group alignments. Even more people judged the parties by their organization and political competency. Nearly half of the survey responses mentioned outright policy criteria. Even the broadest and most frequently used criteria—judging parties by the nature of the times—can provide a meaningful basis of evaluation. In short, far from suggesting that citizens are uninformed and

Table 2.2 Bases of Party Evaluations (in percentages)

Criteria based on	United States	Great Britain	West Germany
Ideological concepts	21	21	34
Social groups	40	41	45
Party organization and competence	49	35	66
Policy concepts	45	46	53
Nature of the times	64	59	86
Political figures	40	18	38
Intrinsic values	46	65	49
No content	14	18	6
Total	319	303	377

Source: Political Action Study, 1974–75.

Note: Totals exceed 100 percent because multiple responses were possible.

unsophisticated, these data display a diversity and complexity of public opinion that often is overlooked.

POLITICS AND THE PUBLIC

This chapter has described trends that are affecting all advanced industrial democracies: the rise of political interest, cognitive skills, and information resources. There are, of course, important differences in these traits across nations. Political interest and involvement apparently are more extensive in the United States than in Britain, France, or Germany. Conversely, politics and public opinion generally are more ideological in Europe than in the United States. Subsequent chapters draw out these national differences in more detail, but this chapter described the increasing political sophistication that is common to most advanced industrial democracies.

Although political sophistication has increased, democratic electorates will never match the political sophistication posited by classic democratic theory and displayed by political elites, such as members of Congress or Parliament. It makes little sense to debate this point. Instead, survey research can be more useful in describing how citizens actually perceive and evaluate politics and reach political decisions—how people deal with the decision-making tasks they face. Despite the criticisms of the naysayers, citizens regularly make political choices and use diverse criteria on which to make these decisions. How are these choices made?

This chapter described a pattern of public opinion that Donald Kinder and David Sears (1985) describe as the "pluralistic roots of political beliefs." People rely on various methods to manage the complexities of politics. Many voters focus their attention on a few issues of particular interest, rather than devote equal attention to all issues. Thus, the electorate is composed of overlapping issue publics, each judging governmental action on different policies. The bases of evaluation also vary within the electorate. Some citizens judge politics by a broad ideological framework, but this is only a minority of the public. Many more people use political cues, such as social-reference groups or party attachments, to guide their behavior. By limiting their issue interests and relying on other decision-making shortcuts, the average voter can balance the costs and benefits of political involvement and still make reasonable political decisions.[9]

Some of the most persuasive work on the diversity of decision making comes from Sniderman, Brody, and Tetlock (1991; also Moon 1990). They find, for example, that better-educated individuals are more likely to use ideological criteria in making political choices; the lesser-educated are more likely to use group references or other political cues to make their decisions. In both cases, the decisions broadly can reflect individuals' interests. Similarly, Arthur Lupia's (1994) research on voting on insurance initiatives in California found that a small attentive public was well informed on the initiatives and made choices appropriate for its expressed interests. In addition, a larger group of voters used group cues (such as which proposals were supported by Ralph Nader and which by the insurance industry) that also led to rational voting choices. This is pluralistic decision making in practice.

This pluralistic model has several implications for our study of public opinion in later chapters. We should not interpret unstable or inconsistent issue opinions as evidence that voters lack any attitudes. Survey questions are imprecise, the public's issue interests are specialized, and a complex mix of beliefs may be related to a single issue (Zaller 1992). In addition, we must be sensitive to the diversity and complexity of mass politics. Simple models of political behavior that assume a homogeneous electorate might be theoretically elegant and empirically parsimonious, but also unrealistic. People function on the basis of diverse criteria and motivations. We should try to model this diversity, instead of adopting overly generalized theories of citizen politics. Finally, we must not underestimate the potential for change. As this chapter has documented, the electorates of advanced industrial democracies have undergone a major transformation during the postwar period. Public opinion reflects a dynamic process, and we should avoid static views of an unchanging (or unchangeable) public.

We should not, of course, be guilty of overestimating the sophistication of the citizenry. There will always be instances in which the public holds ill-advised or ill-informed opinions; some citizens will remain ignorant of all political matters. Such is the imperfect nature of human behavior. A few individuals deserve the rating of full ideologues, and an equally small number are devoid of all bases for making meaningful political choices. The important lesson is not to ignore or belittle the varied criteria citizens rely on in dealing with politics.

The ultimate question, then, is not whether the public meets the maximum ideological standards of classic democratic theory but whether the public has a sufficient basis for rational political action. Phrased in these terms, and based on the evidence presented in this chapter, we can be more optimistic about the political abilities of contemporary publics.

SUGGESTED READINGS

Converse, Philip. The nature of belief systems in mass publics. In *Ideology and Discontent*, edited by D. Apter. New York: Free Press, 1994.

Delli Carpini, Michael, and Scott Keeter. *What Americans Know about Politics and Why It Matters.* New Haven: Yale University Press, 1996.

Kaase, Max, and Ken Newton. *Beliefs in Government.* Oxford: Oxford University Press, 1995.

Lupia, Arthur, and Mathew McCubbins. *The Democratic Dilemma: Can Citizens Learn What They Need to Know?* Cambridge, U.K.: Cambridge University Press, 1998.

Popkin, Samuel. *The Reasoning Voter*, 2d ed. Chicago: University of Chicago Press, 1994.

Sniderman, Paul, Richard Brody, and Philip Tetlock. *Reasoning and Choice.* New York: Cambridge University Press, 1991.

NOTES

1. There were, of course, dissenting voices. Bagehot (1978), Schumpeter (1943), Wallas (1908), and Lippmann (1922) were highly critical of a participatory view of democracy. For a review of this literature, see Eckstein (1984).

2. For other examples of such inconsistencies, see Arnold (1990). Furthermore, the elitist theory ignores the problem of democratic accountability if its assumptions were true and ignores the evidence on the abuses of power among democratically elected elites.

3. For example, subsequent research has questioned the evidence that elites are more politically tolerant than the general public (Jackman 1972; Sniderman et al. 1991).

4. Another source of debate has been methodological, focusing on how sophistication is measured. For a discussion of these points, see Dalton (1996a, 27–31).

5. The European nations used the same question: "Which sources of information are most helpful at election time?" The question in the United States asked about the use of information sources for news about what is going on in the world today.

6. The British, German, and French questions measured general interest in politics, and the questions differed across nations. The American question asked about interest in campaigns. Because of the differences in question wordings, the absolute levels of political interest should not be compared across nations; for such comparisons, see Jennings and van Deth (1989). For trends in political interest in additional nations, see Dalton and Wattenberg (2000, ch. 3).

7. Critics of the public's level of knowledge often ignore parallel findings among elite groups. For instance, Zimmerman (1990, 1991) found that newspaper editors and elected politicians displayed surprisingly low levels of knowledge about historical and scientific facts.

8. This literature is quite diverse in its applications (see Hurwitz and Peffley 1987; Sniderman, Brody, and Kuklinski 1984; Graber 1988; Miller, Wattenberg, and Malanchuk 1986; Rohrschneider 1993a). For a critique of schema theory, see Kuklinski, Luskin, and Bolland (1991).

9. The public's reliance on various decision-making shortcuts, *satisficing* behavior, is common to decision makers in business and government (Cyert and March 1963). Nevertheless, democratic elitists denigrate the public when they adopt this model for political choices.

CHAPTER 3

Political Participation

DEMOCRACY SHOULD BE a celebration of an involved public. Democracy requires an active citizenry because it is through discussion, popular interest, and involvement in politics that societal goals should be defined and carried out. Without public involvement in the process, democracy lacks both its legitimacy and its guiding force. When Germans take the time to cast informed votes, British electors canvass their neighbors, or Americans write their president, the democratic process is at work. The recent global spread of democratization has brought these democratic freedoms to millions of people. The jubilation that accompanied the first democratic elections in Eastern Europe or the open elections in South Africa attests to the value that citizens place on this right.

Even though it seems we should all be celebrating the triumph of democracy—the *End of History* in the words of one analyst (Fukuyama 1992)—by participating in the democratic process, there is great controversy about whether or not citizens are becoming apathetic about their democratic rights. The socioeconomic development of Western democracies and the process of cognitive mobilization should spur increases in political participation. Yet turnout in elections is down in the United States and many other democracies. Moreover, Robert Putnam (1995, 2000) recently has warned that civic engagement is decreasing to dangerous levels in America. A recent bipartisan report on the state of American democracy echoed the sentiments that fewer citizens are politically engaged; they are becoming spectators instead of participants in the democratic process—and democracy will suffer as a result (Bennet and Nunn 1998). Are we celebrating the success of democracy by staying home?

In order to study these questions, we must recognize that there are different forms of citizen input. This chapter examines participation in several methods of "conventional" citizen action: voting, campaigns, group activities, and other methods normally associated with conventional politics. Unconventional forms of participation (protests, demonstrations, etc.) are examined in the next chapter because the sources and motivations of unconventional participation are sufficiently distinct to deserve separate attention.

INTERNET RESOURCE

The Institute for Democracy and Electoral Assistance
(IDEA) has data on election turnout around
the globe:

www.idea.int/voter_turnout/index.html

THE MODES OF PARTICIPATION

Think about what you would do if you wanted to influence the government on a policy that was important to you. We often equate political participation with the act of voting. But if you view politics from the citizen's perspective, participation is not limited to voting, nor is voting necessarily the most effective means of influencing the political process. Instead of waiting several years until the next election, you might try to contact political elites directly, or you might work with others who share your interests, or you might find other ways to advocate your cause. In short, democratic participation can take a variety of forms.

Sidney Verba and his colleagues (Verba, Nie, and Kim 1971, 1978) explored the different forms of conventional political action that citizens might use: voting, campaign activity, communal activity (working with a group in the community), and contacting officials on personal matters (table 3.1). They found that people do not use various activities interchangeably, as many early analysts assumed. Instead, people tend to specialize in activities that match their motivations and goals. Specific kinds of activities frequently cluster together. A person who performs one act from a particular cluster is likely to perform other acts from the same cluster, but not necessarily activities from another cluster. They labeled these clusters of activities as *modes of democratic participation.*

These participation modes differ in the requirements they place on participants and the nature of the action. Verba and his colleagues (1978) classified the differences between modes in terms of several criteria: (1) whether the act conveys information about the individual's political preferences and/or applies pressure for compliance; (2) whether the act is directed toward a broad social outcome or a particular interest; (3) the potential degree of conflict involved in the activity; (4) the amount of effort required; and (5) the amount of cooperation with others required by the act.

Voting, for example, is a high-pressure activity because it determines control of the government, but its policy focus is limited because an election involves many issues. Voting also is a reasonably simple act that requires little initiative or cooperation with others. Involvement in political campaigns makes much greater

Table 3.1 Dimensions of Political Activity and Modes of Activity

Mode of activity	Type of influence	Scope of outcome	Conflict	Initiative required	Cooperate with others
Voting	High pressure/ low information	Collective	Conflictual	Little	Little
Campaign activity	High pressure/low to high information	Collective	Conflictual	Some	Some or much
Communal activity	Low to high pressure/ high information	Collective	Maybe yes/maybe no	Some or much	Some or much
Contacting officials on personal matters	Low pressure/ high information	Particular	Nonconflictual	Much	Little
Protest	High pressure/ high information	Collective	Very conflictual	Some or much	Some or much

Source: Verba, Nie, and Kim (1978, 55) with modifications.

demands on the time and motivation of individuals. Although campaign work occurs within an electoral setting, it can be more policy focused than the simple act of voting. Participation in community groups—communal activity—may require even more effort by the individual and produces a qualitatively different form of citizen input. Citizen groups can control both the methods of action and the policy focus of their activities. Finally, some individuals participate for a very particular reason—to have a pothole fixed or request other government services— that does not address broad policy questions. In short, the important point is that different forms of political participation are not equal: They involve different groups of individuals and wield different influence on the political process.

This clustering of activities seems to be a common feature of democratic politics. A replication of the American survey found essentially the same participation grouping two decades later (Verba, Schlozman, and Brady 1995). The British participation study (Parry, Moyser, and Day 1992) added some activities and found additional modes, but their basic findings are very similar to American research.[1] Thus, our discussion of citizen action focuses on the three most common modes of conventional participation: voting, campaign activity, and communal activity.[2]

Voting

The history of modern democracies has followed a pattern of almost ever-expanding citizen involvement in elections (Rokkan 1970). The voting franchise in most nations initially was restricted to property owners with long residency requirements. The United States was one of the first nations to begin liberalizing suffrage laws. By 1850 virtually the entire white adult male population in the United States was enfranchised. The extension of voting rights proceeded more slowly in Western Europe. These societies lacked the populist tradition that existed in the United States. In addition, social cleavages were more sharply polarized; many European conservatives were hesitant to enfranchise a working class that might vote them out of office. An emerging socialist movement in the 1800s pressed for the political equality of the working class, but mass suffrage often was delayed until war or revolution disrupted the conservative political order. French adult males gained voting rights with the formation of the Third Republic in 1870. Britain limited election rolls until early in the twentieth century by placing significant residency and financial restrictions on voting and by allowing multiple votes for business owners and university graduates. Electoral reforms followed World War I and virtually all British males received voting rights. Germany, too, had limited the franchise and allowed for multiple votes during the Wilhelmine Empire. True democratic elections with mass suffrage began with the creation of the Weimar Republic in 1919.

During the twentieth century, governments gradually extended suffrage rights to the rest of the adult population. Women's right to vote was acknowledged first in Britain (1918); Germany (1919) and the United States (1920) quickly followed. France lagged most of Western Europe in this instance; French women were enfranchised only in 1944. The Voting Rights Act of 1965 removed most of the remaining formal restrictions on the voting participation of American blacks. Finally, in the 1970s all four nations lowered the voting age to eighteen years of age.

The right to vote now extends to virtually the entire adult population in contemporary democracies. There are, however, distinct national differences in the rate at which citizens actually turn out to vote. Table 3.2 presents the rates of voting turnout for twenty-four industrialized democracies from the 1950s to the 1990s. These data display sharp cross-national differences in participation levels across democratic nations. In the United States and Switzerland, for

Table 3.2   Levels of Turnout from the 1950s to the 1990s (percentage voting)

	1950s	1960s	1970s	1980s	1990s
Australia	90	93	93	91	94
Austria	94	93	92	92	84
Belgium	88	86	86	87	85
GREAT BRITAIN	**80**	**76**	**75**	**74**	**75**
Canada	74	77	73	73	69
Denmark	82	87	87	86	84
Finland	86	85	78	75	71
FRANCE	**80**	**77**	**82**	**72**	**69**
GERMANY (WEST)	**87**	**87**	**91**	**87**	**79**
Greece	—	—	78	80	80
Iceland	91	91	90	89	86
Ireland	74	74	76	72	67
Israel	78	80	78	78	77
Italy	94	93	93	89	85
Japan	76	80	78	78	73
Luxembourg	92	90	90	88	87
Netherlands	95	95	84	84	76
New Zealand	91	88	85	89	80
Norway	79	83	82	83	77
Portugal	—	—	88	78	68
Spain	—	—	73	75	76
Sweden	79	86	90	90	85
Switzerland	69	64	53	48	44
UNITED STATES	**61**	**62**	**54**	**52**	**53**
21-nation average	82	82	81	79	76

Sources: Mackie and Rose (1991) and data collected by the author.

instance, national elections involve barely half of the eligible adults. Voting rates are consistently higher in most European nations, especially in Germany, where close to 80 percent of the electorate cast a ballot in Bundestag elections. Turnout ranges between 70 and 90 percent in most British House of Commons elections and French National Assembly elections.

The other significant pattern in table 3.2 is the trend in participation rates over time. Comparing the two end points for the twenty-one nations with a complete time series, twelve have experienced turnout declines of more than 2 percent (including France, Germany, and the United States), seven have had stable turnout levels (plus or minus 2 percent), and one saw a turnout increase of more than 2 percent. More refined analyses indicate that voting rates peaked in the 1960s and then declined, especially in the 1990s (Gray and Caul 2000). Thus, voting participation is generally decreasing across national boundaries.

Voting levels in the United States appear significantly lower than in most other nations, and the decrease in American turnout over the past forty years has exacerbated this pattern. Some analysts cite these statistics as evidence of the American electorate's limited political involvement (and by implication limited political abilities). But a more complex set of factors is at work (Wattenberg in press; Teixeira 1992, chap. 1; Franklin 1996). Voter registration systems and other electoral procedures strongly influence transatlantic differences in turnout. Most Europeans are automatically included on the roster of registered voters, and these electoral registers are updated by the government. Thus, a much larger percentage of the European public is registered to participate in elections. In contrast, most Americans must take the initiative to register themselves, and many eligible voters fail to do so. By many estimates, participation in American elections would increase by at least ten percentage points if the European system of registration were adopted (Wolfinger and Rosenstone 1980). The scheduling of most European elections on weekends also encourages turnout, because more voters can find the time to visit the polls. In addition, most European electoral systems are based on proportional representation (PR) rather than plurality-based single-member districts, as in the United States. Proportional representation stimulates turnout because any party, large or small, can increase its representation in the legislature as a direct function of its share of the popular vote (Blais and Carty 1990; Franklin 1996).

Powell (1986) and Markus Crepaz (1990) show that political competition is another strong influence on turnout rates. Sharp social or ideological cleavages between parties stimulate turnout. When European voters go to the polls, they are deciding whether their country will be run by parties with socialist, green, conservative, ethnic, or even religious programs. These sharp party differences encourage higher voting rates. Robert Jackman (1987) finds that the number of party choices and the structure of legislative power in a system are direct predictors of turnout.

The United States also differs from most other democracies because the American government asks its citizens to vote on far more matters. Whereas the typical European voter may cast three or four ballots in a four-year period, many Americans face a dozen or more separate elections in the space of four years. Furthermore, Americans are expected to vote for a much wider range of political offices. Only one house of the bicameral national legislature is directly elected in Britain, Germany, and France; the French president is one of the few directly elected European heads of state. Local, regional, and even national elections in Europe normally consist of casting a single ballot for a single office. The extensive list of elected offices and long ballots common to American elections are unknown in Western Europe. Finally, direct democracy techniques such as the referendum and initiative are used only sparingly in France and Britain and not at all in German national politics.

Thus, the American political system places unusual demands on the voters to decide on an array of political offices, government bond and tax proposals, and other policy initiatives. Voting in low-information contests, such as those for local nonpartisan offices, is a real challenge for American voters. It is probably no coincidence that the one European country that has a comparable turnout level to the United States—Switzerland—also presents its citizens with extensive voting opportunities (for other reasons why Swiss turnout is so low, see Powell 1982, 119).

Rather than count only the number of people who vote in national elections, an alternative measure of participation focuses on the *amount of electing* being done by the public (Crewe 1981). When the context of American elections is considered, the amount of electing is actually quite high:

> No country can approach the United States in the frequency and variety of elections, and thus in the amount of electing. No other country elects its lower house as often as every two years, or its president as frequently as every four years. No other country popularly elects its state governors and town mayors, or has as wide a variety of nonrepresentative offices (judges, sheriffs, attorneys general, city treasurers, and so on) subject to election. Only one other country (Switzerland) can compete in the number and variety of local referendums, and only two (Belgium and Turkey) hold party "primaries" in most parts of the country. Even if differences in turnout rates are taken into account, American citizens do not necessarily vote less often than other nationalities; most probably, they do more voting. (Crewe 1981, 262)

A simple comparison of the electoral experiences of a typical European and American voter highlights this difference in the amount of voting. For example, between 1995 and 2000 a resident of Oxford, England, could have voted about four times; a resident of Irvine, California, could have cast more than fifty votes in just the single year of 2000.[3]

Turnout rates in national elections thus provide a poor indicator of the overall political involvement of the public. In addition, the simple quantity of voting is less important than the quality of this participation mode. Verba, Nie, and Kim (1978, chap. 3) describe voting as an activity of high pressure because leaders are being chosen, but there is limited specific policy information or influence because elections involve a diverse range of factors. Therefore, the infrequent opportunity of most Europeans to cast a single vote for a prepackaged party is a limited tool of political influence. This influence may increase when elections extend to a wide range of political offices and include referendums, as in the United States. Still, it is difficult to treat elections as policy mandates because they assess relative support for broad programs and not specific policies. Even a sophisticated policy-oriented electorate cannot be assured that important policy options are represented in an election or that the government will follow these policies in the period between elections. Consequently, research shows that many people vote because of a sense of civic duty or involvement in a campaign or as an expression of political or partisan support, rather than to influence policy.

The limits of voting have led some critics to claim that by focusing mass participation on voting, parties and political elites are seeking to protect their privileged position in the policy process and actually limit citizen influence. Even if this skepticism is deserved, voting will remain an important aspect of democratic politics, as much for its symbolic value as for its instrumental influence on policy. Voting is the one activity that binds the individual to the political system and legitimizes the rest of the democratic process. And the decline in voting turnout seems to confirm the popular impression that democratic participation is now waning.

Campaign Activity

Participation in campaigns represents an extension of electoral participation beyond the act of voting. This mode includes a variety of political acts: working for a party or candidate, attending campaign meetings, persuading others how to vote, membership in a party or political organization, and other forms of party activity during and between elections. Fewer people are routinely active in campaigns because this is more demanding than merely casting a vote. Campaign work requires more initiative, and there is greater need to coordinate participation with others (see table 3.1, p. 34). Along with the additional effort, campaign activity can provide more political influence to the individual citizen and convey more information than voting. Campaign activities are important to parties and candidates, and candidates generally are more sensitive to, and aware of, the policy interests of their activists (Verba and Nie 1972, chaps. 17–19).

Campaign activities can take many forms, depending on the context of electioneering in the nation. In the United States, for example, campaigns are now largely media events. Popular involvement in organized campaign activities is limited (table 3.3). Few Americans attend party meetings, work for a party or

Table 3.3 Trends in American Campaign Activity

Activity	1952	1956	1960	1964	1968	1972	1976	1980	1984	1988	1992	1996	2000
Work for a party or candidate	3	3	6	5	6	5	4	4	4	3	3	2	3
Go to a meeting	7	7	8	8	9	9	6	8	8	7	8	5	5
Give money	4	10	12	11	9	10	16	8	8	9	7	7	6
Wear a button or have a bumper sticker	—	16	21	17	15	14	8	7	9	9	11	10	10
Persuade others how to vote	28	28	34	31	33	32	37	36	32	29	38	27	34

Source: American National Election Study, 1952–2000.

candidate, or belong to a party or political club. Putnam (2000, chap. 2) presents additional poll data that indicate a decreased attendance at political meetings and party work since the early 1970s. The most frequent campaign activities are individualistic forms of involvement: giving money to a campaign or trying to persuade others. Personal involvement in campaign discussions has held steady or even increased slightly over the past thirty years.

British campaigns differ in several ways from American elections. British elections do not follow a regular time schedule; the prime minister may dissolve Parliament and call for new elections at almost any time during a legislative term. Therefore, elections are often quickly organized and brief, averaging little more than a month. In addition, British parties depend on a pool of formal party members for the bulk of campaign work. Party members attend political rallies, canvass the constituency during the campaign, and go door-to-door contacting potential voters on election day. Beyond the core of party members, there is limited participation in most campaign activities (table 3.4). Moreover, with declines in the percentage of party members has come a general decrease in organized campaign activities.

Germany's development of a democratic political system during the late twentieth century increased citizen involvement in campaigns and most other aspects of the politics (Ühlinger 1989). Membership in the political parties grew from the 1950s until the 1980s, and participation in campaigns also grew. For example, 11 percent of the public attended a campaign meeting in the 1961 election; by 1976 this figure had nearly doubled (20 percent). Beginning in the 1970s popular displays of party support also became a visible aspect of campaigns. But since the 1980s participation in campaigns has dropped off, much as it has in the rest of Europe (Dalton and Wattenberg 2000, chap. 3). Formal party membership has also decreased over the past decade (Scarrow 2000).

Still, relative to other Europeans, the German public remains politically engaged.[4] In the 1989 European Parliament (EP) election, for instance, German voters closely followed the campaign in the media and nearly one out of ten spoke with a party worker during the campaign—although the EP elections attract much less attention than Bundestag elections (see table 3.5).

The available evidence on party and campaign activity in France is less extensive. Formal party membership increased during the Fifth Republic until the 1980s and then decreased during the 1990s. There are ongoing debates about the general depoliticization of French politics (Boy and Mayer 1993). Attendance at campaign meetings, public displays of party support, and other campaign activities probably have decreased during the past two decades, though firm empirical evidence is limited. Data from the 1989 EP election show that many French voters followed the campaign, but campaign involvement lags slightly behind British and German levels (table 3.5).

Although national histories differ, campaign activity has generally decreased across these four nations. Evidence from a larger set of nations suggests that this

Table 3.4 Trends in British Campaign Activity

Activity	1964	1966	1970	1974	1975	1979	1983	1987	1997
Canvas	3	2	1	2	2	2	2	2	2
Work for party or candidate	8	2	2	2	3	2	2	2	–
Attend meeting (indoors)	8	7	5	5	6	4	3	4	4
Attend meeting (outdoors)	8	3	6	4	3	2	–	–	7
Display poster	–	–	10	9	11	8	12	10	9
Party member	14	–	10	–	8	–	7	9	4
Read electoral address	46	49	53	51	43	56	49	49	62

Sources: 1964–75, 1983–97 from British Gallup Poll; participation data for 1979 and party membership data for all years from the British Election Studies.

Table 3.5   Participation in Various Activities for European Parliament Election
(in percentages)

	Britain	France	Germany
Followed campaign			
Watched TV program on election	50	51	61
Read newspaper report on election	30	26	32
Read a party poster	11	25	35
Listened to radio on election	18	19	19
Read party materials	32	18	16
Read advertisement about election	15	14	23
Active in campaign			
Talked to people about election	32	39	40
Spoke to a party worker	4	5	9
Tried to persuade someone on vote	7	8	3
Attended a public meeting	1	3	7

Source: Eurobarometer 31A (June 1989).

is a common pattern for most advanced industrial democracies (Dalton and Wattenberg 2000, chap. 3). Fewer citizens now attend political rallies, work for a party or candidate, or actively participate in election campaigns (giving money to U.S. campaigns may be the primary counterexample). The expanding electoral role of the mass media may be one factor behind these trends. The media's growing importance as a source of information is lessening the importance of party-organized activities designed to inform the public. The media's role also has encouraged the spread of American-style electioneering to Western Europe. British candidates orchestrate "walkabouts" to generate stories for the evening television news, campaigns focus more attention on candidate personalities than in the past, and televised preelection debates are the norm in Germany and France.

These data seem to provide further evidence of the disengagement of contemporary publics. Although many individuals are still drawn to the excitement and competition of elections, campaign participation now is more often individualistic, such as a display of party support or discussing the elections with friends. The collective activities that once marked election campaigns are now less frequent. Thus, the *level* of campaign activity may be changing as well as the *nature* of the public's involvement.

Communal Activity

The essence of grassroots democracy is represented in communal activity. Communal participation can take a wide variety of forms. Communal activity often involves group efforts to deal with social or community problems, ranging from issues of schools or roads to protecting the local environment. From the PTA to local neighborhood committees, this is democracy in action. The existence of such autonomous groups and independent action defines the characteristics of a civil society that theorists from Thomas Jefferson to the present have considered a foundation of the democratic process. Tocqueville, for example, saw such group activity as a distinctive feature of American democracy:

> The political activity that pervades the United States must be seen to be understood. No sooner do you set foot upon American ground than you are stunned by a kind of tumult; . . . here the people of one quarter of a town are meeting to decide upon the building of a church; there the election of a representative is going on; a little farther, the delegates of a district are hastening to the town in order to consult upon some local improvements; in another place, the laborers of a village quit their plows to deliberate upon a project of a road or a public school. . . . To take a hand in the regulation of society and to discuss it is (the) biggest concern and, so to speak, the only pleasure an American knows. (Tocqueville 1966, 249–50)

Today participation in citizen groups can include involvement in public interest groups with broad policy concerns, such as environmental interest groups, women's groups, or consumer protection.

This mode is distinct from campaigns because communal participation takes place largely outside the electoral setting and lacks a partisan focus. Because participation is not structured by an election, a relatively high level of political sophistication and initiative is required of communal activists (table 3.1, p. 34). Citizens define their own issue agenda, the methods of influencing policymakers, and the timing of influence. The issues might be as broad as nuclear disarmament or as narrow as the policies of the local school district—citizens, not elites, decide. Control over the framework of participation means that communal activities can convey more information and exert more political pressure than the public's restricted participation in campaigns. In short, the communal mode shifts control of participation to the public and thereby increases the citizenry's political influence.

Political scientists are now intensely debating whether or not communal activity and participation in citizen groups is following the same downward spiral as election turnout. In a provocative series of analyses, Putnam (1995, 2000) claims that we are now "bowling alone." He tracks the decline of traditional American social and civic associations across the second half of the twentieth century. Participation in groups ranging from the Elks and Moose clubs to the PTA to bowling leagues has dropped off markedly over the past four decades. Putnam notes that such groups taught skills and norms that spurred democratic political involvement, and with the decline of such associations involvement has stagnated. He tracks a secular decline in the number of Americans who attended a public meeting on town or school affairs, who belonged to a "better government" group, or who served on a committee for a local organization. Instead, too many of us are sitting at home in front of our television sets or computer monitors.

Putnam's critics maintain that he is studying the "old" forms of group activity, and while contemporary publics are not engaged in Elks and Moose lodges, but in self-help groups, neighborhood associations, and issue-oriented groups such as environmental groups and the women's movement (Skocpol and Fiorina 1999). In fact, Putnam gives examples of these new forms of action when he lists the range of social activities held in one California church:

> In January 1991 the weekly calendar of the Crystal Cathedral . . . included sessions devoted to Women in the Marketplace, Conquering Compulsive Behaviors, Career Builders' Workshop, Stretch and Walk Time for Women, Cancer Conquerors, Positive Christian Singles, Gamblers Anonymous, Women Who Love Too Much, Overeaters Anonymous, and Friday Night Live. (Putnam 2000, 66)

These are examples of the new forms of social organization that are not tapped by membership in the traditional social institutions.

The unstructured nature of communal activities makes it difficult to measure participation levels accurately or to compare levels across nations. Still, citizens in the four nations in our study all are engaged in communal activities to a significant degree. Group-based participation has long been a distinctive aspect of the American political culture, and membership in social groups often exceeds that in other democracies. Verba and his colleagues find that American participation in community groups increased from 30 percent in 1967 to 34 percent in 1987 (Verba, Schlozman, and Brady 1995, 72). When Putnam replicated this question in 2000, participation on a community project had increased further to 38 percent of the public.[5] The World Values Survey also finds that the number of Americans who belong to civic associations, environmental groups, women's groups, or peace groups increased from 6 percent in 1980 to 18 percent in 1990—producing a higher rate of membership than in Britain, France, or Germany (figure 3.1).

European political norms traditionally placed less emphasis on group activities, and the structure of European political systems does not encourage direct citizen contact with elected representatives. But there is strong evidence that communal participation has grown in these other democracies over the past few decades. Peter Hall (1999) demonstrates a growth of British participation in social groups, and the World Values Survey similarly finds nearly a doubling of civic participation from 1980 to 1990 (figure 3.1; also see Parry, Moyser, and Day 1992,

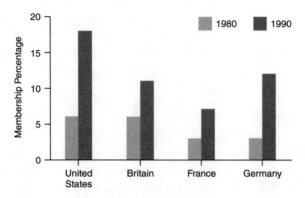

Figure 3.1   Participation in Public Interest Groups, 1980–90

Source: 1980–81 World Values Survey and 1990–93 World Values Survey.

Note: Figure entries are the percentages of those surveyed who belong to a civic association, environmental group, women's group, or peace group in each nation.

44–45). Communal activity also has increased in Germany (Wessels 1997; Offe 2002). Voluntary civic associations were an innovation for German politics in the 1970s, but now these groups have expanded to become a regular aspect of politics. Again, the World Values Survey tracks this increase: In 1980, 3 percent claimed to belong to a civic association or political group; this increased to 12 percent by 1990. By most accounts, communal activity is more limited in France. Tocqueville, for example, contrasted American social cooperation with the individualism of the French political culture. But even in France, the World Values Survey tracks an increase in civic participation from 1980 to 1990.

Putnam has identified important changes in the American political process, but I am not convinced that his findings mean that political involvement of all sorts is declining, or that the patterns he described for the United States apply to other democracies. Especially for the three European nations we examine, participation in social and civic groups seems to be increasing, introducing more direct citizen involvement in the political process. (Furthermore, many of the factors that Putnam uses to explain the American trends also have occurred in Europe, but apparently without the same effects.) Even if Americans are less likely to participate in institutionalized forms of social or political action, there is some evidence that engagement in informal groups, social movements, and local initiatives is filling part of this void (Putnam 2000, chap. 10). In summary, communal political involvement seems to be an increasingly common aspect of political action in contemporary democracies.

WHO PARTICIPATES?

The question of who participates in politics is as important as the question of how many people participate. First, the characteristics of participants help us to interpret the meaning of political activism. For example, policy dissatisfaction might either increase or decrease the likelihood of political action. In one instance, dissatisfaction might stimulate individuals to participate in order to redress their grievances; in another instance, dissatisfaction might lead to alienation and a withdrawal from politics. These two alternatives cast a much different light on how we interpret participation. Second, if participation influences policy results, then the pattern of action suggests which citizens are making their voices heard by policymakers and which interests are not represented. Finally, comparing the correlates of action across nations and modes provides insights into the political process in each nation and how it shapes citizen choices on how to participate.

Verba, Schlozman, and Brady (1995) summarized previous theories of participation in terms of what they call the "civic voluntarism model." The model includes three types of influences on political participation: *personal characteristics, group effects,* and *political attitudes.* Under the first heading, political scientists stress social status (e.g., education and income) as the personal characteristic that is most strongly related to political action. Higher-status individuals, especially the better educated, are more likely to have the time, the money, the access to political information, the knowledge, and the ability to become politically involved. It is not social status, per se, that stimulates participation, but social status is related to skills and orientations that directly influence participation (Nie, Junn, and Stehlik-Barry 1996; Verba, Schlozman, and Brady 1995). So widespread is this notion that social status is sometimes described as the "standard model" of political participation (Verba and Nie 1972, chap. 8). Therefore, social status is the first variable to add to our inventory of the potential causes of participation.

Another personal characteristic is the individual's position in the life cycle. For many young people, politics is a remote world. As individuals age, however, they take on social responsibilities that increase their motivations to follow politics. People become taxpayers and homeowners, their children enter public schools, and they may begin to draw benefits from government programs. Most studies thus find that political involvement increases with age.

Gender is another factor that might affect political activism. Men are often more politically active than women in democracies (Lovenduski 1986). Differences in political resources, such as educational level, income, and employment patterns, explain a large part of this gap (Schlozman, Burns, and Verba 1994). In addition, early life learning often portrays politics as inappropriate to the female role; this undoubtedly lessens the motivation of women to participate and the willingness of the male world to accept female participation. In an age of changing gender roles, we can determine whether or not gender is still an important predictor of participation.

A second group of potential predictors reflect group-based forces. Some group influences may be psychological, such as attachments to one's preferred political party. Because campaigns and elections are largely partisan contests, party attachments can stimulate individuals to act (Verba, Nie, and Kim 1978, chap. 6). A sense of party identification motivates people to vote or participate in campaigns as a display of party support; they are concerned that their party wins. Conversely, people with weak or nonexistent party bonds are less concerned with election results and are less likely to participate.

Participation in social and voluntary groups provides another potential stimulant to action. Experience in the participatory decision making of a social club or volunteer organization develops skills and orientations that carry over to the world of politics (Putnam 2000; Verba, Schlozman, and Brady 1995). Social groups also provide a useful reference structure for judging whether or not participation is a worthwhile activity in stimulating action (Uhlaner 1989). In addition, certain social groups actively mobilize the involvement of their members. Therefore, participation in nonpolitical groups may stimulate political involvement.

Finally, political values are a third possible influence on participation. For example, researchers continue to debate the causal role of political dissatisfaction. On the one hand, policy satisfaction might increase support for the political process and thereby political participation. In these terms, high turnout rates show the public's basic support of the government. On the other hand, dissatisfaction might stimulate efforts to change policy. From this perspective, high turnout rates show widespread public dissatisfaction with the government. Although scholars may disagree on the causal direction of policy dissatisfaction, they regard it as an important potential influence on participation levels.

In a somewhat different vein, participation may be related to policy preferences or ideology (Verba and Nie 1972; Verba, Schlozman, and Brady 1995). Do Democrats participate as much as Republicans, or do they participate in different ways? If participation has an influence on policymakers and the government, then the question of whether activists are drawn equally across political camps has important implications for the representativeness of the democratic process. Political participation that is heavily concentrated among ideological extremists might distort the policy process. Therefore, it is important to consider the political orientations (and policy preferences) of participants.

Beliefs about the citizen's role and the nature of political action also may affect participation rates (Parry, Moyser, and Day 1992, chap. 8).[6] A sense of political efficacy, the feeling that one's political action can affect the political process, can stimulate individuals to participate. Conversely, a feeling of political cynicism can lead to political apathy and withdrawal. If one cannot affect the political process, why bother to try?

Among these three groups of potential predictors, the surveys available for analysis include the following factors:

- Educational level
- Age
- Gender
- Political party attachments
- Union membership
- Satisfaction with the democratic process
- Left/Right position

One of the lessons of the civic voluntarism model is that the effects of these variables overlap. Social status, for example, should independently influence through its impact on voters' cognitive skills, as well as through the values and norms that education stimulates. To determine the separate influence of each variable, we used them in a summary analysis predicting political participation. The analysis measures the causal importance of each factor on political activism, independent of the effects of the other variables. We conducted the analysis separately for voting, campaign activity, and communal activity to compare the causal patterns across participation modes.

Voting

Who is more likely to vote? We compared participation rates in the 1992 U.S. presidential election and in the 1989 European Parliament elections (figure 3.2).[7] The thickness of the arrows in the figure illustrates the magnitude of influence for each factor.

The thick arrows connecting age and voting show that turnout increases significantly with age, especially in the United States ($\beta = .21$), Britain ($\beta = .24$), and France ($\beta = .33$). The figure expresses these causal effects as statistical coefficients, for which the influence of age is estimated independent of the effects of the other predictors in the model. If the simple relationship is expressed in percentage terms, about 80 percent of Americans in their fifties claim to have voted, compared to about 60 percent among twenty-year-olds. Voting turnout follows this life-cycle pattern in these three nations.

Because elections are partisan contests, those who identify strongly with a party are more likely to show up at the polls (and presumably cast a ballot for their own party). Another organizational influence, union membership, shows a weak influence in stimulating turnout.

The other variables in the model display only small differences in participation rates. Voting rates are slightly higher among the better educated in all three European nations, although educational differences are much more pronounced among Americans. Political values—satisfaction with democracy

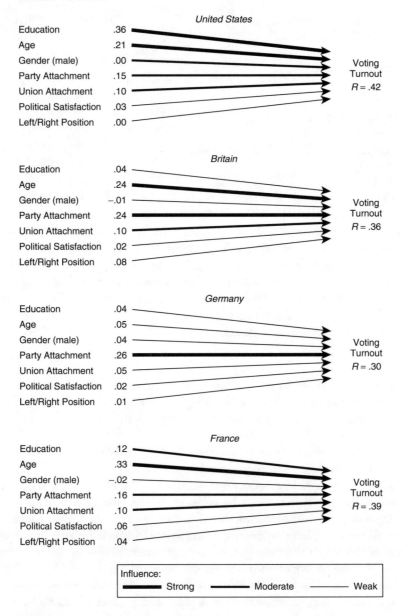

Figure 3.2   Predictors of Voting Turnout

Sources: American National Election Study 1992; Eurobarometer 31A.

Note: Analyses are based on individuals age 18 and older in the United States and 19 or older in the Eurobarometer study.

and Left/Right position—have a negligible impact on turnout.[8] In this most common of political activities, the political bias in participation is minimal.

Campaign Activity

Because the characteristics of campaign activity differ from the simple act of voting, we might expect that the type of people who participate in campaign activity also differs. We combined several measures of campaign activism into a single index.[9] Then we used our standard set of predictors to explain campaign activism.

Figure 3.3 shows that individuals with strong partisan attachments are more likely to be active in campaigns. Because campaign work is an intensely partisan activity, partisan ties exert an even stronger force there than on voting turnout. In percentage terms, for example, 54 percent of the strong partisans in the United States participated in at least one campaign activity, compared to only 33 percent among nonpartisans.

The greater initiative required by campaign activity also means that the political skills and resources represented by education have a greater influence on participation rates. Campaign activists in the United States, Britain, and France are disproportionately drawn from the better educated. At the same time, union involvement also stimulates campaign activity among Europeans, indicating that unions are mobilizing this sector into the political process.

Is there a gender gap? For both voting and campaign activity, gender differences in participation are small and inconsistent. Males vote at a higher rate in Germany and the United States; females are more frequent voters in Britain and France. The effects of gender on campaign activity are equally limited and varied across nations. Furthermore, other research suggests that gender differences in participation may be decreasing (Inglehart 1990, chap. 10). The gender image of politics may be lessening as more women enter the political process and gender roles in society narrow.

Communal Activity

Participation in citizen-action groups requires a great deal of initiative and sophistication from the participant. As a result, figure 3.4 shows that the better educated are much more likely to participate in communal activities in all three European nations.[10] The other personal factors—age and gender—generally exert little influence. The one exception is in Germany, where the young are more active in citizen groups. This may reflect younger Germans' inclination toward more direct, participatory styles of political action.

Working with a community group is distinct from voting and campaign activity because communal participation is generally not a partisan activity. In fact, in many instances participants are drawn to communal groups because they lack strict party allegiances. Consequently, the figure shows that party ties have

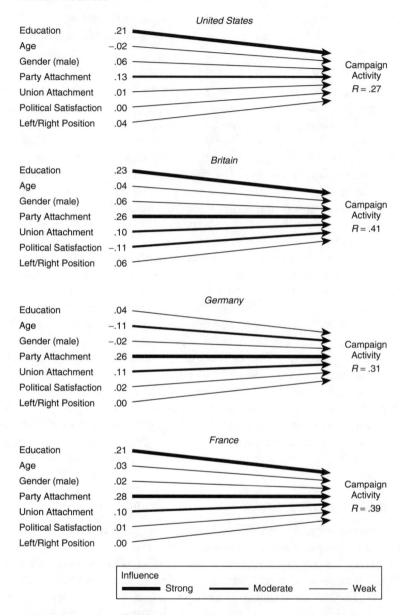

Figure 3.3   Predictors of Campaign Activity

Sources: American National Election Study 1992; Eurobarometer 31A.

Note: Analyses are based on individuals age 18 and older in the United States and 19 or older in the Eurobarometer study.

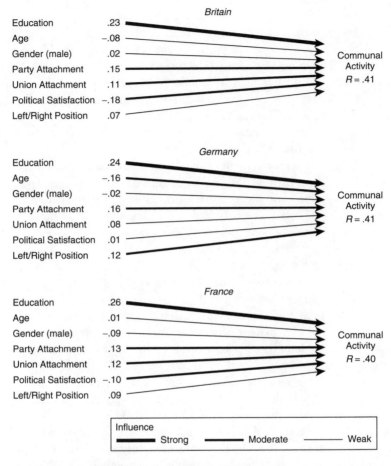

Figure 3.4   Predictors of Communal Activity

Source: Eurobarometer 31.

less impact on communal participation than on voting or campaign activities. We also find that union membership is less influential there than on the other two participation modes because citizen-action groups lie outside the normal domain of union-based politics.

Broad political orientations exert only a limited influence on communal activity. In Britain, those who are satisfied with the functioning of democracy are less likely to participate (ß = .13); but in France the satisfied are actually more active, and in Germany this variable has little influence. Leftists have a slight tendency to be more involved in citizen groups, but these differences are modest in each nation.

The group differences in activity for the three participation modes are fairly similar across nations, but two national deviations deserve attention. For all three modes, educational differences in participation are greater in the United States than in the other nations. American differences in voting by education (ß = .36), for instance, are far greater than in Britain (ß = .04), Germany (ß = .04), or France (ß = .08). Moreover, educational differences in turnout are increasing in America (Teixeira 1992; Wattenberg in press). We expect some differences in participation rates between social strata, but too large a gap implies that certain groups are excluded from the democratic process.

Most European democracies have avoided the problem of large social-status differences in voting turnout. Strong labor unions and working-class parties mobilize the working class and the less educated so that participation rates are more similar across social strata. Indeed, union membership is more strongly related to participation among European electorates, and the extent of union membership is much greater among the European working class. The weakness of these same organizations in the United States, when coupled with the restrictive registration requirements of the American electoral system, has created a serious participation gap between social groups. Frances Fox Piven and Richard Cloward (2000) even go so far as to argue that this class bias was an intentional consequence of the U.S. system of voter registration. Regardless of the intent, the U.S. electoral system limits participation by the poor and the less educated. This large participation gap in the United States shows the need for some method of equalizing the involvement of all social groups in American politics.

A second national difference involves the age variable. In Germany, the young participate more than the old in campaign and communal activities—a direct reversal of the normal life-cycle pattern. This age relationship reflects German historical conditions. In the 1970s Germany experienced a "participatory revolution" that greatly increased public involvement in politics, and the young were at the forefront of this revolution (Kaase 1982). The persisting tendency for the young to be politically more active reflects the continuation of this process and the ability of alternative groups, such as the Green Party, to attract the young into the political process.

CHANGING PUBLICS AND POLITICAL PARTICIPATION

There are a variety of ways in which people can become involved in the democratic process, and we have demonstrated these differences in this chapter. Voting turnout is high in most Western democracies, averaging more than 70 percent in most nations. In addition, a sizable proportion of the populace is involved in more demanding political activities, such as campaigns, communal participation, or directly contacting government officials.

Each of our four nations displays a different mix of these various methods of citizen influence. Americans come closest to the pattern of multidimensional participants. Turnout in elections is low, but Americans are active in campaigns and community activities at relatively high levels. Germans also are a relatively participatory public. Turnout rates are much higher than in the United States, and Germans are involved in campaign and communal activities. The British patterns of participation focus on voting, with modest involvement beyond the ballot box. In their more extensive analysis of British participation patterns, Geraint Parry and his colleagues (1992, chap. 10) note with some dismay that a quarter of the British public are almost completely inactive, and less than 2 percent are active across several modes. Based on the limited available evidence, the French appear to have limited involvement in group and campaign activities, focusing their conventional participation on voting.

Our findings show that contemporary electorates are involved in politics. Yet a paradox remains. Measures of political information, interest, and sophistication in chapter 2 display a clear increase over the past few decades. Several scholars have pointed out that rising levels of education and increased media consumption should increase participation (Teixeira 1992; Wattenberg in press). In overall terms, however, conventional participation levels are not increasing significantly; in some areas participation actually has declined. Voting turnout rates have decreased for most advanced industrial democracies. And campaign activity has displayed a similar erosion. Brody (1978) refers to this as the "puzzle of political participation." Why are some aspects of political participation decreasing, if the public's political skills and resources are increasing?

This is a paradox with many possible explanations. Steven Rosenstone and John Hansen (1993) suggest that the decline in American turnout is due to the decreasing ability of political organizations to mobilize individuals into action (also see Abramson and Aldrich 1982). The political parties are less active in bringing individuals to the polls and getting the public involved in campaigns. Growing social isolation and the decline of community is another explanation (Putnam 2000; Teixeira 1992, chap. 2). Although these arguments carry some weight, they are partially circular in their logic. People are less active in partisan politics because fewer people are actively involving others in politics; people are less politically active because they are also less active in nonpolitical groups.

I think it is necessary to look beyond the electoral arena and reconsider how political sophistication and participation patterns are interrelated. Increasing political sophistication does not necessarily imply a growth in the level of all forms of political activism; rising sophistication levels may be more important in changing the *nature* of participation. Voting, for example, is an area in which elites and political organizations traditionally can mobilize even disinterested citizens to turn out at the polls. High turnout levels often reflect the organizational skills of political groups rather than the public's concern about the election. Moreover, citizen input through this participation mode is limited by the institutionalized structure of elections, which narrows (and blurs) the choice of policy options and limits the frequency of public input. A French environmental group bluntly stated its disdain for elections with a slogan borrowed from the May Revolts of 1968: *Élections—piège à cons* (Elections—trap for idiots). An increasingly sophisticated and cognitively mobilized electorate is not likely to depend on voting and campaign activity as the primary means of expanding its involvement in politics.

The growing political skills and resources of contemporary electorates have had a more noticeable impact on increasing participation in areas in which activity is citizen initiated, less structured, and more policy oriented (Dalton 1984; Inglehart 1990, chap. 10). The self-mobilized individual favors referendums over elections and communal activity over campaign work. The use of referendums and other forms of direct input has increased in most advanced industrial democracies in recent years (Butler and Ranney 1994; Scarrow 2001). Similarly, participation in citizen lobbies, single-issue groups, and citizen-action movements is increasing in nearly all advanced industrial democracies (Meyer and Tarrow 1998). Verba, Schlozman, and Brady (1995, chap. 3) similarly find that issue-based contacting of political elites has significantly increased among Americans.

In summary, the trends in political activity represent changes in the style of political action, and not just changes in the level of participation. The new style of citizen politics seeks to place more control over political activity in the hands of the citizenry. These changes in participation make greater demands on the participants. At the same time, these activities can increase public pressure on political elites. Citizen participation is becoming more closely linked to citizen influence.

Suggested Readings

Burns, Nancy, Kay L. Schlozman, and Sidney Verba. *The Private Roots of Public Action.* Cambridge, Mass.: Harvard University Press, 2001.

Conway, M. Margaret. *Political Participation in the United States.* 3d ed. Washington, D.C.: CQ Press, 2000.

Parry, Geraint, George Moyser, and Neil Day. *Political Participation and Democracy in Britain.* Cambridge, U.K.: Cambridge University Press, 1992.

Putnam, Robert. *Bowling Alone: The Collapse and Renewal of American Community.* New York: Simon & Schuster, 2000.

Teixeira, Ruy. *The Disappearing American Voter.* Washington, D.C.: The Brookings Institution, 1992.

van Deth, Jan, et al., eds. *Social Capital and European Democracy.* New York: Routledge, 1999.

Verba, Sidney, Kay Schlozman, and Henry Brady. *Voice and Equality: Civic Voluntarism in American Politics.* Cambridge, Mass.: Harvard University Press, 1995.

Wattenberg, Martin. *Where Have All the Voters Gone?* In press.

Notes

1. Parry, Moyser, and Day (1992) add items on protest and political violence that form another mode in their study of British participation. Westle (1992) reviews the broader European literature on this topic.

2. Verba and Nie (1972) originally found only 4 percent of the American public is active primarily through contacting officials on personal matters. These individuals tend to be sophisticated, but also unconcerned with broad political issues. Because of the very small

size of this group, we do not include this fourth participation mode. Parry and his colleagues (1992, chap. 3) find that contacting is more common in Britain, especially for the new examples of local contact that they included in their study. Similarly, Verba, Schlozman, and Brady (1995, chap. 3) find that the frequency of issue-based contacting among Americans almost doubled between 1967 and 1987, involving almost a quarter of the public. So this participation mode is expanding.

3. The British votes include local council, county, the 1997 House of Commons election, and the 1999 European Parliament election. The American votes include both primary and general elections: four votes in the primary for federal offices and two for state offices (these six offices were filled in the general election), two votes for judges, four for the junior college school district, four for city government, four for the water district, and more than thirty initiatives and referendums.

4. Comparisons between eastern and western Germany suggest that citizens in both regions participate at roughly the same levels. Easterners lag a bit behind on measures of party and campaign involvement but display comparable levels of voting turnout and political interest (Dalton 2002; Westle 1992).

5. Information on the 2000 Social Capital Survey is available at www.cfsv.org/community-survey/index.html

6. Even though feelings of efficacy are important, a valid measure was not available in the surveys we analyzed, so this is not included in the models discussed. For more on the impact of efficacy, see Wattenberg (in press) and Parry, Moyser, and Day (1992).

7. The analyses in figures 3.2, 3.3, and 3.4 are based on multiple regression analyses; figure entries are standardized regression coefficients. The European Parliament elections attract less interest than national parliamentary elections, which may affect our findings. Turnout as reported by our respondents is 54 percent for Britain, 75 percent for Germany, and 54 percent for France. But these turnout rates are also more comparable to U.S. elections. We decided to use this election because it was held simultaneously in all three European nations and we have comparable public opinion data from the Eurobarometer survey (the subsequent European Election Studies unfortunately did not ask about participation in the campaigns).

8. Political satisfaction in the European samples was measured by a question on the respondent's satisfaction with the way democracy functions in the nation. In the United States, satisfaction was measured by a question on trust in government.

9. Campaign activity in the European samples was drawn from Eurobarometer 31A (table 3.5). Activism was measured by a count of participation in the following actions: talked to friends about the campaign, spoke to a party worker, attended a meeting, read party material, or tried to persuade others. Campaign activity in the American survey was measured by a count of the activities listed in table 3.3 (p. 40).

10. The measure of communal participation is taken from Eurobarometer 31. Respondents were asked about "taking part in citizens' action groups." We coded these responses: (1) would never do, (2) would do under exceptional circumstances, (3) would do for important matters, and (4) have done. Comparable recent data are not available for the United States.

CHAPTER 4
Protest Politics

OCCASIONALLY, CITIZEN PARTICIPATION bursts beyond the bounds of conventional politics to include demonstrations, protests, and other forms of unconventional activity. The protests that accompanied the civil rights demonstrations in the United States during the 1960s, the environmental protests of the last decades of the twentieth century, and the people-power protests that brought democracy to Eastern Europe illustrate how the public can force political systems to respond, to change, and to grow.

Protest is not new to Western democracies. The United States has repeatedly experienced political conflict throughout its history (Tilly 1969). The colonial period saw frequent revolts against taxation, property restrictions, and other government policies. When rural elements allied themselves with the urban poor and bourgeoisie, an American revolution against British control became inevitable. After independence, political conflict continued with the growth of workers' movements and agrarian/populist movements in the 1800s. Suffragettes, labor unions, and other political groups used large-scale, nonviolent protests and demonstrations throughout the past century.

A revolutionary tradition is even more deeply ingrained in the French political culture. Many French Leftists trace the foundations of French democracy to the revolutions of 1789, 1830, and 1848, as well as the Paris Commune of 1871. Between these dramatic political events, French society displayed a high level of protest and collective violence for most of the nineteenth century (Tilly et al. 1975, chap. 2). Food riots and similar conflicts were widespread in the mid-1800s, and industrial conflict developed during the second half of the century and the early 1900s. A call to the barricades stirs the hearts of many French citizens, contributing to historically high levels of unconventional political activity. In the words of one expert, protest in France is a national way of life.

Protest and collective action occurred on a more limited scale in Germany and Britain, although political conflict was still fairly common. Conflicts over industrial policy during the Wilhelmine Empire and Weimar Republic often manifested themselves in mass protests. Even Britain, with its tradition of grad-

INTERNET RESOURCE

Visit the Initiative and Referendum Institute for information on the use of referendums in the United States and other democracies:

www.iandrinstitute.org

ual political change, has a history of violence and political conflict that is often overlooked by political scientists (Marsh 1977, chap. 2).

The history of Western democracies is thus marked by repeated episodes of protest and vigorous political dissent by the citizenry. This record persists to the present. For example, the 1960s and early 1970s were a time of student protest and social unrest in most Western democracies. This spread to protests and spectacular actions designed to advance the goals of the environmental movement, the women's movement, and other new citizen-action groups. Environmentalists, for example, hang banners on smokestacks; organize large public events; orchestrate die-ins; and openly confront whalers, seal hunters, and others who threaten the environment. These tactics have been adopted by other more established groups that see unconventional politics as an effective political tool for gaining supporters and exerting pressure on policymakers. Thus, some analysts argue that a new pattern of protest is becoming a regular form of political action in advanced industrial societies (Meyer and Tarrow 1998; McAdam et al. 2001).

Historically, protest and collective action were often the last desperate acts of the public, arising from feelings of frustration and deprivation. Protest was concentrated among the socially disadvantaged, repressed minorities, or groups alienated from the established political order. Unconventional action was an outlet for those who lacked access through conventional channels.

Protest remains a political resource of minorities and repressed groups, and demonstrations by racial minorities (foreign workers in Europe), the economically disadvantaged, and similar groups will continue. Perhaps the most graphic illustration of this form of protest was the democratic revolution that spread through Eastern Europe in late 1989, the Philippines, South Africa, and other democratizing nations. When citizens are blocked from exercising political influence through legitimate participation channels, protest politics exists as an option.

Within advanced industrial societies, however, the use of protest has changed in at least three ways. First, protest broadened from the disadvantaged to include a wider spectrum of political groups. From the student movements of the 1960s, protest has become an accepted form of activity by a wide range of political groups. Gray Panthers protest for senior citizen rights, consumers are active monitors of industry, environmentalists call attention to ecological problems, and citizen groups of all types are proliferating.

Second, with the changing social base of protest came a shift in the focus of unconventional political action. Protests and demonstrations historically were indicators of revolutionary ferment and often challenged the basic legitimacy of political institutions. Food riots, tax revolts, and socialist worker uprisings exemplify this antigovernmental activity. The new forms of protest in advanced industrial societies are seldom directed at overthrowing the established political order—the affluent and well-educated participants are some of the primary beneficiaries of this order. Reformism has replaced revolutionary fervor.

Third, before modern times, collective political action was often a spontaneous event, such as an unorganized crowd attacking a tax collector or staging a food riot. Modern protest behavior is a planned and organized activity. Political groups consciously plan protests when these activities will benefit their cause. Modern protests are often orchestrated events, with participants arriving in chartered buses to planned staging areas complete with demonstration coordinators, portable toilet facilities, and accommodations for the media. Protest is simply another political resource for mobilizing public opinion and influencing policymakers.

Many people claim that the period of protest is passing; just the opposite is true. As protest becomes less unconventional, it also becomes less noticeable and newsworthy. The growing use of protests in European societies and the spread of single-issue groups in the United States should convince us that protest politics will continue. Furthermore, an infrastructure now exists for continued protest activities for other issues. The creation of citizen lobbies, environmental groups, consumer activists, and other groups provides a basis for organizing future protests. The existence of these new opposition groups may be crucial in permanently changing the style of citizen politics.

The spread of protest politics not only expands the repertoire of political participation, it also represents a style of political action that differs markedly from conventional politics (see table 3.1, p. 34). Protest can focus on specific issues or policy goals—from protecting whales to protesting the policies of a local government—and can convey a high level of political information with real political force. Voting and campaign work seldom can focus on a single issue because parties represent a package of policies. Instead of participating within a framework defined by elites, protest gives participants control over the action. The public controls the timing and location of protest activities. Sustained and effective protest is a demanding participation mode that requires initiative and cooperation with others. Thus, the advocates of protest argue that the public can strengthen its political influence by adopting a strategy of direct action.

MEASURING PROTEST

Although protest and other forms of collective action are a regular feature of democratic politics, these activities were absent from early empirical studies of political participation. This partially reflected the low level of protest that existed in the 1950s and early 1960s, as well as the unconventional nature of these activities. The growing wave of protest in recent years stimulated several studies to fill this void in our knowledge.

The first task was to measure unconventional political participation. Edward Muller (1972) and Alan Marsh (1974) developed a model of this participation mode. They ordered the various forms of unconventional participation along a continuum from least to most extreme. This continuum is marked by several thresholds (figure 4.1). The first threshold indicates a transition between conventional and unconventional politics. Signing petitions and participating in lawful demonstrations are unorthodox political activities but are still within the bounds of accepted democratic norms.

Ian McAllister (1992, 63–69) emphasized the importance of the second threshold because it marks the change to techniques that are direct action and are only semilegal, such as boycotts. Activities at this level or beyond exceed the boundaries of conventional, institutionalized political action. A third level of political activities involves illegal, but nonviolent, acts. Unofficial strikes or a peaceful occupation of a building are examples of this step. Finally, a fourth threshold includes violent activities that can include personal injury or physical damage. At this fourth level, political action exceeds what is accepted or tolerable in a democracy. Research

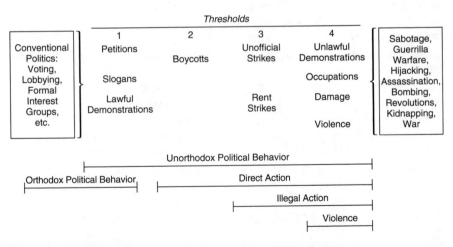

Figure 4.1 Conceptual Diagram of Unconventional Political Behavior

Source: Marsh (1977, 42), with modifications.

shows that unconventional political action is cumulative. Individuals active at any threshold also generally participate in milder forms of protest.

To provide a first overview of unconventional political activity, table 4.1 describes cross-national levels of action. The column on the left ranks nations according to the percentage of citizens who have signed a petition—the most modest and most common form of unconventional action. Indeed, by democratic standards this is a conventional part of politics. The column on the right ranks nations by public involvement in any of four more-challenging types of unconventional action: attending a lawful demonstration, joining in boycotts, joining unofficial strikes, or occupying buildings.

Signing a petition is clearly a very mild form of unconventional action and involves a large share of the citizenry in most Western democracies. The petition has a long and venerable heritage in British and American politics, and political groups of every orientation use it (Parry, Moyser, and Day 1992). One can hardly enter a Kmart or a Marks & Spencer without being asked to sign a petition.

Table 4.1   Cross-National Levels of Unconventional Political Participation (percentage active)

Signed a petition		Participated in a challenging act	
Australia	79	Sweden	46
Canada	77*	Italy	37*
GREAT BRITAIN	**75***	**FRANCE**	**36***
Sweden	72	Norway	34
UNITED STATES	**71**	**GERMANY (West)**	**33**
Switzerland	68	Canada	32*
GERMANY (West)	**66**	Australia	30
Norway	65	**GERMANY (East)**	**27**
GERMANY (East)	**57**	Netherlands	27*
Japan	55	**GREAT BRITAIN**	**25***
FRANCE	**51***	**UNITED STATES**	**25**
Netherlands	49*	Finland	22
Austria	46*	Spain	22
Italy	42*	Japan	13
Finland	39	Austria	13*
Spain	22	Switzerland	12

Source: 1995–98 World Values Survey. Nations marked by an asterisk are from the 1990–91 World Values Survey.

Notes: Entries in the second column are the percentage of respondents who have engaged in at least one of the following acts: a lawful demonstration, a boycott, an unofficial strike, or occupying a building.

Thus, most Americans (71 percent) and Britons (75 percent) have signed a petition. This form of political action also is commonplace in most other Western democracies. Indeed, the breadth of usage is so wide that one might ask whether this is an unconventional political activity.

A more telling test of the public's willingness to exceed conventional political bounds is participation in the four challenging acts in the right column of the table. The French have a relatively high level of unconventional political action, exceeded only by the Italians and Swedish citizens. More than one-third of the French public has participated in at least one of the four unconventional activities, and nonparticipants show a widespread willingness to engage in these activities. This verifies our earlier description of the French as disdaining conventional politics and relishing protest. In a much earlier work, William Kornhauser (1959) argued that the very weakness of social groups and conventional participation channels in France encourages support for protest. Michel Crozier (1964) described a French aversion to interpersonal interaction that also restricts political participation. Indeed, the French rank relatively low in the signing of petitions, a political activity that requires face-to-face contact. To this is added a cultural tradition that enshrines France's revolutionary tradition. In just the single year following the 1990 French survey, there were large-scale protest actions by farmers opposed to meat imports, royalists clashed with police, youths protested in Narbonne, Arab minority groups protested in Paris, environmentalists demonstrated about Chernobyl, the police staged their own protest, and state employees called a general strike. French protest knows few social bounds.

Most other European democracies display a modest level of unconventional political action, involving 20 to 30 percent of the public in at least one of these activities (Topf 1995b). Mediterranean and Scandinavian nations are found at the top of this ranking, and the Japanese display a marked aversion to these political activities. It is surprising to find that relatively few Britons and Americans engage in challenging activities, although they often sign petitions. We return to this point shortly.

Many western Germans have participated in one of these activities, since protest is an accepted form of action by groups ranging from neighborhood associations to the environmental movement. In the 1990 survey, conducted just after Germany unified, unconventional participation was exceptionally high in eastern Germany. The "peaceful revolution" in 1989 was not so peaceful; it required massive public demonstrations to topple the old regime. Since then, easterners have become engaged in the democratic process of the Federal Republic, and protest activity in the east has declined. By 1995 most residents of the former German Democratic Republic had signed a petition (57 percent) and a quarter had participated in at least one challenging action (27 percent).

On the whole, most people participate in some form of unconventional political action, even if only in the most mild form of signing a petition. Participation in higher forms of unconventional politics—such as participating in a lawful demonstration or joining a boycott—actually rivals conventional political activity (see chapter 3).

Is the era of protest passing? In his critique of American civic engagement, Putnam (2000) suggests that protest is declining in the United States along with other forms of action. Certainly protest seems less newsworthy than it was a decade or two ago. But because protest and demonstrations have broadened in their usage, the overall levels of unconventional action have risen in most advanced industrial democracies. Table 4.2 tracks the development of unconventional activities over time for our four core nations. With the exception of eastern Germany, unconventional political activities have grown in these four nations.[1] Furthermore, the beginning of this series in 1974 undoubtedly misses the growth of such unconventional activities that occurred during the 1960s. In addition, Ronald Inglehart (1997, chap. 8) shows that there has been a general increase in protest activities for the larger set of advanced industrial societies from the 1980s to the 1990s. This growth of protest probably results from a general increase in small demonstrations over highways, schools, neighborhood issues, and other specific concerns, rather than a few large-scale movements. Protest is becoming a more common political activity in advanced industrial democracies. The era of protest politics is not passing.

These time trends might explain why the United States ranks so low in recent cross-national comparisons (table 4.1, p. 62) despite its reputation for a high level of protest activity. The American public had high levels of protest in the first systematic studies of unconventional political action (Barnes, Kaase et al. 1979). These activities have gradually increased in the United States, but their use has spread even more rapidly in Britain, Germany, and other Western democracies. For instance, the percentage of Americans participating in a boycott grew from 14 percent in 1975 to 19 percent in 1995; Germans began at only 4 percent but increased to match the United States (18 percent). American participation has not declined; participation in other nations has grown at a faster rate and thus has overtaken American activity levels.

Although we have generally spoken about protest in positive terms, the dark side of unconventional politics occurs when citizens pass the fourth threshold and engage in violent behavior. The abortion clinic bombers or the terrorist activities of the Irish Republican Army go far beyond the tolerable bounds of politics. These actions are fundamentally different from the protest behavior of most citizens. Table 4.2 contains evidence on the extent of violent political action in our four nations. Although protest politics is widely accepted, the number of people who participate in violent activities is minimal. In 1981, for example, 44 percent of the French public had signed a petition and 26 percent had participated in a lawful demonstration, but only 1 percent had damaged property or engaged in personal violence. Citizens want to protest the actions of the democratic political process, not destroy it.

Table 4.2 Unconventional Participation (in percentages)

	United States				Great Britain			West Germany				East Germany		France	
	1975	1981	1990	1995	1974	1981	1990	1974	1981	1990	1995	1990	1995	1981	1990
Sign a petition	58	61	70	71	22	63	75	30	46	55	66	69	57	44	51
Participate in lawful demonstrations	11	12	15	16	6	10	13	9	14	25	26	53	22	26	31
Join in boycott	14	14	17	19	5	7	14	4	7	9	18	3	11	11	11
Participate in unofficial strike	2	3	4	4	5	7	8	1	2	2	4	2	1	10	9
Occupy building	2	2	2	2	1	2	2	*	1	1	2	1	2	7	7
Damage property	1	1	—	—	1	2	—	*	1	—	—	—	—	1	—
Personal violence	1	2	—	—	*	1	—	*	1	—	—	—	—	1	—

Sources: 1974–75 Political Action Study; 1981 World Values Survey; 1990–91 World Values Survey; 1995–98 World Values Survey.

Notes: Table entries are the percentages who say they have done the activity. The asterisks signify less than 1 percent; the dashes indicate that the question was not asked in this survey.

Who Protests?

Why do citizens protest? Every protester has an individual explanation for his or her action. Some people are stimulated by a commitment to an issue or ideology. Other protesters are motivated by a general opposition to the government and political system and search for opportunities to display their feelings. Still others are caught up in the excitement and sense of comradeship that protests produce or simply accompany a friend to be where the action is. Social scientists have tried to systematize these individual motivations to explain the general sources of protest activity.

The *deprivation approach* maintains that protest is primarily based on feelings of frustration and political alienation. Analysts since Aristotle have seen personal dissatisfaction and the striving for better conditions as the root cause of political violence. For Aristotle, the principal causes of revolution were the aspirations for economic or political equality on the part of the common people who lack it or the aspirations of oligarchs for greater inequality than they had. Much later, Tocqueville linked the violence of the 1789 French Revolution to unfulfilled aspirations expanding more rapidly than objective conditions, thereby increasing dissatisfaction and the pressure for change. Karl Marx similarly posited personal dissatisfaction and the competition between the haves and have-nots as the driving force of history and the ultimate source of political revolt.

Modern social scientists have echoed and quantified these themes. The theory has a psychological base: Frustration leads to aggression. Therefore, dissatisfaction with society and politics can lead to political violence. The seminal study in the area is the work of Ted Robert Gurr (1970). He stated that "the primary causal sequence in political violence is first the development of discontent, second the politicization of discontent, and finally its actualization in violent political action against political objects and actors" (Gurr 1970, 12–13). Gurr based his conclusions on analyses of cross-national levels of political violence. Analyses of public opinion data also show that policy dissatisfaction increases the likelihood of participation in protest activities (Norris 1999b).

This model implies that political dissatisfaction and alienation should be major predictors of protest. Indirectly, the theory suggests that unconventional political activity should be more common among lower-status individuals, minorities, and other groups who have reasons to feel deprived or dissatisfied.

A second general explanation of protest is termed a *resource model* (Tilly 1975). This model does not view protest and collective action as an outburst by a frustrated public. Instead, protest is another political resource (like voting, campaign activity, or communal activity) that individuals may use in pursuing their goals. Unconventional action is seen as a normal part of the political process as competing groups vie for political power.

The resource model provides alternative suggestions of who resorts to protest behavior. The model implies that protest activity should be higher among the better educated and politically sophisticated, those who have the political skills and resources to engage in these demanding forms of activity. One also might view involvement in other social groups as providing resources and experiences that encourage activities across other participation modes (Verba, Schlozman, and Brady 1995). In addition, a belief that protest will be effective should significantly increase the likelihood that individuals will participate. Indeed, one of the most interesting studies of protest found that participants in the American ghetto riots in the 1960s were actually more efficacious than nonparticipants (Aberbach and Walker 1970).

In addition to these broad theories of protest, several personal characteristics might stimulate unconventional action. Research has shown a strong tendency toward higher levels of protest among the young. Gender also might influence unconventional political participation (Schlozman, Burns, and Verba 1994). The confrontational style of protest politics may involve a disproportionate number of men, although there is evidence that this pattern is changing with a narrowing of gender roles.

Finally, we are interested in the political orientations of protesters. Unconventional action is often seen as a tool for liberals and progressives who want to challenge the political establishment and who feel the need to go beyond conventional politics to have their views heard. At the same time, protest activity has broadened across the political spectrum, and protest may no longer be the primary domain of the Left. For every pro-choice protest, there is now a pro-life demonstration. For groups that protest for liberal causes, there is counter-mobilization among conservatives. Thus, we should consider whether or not there remains a political bias in the use of unconventional political action.

We used the six predictors of conventional political participation from chapter 3 to tap these contrasting models of protest behavior: education, age, gender, union attachments, political satisfaction, and Left/Right position (figure 4.2).[2]

Political dissatisfaction has a stronger impact on the willingness to engage in protest than on most forms of conventional participation (compare to figures 3.1, 3.2, and 3.3). Yet dissatisfied citizens are only slightly more willing to protest than those who are satisfied with the government's performance. Furthermore, the pattern of other predictors tends to undercut the dissatisfaction model. For example, the willingness to protest is more common among males and the better educated than among women and the less educated.[3]

In short, protest in advanced industrial democracies is not simply an outlet for the alienated and deprived; just the opposite often appears. The general pattern of protest activity is better described by the resource model. Protesters are individuals who have the ability to organize and participate in political activities of all forms, including protest. The clearest evidence of this is the strong tendency for the better educated to engaged in protest in all four nations.[4]

In one important area, however, the correlates of protest differ from conven-

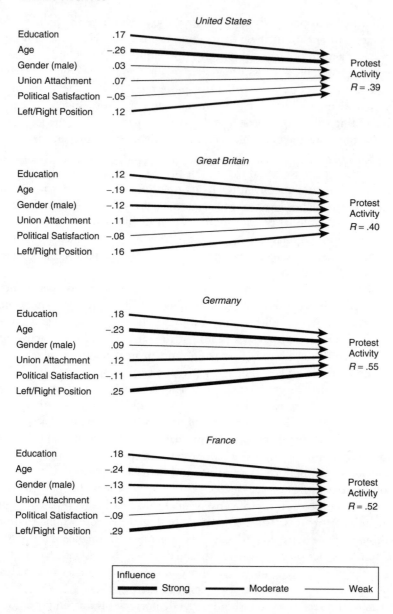

Figure 4.2   Predictors of Protest Activity

Source: 1990–91 World Values Survey.

tional activity. Conventional participation routinely increases with age, as family and social responsibilities heighten the relevance of politics. In contrast, protest is the domain of the young. In the United States, for example, two-thirds of those in their twenties have participated in at least one protest activity, compared to less than half of those in their sixties. Age is among the strongest predictors of the willingness to engage in unconventional activity.

Political scientists differ in their interpretations of this age relationship. On the one hand, this pattern may reflect life-cycle differences in protest activity. Youth is a period of enthusiasm and rebellion, which may encourage participation in protests and other unconventional activities. Young people also may be more available to protest because of their free time and concentration in university settings. This explanation would predict that an individual's protest activity should decline with age.

On the other hand, age differences in protest may represent a generational pattern of changing participation styles. That is, today's young people protest not because of their youth but because their generation has adopted a new style of political participation. The increasing educational levels, political sophistication, and participation norms among younger generations are producing support for direct-action techniques. If this is true, age differences in protest represent a historical change in participation patterns. Thus, youthful protesters should gradually mature into middle-age activists and not fade with the passage of time.[5]

Age differences in protest probably represent a combination of life-cycle and generational effects. Attempts to assess the relative importance of either explanation stress the primacy of generational effects (Barnes, Kaase et al. 1979, 524; Jennings 1987). Protest levels among the younger generations may decrease as these individuals move through the life cycle, but younger generations probably will remain more involved than their elders in direct action. In the long run, this process implies a further increase in unconventional political activities.

Another important correlate of unconventional action is Left/Right position. Although protest politics has spread throughout the political process and is used by groups on the Left and Right, the willingness to engage in these activities remains more common among leftists in each nation. These effects are stronger than the ideological biases in conventional forms of political action and are consistent even though one nation was headed by a leftist government (France) and the other three by conservative governments. Protest politics is still disproportionately the domain of the Left.

PARTICIPATION AND CONTEMPORARY DEMOCRACIES

Putnam (1995, 2000) has recently argued that citizen involvement in society and politics is waning, and this has serious and dangerous consequences for democracy. The evidence of this chapter and the last questions this conclusion. Citizen interest and participation in the political process are not generally decreasing in advanced industrial societies—rather, *the forms of political action are changing.*[6] The old forms of action—voting, party work, and campaign activity—are in decline. Conversely, participation in citizen-initiated and policy-oriented forms of political activity has increased. Chapter 3 discussed the growth of citizen-action groups, communal participation, and direct-democracy methods. This chapter documents the expansion of protest politics.

Protest politics can take many forms. The most dramatic examples are the attention-getting events of large groups that stimulate public interest in an issue or organization. Greenpeace, for instance, has become famous for using its rubber boats to disrupt whaling and protect the harp seals from hunters, as well other spectacular actions. Such dramatic actions have been adopted and expanded by other environmental organizations. But the larger significance of protest politics lies in its adoption by a variety of other citizen groups. The use of protests has broadened to include consumer groups dissatisfied with a company's product, taxpayers dissatisfied with the action of local government, and students dissatisfied with university policies. The general acceptance of protest politics is what has transformed the style of citizen politics.

Increases in these activities are especially significant because they place greater control over the locus and focus of participation in the hands of the citizenry. Political input is not limited to the issues and institutionalized channels determined by elites. A single individual, or a group of citizens, can organize around a specific issue and select the timing and method of influencing policymakers. These direct-action techniques also are high-information and high-pressure activities. They, therefore, match some of the participation demands of an increasingly educated and politically sophisticated public, far more so than participation in voting and campaign activities.

A major goal of democratic societies is to expand citizen participation in the political process and thereby increase popular control of political elites. Therefore, increases in communal participation, protest, and other citizen-initiated activities generally are welcomed. This changing pattern of political action is an important element of the new style of citizen politics in advanced industrial democracies.

In addition, however, these changing participation patterns create some new problems for modern democracies. The growing complexity and technical nature of contemporary issues require that citizens have substantial political sophistication to cope with the world of politics. Moreover, participation in citizen-initiated activities is more demanding on the individual than voting or campaign activity. Electoral participation by the less sophisticated is often mobilized by political groups (such as unions or religious/ethnic associations). Communal activity and unconventional politics require greater personal initiative. Consequently, involvement in politics is becoming even more dependent on the skills and resources represented by social status.

This situation may increase the participation gap between lower-status groups and higher-status individuals. As the better educated expand their political influence through direct-action methods, less-educated citizens might be unable to compete on the same terms. The politically active may become even more influential, while the less active may see their influence wane. Ironically, overall increases in political involvement may mask a growing social-status bias in citizen participation and influence, which runs counter to democratic ideals.

Some evidence of this problem can be seen in the relationship between educational level and political activity. Differences in voting turnout by education, for example, are modest. Differences in communal participation and protest by educational level are substantial; the better educated are the benefactors of these new participation opportunities. The solution to this problem is to raise the participation levels of lower-status groups, not limit the activity of the better educated. Political leaders must facilitate participation by a broader spectrum of the public and lower the remaining barriers to participation. The dictum of "maximum feasible citizen participation" needs to be followed more closely.[7]

Direct-action methods pose another challenge to contemporary democracies. By their very nature, direct-action techniques disrupt the status quo. These activities occasionally challenge the established institutions and procedures of contemporary democracies. This led some critics to ask whether rapidly expanding citizen participation, especially in protest activities, is placing too many demands on already overburdened political systems (Huntington 1981; Crozier, Huntington, and Watanuki 1975). Policy cannot be made in the streets, they argue. Efficient and effective policymaking requires a deliberative process in which political elites have some latitude in their decisions. A politicized public with intense policy minorities lobbying for their special interests would strain the political consensus that is a requisite of democratic politics. Indeed, as citizen demands for influence are increasing, a survey of Washington political elites suggests that those who make and implement policy doubt the abilities of the American public.[8]

In short, these analysts argue that it is possible to get too much of a good thing—political participation. Indeed, they cite the empirical evidence accompanying the elitist theory of democracy in taking this position (chapter 2). Citizen activism must be balanced against the needs for government efficiency and rational policy planning. Hence, they believe that the expansion of participation in recent years may have upset this balance, leading to problems of governability in Western democracies. These arguments were commonplace in the 1980s, and even with the democratization wave of the 1990s, there are still too many who would limit the rights of others.

Cautions about the excess of participation display a disregard for the democratic goals they profess to defend; they share more in common with the former regimes of Eastern Europe than with real democratic principles. The associate editor of *The Economist* noted the irony of worrying about the excesses of democracy as we simultaneously celebrated the fall of communism:

> The democracies must therefore apply to themselves the argument they used to direct against the communists. As people get richer and better educated, a democrat would admonishingly tell a communist, they will no longer be willing to let a handful of men in the Politburo take all the decisions that govern a country's life. The same must now be said, with adjustment for scale, about the workings of democracy. As the old differences of wealth, education and social condition blur, it will be increasingly hard to go on persuading people that most of them are fit only to put a tick on a ballot paper every few years, and that the handful of men and women they thereby send to parliament must be left to take all the other decisions. (Beedham 1993, 6)

Contemporary protest and calls for direct citizen input are not antidemocratic behavior. Indeed, they frequently are attempts by ordinary citizens to pressure the political system to become more democratic. More often than not, the protesters are pressing political elites to open the political process and be responsive to new issue interests. Furthermore, very few citizens subscribe to the extreme forms of violent political action that actually might threaten the political system.

I favor a Jeffersonian view of the democratic process. The logic of democratic politics is that expanding political involvement also can expand citizens' understanding of the political process. Citizens learn about the responsibilities of governing and the choices facing society by becoming involved—and that makes them better citizens. Parry and his colleagues (1992, chap. 13), for instance, provide empirical evidence that participation increases the public's knowledge about politics. A recent comparative study of environmental groups similarly stressed the educational role of citizen-action groups (Pierce et al. 1992). In the long run, involving the public can make better citizens and better politics.

Ironically, some evidence from Britain indicates that active citizens also become more critical of politicians and the political process (Parry, Moyser, and Day 1992, chap. 13). Thus, the educational role of participation can lead to further challenges to the political status quo. These demands can introduce new strains on the democratic process. But one would hope that a responsive political system could build positive experiences with the democratic process. Moreover, the democratization process makes progress by addressing the demands of a critical public.

Contemporary democracies clearly face important challenges, and their future depends on the nature of the response. The response should not be to push back the clock, to re-create the halcyon politics of a bygone age. Democracies must adapt to survive, maximizing the advantages of increasing citizen participation while minimizing the disadvantages. The experience of the past several years suggests that this is the course we are following. Institutions are changing to accommodate increased citizen participation. German administrative regulations now require consultation with citizen groups as part of the political process. Public access and advice have become much more open in the United States. Citizen-action groups are winning legal standing to bring lawsuits to protect the public interest. Politicians and bureaucrats are becoming more comfortable with an expanded form of democracy. Democracy is threatened when we fail to take the democratic creed literally and reject these challenges.

SUGGESTED READINGS

Barnes, Samuel, Max Kaase et al. *Political Action.* Beverly Hills, Calif.: Sage, 1979.
Jennings, M. Kent, and Jan van Deth, eds. *Continuities in Political Action.* Berlin: deGruyter, 1989.

NOTES

1. When Putnam recently asked a differently phrased protest question that replicated an earlier study by Verba, Schlozman, and Brady (1995), the percentage of Americans who had participated in a protest or demonstration during the past year had remained constant at 6 percent in 1987 and 7 percent in 2001. For information on the 2000 Social Capital Survey, see www.cfsv.org/communitysurvey/index.html

2. The protest measure is a simple additive scale of the respondent's willingness to participate in the four challenging activities of table 4.1. The model differs slightly from those in chapter 3 because the World Values Survey lacked a measure of party attachments and had a different measure of political satisfaction (support for radical social change). The analyses in figure 4.2 are based on multiple regression; figure entries are standardized regression coefficients.

3. We conducted comparable analyses with Eurobarometer 31, which allowed us to match the predictors of chapter 3 but without data for the United States. Our measure of unconventional action in willingness to engage is the same four activities as in figure 4.2. The results are generally consistent with those from the World Values Survey:

Predictor	Great Britain	West Germany	France
Education	.15	.22	.21
Age	−.08	−.17	−.14
Gender (Male)	.04	.06	.11
Party attachment	.14	.05	.20
Union attachment	.15	.08	.17
Political satisfaction	−.14	.00	−.03
Left/Right position	.18	.11	.19
R =	.44	.39	.49

4. Union activity is also related to unconventional political action. This relationship, however, is generally less than for conventional action. In addition, the different union measure in the World Values Survey produces very few union activists (about 10 percent) and thus might accentuate the influence of this factor.

5. For evidence on the endurance of this new style of protest politics, see Jennings's (1987) national study of youth and Putnam's (2000) generational comparisons of protest. Putnam's findings suggest that the generational shift toward greater protest activity has reversed among the youngest age groups.

6. The cross-national evidence strongly suggests that political involvement is not generally decreasing (Putnam, 2002) although Putnam's (2000) impressive array of evidence suggests that this may be occurring in the United States. I would argue, however, that Putnam's data are less able to tap the new forms of political action we have discussed in chapters 3 and 4, and since these forms of activity have grown less dramatically in the United States than in other Western democracies, they are more difficult to document with indirect measures.
7. This term is identified with the Great Society programs initiated by the Johnson administration to increase the participation of minorities and low-income groups. These institutionalized participation channels have been adopted by a range of citizen groups and governments in the United States and other democracies.
8. The Pew Research Center (1998b) surveyed members of Congress, top presidential appointees, and members of the Senior Executive Service to find out how leaders view the public. Among members of Congress, just 31 percent think Americans know enough about issues to make wise decisions about public policy. Even fewer presidential appointees (13 percent) and senior civil servants (14 percent) believe this.

PART TWO

Political Orientations

CHAPTER 5

Values in Change

HUMAN VALUES DEFINE the essence of our lives. Our values tell us what is important to us and to society and provide the reference standard for making our decisions. We structure our lives around our beliefs about what is important to us, whether it is the choice of careers, a marriage partner, or a movie on Saturday night.

Politics often involves human values. Values identify what people believe are, or should be, the goals of society and the political system. Shared values help define the norms of a political and social system. The clash between alternative values creates a basis for political competition over which values should shape public policy. For instance, are welfare programs constructed in terms of values of economic efficiency or in terms of empathy for the living conditions of families in need? Are issues of criminal justice based on concerns about protecting the security of the populace or about protecting the rights of the accused? In a real sense, politics regularly involves conflicts over values.

I believe that the new style of citizen politics includes a fundamental shift in some of the basic political values of many people. A comparison of contemporary societies to those of a generation ago would uncover strong evidence of changing social norms. Hierarchical relationships and deference toward authority are giving way to decentralization, self-expression, and more participation in the decisions affecting one's life. Previous chapters described how participatory norms are stimulating greater political involvement, but the consequences of value change are much broader. The new values affect attitudes toward work, lifestyles, and the individual's role in society.

The definition of societal goals and the meaning of "success" are also changing. Until recently, many Americans measured success almost solely in economic terms: a large house, two cars in the garage, and other signs of affluence. The late Malcolm Forbes said that life was a contest, and the winner was the person who accumulated the most possessions before he or she died. In Europe, the threshold for economic success might have been lower, but material concerns were equally important.

INTERNET RESOURCE

Visit the World Values Survey Web site for
information on this global survey of values:

wvs.isr.umich.edu/

Once affluence became widespread, however, many people realized that
bigger is not necessarily better. The consensus for economic growth is now
tempered by a concern for improving the quality of life. A new concern for
protecting environmental quality spread throughout society. Instead of just
income, careers are measured by the feeling of accomplishment and freedom
they offered. Social relations and acceptance of diversity are additional examples
of values in change. Progress on racial, sexual, and religious equality is transforming American and European societies.

Evidence of value change is all around us, if we look. We think in the present, however, and so the magnitude of these changes is not always appreciated. One
can get a sense of these changes by comparing contemporary American lifestyles
to the images of American life depicted on vintage television reruns from the 1950s.
Series such as *Ozzie and Harriet, Father Knows Best,* and *Leave It to Beaver* reflect
many values of a bygone era. How well would the Nelsons or the Cleavers adjust
to a world with women's liberation, the new morality, racial desegregation, rap
music, and alternative lifestyles? Imagine the Cleavers and the Bundys as next-
door neighbors—or Wally Cleaver hanging out with Beavis and Butthead.

This chapter examines the evidence that values are systematically changing
in advanced industrial societies. Then we consider some of the implications of
this process of value change for democratic politics.

THE NATURE OF VALUE CHANGE

We study citizen values because they provide the standards that guide the attitudes and behaviors of the public. Values signify a preference for certain personal
and social goals, as well as the methods to obtain these goals. One individual may
place a high priority on freedom, equality, and social harmony—and favor policies that strengthen these values. Others may stress independence, social recognition, and ambition in guiding their actions.

Many personal and political decisions involve a choice between several
valued goals. One situation may create a choice between behaving independently
and obediently or between behaving politely and sincerely. A national policy
may present contrasts between the goals of world peace and national security or

between economic well-being and protection of nature. People develop a general framework for making these decisions by organizing values into a value system, which arranges values by their importance to the individual. Citizen behavior may appear inconsistent and illogical (see chapter 2) unless the researcher considers the values of each person and how he or she applies these values in specific situations. To one citizen, busing taps values of social equality and civil rights; to another, it concerns freedom and providing for one's family. Both perspectives are correct, and attitudes toward busing are determined by how people weigh these conflicting values.

Value systems should include the salient goals that guide human behavior. Milton Rokeach (1973) developed an inventory of eighteen instrumental values dealing with the methods of achieving desired goals and eighteen terminal values defining preferred end-state goals. A complete list of important human goals should be much longer, and a complete list would be necessary to explain individual behavior fully.

Social scientists have focused their attention on questions of value change as the evidence of the public's changing priorities became apparent in several areas. In reaction to the individualization of society, David Riesman and others stressed the shift from group solidarity and other-directed values to self-actualizing and inner-directed goals (Riesman 1950; Sennet 1978). Alex Inkeles and David Smith (1974) described a more general process of value change, linking developed and modern societies, and this has been updated by more recent research on modernizing societies (Inglehart 1997; Inglehart and Baker 2000).

Inglehart has developed the most systematic attempt to describe the value changes that are transforming advanced industrial societies (Inglehart 1977, 1990; Abramson and Inglehart 1995). Inglehart bases his theory of value change on two premises. First, he suggests that basic value priorities are determined by a *scarcity hypothesis*: Individuals "place the greatest value on those things that are in relatively short supply" (Inglehart 1981, 881). That is, when some valued object is difficult to obtain, its worth is magnified. If the supply increases to match the demand, then the object is taken for granted and attention shifts to things that are still scarce. For example, water is a precious commodity during a drought, but when the rains return to normal, the concern over water evaporates. Similarly, the modern concern for clean water arose when pollution became widespread and the availability of clean water became uncertain. This general argument can be applied to other items valued by society.

The second premise of Inglehart's theory is a *socialization hypothesis*: "To a large extent, one's value priorities reflect the conditions that prevailed during one's preadult years" (Inglehart 1981, 881). These formative conditions include both the immediate situation in one's own family and the broader political and economic conditions of society. Value change may continue after this formative period as people move through the life cycle or are exposed to new experiences.

Nevertheless, Inglehart assumes that later learning must overcome the inertia of preexisting orientations.

The combination of both hypotheses—scarcity and socialization—produces a general model of value change. An individual's basic value priorities are initially formed early in life and emphasize those desired goals that are in short supply. Once these values develop, they tend to endure in the face of later changes in social and family conditions.

Chapter 1 described how advanced industrial societies are now characterized by unprecedented affluence, greatly increased educational levels, expanding information opportunities, an extensive social welfare system, and other related characteristics. These characteristics changed dramatically during the late twentieth century. We have linked these trends to the growing sophistication, cognitive mobilization, and participation of modern electorates. In addition, Inglehart maintains that these social forces are changing the public's basic value priorities because these trends are altering the socioeconomic conditions of these nations. The relative scarcity of valued objects is changing, and with this comes parallel changes in what the public values most.

To generalize the scarcity hypothesis into a broader theoretical model, Inglehart drew on the work of Abraham Maslow (1954).[1] Maslow suggested a hierarchical ordering of human goals. People are first driven to fulfill basic subsistence needs: water, food, and shelter. When these needs are met, the search continues until enough material goods are acquired to attain a comfortable margin of economic security. Having accomplished this, individuals may turn to higher-order needs, such as the needs for belonging, self-esteem, participation, self-actualization, and the fulfillment of aesthetic and intellectual potential. Thus, social conditions generally predict the broad societal pattern in the choice of values.

The inaugural series of the CBS television show *Survivor* presented the Maslovian value hierarchy in practice. Once the relatively affluent American participants reached the island, their priorities shifted toward subsistence needs: finding water, ensuring there was enough rice for the day, and maybe even hunting rats for additional protein. The aesthetic and quality-of-life concerns they probably voiced at home were subjugated to the needs to survive. This is Maslow as Robinson Crusoe.

Inglehart applied the logic of Maslow's value hierarchy to political issues (figure 5.1). Many political issues, such as economic security, law and order, and national defense, tap underlying sustenance and safety needs. Inglehart describes these goals as *material* values. In a time of depression or civil unrest, for example, security and sustenance needs undoubtedly receive great attention. If a society can make significant progress in addressing these goals, then attention can shift toward higher-order values. These higher-order goals are reflected in issues such as individual freedom, self-expression, and participation. Inglehart labels these goals as *postmaterial* values.

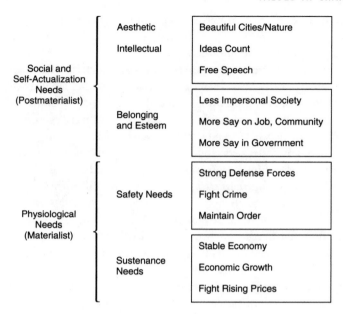

Figure 5.1   The Maslovian Value Hierarchy

Source: Inglehart (1977, 42).

Inglehart contends that this material/postmaterial continuum provides a general framework for understanding the primary value changes now occurring in advanced industrial democracies. Other researchers note the broad nature of value change and describe the process as a transition from "Old Politics" values of economic growth, security, and traditional lifestyles to "New Politics" values of individual freedoms, social equality, and the quality of life. One sign of the significance of this concept is the large number of other studies that have examined the logic and method of the postmaterial theory (see the extensive literature cited in van Deth and Scarbrough 1995).

The major challenges to Inglehart's theory of value change have come in two areas. First, several studies question whether socioeconomic conditions are linked to citizen values as Inglehart predicts. For example, Harold Clarke and Nitish Dutt (1991) demonstrate that Inglehart's simple value index is closely related to the ebb and flow of economic conditions instead of consistently reflecting the conditions of earlier formative environments. Raymond Duch and Michael Taylor (1993, 1994) similarly raise questions about whether or not formative conditions are the key determinants of values (also see Inglehart's response, Abramson and Inglehart 1994). In large part, I see these as narrow methodological questions about the measurement of values, or whether educational attainment primarily represents formative conditions or present social position. But these results do sensitize us to the fact that values are dependent on formative conditions *and* present circumstances.

A second critique asks if advanced industrial societies are changing only along the single material/postmaterial dimension. Scott Flanagan (1982, 1987) argued that citizen values are shifting along at least two dimensions. One dimension involves a shift from material to noneconomic values; a second dimension involves a shift from authoritarian to libertarian values (also see Nevitte 1996). Braithwaite and his colleagues (1996) similarly suggest that advanced industrial societies are experiencing a transition from security-based to harmony-based values. Undoubtedly Inglehart's framework oversimplifies the process of value change, since societies are changing in multiple ways that tap different parts of people's value systems. This is clearly an area in which further research is warranted. But Inglehart's framework generally overlaps with the value dimensions that these other researchers have suggested. Flanagan's two dimensions, for example, can be seen as subelements of Inglehart's broader framework. Regardless of how we conceptualize this process, there is general agreement that the value priorities of modern publics have been changing.

THE DISTRIBUTION OF VALUES

When we measure citizen values, we must realize that most people attach a positive worth to both material and postmaterial goals. The average person prefers both economic growth and a clean environment, social stability, and individual freedom. Politics, however, often involves a conflict between separately valued goals. Therefore, rather than study one set of values in isolation from another, we must identify which goals take priority in the public's mind when values come in conflict.

Survey researchers use a variety of methods to measure public values. Indeed, because values are deeply held and relatively pure feelings, it is complicated to tap them with a simple public opinion survey question. In addition, researchers debate whether we should measure values in terms of personal life conditions or phrased as political goals that are linked to political behaviors. This measurement debate is ongoing (van Deth and Scarbrough 1995; Bean and Papadakis 1994).

Following Inglehart's model of the Maslovian value hierarchy, the 1990–91 World Values Survey assessed value priorities by asking respondents to rank the importance of twelve possible political goals. Table 5.1 presents the top priorities of American, British, French, and German citizens across these items.

Most citizens on both sides of the Atlantic cite material goals as their first priority. Americans most often emphasize economic growth, a stable economy, and crime prevention. Europeans stress the same material needs. The responses from East Germans are especially insightful. After suffering through a decade of mounting economic and social problems, East Germans placed heavy stress on

Table 5.1   Distribution of Value Priorities (in percentages)

	United States	Great Britain	France	West Germany	East Germany
High level of economic growth (M)	76	67	72	65	86
A stable economy (M)	71	62	47	66	86
More say in work/ community (PM)	55	69	68	59	59
Fight against crime (M)	65	64	55	49	45
Protect free speech (PM)	48	45	63	61	51
Maintain order in nation (M)	57	46	44	55	60
More say in government (PM)	55	51	38	50	58
More humane society (PM)	33	43	57	55	47
Fight rising prices (M)	44	52	50	28	27
Make cities/country beautiful (PM)	23	36	38	42	49
Ideas count more than money (PM)	27	27	35	25	18
A strong defense (M)	38	19	12	12	2

Source: 1990–91 World Values Survey.

Note: Table entries are the percentage of respondents who listed the item as first or second choice among items presented in sets of four. Missing data were included in the calculation of percentages.

the need to improve economic conditions. Consistent with Maslow's theory, economic needs and security take precedence over postmaterial goals such as participation, free speech, and the environment—even though these were also severe problems in East Germany. As Bertolt Brecht once wrote: "Erst kommt das Fressen, dann die Morale" (first comes the food, then morals). Among the Western democracies, however, many people also give high rankings to post-material goals such as participating in job-related and political decision making and protecting free speech. A majority of West Germans and the French greatly value progress toward a more humane society.

Using the choices made among these twelve items, we created a single index that scores individuals by the relative weight they attach to postmaterial goals.[2] Materialists place high priority on the six economic and security goals (marked "M"), whereas postmaterialists stress participation and the other postmaterial goals (marked "PM"). Table 5.2 displays the percentage of postmaterialists on this twelve-item index over time.[3]

In the early 1970s postmaterialists were a relatively small minority in every nation. Using the twelve-item index, only 13 percent of Germans and 18 percent

Table 5.2   The Shift in Postmaterial Values over Time (percentage postmaterial on 12-item index)

Country	1973	1990	1995
Belgium	38	38	—
GREAT BRITAIN	18	19	—
Canada	—	29	—
Denmark	19	32	—
FRANCE	33	27	—
GERMANY (East)	—	23	24
GERMANY (West)	13	36	43
Ireland	15	23	—
Italy	16	33	—
Japan	—	31	29
Netherlands	35	39	—
Spain	—	37	29
Sweden	—	31	26
UNITED STATES	—	21	20
Norway	—	17	20
8-nation average	23	31	—

Sources: 1973 European Communities Study; 1974 Political Action Study for first U.S. time point; 1990–91 World Values Survey; 1995–98 World Values Survey.

Note: Entries are the percentage of respondents in each nation who place a higher priority on postmaterial goals, using the 12-item values index (table 5.1).

of the British scored high on the postmaterial scale. The proportion of materialists was even more pronounced with Inglehart's four-item index (Inglehart 1977, 1990). The greater number of materialists is not surprising. The conditions fostering value change should take several generations to accumulate, and in historical perspective the development of advanced industrialism is a relatively recent phenomenon.

By the 1990s the proportion of postmaterialists had increased in each nation for which long-term data are available. The percentage of postmaterialists in western Germany, for example, increased to 43 percent by 1995. A much more extensive time series is available for the more frequently used four-item postmaterial index (Abramson and Inglehart 1995; Inglehart 1997). These trend data show a general shift toward postmaterial values for a large set of advanced industrial societies.

Evidence from other sources underscores this value shift among Western publics. For instance, between 1949 and 1975 Germans reversed the priority they attach to two freedoms: freedom from want and freedom of speech (Dalton 1989,

118). In the insecure climate of the immediate postwar period, 35 percent of West Germans emphasized freedom from want and 26 percent gave priority to free speech. After the Economic Miracle had transformed German lifestyles, only 23 percent stressed freedom from want and 54 percent emphasized free speech. Similar trends are apparent in the values German parents say they would emphasize in raising their children (Nevitte 1996).

Even if one is uncertain about the exact proportion of postmaterialists because of the debate on how to measure these values, the trend toward post-material goals is clear. Larger proportions of the public—often a third—now espouse a priority for postmaterial goals in most advanced industrial democracies. Because many of the remaining individuals favor a mix of both values, the number of people exclusively preferring material goals is a minority in most nations. Thus, value priorities in these societies are now characterized by a mix of material and postmaterial objectives.

For more than two decades I have heard repeated arguments that post-materialism is a "sunshine" issue that will fade with the next economic downturn or period of political uncertainty. In the 1970s OPEC increases in oil prices stimulated global recessions that some claimed would end the liberalism of the 1960s. The 1980s were heralded as the "me" decade. Despite these potential countertrends, public opinion surveys document the slow and relatively steady growth of postmaterial values over time. An evolutionary change in values is transforming the nature of citizen politics.

MODELING THE PROCESS OF VALUE CHANGE

How do we know expressed support for postmaterial goals really reflects an ongoing process of societal value change? At first, the evidence was tentative. With time, however, the evidence in support of postmaterial value change has mounted. The trends cited previously provide one sort of evidence.

The most telling evidence supporting the postmaterial thesis comes from analyses that test the two hypotheses underlying Inglehart's theory. The scarcity hypothesis predicts that the socioeconomic conditions of a nation are related to the priorities of its citizens. The socialization hypothesis predicts that values become crystallized early in life; thus, the overall values of a society reflect the conditions decades or more earlier, when values were being formed.

We can test these hypotheses by comparing national levels of postmaterial values to the socioeconomic conditions of each nation. If scarcity breeds a concern for materialist values, then these concerns should be more common in nations with lower living standards. Conversely, the affluence of advanced industrial societies should increase support for postmaterial goals among these publics. Moreover, according to the socialization hypothesis, these effects should occur with some time lag. Thus, the best predictor of values should be national conditions a generation ago, when values were forming.

Figure 5.2 displays a clear relationship between national affluence (GNP per capita in 1965) and the distribution of material/postmaterial values in 1990–91 for thirty-three nations.[4] In general, postmaterialists are most common in nations (including the four core nations in this book) that had relatively high living standards during the formative years of the average adult surveyed in 1990. In contrast, there are low levels of postmaterialism in less affluent nations, such as Nigeria, India, China, and other less developed nations (including several nations in Eastern Europe). Moreover, this is not simply a correlation between contemporaneous measures as Abramson and Inglehart presented (1995, 128); we are comparing economic conditions a generation ago with value priorities in the 1990s.

Prior research has noted the curvilinear relationship between economic conditions and value change (Abramson and Inglehart 1995; Dalton 1977).[5] As can be seen in figure 5.2, the greatest shift in values occurs during the transition from a subsistence economy to an advanced industrial society, such as that found in postwar Western Europe. Once this level of affluence is achieved, further increases in well-being produce progressively smaller changes in values. This implies that the process of value change will continue at a slower rate in the future, but a gradual shift in values should continue.

Another test of the postmaterial theory involves generational patterns in the distribution of values. Older generations, reared in the years before World War II, grew up in a period of widespread uncertainty. These individuals suffered through the Great Depression in the 1930s and endured two world wars and the social and economic traumas that accompanied these events. Given these circum-

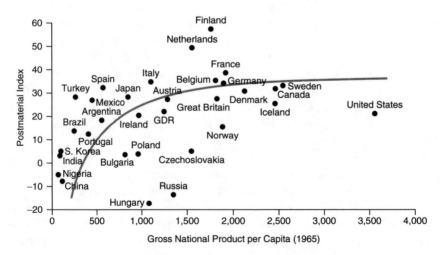

Figure 5.2   Formative Economic Conditions and Postmaterial Values

Sources: Taylor and Hudson (1972, 314–21); Abramson and Inglehart (1995, 124–25).

stances, older generations in most Western democracies should have been social-ized into a greater concern with material goals: economic growth, economic security, domestic order, and social and military security.

Conversely, younger generations in Europe and North America were raised in a period of unprecedented affluence and security. Present-day living standards are often several times higher than those experienced before World War II. The rapid growth of the welfare state now protects most people from even major economic problems. Postwar generations also have a broader worldview, reflect-ing their higher educational levels, greater exposure to political information, and more diverse cultural experiences. Furthermore, the end of the Cold War caps one of the longest periods of international peace in modern European history. Under these conditions, the material concerns that preoccupied prewar genera-tions should diminish in urgency. Growing up in a period when material and security needs seem relatively assured, younger generations should shift their attention toward postmaterial goals.

Furthermore, Inglehart's socialization hypothesis predicts that values formed early in life should persist through the lifespan. That is, if values are enduring, different age groups should retain the mark of their formative generational expe-riences even if family or societal conditions change. Older Europeans should still stress security concerns even if their present lifestyles include a high level of afflu-ence. Generations socialized in the affluence of the postwar economic miracle should retain their greater concern for postmaterial values even as they age and assume greater family and economic responsibilities.

Thus, a crucial test of the value-change thesis involves tracking the value priorities of generations over time. Figure 5.3 describes the value priorities of several European generations from 1970 until 1992 using Inglehart's four-item value index.[6] The oldest cohort, ages 65–85 in 1970 (born between 1886 and 1905), is located near the bottom of the figure. In 1970 the proportion of mate-rialists in this cohort outweighs postmaterialists by nearly 50 percent. In contrast, the youngest cohort in 1970 (born between 1946 and 1955) is almost evenly balanced between material and postmaterial values.

Not only is the relative ranking of generations important evidence in support of Inglehart's theory, but so is the persistence of this pattern over time. The level of values fluctuates over time in response to random sampling variation and the sensi-tivity of the four-item values index to inflation levels (which I consider a method-ological imperfection in the four-item measure).[7] Most important, the generational gaps in value orientations remain fairly constant over time—seen in the parallel movement of each generation—although all cohorts are moving through the life cycle. The youngest age group from 1970, for example, is approaching middle age by the end of the survey series (ages 37–46), yet its postmaterial value orientations do not lessen significantly between 1970 and 1992. Life-cycle experiences normally modify, but do not replace, the early learning of value priorities.

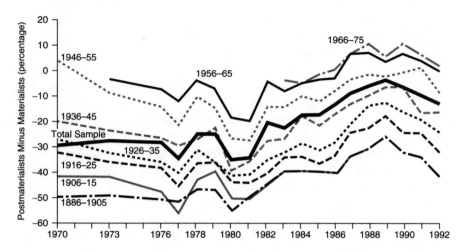

Figure 5.3   Distribution by Age Cohort of European Value Priorities over Time

Source: Redrawn from Ronald Inglehart and Paul Abramson, "Economic Security and Value Change, 1970–1993" (*American Political Science Review* 88:340). Used by permission of the authors and publisher.

Note: The data represented are based on a combined weighted sample of European Community surveys carried out (in the years indicated along the *x* axis) in West Germany, France, Britain, Italy, the Netherlands, and Belgium, using the four-item materialist/postmaterialist values index. The total sample size was 222,699. The values plotted are the percentage of postmaterialist minus percentage of materialist aggregated scores for eight cohorts defined by their birth years and for the total six-nation sample.

The size of the generational differences in values across nations provides supplemental support for the value-change thesis. West Germany, for example, experienced tremendous socioeconomic change during the past few generations. Consequently, the value differences between the youngest and oldest German cohorts are larger than for many other nations. Conversely, in nations that experienced less socioeconomic change over the past several decades, age groups should display smaller differences in their values. Abramson and Inglehart (1995, 134) demonstrated that there is a strong relationship between rates of economic growth and the size of the age gap in value priorities. Large social changes produce large changes in values.

Education is another indirect measure of an individual's economic circumstances during adolescence, when value priorities were being formed, because access to higher education often reflects the family's social status during an individual's youth.[8] In addition, education also may affect value priorities because of the content of learning. Contemporary Western educational systems generally stress the values of participation, self-expression, intellectual understanding, and other postmaterial goals. Moreover, the diversity of the modern university milieu may encourage a broadening of social perspectives. And finally, the effects of education overlap with those of generation; the young are better educated than the old.

Figure 5.4 presents the differences across educational groups in the percentage scoring high on postmaterial values on the twelve-item index. In every nation, there is a strong positive relationship between educational level and support for postmaterial goals. In France, for instance, only 21 percent of the lesser educated are postmaterialists, compared to nearly half of those with higher education (48 percent). One could argue that the American and East German educational systems were the most egalitarian of those portrayed in the figure, and thus the link between educational level and early life conditions is weaker in these two nations—consequently the relationship between education and values is also weaker.

The concentration of postmaterial values among the young and better educated gives added significance to these orientations. If Inglehart's theory is correct, the percentage of postmaterialists should gradually increase over time, as older materialist cohorts are replaced by younger, more postmaterialist generations.[9] Similarly, if expanding educational opportunities continue to increase the public's educational level, support for postmaterial values should continue to grow. Furthermore, because postmaterialists are more active in politics, their political influence is greater than their numbers imply. Indeed, among the group

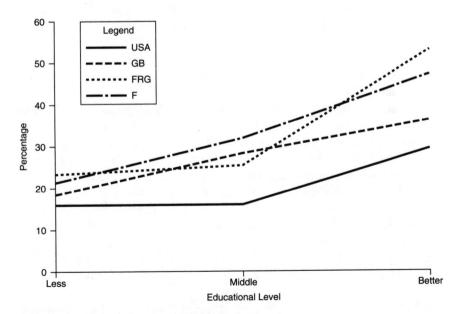

Figure 5.4   Postmaterialists by Educational Level

Source: 1990–91 World Values Survey.

of future elites—university-educated youth—postmaterial values predominate.[10] As these individuals succeed into positions of economic, social, and political leadership, the impact of changing values should strengthen. Value change thus has the appearance of an ongoing process.

THE CONSEQUENCES OF VALUE CHANGE

Although postmaterialists now constitute only a minority of the population in most advanced industrial democracies, the impact of their values is already apparent, extending beyond politics to all aspects of society. Indeed, one of the most impressive aspects of Inglehart's book *Culture Shift in Advanced Industrial Society* (1990) is the range of political phenomena he links to postmaterialism.

At the workplace, for example, these new value orientations fuel demands for a more flexible and individually oriented work environment. Rigid, hierarchical, assembly-line systems of production are being challenged by worker participation (codetermination), quality circles, and flexible working hours. Postmaterial values prompt a shift from materialist occupational goals (security and a good salary) to qualitative goals (a feeling of accomplishment and sense of responsibility). Many business analysts bemoan the decline of the work ethic, but it is more accurate to say that the work ethic is becoming motivated by a new set of goals.

Social relations are changing in reaction to these new value orientations. Neil Nevitte (1996) quite convincingly demonstrates that deference to authority of all forms is declining, as individuals are more willing to challenge elites. Bosses, army officers, university professors, and political leaders all decry the decline in deference to their authority. But the postmaterial credo is that an individual earns authority; it is not bestowed by a position. Similarly, many citizens are placing less reliance on social norms—class, religion, or community—as a guide for behavior. Parents in advanced industrial societies also are stressing greater independence as they educate their children. The public's behavior in all aspects of social and political life is becoming more self-directed. This shows in the declining brand-name loyalty among consumers and the decline of political party loyalty among voters. In short, contemporary lifestyles reflect a demand for greater freedom and individuality, which appears in fashions, consumer tastes, social behavior, and interpersonal relations.

This broader process of value change includes religious values and sexual mores (Inglehart 1997; Nevitte 1996). Materialists are significantly more likely to hold restrictive attitudes on sexually related issues, such as extramarital sex, abortion, or homosexuality. In short, materialists are not just concerned with economic matters; these values tap a broader collection of traditional social norms.

Focusing our attention on the realm of politics, postmaterial values are often linked to the new social movements of advanced industrial societies. Postmaterialists champion a new set of political issues—environmental quality, nuclear energy, women's rights, and consumerism—that the political establishment often overlooked. Debates in Washington about acid rain, the safety of nuclear plants, and gender equality have close parallels in the capitals of Europe. Proponents of these issues have similar characteristics: They are young, better educated, and postmaterialists.

Table 5.3 displays the relationship between values and support for new social movements. In the Western democracies, support for groups opposing nuclear power and groups supporting women's rights is significantly higher among post-materialists. Postmaterialists are roughly twice as supportive as materialists, and this gap widens if we examine participation in movement activities (Dalton 1994a, chap. 3; Inglehart 1990). Postmaterialists have revived political interest in other issues—codetermination and social equality—and reinterpreted them in terms of new value perspectives. These new issues have been added to the polit-ical agenda of contemporary democracies. Perhaps even more important, a new set of public interest groups and political movements advocating these issues are part of the contemporary political process.

Eastern Germans are an exception to the general pattern. Support for these challenging groups is not significantly related to value priorities in the east. In part, this is a reflection of the predominance of economic concerns in the east; in part, this is because postmaterial values had not yet become politicized in their politi-

Table 5.3   Support for Social Movements by Value Type (in percentages)

	VALUE TYPE				Correlation
	Materialist ——— Postmaterialist				
Strongly Approve of Antinuclear Groups					
United States	18	22	24	37	.12
Great Britain	14	14	18	30	.16
France	19	23	29	29	.09
Germany (West)	19	25	29	55	.26
Germany (East)	47	42	38	44	.01
Strongly Approve of Women's Groups					
United States	24	30	28	46	.12
Great Britain	15	17	17	23	.05
France	16	22	23	21	.06
Germany (West)	11	11	16	31	.21
Germany (East)	25	33	27	28	−.01

Source: 1990–91 World Values Survey.

Notes: Table entries are the percentage of respondents expressing strong approval for each group. Correlations are *tau-b* coefficients; each is statistically significant at .05 level or better except for the two eastern German correlations.

cal thinking in this 1990 survey. In addition, it is clear that easterners are respond-ing to a different political context. For instance, support for the antinuclear movement is exceptionally high in eastern Germany, which is probably a reflec-tion of widespread public worries about the safety of the Russian-style nuclear power plants used in the east that transcend the specific value orientation of the individual.

Value change also affects patterns of political participation. Postmaterial values stimulate direct participation in the decisions affecting one's life—whether at school, in the workplace, or in the political process. Postmaterialists are more interested in politics than are materialists and more likely to translate this interest into political action. In the 1990–91 World Values Survey, for example, postmaterialists are more likely than materialists to say they discuss politics and follow political matters.

The participatory orientation of postmaterialists adds to the puzzle of partic-ipation noted in chapter 3: If postmaterialism supposedly stimulates political involvement, why are voting and some other forms of action declining? Our answer to this puzzle reinforces the contention that the style of political action is changing in advanced industrial societies. The participatory orientation of postmaterialists has not affected all participation modes equally (Inglehart 1979). Postmaterial values are not stimulating voting or campaign activity, and in some nations voting turnout is actually lower among postmaterialists.[11] This is partially because the established parties have responded ambiguously to new issue demands. In addition, postmaterialists are skeptical of formal hierarchical organ-izations, such as most political parties.

Instead, postmaterial values stimulate participation in citizen initiatives, protests, and other forms of unconventional political activity. In the 1990 World Values Survey, for instance, postmaterialists are more than twice as likely as mate-rialists to participate in protests (figure 5.5). These nonpartisan participation opportunities provide postmaterialists with a more direct influence on politics, which matches their value orientations. Most postmaterialists also possess the political skills to carry out these more demanding forms of political action. As chapters 3 and 4 noted, along with increasing levels of citizen involvement has come a change in the form of political participation.

Value Change and Value Stability

This chapter has emphasized the changing values of Western publics, but a more accurate description would stress the increasing diversity of the public's value prior-ities. More people still give primary attention to material goals, and socioeconomic issues deriving from these values will continue to dominate political debate for decades to come. The persistence of traditional values should not be overlooked.

At the same time, postmaterial values are becoming more common. A sizable proportion of the public is willing to sacrifice further economic growth for a clean environment. Many people value the opportunity to participate in the decisions

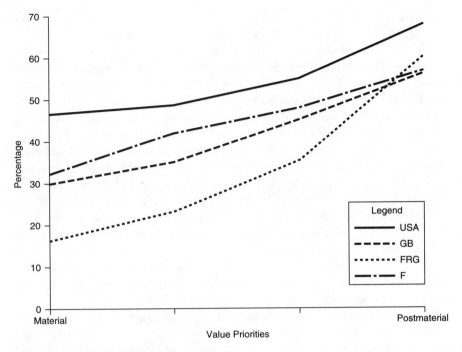

Figure 5.5   Protest Potential by Value Priorities

Source: 1990–91 World Values Survey.

Note: On the vertical dimension are plotted the percentages of respondents willing to perform two or more unconventional activities.

affecting their lives more than they value institutions and procedures that ensure stability and order at the possible cost of citizen input. Public values are changing.

The current mix of values sometimes makes it difficult for political analysts and politicians to know what the public wants. For nearly every example of the persistence of traditional material value patterns, there is now a counterexample reflecting postmaterial values. For every citizen lobbying a local town council to stimulate the economy, there is another who worries that growth will mean a loss in green space or a loss in the quality of life. The diversity of values marks a major change in the nature of citizen politics: Political debates again involve questions of goals and not just means to reach consensual goals.

The mix of values also makes it difficult for journalists and political analysts to discern the public's priorities when ultimate goals are being debated. At times, such as during the 1960s, media reports made it seem that every young person was joining the counterculture. In the 1980s images of the yuppie in pursuit of an MBA and a BMW were equally common. Now Generation X is defined, in part, by the lack of either identity. The strength of empirical research is that we can track the values of the public in a more scientific manner. And what we find is a slow evolution toward greater priority for postmaterial goals.

This process of value change should have several consequences for contemporary politics. Value change is shifting the issues of contemporary political debate. Concerns for environmental protection, individual freedom, social equality, participation, and the quality of life have been *added* to the traditional political agenda of economic and security issues. Some of the most telling evidence comes from Jeffrey Berry's study of legislation in the U.S. Congress. He finds that the majority of the Congressional agenda was concerned with materialist issues in 1963, and this shifted to a predominately postmaterialist agenda by 1991 (Berry 1999, chaps. 4–5). Similarly, Inglehart has tracked a marked increase in the attention that political parties devote to environmental and other New Politics issues over time (Inglehart 1997). For now and the foreseeable future, politics in most advanced industrial societies will be addressing a significant postmaterial agenda.

Inevitably, changes in value priorities carry over to the institutions of the political process. Nevitte (1996) has recently restated the political science premise that the values of society are eventually reflected in the values and institutions of the political system. Today political parties are no longer the sole or even the primary agents of political representation in modern democracies. Citizen interest groups have proliferated in the United States and Europe (Berry 1989; Meyer and Tarrow 1998). The public's participatory demands have led to reforms within established political parties to increase the role of members, such as the convention reforms of the U.S. Democratic Party or the increased role for constituency associations in the British Labour Party. Postmaterialists have promoted the institutional reforms we discussed in the conclusion to chapter 4: greater use of initiatives and referendums, the opening up of administrative processes, and the expansion of the legal rights of citizen groups. Public interest groups are now widely involved in the American policymaking process, from the national government down to local governments and administrative boards (Berry 1999). These institutional reforms increase the political influence of these groups, as well as producing even more fundamental changes in the process itself that affect all participants. Postmaterial groups are agents for expanding the democratization process in advanced industrial democracies.

One other question involves the impact of these new values on the political parties and citizen voting behavior. Most of the established political parties are primarily oriented to traditional social divisions, and at least initially they resisted attempts to incorporate postmaterial issues into a partisan framework. Since the first edition of this book, several of the established political parties have become more sensitive to postmaterial issues. A decade ago, few politicians claimed to speak for the environment. Today politicians of all colors claim to be green at election time. But it is still unclear whether the political parties will deliver on these promises once elected or will focus on their traditional materialist constituencies (see chapters 7 and 8).

Only a few skeptics still doubt that value priorities are changing among Western publics; the evidence of change is obvious. It is more difficult to anticipate the many consequences of these new values. By monitoring these trends, however, we may get a preview of the nature of citizen politics in advanced industrial democracies.

SUGGESTED READINGS

Abramson, Paul, and Ronald Inglehart. *Value Change in Global Perspective.* Ann Arbor: University of Michigan Press, 1995.
Clark, Terry Nichols, and Vincent Hoffmann-Martinot, eds. *The New Political Culture.* Boulder, Colo.: Westview Press, 1998.
Harding, Steve. *Contrasting Values in Western Europe.* London: Macmillan, 1986.
Inglehart, Ronald. *Culture Shift in Advanced Industrial Society.* Princeton, N.J.: Princeton University Press, 1990.
Nevitte, Neil. *The Decline of Deference.* Petersborough, Can.: Broadview Press, 1996.
Van Deth, Jan, and Elinor Scarbrough, eds. *The Impact of Values.* New York: Oxford University Press, 1995.

NOTES

1. Inglehart's early work was closely linked to the Maslovian value hierarchy, but this is less prominent in his more recent research. As Inglehart has broadened his interests and empirical evidence beyond advanced industrial societies, he has become more sensitive to how cultural forces and local conditions can shape which goals are considered scarce and thus valued by the public.
2. Inglehart normally uses a four-item subset of the twelve items to construct a single index of material/postmaterial values (Inglehart 1977, 1990, chap. 2). The disadvantage of this index is that it is based on only four items, and this provides a narrow basis for tapping a broad dimension of human values. For instance, several analysts, including Inglehart, have shown that the four-item index is sensitive to current inflation levels because one item deals with the "fight against rising prices." The advantage of the four-item measure is that it has been used over more than three decades in European opinion surveys and on a limited basis in several dozen other nations. The analyses in this chapter primarily rely on the more robust twelve-item index.
3. The twelve items were presented to respondents in groups of four. We counted the number of material items and postmaterial items selected as first or second priorities in each set of four. Our index is the difference between the number of material and postmaterial choices.
4. We use 1965 GNP/capita because this is roughly when values were being formed for many of the adults surveyed in 1990. In addition, we used Abramson and Inglehart's (1995, 124–25) summary index of values in order to be directly comparable to their analysis of the relationship between current GNP/capita and values.
5. There is a strong relationship ($r = .44$) between GNP/capita in 1965 and values in 1990, and this correlation is even stronger if modeled as a curvilinear relationship ($r = .49$).
6. Figure 5.3 is based on the combined results of samples from six nations: Britain, West Germany, France, Italy, Belgium, and the Netherlands. The nations were combined to produce age-group samples large enough to estimate values precisely. For a full discussion of these data, see Abramson and Inglehart (1995).
7. One weakness of the Inglehart measure is that it attempts to measure basic values with items

dealing with specific political issues. Thus, it is not surprising that the four-item index is sensitive to inflation rates because one of the items taps concern about rising prices (Clarke and Dutt 1991; Clarke et al. 1999). A broader measure of values, such as Inglehart's twelve-item index or the social priorities question of Flanagan (1982), would be less susceptible to these measurement problems because these measures would come closer to tapping basic values.

8. Duch and Taylor (1993) use extensive multivariate analysis to argue that formative conditions do not influence current value priorities. Abramson and Inglehart (1995) have challenged this interpretation, arguing that Duch and Taylor have distorted the results by their selection of time points and misinterpret the meaning of educational effects (also see Duch and Taylor 1994). I believe the evidence of generational change is predominant and that educational effects are another measure of formative life conditions, especially in Europe.

9. Even during this relatively brief time span, generational turnover has contributed to a postmaterial trend (Abramson and Inglehart 1995). For instance, in 1970 the pre–World War I generation constituted about 16 percent of the West German public; by 1980 this group constituted about 5 percent; and by 1990 they had essentially left the electorate. In the place of these older citizens, young Germans, socialized in the affluent post–World War II era, had entered the electorate.

10. Inglehart (1981) finds that European political elites (candidates for the European Parliament) are nearly three times more postmaterialist than the total public. Postmaterialists are also more common among younger elites.

11. Crepaz (1990) shows that the presence of a green or New Left party increases voting rates, presumably by encouraging postmaterialists to turn out at the polls.

CHAPTER 6

Issues and Ideological Orientations

ISSUES ARE THE currency of politics. People's issue opinions identify their priorities for government action and their expectations for the political process. Political parties are largely defined by their issue positions, and elections provide the public with a means of selecting between competing issue programs offered by the candidates and parties. As citizens become more sophisticated and involved in the political process, issue beliefs are an increasingly important influence on voting choice and the policy process. Moreover, researchers find a significant relationship between the public's issue preferences and policy outcomes at the state and federal levels (Erikson, Wright, and McIver 1994; Shapiro and Jacobs 1989). Issues are what politics is about.

Issue opinions also represent the translation of broad value orientations into specific political concerns. Issues are partially determined by the values examined in the last chapter, as well as by factors external to the individual: the cues provided by political elites, the flow of political events, and the application of abstract values to specific situations. For example, a person may favor the principle of equal rights for all citizens, but attitudes toward voting rights, job discrimination, school busing, open housing, and other civil rights legislation represent different mixes of values and practical concerns. Consequently, issue opinions are more changeable and varied than broad value orientations.

Another important characteristic of issues is that people focus their attention on a few areas—they are members of one or more *issue publics* (see chapter 2). Some people are especially concerned with education policy; others are more interested in foreign affairs, civil rights, environmental protection, or another issue. In general, only a minority of the public is interested and informed on any specific issue, although most people are members of at least one issue public. Members of an issue public are relatively well informed about the issue and follow the actions of politicians and the political parties on the issue. The salient issue for an individual has a strong impact on his or her political behavior.

Issue opinions are a dynamic aspect of politics, and the theme of changing popular values can be carried over to the study of issues. In some areas, contemporary publics are obviously more liberal than their predecessors. The issues of

women's rights, environmental protection, social equality, and individual lifestyles
were unknown or highly divisive a generation ago; a growing consensus now
exists on many of these issues. In other areas, people remain divided on the goals
of government. Discussions of tax revolts, neoconservative revival, and supply-
side economics suggest that conservative values have not lost their appeal for
many people. This chapter describes the present issue opinions of Western publics
and highlights, where possible, the trends in these opinions.

DOMESTIC POLICY OPINIONS

At one time, domestic policy was synonymous with concern over economic matters,
and economic issues still rank at the top of the public's political agenda for most
elections. More recently, however, the number of salient domestic issues has proliferated. Many people are now concerned with noneconomic issues such as social
equality, environmental protection, and citizen participation. This section provides
an overview of the wide-ranging domestic policy concerns of the citizenry.

Socioeconomic Issues and the State

For most of the twentieth century, the political conflicts that emerged from
industrialization and the Great Depression dominated politics in democratic
party systems. This debate revolved around the question of the government's
role in society and the economy, especially the provision of basic social needs.

A prime example of this policy area is the set of government-backed social
insurance programs that most governments introduced in the early 1900s; comparable American programs flowed from Roosevelt's New Deal in the 1930s. These
social programs protected individuals from economic calamities caused by illness,
unemployment, disability, or other hardships. In some nations, the government's
involvement in the economy also included public ownership of major industries
and active efforts to manage the economy.

Labor unions favored the extension of government social policy as a way to
improve the life chances of the average person. Business leaders and members of
the middle class frequently opposed these policies as an unnecessary government
intrusion into private affairs. At stake was not only the question of government

involvement in society but also the desirability of certain social goals and the distribution of political influence between labor and business. To a large extent, the terms *liberal* and *conservative* were synonymous with one's position on these questions. Attitudes toward these issues provided the major source of political competition in most elections. Class-based opinions on socioeconomic issues were the primary policy concerns of many voters.

Despite expanding government policy efforts in these areas, or perhaps because of them, new questions about the scope of governmental activity were raised in the 1980s. Conservative politicians on both sides of the Atlantic championed a populist revolt against big government (Pierson 1994). Margaret Thatcher, Ronald Reagan, and Helmut Kohl attempted to turn back the growth of government, privatizing government-owned businesses or government-run programs and reducing government social programs. Political observers interpreted their electoral successes as evidence of a new conservative trend in public attitudes toward government.

Abundant evidence exists that support for the principle of big government has lessened in recent years. For instance, between 1964 and 1980 the number of Americans who believed that the federal government was too powerful rose from 30 to 49 percent. The American public also became more critical of taxation levels and the use of tax money. The Gallup surveys show that in the 1950s less than half of the American public believed they were paying an unfair amount of taxes; by the late 1970s more than three-quarters believed their share of taxes was too high. Similarly, the American National Election Study finds an increase in the proportion believing that government "wastes a lot" of tax dollars, from 47 percent in 1964 to 61 percent in 1998. These opinions fueled popular support for the tax revolt that spread across America in the 1980s. Concerns about taxes diminished slightly as governments responded, although most Americans still believe their taxes are too high (Page and Shapiro 1992, 160–63; Niemi, Mueller, and Smith 1989, chap. 3). Perhaps the strongest indicator of these opinions has been the Republican Party's success in appealing to the antitax sentiments of many voters.

Some signs of a growing cynicism about big government also appear among Europeans. Longitudinal British public opinion trends uncover increasing criticism of big government beginning in the late 1970s (Heath and McMahon 1992). British desires for the denationalization of some industries grew during the early Thatcher years, which paralleled the Thatcher government's privatization of British Petroleum, British Gas, British Airways, British Telecom, and a host of other government-owned enterprises.[1] Thatcher also advocated a cutback in social programs, tax cuts, and a general reduction in the scope of British government that challenged the collectivist consensus of the postwar era. Similar doubts about government also were visible in German political attitudes. Helmut Kohl's administration reduced the scope of government activity by selling off shares of government-owned firms and reducing the benefits of Germany's generous welfare state. The French government expanded governmental activity under a new socialist government at the beginning of the 1980s, but by the end of the decade a retrenchment in governmental activity had begun.

Despite this neoconservative policy activity, recent public opinion surveys show that many people still believe the government is responsible for promoting individual well-being and guaranteeing the quality of life for its citizens (Borre and Scarbrough 1995). Table 6.1 displays the percentage of citizens who think the government is "definitely responsible" for dealing with specific social problems. The British and the French have very high expectations of government: Half believe the government is definitely responsible for providing for health care, providing a decent standard of living for the elderly, and maintaining strict environmental laws. Strong support also exists for governmental action on price controls, availability of housing, and even giving aid to college students. Eastern Germans, who were conditioned by the GDR to expect big government, are actually very similar to the British and the French in their reliance on the govern-

Table 6.1   Governmental Responsibility for Dealing with Policy Areas
            (in percentages)

	United States	Great Britain	France	West Germany	East Germany
Provide health care for sick	39	82	53	51	66
Provide decent living standard for the elderly	38	73	51	48	64
Strict environmental laws	46	63	67	58	72
Give aid to needy college students	35	38	59	27	43
Keep prices under control	25	44	42	23	43
Provide job for everyone who wants one	14	29	40	28	57
Reduce income differences between rich and poor	17	36	49	25	48
Provide housing for those who need it	20	37	44	20	38
Provide a decent living standard for the unemployed	13	29	34	17	38
Provide industry with help	17	41	36	16	27
Average	26	47	48	31	50

Source: 1996 International Social Survey Program.

Note: Table entries are the percentage of respondents who say that each area should definitely be the government's responsibility. Missing data were excluded in the calculation of percentages.

ment to guarantee basic social needs. Many western Germans also believe the government is responsible in these policy areas, though to a lesser degree than easterners.[2] Data from the other European nations show that support for governmental action to resolve social needs is a core element of the European political culture (Taylor-Gooby 1998).

In comparison to most Europeans, Americans are more reserved in their acceptance of governmental action. Even in areas in which the government is a primary actor, such as care of the elderly and unemployment, only a minority of Americans view these problems as definite governmental responsibilities (table 6.1). The United States is a major exception among Western democracies in its limited support for activist government. Public ownership of a significant portion of the economy was never attempted, and most Americans oppose nationalization on even a limited scale (Niemi, Mueller, and Smith 1989, chap. 1). Popular support for basic social programs remains underdeveloped by European standards. These conservative socioeconomic attitudes of Americans are often explained by the individualist nature of American society and the absence of a socialist working-class party.

Another measure of citizen expectations of their government involves preferences for governmental spending. One of the great contradictions of public opinion is that even as people have grown more critical about taxes and the overall size of government, support for increased spending on specific policy programs remains widespread. Table 6.2 displays the difference between the percentage of Americans who favor more governmental spending in a policy area and those who want to spend less. These data describe a long-term consensus for increased governmental spending on education, crime prevention, health care, preventing drug addiction, and environmental protection. Only welfare, the space program, and foreign aid are consistently identified as candidates for budget cuts. Moreover, although specific spending priorities change over time, the average preference for increased governmental spending listed across the bottom of the table has varied surprisingly little across six administrations.

Americans' priorities for spending on specific programs do, however, respond to changes in the federal budget and the political context in a manner consistent with Benjamin Page and Robert Shapiro's (1992) description of a rational public. For instance, the perceived military weakness of the Carter administration was reflected in calls for greater defense spending; 56 percent of Americans thought the government was spending too little on defense in the spring of 1980. This attitude supported the large defense expenditures of the early Reagan administration. Then, as examples of Pentagon waste became commonplace (accounts of $500 hammers and $7,000 coffeepots), popular support for defense spending was replaced by endorsement of the status quo or even a cut in defense budgets. Similarly, limitations on social spending enacted by the Reagan administration exceeded the wishes of many Americans. Between 1980 and 1991 support increased for *more* spending

Table 6.2 Budget Priorities of the American Public over Time (in percentages)

Priority	1973	1976	1980	1984	1988	1991	1996	2000
Halting rising crime rate	60	57	63	62	64	59	61	55
Protecting the nation's health	56	55	47	51	63	66	60	69
Dealing with drug addiction	59	51	52	57	64	50	48	53
Protecting the environment	53	45	32	54	60	63	50	55
Improving the educational system	40	41	42	59	60	62	65	67
Solving problems of big cities	36	23	19	31	36	35	45	40
Improving the condition of blacks	11	2	0	19	19	20	13	21
Military and defense	−27	−3	45	−21	−22	−13	−15	−2
Welfare	−31	−46	−43	−16	−19	−15	−43	−19
Space exploration program	−51	−51	−21	−27	−16	−26	−32	−29
Foreign aid	−66	−72	−64	−65	−63	−68	−69	−52
Average	13	9	16	19	22	21	16	23

Source: NORC General Social Survey.

Note: Table entries are the percentages of respondents saying "too much" being spent on the problem minus the percentages saying "too little."

in the areas of health care, environmental protection, education, urban problems, and minority aid. The Clinton administration entered office with a public that supported more spending on health care and other social programs.

Cross-national opinion polls indicate that budgetary support for specific policy programs such as health care, environmental protection, education, housing, and social services is widespread among Europeans as well (table 6.3). Britons favor increased spending in most areas, especially on policies identified with the welfare state. Western Germans display modest support for increased spending, but this is in the context of already large public expenditures and the economic uncertainties accompanying German unification. The legacy of the German Democratic Republic is evident in eastern Germans' commitment to big government, though it is important to note that the eastern German opinions are not much different from those of the British. The other European nations in this survey display general support for increased governmental spending (Kaase and Newton 1998). Americans also favor increased spending on various governmental programs, despite their general reservations about the scope of government.

This paradox between the public's general skepticism of government and its endorsement of increased spending on specific areas reflects a common contradiction in public opinion. The motto for government is clear: Tax less and spend more. Seymour Lipset and Everett Ladd (1980) describe this paradox as the combination of "ideological conservatism" and "programmatic liberalism." The attitudes of Americans and Europeans remain an ambiguous mix of support and denial of governmental action.

Table 6.3   Cross-National Comparison of Citizen Budget Priorities
(in percentages)

Priority	United States	Great Britain	France	West Germany	East Germany
Education	72	84	56	44	58
Health	61	91	36	47	69
Police and law enforcement	51	72	26	51	69
Old age pensions	41	79	23	49	58
Environment	36	39	37	53	51
Unemployment benefits	5	16	−12	11	51
Culture and arts	−31	−59	−21	−27	6
Military and defense	−12	−14	−59	−58	−69
Average	28	39	11	21	36

Source: 1996 International Social Survey Program.

Note: Table entries are the percentages of respondents saying "too much" being spent on the problem minus the percentages saying "too little."

The most accurate description of popular attitudes toward government might be that citizens are now critical of "big" government, but they also are accustomed to, and depend on, the policies of the modern state. When people confront the choice between cutting taxes and maintaining government services, many surveys find that a plurality prefer the services option even during the midst of the so-called tax revolt. This mix of opinions thus limits initiatives for dramatic increases in public spending, such as Clinton's proposals for national health care, as well as limiting initiatives that would generate major reductions in the current scope of government, such as the massive tax cut first proposed by the Bush administration.

Race and Equality

In recent years many people have developed a greater concern for social equality issues. After generations of dormancy, the issues of civil rights and racial equality inflamed American politics in the mid-1960s. For most of the decade the civil rights issue preoccupied the attention of many Americans and was a major source of political conflict. The importance of the racial issues has continued to the present. In addition, the success of the civil rights movement among African Americans encouraged similar activity among Latinos, Asian Americans, and other minorities.

European experience with ethnic and racial equality is more limited because most of these nations were homogeneous in their ethnic composition. This situation began to change in the 1960s (Hollifield 1993). Decolonialization by Britain and France led to a steady inflow of black and brown immigrants from former colonies. Labor force shortages led the West Germans to invite "guestworkers" from less developed Mediterranean countries to work in German factories. Nonwhites now account for 5 to 10 percent of the population in these three nations, and as much as a quarter of the workforce in some cities. During the past decade European societies have experienced some of the same social divisions based on race and ethnic origin that exist in the United States. Governments usually addressed these problems responsibly, but a public backlash against minorities frequently surfaced. For example, Britain experienced several race riots and other racially related political conflicts. Tensions between the French and North Africans erupted into violence in southern France, and the National Front Party espouses antiforeigner policies. German unification was accompanied by a surge of violence against foreigners and the emergence of the xenophobic Republikaner Party.

Although racial and ethnic conflicts are still a part of contemporary politics, the trends in racial attitudes over the past generation document a massive change in the beliefs of Americans. In the 1940s a majority of white Americans openly endorsed racial segregation in education, housing, transportation, and employment (figure 6.1). The values of freedom, equality, and justice that constitute the American creed did not apply to blacks. A phenomenal growth in support for

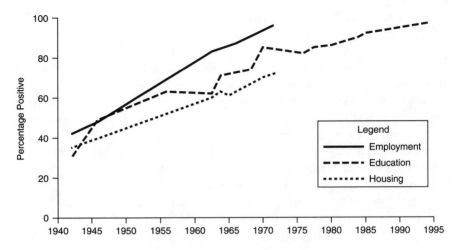

Figure 6.1 Support for Racial Integration in America

Sources: Adapted from Smith and Sheatsley (1984) and updated from Schuman et al. (1997).

Note: Figure entries are the percentage of respondents favoring integration in each area.

racial integration occurred over the next four decades. Integration of housing, education, and employment won widespread endorsement. Colin Powell's stature as secretary of state in the Bush administration illustrates how much has changed.

In a provocative book on public opinion, Paul Sniderman and Thomas Piazza (1993) examine racial attitudes in contemporary America. They show that as racial integration became accepted, the politics of race broadened to include a new set of issues: affirmative action, governmental social programs, and equity principles. The American public remains divided on many of these new racial issues. Some of the actions aimed at redressing racial inequality—affirmative action policies (such as school busing and preferential treatment) and racial quotas—are opposed by most Americans (Schuman et al. 1997). The current controversies over affirmative action programs illustrate this discontent. Many political analysts claim that these divided opinions are signs of a new racism in America. Based on an innovative set of survey experiments, Sniderman and Piazza conclude that although a minority of Americans still harbor racial prejudice, the contemporary clash over racial policies is more attributable to broader ideological conflicts over the scope of government, beliefs about equality, and other political values.

European attitudes toward racial issues are still evolving. Racial tensions were once considered the unique American dilemma, but no longer. The process of European unification and the globalization of national economies are increasing the racial and ethnic diversity of almost all advanced industrial societies. At first Europeans reacted ambiguously and tenuously to these new residents, but gradually tensions based on different economic conditions, values, and life perspectives developed—at least among portions of the European public. European public opinion surveys routinely find that most citizens in northern European nations believe that too many immigrants were allowed into their country (McCrone and Surridge 1998; Eurobarometer 30).

Table 6.4 summarizes a variety of questions dealing with attitudes toward immigrants. It is first apparent that citizens in all four nations are concerned about issues of immigrant and minority relations. Two-thirds or more say that immigration is a major problem in their nation and that the levels of immigration should be reduced. Additional questions illustrate some of the bases of these concerns: Many people believe that immigrants raise crime rates or take jobs away from the native population. At its worst, a fifth to a third of the various European publics believe that immigrants should be returned to their nation of origin. These sentiments are likely a mix of objective concerns as well as preju-

Table 6.4 Cross-National Comparison of Attitudes toward Immigrants (in percentages)

	United States	Great Britain	France	West Germany	East Germany
Immigration is a problem	—	63	74	86	86
Critical Opinions					
Should decrease number of immigrants	64	68	—	76	79
Immigrants increase crime	33	26	—	55	68
Immigrants take jobs	48	50	—	26	53
Illegal immigrants should be sent home	—	55	69	77	76
All immigrants should be sent home	—	18	21	34	35
Positive Opinions					
Europe should take strong stand against racism	—	83	78	76	90
Immigrants open society to new ideas	64	68	—	76	79
Immigrants should have same rights	—	69	70	50	64
Immigrants good for economy	34	17	—	39	32

Sources: 1995 International Social Survey Program; Eurobarometer 39 (March 1993) and 47.1 (March 1997).

Note: Table entries are the percentages of respondents agreeing with each statement.

dicial fears as different cultures are intermixing (Sniderman et al. 2000). And for both the United States and Europe, the 1990s were a period of substantial new migration that tested the tolerance of these societies.

At the same time, tolerance toward immigrants is apparent in other survey items in the lower half of the table. The vast majority of Europeans believe that European institutions should take a strong stand against racism—rising to 90 percent in eastern Germany where racial conflict flared up after unification. Most citizens also believe that immigrants open their society to new ideas and that immigrants should have the same rights as others. It is this juxtaposition of abstract support for the principles of equality and tolerance with the fears over concrete problems in the clash between different cultures that makes racial and ethnic conflicts so difficult for Americans and Europeans.

Although the climate of opinion now endorses racial equality, one must be cautious not to overlook the real racial problems that still exist in many nations. Support for the principle of equality coexists with the remnants of segregation in the United States; racial conflict can still flare up in Brixton, Liverpool, or Marseilles. Problems of housing segregation, unequal education, and job discrimination are real. Public opinion alone is not sufficient to resolve these problems, and undoubtedly some survey respondents overstate their racial tolerance. And yet the shift of social norms in support of racial equality makes these problems more solvable than when discrimination was openly acclaimed.

Gender Issues

Another social dimension concerns equality between men and women. A short generation ago traditional gender roles were deeply entrenched on both sides of the Atlantic. American women faced limited career opportunities and German housewives were expected to devote their efforts to *Kinder, Kirche, und Küche* (children, church, and kitchen). The status of women in Britain, France, and other advanced industrial societies was equally constrained.

These traditional attitudes underwent a profound transformation in the latter half of the twentieth century. The women's movement grew most rapidly in the United States, and a parallel growth of women's groups has occurred in Europe (Lovenduski and Norris 1996). These groups, and individual women, raised society's consciousness about the different treatment of men and women and changed societal values. Political action led to legislation equalizing the rights of both genders. The public at large became more sensitive to gender issues, and social norms have gradually changed (Rochon 1998).

Most Americans now express belief in equal opportunities for men and women. For example, one survey question asks whether or not one approves of a married woman working if she has a husband to support her, by implication condoning the norm that married women belong at home (figure 6.2). In 1938 when this question was first asked, only 22 percent of Americans approved of a woman working in these circumstances; this increased to 80 percent or more by

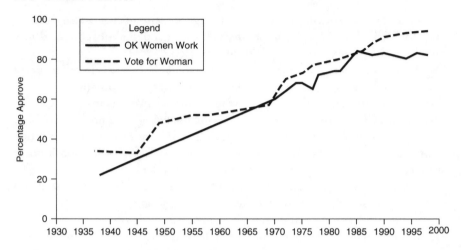

Figure 6.2   Support for Women's Equality

Source: The Gallup Organization, 1938–75; General Social Survey, 1972–96.

the end of the 1980s. Similarly, Gallup data show a striking increase in the number of Americans who say they would vote for a woman as president. In 1936 only 31 percent expressed this view; by the 1980s this figure reached more than 80 percent. The American National Election Study asked a more focused question on whether a woman's place is in the home; the percentage agreeing with this view has steadily decreased since it was first asked in 1972.

Table 6.5 provides evidence on how Americans and Europeans think about gender-related issues (also see Scott, Braun, and Alwin 1998). The top panel in the table displays opinions on the balance between the careers and family life for women. Most people believe that working women can establish close ties with their children and that a job can establish a woman's independence. Yet there are also some common concerns about a woman undertaking a career; many people—both men and women—believe that a young child will suffer if the mother works. A large number of people in each nation, including a significant minority of women, believe that women are primarily oriented toward family life over a career. Even in eastern Germany, where the state made exceptional efforts to involve women in the workforce and politics on equal terms, the same mixed attitudes toward the role of women appear.

These findings initially suggest that gender norms are changing, and in one sense it is amazing that gender roles developed over centuries have changed so rapidly. At the same time, this transformation has been incomplete. Evidence from European surveys indicates that most men believe that women are primarily responsible for housework and a man has more right to a job (Scott, Braun, and Alwin 1998). Other survey data indicate that many working women believe their situation is worse than men's regarding wages, promotion prospects, job opportunities, and job security (Eurobarometer 19). Traditional images of the role of women still exist in the minds of many people. Ultimately, the legacy of the women's movement might be the creation of a choice for women—both work and family are now accepted options—instead of limiting choice to a single role.

The last panel of table 6.5 displays broad support for the political equality of women. Most Europeans approve of the women's movement; this reflects an increase in support over the prior decade. Large majorities also reject the notion that politics is better left to men, and most express equal confidence in male and female politicians. If comparable data were available from American surveys, we would expect similar results. Although women remain underrepresented within the top stratum of political officials, old stereotypes of politics as an exclusively male domain have eroded.

Table 6.5   Attitudes toward Gender Equality (in percentages)

	United States	Great Britain	France	West Germany	East Germany
Situation of women has improved	70	68	60	68	—
Work and Family					
Working/nonworking mothers can establish same relationship with children	70*	68	73	39*	56
Having a job is best way for woman to be independent	55*	65*	76*	67*	70*
Preschoolers suffer if mother works (Disagree)	47	45	33	15	21
A job is all right, but women really want home/children (D)	40*	49*	29*	42*	46
Being a housewife is as fulfilling as a job (D)	24*	35*	35*	39*	60*
Average	47	52	49	40	51*
Political Attitudes					
Approve of women's movement	81	63	62	62*	76
Country would be better governed if more women politicians	57	51	59	51	—

Source: 1990–91 World Values Survey; first and last items are from the "Men and Women Study 1995."

Note: Table entries are the percentage of respondents who agree (or disagree) with each statement. Items where there are substantial differences between genders (Cramer's V greater than .10) are denoted by an asterisk.

Environmental Protection

Environmental protection represents one of the new issue concerns of advanced industrial democracies. Environmentalism was initially stimulated by a few very visible ecological crises; these concerns then persisted and expanded. Separate issues were linked together into environmental programs, citizen groups mobilized in support of environmental issues, and new green parties formed in several nations (Dalton 1994a; Richardson and Rootes 1995). Gradually there developed a scientific and political awareness of how human activity and economic development could pose threats to the natural environment, which lessened the quality of life and could pose a threat to the sustainability of our progress.

The broadest sign of public concern is an interest in environmental issues. The first row in table 6.6 indicates environmental concern is widespread in all these nations. Even when phrased in negative terms to dissuade easy agreement, most people agree that protecting the environment is an urgent problem. Other research finds that interest in a host of environmental issues has reached the publics' consciousness (Dalton and Rohrschneider 1998). Issues of global warming, the ozone hole, and biodiversity have become global concerns (except at 1600 Pennsylvania Avenue). Environmental protection is a priority issue for many citizens.

Widespread interest in environmental issues also translates into support for environmental protection. Contemporary public opinion nearly unanimously endorses stronger measures to protect the environment (table 6.6). In a survey conducted by Gallup before the 1992 environmental summit in Rio de Janiero, more than 90 percent of the public in these nations favor stronger environmental protection laws for business and industry. Nearly equal numbers favor laws requiring that all citizens conserve resources and reduce pollution (also see Dunlap et al. 1992). Significantly, strong support for environmental action also exists among eastern Germans, where years of environmental neglect have created severe damage to human health and the environment.

Many political analysts discount these environmental opinions because such popular views can be expressed in a survey without concern for the actual costs of a policy. Thus, survey researchers ask people to balance their environmental beliefs against the potential economic costs of environmental protection. The data in the middle panel of table 6.6 indicate that most people say they would give up part of their income or pay higher taxes to prevent pollution. On another question, 58 percent of the American public favor protection of the environment even if it risks holding back economic growth; majorities in Europe agree (also see Dalton and Rohrschneider 1998).

Another sign of public support for environmental reform is environmentally friendly behavior. The Gallup Health of the Planet study found that a majority of Americans say they avoid products that might harm the environment. The percentage of green consumers is also high in Europe, where waste problems and recycling efforts are more common than in the United States. The 1994 Interna-

Table 6.6   Environmental Attitudes (in percentages)

	United States	Great Britain	France	West Germany	East Germany
Protecting the environment is urgent problem	68	73	76	82	86
Policy Support					
Favor stronger laws for business and industry*	90	93	—	94	—
Favor stronger laws for citizens*	82	83	—	86	—
Nuclear power stations are very dangerous for environment	54	49	—	68	63
Trade-Off Questions					
Would give up part of income to prevent pollution	72	64	59	46	60
Would pay more taxes to prevent pollution	61	65	52	46	61
Action					
Approve of environmental movement	91	91	91	97	98
Avoid products that harm the environment*	57	75	—	81	—

Source: 1990–91 World Values Survey and 1992 Gallup Health of the Planet Survey; the items from the Gallup survey are denoted by an asterisk. The question on nuclear power is from the 1993 International Social Survey.

Note: Table entries are the percentage of respondents who agree with each statement. Missing data was included in the calculation of percentages.

tional Social Survey found that 85 percent of western Germans say they sort their trash for recycling, as do 77 percent of eastern Germans (60 percent of Americans say they recycle). The same survey showed significant numbers who claim to have signed an environmental petition: United States, 31 percent; Great Britain, 37 percent; western Germany, 31 percent; and 28 percent in eastern Germany. Even more striking, these publics almost unanimously support ecology and nature conservation groups, with approval ratings above 90 percent in each nation.

Environmental attitudes indicate that citizens are now interested in new political issues, especially issues tapping the noneconomic concerns typical of postmaterial values. In earlier periods, economic needs superseded concerns about the environment. Today many people say they are willing to sacrifice financially to improve the environment. These concerns reflect more than just a growing awareness of the hidden health and economic costs of pollution. In a broad cross-national study of attitudes toward the environment, Ronald Inglehart (1995) notes that the citizens in prosperous countries with relatively cleaner environments are most willing to make sacrifices for the environment. Material success allows the citizens in these nations to shift attention to the quality of their lives.[3] Similarly, support for environmental protection is more common among the young, better-educated, and postmaterial sectors of society. Environmentalism thus reflects the processes of value change that are part of the new style of citizen politics.

Social and Moral Issues

A final set of domestic issues involves the turbulent debate over social and moral norms that involve interpersonal relations and life choices. In the late 1960s and early 1970s young people began to question traditional values with symbolic statements, such as the use of drugs or the choice of hairstyles, clothing, and music. This movement tested the extent of individual freedom on matters such as abortion, divorce, homosexuality, and pornography. Thus, these issues entered the political debate in a variety of ways.

Social issues differ from most other issues because of their moral content. The critic of abortion or homosexuality views the issue in terms of moral right and wrong; unlike the negotiable monetary benefits of economic issues, principles are at stake. Several consequences follow from the moral base of social issues. People find it is difficult to compromise on social issues because political views are intensely felt, and the issue public for social issues is often larger than might otherwise be expected. In addition, the active interest groups on social issues are religious organizations and Christian Democratic parties, not labor unions and business groups. Religious values are an important determinant of opinions on social issues.

Table 6.7 presents public opinion on several social and moral issues. Until recently traditional value orientations led many people to be highly critical of divorce. Scandal, dishonor, and religious isolation often accompanied the divorce decree. The table indicates that attitudes have changed dramatically; nearly everyone now believes that divorce is sometimes justified. As attitudes toward divorce have become more tolerant, legislation has removed the stigma of divorce and provisions discriminating against women.

Attitudes toward sexual relations evoke differing responses, depending on the context. What stands out most dramatically in the table is the more conservative orientation of Americans compared to all the European respondents. Americans are more critical toward extramarital sex and sexual relations generally. Despite the political activity of gay and lesbian groups, widespread negativity toward homosexuals remains. A majority of the public in each nation believes that homosexual relations are wrong.[4]

Abortion also has been a divisive social issue in several nations. Proponents and opponents of the issue are intense in their issue beliefs and oriented toward

Table 6.7   Attitudes on Social and Moral Issues (in percentages)

	United States	Great Britain	France	West Germany	East Germany
Divorce is sometimes justified	81	87	89	93	87
Premarital sex is wrong	61	34	26	31	21
Extramarital sex is wrong	99	98	94	90	90
Homosexual relations are wrong	75	66	64	61	62
Abortion Attitudes					
Abortion is not wrong					
If child may have birth defect	47	63	81	49	65
If parents are poor	31	34	53	17	36
Religious Attitudes					
Believe in God	92	68	52	62	26
Believe in life after death	81	59	51	55	15
Believe in heaven	86	53	33	46	22
Believe in hell	74	32	20	36	11
Believe in miracles	79	38	37	62	38
Average	83	50	39	52	22

Sources: 1996 and 1998 International Social Surveys; the divorce question is from the 1990 World Values Survey.

Note: Missing data were not included in the calculation of percentages.

political action. Furthermore, this issue has periodically been the subject of major legislative or judicial action in all four nations. Contemporary publics believe that abortion is sometimes justified, such as when the health of the baby is at risk. (Other surveys show broad support for abortion when the health of the mother is endangered.) Fewer people approve of abortion when it is based on economic factors. Despite the dramatic ebbs and flows in public events on this issue, attitudes have changed only slightly over the past two decades (Page and Shapiro 1992; Ashford and Timms 1992).

The findings in table 6.7 lead to two broad conclusions. First, Americans are generally more conservative than Europeans on social and moral issues. This pattern is likely the result of national differences in religious feelings, as seen in the bottom panel in the table. Despite the affluence, high mobility rates, and social diversity of Americans, the United States is among the most religious of Western societies. American church attendance and religious feelings are among the highest in the world. A full 81 percent of Americans consider themselves religious, compared to barely half of Europeans. Even more striking are the patterns on other religious beliefs: Two-thirds of Americans believe in the existence of hell, compared to only a third of Britons and less than a fifth of Germans and the French. The secular policies of the GDR created an even more secular society in eastern Germany.[5]

Second, public opinion has generally become more tolerant on social issues as the processes of modernization and secularization have transformed Western societies. Long-term opinion series for the United States and Germany indicate a gradual liberalization of attitudes toward sexual relations and homosexuals over the past generation (Noelle-Neumann and Piel 1984; Page and Shapiro 1992).

Underlying these longitudinal changes has been the diminishment of religious values among the advanced industrial democracies. Virtually all these societies are becoming more secular: Church attendance has decreased and religious attachments have weakened. For example, the 1980 World Values Survey found that nearly half of the public in each European nation said that God played an important part in their life; more than 80 percent of Americans expressed this same opinion. Even in the short span of ten years, these feelings of religiosity dropped off markedly in each nation. If comparable data were available for the 1950s or 1960s, the value shift would be markedly greater.[6]

This change in values has had mixed effects on advanced industrial societies. The decline in religiosity may prompt greater tolerance of different lifestyle choices, especially involving abortion rights and alternative lifestyles. At the same time, weakening religious attachments are probably linked to declining respect and acceptance for authority, as well as an erosion in moral and ethical standards. A more secular public sees humankind in a different light.

FOREIGN POLICY OPINIONS

Foreign policy has probably undergone the most dramatic political changes in the few years between the last two editions of this book. After decades of silent conflict during the Cold War, the collapse of the Soviet Union dramatically reshaped the international order. Similarly, the democratic revolution that spread throughout Eastern Europe altered the international distribution of power and values in a fundamental way. Terrorism is a new threat. There is a new world order, even if governments are unsure about its content and people are unsure about their opinions. This section traces some of these changes.

Conflict and Cooperation

Although the Cold War is over, the world can still be a brutish place. Regional and local conflicts—such as in Bosnia, Somalia, or the Persian Gulf—threaten individual and international security. Yet the end of the Cold War has transformed peace and conflict issues in the current world. Potential conflict between the superpowers no longer is the central theme of international relations; public attention has shifted toward other sources of international conflict. In a cross-national survey conducted in early 1994, a majority of Americans, Germans, and Britons believed the world had become a *more dangerous* place since the end of the Cold War (table 6.8).

Table 6.8   Attitudes on Foreign Policy Issues (in percentages)

	United States	Great Britain	France	Germany
Security Issues				
World has become more dangerous since end of Cold War	67	51	—	50
Nuclear weapons are no longer necessary	—	50	39	78
International Cooperation				
UN peacekeeping missions will become more important in future	67	72	69	48
Important to cooperate with others through UN	89	91	—	85
UN should send troops to conflict areas to achieve peace	63	72	—	67
European Unification				
EU membership a good thing (net approval)	—	5	32	35
Favor single currency (euro)	—	25	64	55
Favor EU policymaking (avg. support for various areas)	—	36	56	55
Favor a common foreign policy	—	56	78	76
Favor EU expansion (avg. support for 15 nations)	—	41	34	38

Sources: European Union items are from Eurobarometer 52 (October–November 1999); other items are from *Index to International Public Opinion* (various years from 1995–99).

The changing nature of citizen orientations toward military and security issues is apparent in perceptions of the North Atlantic Treaty Organization (NATO). NATO was once the bulwark of Western defense and was roundly supported by the public in most member states (Smith and Wertman 1992). Today NATO's main threat from the East has largely vanished, and NATO has given associate status to several Eastern European nations. Surveys conducted by the U.S. Information Agency find that most Europeans express a continuing need for NATO (McIntosh and MacIver 1994). At the same time Europeans also seem to be distancing themselves slightly from the alliance with the United States. Roughly a third of the public in Britain, Germany, and France believe that U.S. involvement is no longer needed in the defense of Europe. Continuing their previous tendencies, the French are often openly skeptical about American involvement in Europe and the foreign policy goals of the United States.

Most surveys indicate that Western democratic publics now place less stress on conflict with Russia as the basis of international tensions. Instead, the Middle East, terrorism, and other threats are seen as more pressing. Perhaps because of these changing perceptions of the threat and the end of superpower conflict, citizens are more likely to endorse cooperative international efforts, such as through the United Nations. Table 6.8 indicates, for example, that most people expect UN peace-keeping missions to become more common in the future and they support this development. Nearly two-thirds of Americans approve of sending UN troops to enforce peace in the world's trouble spots. Because of the past criticism the United Nations received from some prominent American politicians, this support may be an indicator of a new internationalism. There is also broad support for the UN among the British and German respondents in the same survey.

Another example of internationalism is the process of economic, social, and political integration of Europe that has occurred within the institutional frame-work of the European Union (EU). Longitudinal data indicate that most of the French and German public supported the process of integration from the outset (Gabel 1998; Reif and Inglehart 1991). Approval of the EU has been less certain among the British but gradually expanded in the 1980s. Table 6.8 indicates that most Europeans support the principle of European unification; those who think the EU is a "good thing" outnumber those who say it is a "bad thing" by a sizable margin in Germany and France, although the British remain less certain. The Germans and the French are relatively positive about the Union expanding its policy role in the creation of a single European currency (the euro) and across a variety of other policy areas—again, British support is more temperate. The goal of expanding the EU to include the new democratic nations of Eastern Europe also evokes mixed responses. On the whole, however, Europeans are increasingly likely to think of the EU as a forum for European policymaking.[7]

We are still in a period when international politics are in flux, and new threats to world order have emerged with the ending of the Cold War. Although it is too early to discern the exact shape that foreign policy opinions will take in this new context, it appears that Western publics are broadening their perspectives and thinking about foreign policy in more cooperative and international terms. As one illustration, a 1995 survey found that a substantial proportion of the public in Britain, Germany, and France believed that nuclear weapons were no longer necessary, and a differently worded question in the United States found nearly half of Americans shared these views.[8] Perhaps our thinking about international relations has entered a new era.

LEFT/RIGHT ORIENTATIONS

People are changing their opinions on many issues. Opinions on equality issues display a dramatic shift over the past generation; overt discrimination against racial minorities, women, and other minority groups is no longer condoned by most people. Tolerance of nonconformity is also more common, whether the objects of tolerance are political or social minorities (McCloskey and Brill 1983; Thomassen 1995). Liberal attitudes toward new issues such as environmental quality and alternative lifestyles are also commonplace. Moreover, there is a broad consensus in support of the basic social programs provided by the modern state, although voters do not endorse a further growth in these programs and would welcome a restriction in the size of government.

Still, it is difficult to use specific issue opinions to make sweeping generalizations about the changing political orientations of the public. Citizens are now interested in a wider range of issues than just socioeconomic concerns, and so a general assessment of overall political tendencies must weigh several different issues. The rate of social change across various issue interests is uneven. Support for environmental protection has grown rapidly over time, whereas attitudes toward abortion have been more stable. Finally, the content of ongoing political controversies also changes over time. For instance, the racial issues that were intensely fought over in the 1960s—school desegregation, open housing, and public accommodations—now register overwhelmingly liberal responses; but new racial issues—quotas and affirmative action programs—divide the American public. This represents progress in the development of racial tolerance, but racial policy remains politically contentious. One of the major points we have (re)learned from recent political trends is that new issues of conflict inevitably replace old consensual issues.

One way to generalize about the overall political orientations of Western publics is to examine broad ideological orientations that extend beyond specific issues. Political scientists frequently measure such broad orientations in terms of Left/Right attitudes (Fuchs and Klingemann 1989). Political issues are often discussed or summarized in terms of Left/Right or liberal/conservative philosophies. Republicans attack what they call the "loony Left" while Democrats rail against the "reactionary Right." These labels provide the reference points that help voters interpret and evaluate political activities. The ability to think of oneself in Left/Right terms does not imply that citizens possess a sophisticated conceptual framework or theoretical dogma. For many individuals, Left/Right attitudes are a summary of their positions on the political issues of greatest concern (also see chapter 10 on issue voting).

Figure 6.3 presents the distribution of Left/Right orientations across nations. The survey asked respondents to place themselves on an 11-point scale labeled from "Left" to "Right." The figure plots the average Left/Right self-placement of electorates from ten Western democracies, comparing results from the Comparative Study of Electoral Systems (1996–98).

The United States is one of the more conservative nations in overall Left/Right terms; few advanced industrial democracies are more rightist (for

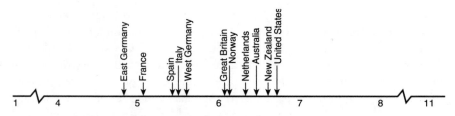

Figure 6.3 National Differences in Left/Right Self-Placement

Source: Comparative Study of Electoral Systems (1996–98).

Note: The Left/Right scale was coded from (1) Left to (11) Right; the French and Italian data are taken from Eurobarometer 47, which used a 10-point scale adjusted to a comparable 11-point score.

additional nations, see Inglehart 1997). This reaffirms an impression derived from many of the specific issue areas examined in this chapter. Britain, western Germany, and most other advanced industrial democracies are clustered around the midpoint of the scale. At the liberal pole are several Mediterranean nations—France, Italy, and Spain—that have significant leftist traditions. They are now joined by eastern Germans and presumably by other democratizing nations in Eastern Europe that display traces of their socialist past (Rose, Mishler, and Haerpfer 1998).

There is some evidence that broad Left/Right attitudes are moving in a more liberal direction over time. The World Values Survey finds such a leftward tilt in opinions between the early 1980s and the early 1990s (Inglehart 1997). Generational comparisons provide even stronger indication of political change. The young are consistently more liberal than their elders (Ashford and Timms 1992, app.). This generation gap suggests that democratic publics are gradually becoming more liberal in their overall political orientations.[9] But even these data tell only a partial story.

As we suggested previously, the content of Left and Right reflects the issues of salience to the public, and this is another source of political change. The meaning of Left and Right varies across age and political groups (Inglehart 1984; Fuchs and Klingemann 1989). For older citizens, these terms are largely synonymous with attitudes on socioeconomic issues: *Left* means support for social programs, working-class interests, and the influence of labor unions; *Right* is identified with limited government, support for middle-class interests, and the influence of the business sector. Among the young, the New Politics issues of environmental protection, social equality, and lifestyle freedoms are added to socioeconomic interests. For the young, the term *Left* can mean opposition to nuclear energy, support for sexual equality, a preference for disarmament, or endorsement of social programs.

Therefore, it is difficult to speak in simple terms about whether contemporary publics are becoming more liberal or more conservative in an overall sense. Indeed, the best longitudinal evidence from the United States suggests that these broad orientations shift in both directions, depending on the issues of controversy and the political currents of the time (Stimson 1999). James Stimson shows that the 1960s were a period of liberal ascendance, whereas the 1980s were a decade of conservative swing. But underlying these overall trends, it appears that the Left/Right placement of young citizens differs from that of their elders, and the meaning of Left and Right in political discourse is also changing.

PUBLIC OPINION AND POLITICAL CHANGE

A significant feature of contemporary issue opinions is that more people are interested in more issues. Opinions on socioeconomic issues were once the predominate concern of voters and political elites; one could realistically describe political competition in terms of a single overarching policy area, such as the New Deal in the United States or capitalist/socialist conflicts in Europe. In recent years the number of the public's distinct issue interests has increased. Socioeconomic matters still attract widespread attention. In addition, issues of social equality, environmental protection, social morals, and foreign policy capture the interest of large numbers of citizens.

The expansion of the boundaries of politics to include these new issues has several implications for the nature of contemporary politics. Governments have increased the scope of their activity. Governments are now worried not only about economic policy but also about whether or not the environment is clean and whether or not personal life choices are tolerated. This expansion of the government's role has rekindled ongoing debates about the appropriate scope of government, although the policy content of the current debate is much different from prior debates about the economic role of the state.

This proliferation of issue publics also changes the structure of political representation and decision making. Issue publics focus the public's political efforts to maximize their representation on key issues. The proliferation of issue publics probably increases the complexity of the governing process, however. A majority of (differing) voters want government to spend more on (differing) specific programs; a majority also want government to tax them less. Policymakers thus see conflicting signals emanating from the public, without a method (or perhaps motivation) to resolve these conflicts systematically. Governmental responses to the demands of one issue public may conflict with the demands of another issue group. Policy proliferation can lead to issue-by-issue decisions rather than broad programmatic planning. One of the challenges facing contemporary governments is how to adapt the democratic process to this different pattern of interest representation.

What can we say about the overall political orientations of contemporary publics? Journalists and social commentators frequently refer to a liberal or conservative mood sweeping a nation. The early 1960s and early 1970s supposedly were a time of radical change and liberal ascendance. Similarly, discussions of the new conservative mood in Western democracies became commonplace in the 1980s, exemplified by the electoral strength of Reagan, Thatcher, Kohl, and Chirac. Clinton's victory in 1992 was called a signal of a new era, and just two years later the Republican congressional victories supposedly marked another new era, which quickly came to an end with Clinton's reelection in 1996. The pundits were then surprised again when George W. Bush won election in 2000, with Republicans initially controlling both houses of Congress (while Blair and Schröder's victories moved Britain and Germany to the Left).

Tested against actual public opinion data, such generalizations are often difficult to substantiate. The counterculture movement of the 1970s was not as widespread as the media would suggest, and the conservative revival of the 1980s was equally overdrawn. Opinion change does not follow a simple predictable course, and the visible public actions of political groups can distort our images of the broader currents of public opinion.[10] Furthermore, there are many issues of potential interest to the public, and not all of them move in a consistent direction over time.

Still, some general trends emerge from our findings. One apparent trend has been the shift toward what might be termed *libertarian attitudes*. Contemporary publics are becoming more tolerant of individual diversity and more concerned with the protection of individual freedoms. This applies to the rights of minorities and women as well as a general acceptance of individual freedom in social relations. These trends are manifested in attitudes toward social equality, moral issues, and the quality of life. Paralleling these changes have been a decline in respect for authority and concern with social order.

The counterevidence is *socioeconomic attitudes*. Concerns about the excessive cost and bureaucracy of government are now commonplace (even if people favor greater governmental spending on a wide variety of programs). The end of socialism and the retrenchment of the welfare state in the West have made it impossible for the Left to attain its traditional goals of state control of the economy and state guarantees of basic social needs. There has been a conservative shift on these aspects of the socioeconomic issue.

In a period of increasing issue proliferation, such conflicting trends are not surprising. There can be a gradual liberalization of political values on social issues, with a conservative gain on socioeconomic matters. But even this generalization would be difficult to sustain because the meaning of such ideological/ programmatic labels has changed as part of this process. No longer does liberalism stand for the creation of social programs, the nationalization of industry, and peaceful coexistence with the communist world. It might just as well mean protection of a clean environment or women's rights legislation. No longer does conservatism represent the prohibition of governmental social programs or the defeat of the Soviet empire. It might mean advocacy of term limits or supporting family policies.

The content of contemporary political debate is therefore difficult to compare to the political conflicts of the New Deal era of the 1930s or even the Great Society of the 1960s. Perhaps this shift in the content of the political debate is what most directly indicates how advanced industrial societies are modernizing and progressing politically as the new millennium begins.

SUGGESTED READINGS

Borre, Ole, and Elinor Scarbrough, eds. *The Scope of Government.* New York: Oxford University Press, 1995.

Jowell, Roger, et al., eds. *British—and European—Social Attitudes: The 15th Report.* Brookfield, Vt:. Ashgate Publishing, 1998.

Niedermayer, Oskar, and Richard Sinnott, eds. *Public Opinion and International Governance.* New York: Oxford University Press, 1995.

Schuman, Howard, Charlotte Steeh, Lawrence Bobo, and Maria Krysan. *Racial Attitudes in America: Trends and Interpretations.* Rev. ed. Cambridge, Mass.: Harvard University Press, 1997.

Stimson, James. *Public Opinion in America: Moods, Cycles, and Swings.* 2d ed. Boulder, Colo.: Westview Press, 1999.

NOTES

1. As the Conservative government sold off public enterprises, the public responded to this changing political context; support for further privatizations decreased over this same time span (Heath and McMahon 1992, 118–19).
2. A majority of Westerners do hold the government responsible for two key provisions of the welfare state: providing health care and a decent living standard for the elderly. For more on East-West contrasts, see Bauer-Kaase (1994).
3. Support for environmental action also might be stimulated by pressing environmental problems that threaten human health and the ecosystem. Thus, we would attribute eastern German support for environmental action to these grievances more than to postmaterial sentiments among the public.
4. Other data from the World Values Survey suggest that opinions toward homosexuals are more evenly divided and are becoming more tolerant over time (Ashford and Timms 1992).
5. Religious attitudes illustrate the occasional inconsistency of public opinion. Citizens in all five surveys are more likely to believe in heaven than in hell (is this wishful thinking?). Eastern Germans are also more likely to believe in miracles than in the existence of God.
6. Most advanced industrial societies also have experienced a long-term trend toward secularization. Church enrollment, for instance, has dropped off in most nations, as well as other forms of involvement in the churches (Franklin, Mackie, and Valen 1992, chap. 1).
7. The European Union maintains a Web site with current reports from its regular monitoring of European public opinion: http://europa.eu.int/comm/dg10/epo/
8. These data are from the Index to International Public Opinion 1995–96, pp. 563 and 641.

9. These generational differences might be due to life-cycle effects, implying that younger people will become more conservative as they age. We could determine this if we had access to data over a longer time period, but the length of the available series is too brief for this purpose. Even if longer-term data were available, however, this would not address questions about the changing content of Left and Right terms as discussed in the following paragraphs.

10. Elections provide a poor indicator of ideological trends except in a very long-term perspective. Elections measure the positions of parties and candidates relative to the electorate, but not the overall distribution of opinion on any specific issue. A party that moves too far Left can lose votes, just as one that moves too far Right. Furthermore, the combination of issues in an election makes it difficult to make simple estimations of the voters' intentions on specific policies.

PART THREE

The Electoral Connection

CHAPTER 7

Elections and Political Parties

CITIZENS USE VARIOUS ways to influence politics, but the electoral connection through political parties is still the primary basis of public influence in representative democracies. Elections are one of the few methods that enable a society to reach a collective decision based on individual preferences. The choice between parties aggregates the preferences of individual voters, thereby converting public opinion into specific political decisions. Other forms of citizen participation may exert substantial influence on government, but they lack this representative quality.

Elections also are important because of what they decide. Electoral outcomes determine who manages the affairs of government and makes public policy.[1] The selection of leaders and the ability to "throw the rascals out" at the next election are the public's penultimate power. Political elites may not always act as they promise, but the selection of a government provides some popular control over these elites.

Elections attract disproportionate attention from social scientists for several other reasons. Elections involve most of the public, so they enable us to see how most people make political decisions. Voting also provides an opportunity to study how political attitudes are linked to actual behavior—the casting of a ballot. Hence, voting choices are likely to be relatively well thought out, intelligible, and predictable. The electoral connection is thus a good setting for studying political thoughts and behavior that is more developed than simply a response to a public opinion survey. If there is one political act that provides a window into the mind of most citizens, it would be voting.

To study elections, one must start by understanding the political parties that provide the foundation of the electoral process. Parties are the primary institutions of representative democracy, especially in Europe (Katz and Mair 1994; Ziegler 1993). Parties define the choices available to voters. Candidates in most European nations are selected by the parties and elected as party representatives, not as individuals. Open primaries and independent legislators are virtually unknown outside the United States. A large proportion of Europeans (including the Germans) vote directly for party lists rather than individual candidates.

INTERNET RESOURCE

Virtually all democratic political parties have
Web sites that can be found at

www.electionworld.org

Political parties also shape the content of election campaigns. Party programs help define the issues that are discussed during the campaign (Budge, Robertson, and Hearl 1987). In many European nations, the parties, not individual candidates, control advertising during the campaign. Political parties and party leaders thus exercise a primary role in articulating the public's concerns.

Once in government, parties control the policymaking process. Control of the executive branch and the organization of the legislative branch are decided on the basis of party majorities. The parties' control is often absolute, as in the parliamentary systems of Europe, where representatives from the same party vote as a bloc (Bowler, Farrell, and Katz 1999). American parties are less united and less decisive, but even here parties actively structure the legislative process. Because of the centrality of political parties to the democratic process, political scientists describe many European political systems as a system of "responsible party government."

Political parties thus provide the focus for our study of the electoral connection, and ultimately the workings of democratic representation. In 1942 E.E. Schattschneider, a well-known political scientist, concluded that "modern democracy is unthinkable save in terms of political parties democracy." Similarly, James Bryce (1921, 119) stated that "parties are inevitable. No one has shown how representative government could be worked without them." These are refrains echoed by many contemporary political scientists.

This chapter summarizes the history and social bases of contemporary party systems. This discussion presents a framework for understanding the party options available to the voters, as well as the characteristics of the major parties as political organizations and agents of representative democracy.

AN OVERVIEW OF FOUR PARTY SYSTEMS

To introduce the party systems in our four core nations, we begin by describing the characteristics of each of the major parties in each nation. Parties vary in their size, structure, and governmental experience, as well as in their political orientations.[2]

As table 7.1 shows, the American party system is atypical in many ways. The single-member district electoral system encourages the development of a two-party system of Democrats and Republicans because seats are awarded only to

Table 7.1   Party Characteristics

Party	Year founded	Vote share	Leg. seats	Internal structure	Years in government (1970–2000)
United States					
Democrats	1832	47.9	212	Decentralized	23
Republicans	1856	47.9	221	Decentralized	7
Great Britain					
Labour	1900	40.7	413	Centralized	12
Liberal Democrats	1987	18.3	52	Decentralized	0
Conservatives	1830	31.7	166	Mixed	18
Germany					
Party of Democratic Socialism (PDS)	1990	5.1	36	Centralized	0
Social Democrats (SPD)	1863	40.9	298	Centralized	14
Greens	1980	6.7	47	Decentralized	0
Free Democrats (FDP)	1948	6.2	43	Decentralized	28
Christian Democrats (CDU)	1950	35.2	245	Mixed	16
Republikaner	1983	1.1	0	Personalistic	0
France					
Communist Party (PC)	1920	9.9	38	Centralized	0
Socialists (PS)	1905	23.5	241	Centralized	13
Greens	1978	6.8	7	Decentralized	0
RPR	1947	15.7	134	Mixed	17
UDF	1978	14.2	108	Mixed	17
National Front	1972	—	1	Personalistic	0

Source: Compiled by the author; election statistics from http://www.electionworld.org

the largest vote-getter in the district. A party system based on only two parties is unusual, since most democracies have multiparty elections and thus multiparty coalitions are necessary to form a government majority. In the United States, in contrast, power shifts back and forth between the two major parties. In congressional elections, the Republicans' dramatic breakthrough in the 1994 elections ended forty years of Democratic rule. The Republicans still held control of both the House and the Senate following a close vote in the 2000 elections; then the Senate shifted to the Democrats in 2001. The fluctuations in congressional vote totals over time are relatively small, averaging less than a 3 percent vote change between elections.

The results of presidential elections are more varied, however. For instance, Lyndon Johnson won a huge Democratic landslide in 1964, and Ronald Reagan won an equally impressive Republican majority in 1984. Presidential elections are heavily influenced by the candidate's own attributes, instead of merely partisan considerations. Therefore, our cross-national analyses of electoral patterns in subsequent chapters study American congressional elections because they are more similar to Western European parliamentary contests.

Another distinctive aspect of the American political system is the decentralized nature of party organizations. Because of the federal system of American government, instead of one Democratic Party (or Republican Party), there are really fifty: one in each state. National party meetings are something like medieval gatherings of feudal states, rather than the actions of a unitary organization. The presidential nominating convention is not controlled and directed by a national party but is taken over every four years by the personnel of the winning candidate. Even in Congress, American legislators are more likely to cross party lines than are parliamentarians in disciplined party systems. This means there is considerably more diversity and fluidity within the American party system. The institutional weakness of the parties is also apparent in their small memberships (chapter 3).

Britain presents a different partisan pattern. Britain is often described as a two-and-a-half-party system: the Labour Party is the major force on the Left, and the Conservative Party is the representative of the Right. In addition, the Liberal Democrats are located near the center of the political spectrum. The Labour and Conservative parties each routinely receive between 40 and 50 percent of the national vote, whereas the small Liberal Democrats in the center garner 10 to 15 percent.[3]

The diversity of the British party system has increased during the past two decades. Revived regional movements strengthened the nationalist parties in Scotland (Scottish Nationalist Party) and Wales (Plaid Cymru) in the 1970s. Thatcher's polarized politics of government retrenchment stimulated the creation of a new centrist party, the Social Democratic Party (SDP), in the early 1980s. By the end of the 1980s the SDP had merged with the Liberal Party to form the Liberal Democrats. The development of regional parliaments in Scotland and Wales in the 1990s further strengthened parties representing these regional interests. Despite these changes in the party system, the competition between Labour and the Conservatives still structures British electoral competition at the national level.

The British political parties also are more highly organized and centralized than the major American political parties. The national parties' organizations in Britain play an important role in selecting candidates and determining the strategies and activities of election campaigns. This is because Britain, like most other democracies, lacks the system of primaries that are used to select candidates in the United States. Once elected, British Members of Parliament (MPs) generally follow party lines in policy debates and in their voting behavior. Thus, party unity has great rewards.

Another feature of parliamentary systems is the constant emphasis on the party rather than the individual politicians. For instance, British voters do not cast a vote directly for the chief executive (the prime minister), as Americans cast a vote for president. Under the procedures of its parliamentary system, the party group that controls Parliament is able to elect the prime minister who heads the executive branch. Even when it comes to electing a local district representative, British voters choose a party, often without knowing much about the candidate who represents the party in the district. The British political system is based on a model of strong party government.

The German party system is even more diverse. The German electoral system is based on proportional representation: A party's share of the votes determines its share of the seats in Parliament.[4] As a result, Germany has a multiparty system with two major parties and several smaller parties. The Christian Democrats (CDU/CSU) are the major conservative party and the Social Democrats are the major leftist party. The CDU/CSU controlled the government for the first two decades of the Federal Republic and again from 1982–98. The SPD is the historical successor to the pre–World War II Socialist Party. The SPD controlled the national government from 1969 until 1982, and again since the 1998 election in coalition with the Green Party.

Several smaller parties also compete in German elections. The Greens emerged on the partisan stage in the 1980s as representatives of a postmaterial agenda (Poguntke 1993). Now in coalition with the SPD, the Greens use their position within the government to advocate a variety of New Politics causes. The small Free Democratic Party (FDP) captures between 5 and 10 percent of the vote. It has been a junior coalition partner in most governments since the Federal Republic was formed.

German unification further changed the political landscape. Unification added millions of new voters from the East, and the Party of Democratic Socialism (PDS) emerged as a successor to the communist and socialist values of the German Democratic Republic. In 1998 the PDS won just over 5 percent of the national vote, although most PDS voters resided in the East. The Republikaner are a right-wing party that advocates nationalist and antiforeigner sentiments. The Republikaner have not won seats in the national Parliament, though their presence has affected the climate of political debate in contemporary Germany.

The German political system emphasizes the role of political parties to a greater degree than that in the United States. For example, parties control the candidate selection process. In Bundestag elections, the voter casts two votes. The first vote (*Erststimme*) is for a candidate from the district. The district candidates are nominated by a small group of official party members or by a committee appointed by the membership. The second vote (*Zweitstimme*) is directly for a party, which leads to the selection of half the Bundestag deputies from lists created by the parties. In addition, election campaigns are generously financed by the government, and government funding and access to public radio and television are allocated to the parties and not the individual candidates. Government funding for the parties also continues between elections, to help them perform their educational functions as prescribed in the Basic Law. Within the Bundestag, parties caucus in advance of major legislation to decide the party position and most legislative votes follow strict party lines. With the notable exception of the Greens, the German political parties are highly organized and centralized institutions. Therefore, it is not surprising to hear Germany described as a system of "party government."

France is an even more highly fragmented multiparty system. Instead of one party on the Left, there are several: the Communist Party (PC), the Socialist Party (PS), and several smaller Left extremist parties. Instead of one major party on the Right, there are several: the Rally for the Republic (RPR) and the Union for French Democracy (UDF). During the 1980s the National Front (FN) emerged as an extreme right-wing party that attracts voters opposed to social changes occurring in France. A new environmental party also formed in the early 1980s, then reformed in mid-decade, and reformed again in the early 1990s. Now running under the label of the Green Party, it attracts the support of a small number of young, postmaterial voters. Add to this mix a miscellaneous assortment of small centrist or extremist parties. In the 1997 election, more than seven party groups won representation in Parliament and many more ran for office.

The electoral history of the Fifth Republic is one of party change and electoral volatility. The Gaullist Party, now RPR, was originally the major party on the right and participated in conservative governments for the first two decades of the Fifth Republic. Eventually it was joined by the UDF as another major conservative party. The tide shifted toward the Left in the 1980s, especially toward the Socialists, with their broad program of Old Politics and New Politics reforms. The leader of the Socialist Party, François Mitterrand, was elected president in 1981, and this was followed by a socialist majority in legislative elections. The conservatives temporarily gained control of Parliament from 1986 to 1988 and then a Left majority reestablished itself. The conservatives (RPR and UDF) swept the parliamentary elections of 1993 and won the presidency in the 1995 elections. In short, the French party system is exceptionally fluid.

It is difficult to describe the French system in terms of a theoretical model of responsible party government. On the one hand, the French party system offers voters greater ideological choice than is available to American, British, or German voters. Political parties also play a major role in running political campaigns and directing the activities of Parliament. On the other hand, the fragmentation of the party system necessitates coalitional politics in which parties are forced to negotiate and compromise on their programs. This weakens the chain of party responsibility found in British or German governments. Moreover, it is often the party leader, rather than the national party organization, who defines a party's goals and strategies. French parties are often highly personalistic, even for a highly centralized party such as the PC. The French party system thus might be characterized as a party system in constant transition.

THE HISTORY OF PARTY SYSTEMS

Discussions of political parties normally focus on the present: the policy positions and political leaders that define current party images. We often think of each election in terms of the issues of the day. But across elections, parties normally take consistent positions that reflect their historical roots based either in an ideology or a connection with enduring social interests. At the same time, many voters repeatedly support the same party across elections for the same reasons. The Democratic tendencies of American Catholics, for example, result from their class position when they first emigrated to America and the history of how Catholics were integrated into society and politics. The Republican leanings of Cuban Americans can be traced to their unique historical experiences, which linked them to the Republican Party.

Seymour Martin Lipset and Stein Rokkan (1967) described the development of modern party systems in terms of the historical conditions of national and socioeconomic development. They maintained that two successive revolutions in the modernization of Western societies—the *National Revolution* and the *Industrial Revolution*—created divisions among certain social groups that still structure partisan competition today. Although their discussion deals primarily with Western Europe, the approach is relevant to other Western democracies including the United States.

The National Revolution involved the process of nation building that transformed the map of Europe in the eighteenth and nineteenth centuries. The National Revolution spawned two sets of competing social groups (social cleavages). The *center–periphery* cleavage pitted the dominant national culture against ethnic, linguistic, or religious minorities in the peripheral regions. It involved conflicts over values and cultural identities. For example, were Alsatians to become Germans or French? Was Scotland a separate nation or a region within Britain? The diverse state histories within the United States generated similar tensions between regional cultures, even leading to a civil war.

This cleavage is visible today in persisting regional differences in political orientations: between the English, Welsh, and Scots; between Bretons and the Parisian center; between the "Free State of Bavaria" and the Federal Republic of Germany; between the "old" Federal Republic and the new German Länder in the East; and between the distinct regional cultures in the United States.

The second cleavage is the *church–state* conflict that casts the centralizing, standardizing, and mobilizing forces of the national government against the traditional influence of the Catholic Church. In the face of a growing secular government, the church often sought to protect its established privileges by resisting the new national government. Furthermore, Protestants often allied themselves with nationalist forces in the struggle for national autonomy. Contemporary divisions between religious denominations and between secular and religious groups are a continuation of these earlier social divisions.

The Industrial Revolution in the nineteenth century also generated two new social cleavages. The *land–industry* cleavage pitted the rural and agrarian interests against the economic concerns of the rising class of industrial entrepreneurs. For instance, the Ruhr industrialists challenged the power of the Prussian Junkers; the landed gentry of Britain and the United States were challenged by the barons of industry. We see this cleavage in contemporary conflicts between rural and urban interests.

As industrialization progressed, a second cleavage developed between *owners* and *workers* within the industrial sector. This cleavage furnished the basis of class conflict between the working class and the middle class composed of business owners and the self-employed. The struggle for the legitimization and representation of the working-class movement often generated intense political conflict in the late nineteenth and early twentieth centuries. Today this cleavage is seen in the political competition between business associations and labor unions, and more generally between members of the middle class and the working class.

These historical events may seem far removed from contemporary party systems, but Lipset and Rokkan (1967) claimed that a linkage exists. These four cleavages define the major bases of social conflict existing within these nations. As social groups that were related to these cleavages developed—such as labor unions or farmer associations—they won access to the political process before the extension of the voting franchise. When mass voting rights were granted to most Europeans around the turn of the century, this structure of group competition was already in place. In most instances, new voters were mobilized into supporting the party groups that already were politically active. New voters thus entered the electorate with preexisting partisan tendencies. The Conservative Party in Britain, for example, became the representative of the middle-class establishment, and the Labour Party catered to the interests of the working class. The working class in France and Germany supported the Communist and Socialist Parties. The American party system developed more gradually because the voting franchise was granted earlier and social groups were less polarized; still, the modern party system reflects political cleavages that are connected to the Civil War and the Great Depression. The Democratic Party, for instance, still draws on the New Deal coalition that formed the basis of the party in the 1930s.

The formation of mass political parties thus tended to institutionalize the existing group alignments, creating the framework for modern party systems. Once voters formed party loyalties and interest groups established party ties, these became self-perpetuating relationships. At each election, parties turned to the same social groups for their core support, and most voters in these groups habitually supported the same party. In one of the most often cited conclusions of comparative politics,

Lipset and Rokkan (1967) stated: "the party systems of the 1960s reflect, with but few significant exceptions, the cleavage structures of the 1920s" (p. 50).

Early electoral research substantiated Lipset and Rokkan's claims. Regional voting patterns from early in this century were mirrored in recent election returns. Survey research found that social cleavages, especially class and religious differences, exerted a potent effect on voting. Richard Rose and Derek Urwin's (1969, 1970) comparative studies of postwar party systems found striking stability in electoral results because voting choices were frozen around the cleavages that Lipset and Rokkan described.

As this theme of partisan stability became the conventional wisdom, dramatic changes began to affect these same party systems. The established parties were presented with new demands and challenges, and the evidence of partisan change mounted (Dalton, Flanagan, and Beck 1984).[5] New parties emerged to compete at elections, and some of the established parties fragmented. Voting results became more changeable from election to election, and voter choices appeared less frozen and predictable.

At the root of this development was a weakening relationship between traditional social cleavages and partisan choice. In their comparative study of Western democracies, Mark Franklin and his colleagues (1992) found broad evidence that traditional social divisions were losing their ability to predict voting choices (also see chapter 8). Because of this erosion in traditional social group–based voting, voting choices became more fluid. Voting is now characterized by higher levels of partisan volatility at the aggregate and individual levels. Popular attachments to political parties weakened and discussions of the crisis of party systems became commonplace (see chapter 9). In sum, the major research question changed from explaining the persistence of contemporary party systems to explaining their instability.

Several unique national circumstances contributed to these patterns: the Vietnam War and Watergate in the United States, regional and economic tensions in Britain, and the Green movement in Germany. The party systems of Europe and North America also experienced their normal share of political crises and economic problems that often rocked the incumbent parties.

In addition, however, a common set of new postmaterial issues emerged on the political stage in these nations (chapter 5). The established parties faced the new issues of environmental protection, social equality, nuclear energy, sexual equality, and alternative lifestyles. People demanded more opportunities to participate in the decisions affecting their lives and pressed for a further democratization of society and politics. Once these trends began, they evoked a conservative counterattack that opposes the liberalization of social norms, women's rights, environmentalism, and related issues. These new postmaterial conflicts are now an important aspect of contemporary politics.

A major factor in the destabilization of modern party systems was the initial inability or unwillingness of the major parties to respond fully to the new demands. As a result, several new parties formed specifically to represent the new political perspectives. The first wave included environmental parties, such as the Green parties in Germany and France or Left-libertarian parties (Richardson and Rootes 1995; Müller-Rommel and Pridham 1991). This stimulated a counterwave of New Right parties, such as the National Front in France or the Republikaner in Germany (Betz 1994; Ignazi 1992). It is unclear whether these parties reflect temporary adjustments to new issues or a more long-lasting realignment of political conflict. American history is filled with third-party movements eventually incorporated into the established parties. Is the present partisan instability in advanced industrial democracies just another case of this recurring pattern?

Party systems are in a state of flux, and it is difficult to determine how fundamental and long-lasting these changes will be. It is clear, however, that the new political conflicts of advanced industrial societies have contributed to this situation. While we wait for history to determine the significance of these trends, we can look more closely at the political alignments that now exist in America, Britain, Germany, and France.

The Structure of Political Alignments

Most parties and party systems are still oriented primarily toward the traditional political alignments described by Lipset and Rokkan (1967). We shall refer to these alignments collectively as the *Old Politics* cleavage. The Old Politics cleavage is based on the political conflict between Old Left and Old Right coalitions. Lipset and Rokkan considered the class cleavage to be the primary factor in structuring the Old Politics cleavage because class issues were the most salient during the extension of the franchise. The Old Left therefore identifies itself with the working class and labor unions, as well as secular groups and urban interests. The Old Right is synonymous with business interests and the middle class; in some nations, this conservative coalition also includes religious and rural voters. When political issues tap the concerns of the Old Politics cleavage—for example, wage settlements, employment programs, social security programs, or abortion legislation—class and religious characteristics are strongly related to voting preferences.

The political conflicts of advanced industrial societies also include a new dimension of postmaterial cleavage (chapter 5). This *New Politics* dimension involves conflict over new issues such as environmental quality, alternative lifestyles, minority rights, participation, social equality, and other postmaterial issues. This dimension represents the cleavage between proponents of these issues, the New Left, and citizens who feel threatened by these issues, the New Right.

The Old Politics cleavage is likely to remain the primary basis of partisan conflict in most advanced industrial democracies for the immediate future. The New Politics dimension is significantly affecting these party systems, however, because it can cut across the established Old Politics cleavage. Despite their differences, labor unions and business interests occasionally join forces to fight the opponents of nuclear energy. Farmers and students sometimes become allies to oppose industrial development projects that may threaten the environment. Fundamentalist blue-collar and white-collar workers unite to oppose changes in moral codes. The emergence of New Left and New Right interests may restructure social group alignments and party coalitions in new and contrasting ways. In sum, the simple dichotomy between Old Left and Old Right is no longer adequate to describe present patterns of political competition. The contemporary political space is now better described by at least two (or more) dimensions.

We can illustrate the separation of the Old Politics and New Politics cleavages with examples drawn from the American experience. For much of the twentieth century, the Old Politics cleavages defined the primary basis of party competition in the U.S. party system. The New Deal coalitions created by the Great Depression determined the social bases of party support: the Democratic Party and its working-class supporters against the Republicans and big business. Religious differences were muted because of the formal separation of church and state in the United States.

In the 1960s the New Politics introduced a new set of issues into the American political process. Student protesters, the women's movement, and the alternative lifestyles movement challenged the symbols of the political establishment. Herbert Weisberg and Jerold Rusk (1970) described how this cultural conflict introduced a new dimension of cleavage, as represented by dissident Democratic candidates in the late 1960s and early 1970s. New Politics issues entered the agenda of subsequent campaigns. Rusk and Weisberg found, however, that Democrats and Republicans were not clearly divided on New Politics issues; these issues divided parties internally rather than separating them politically.[6] Another study of party cleavages in 1974 found that the Democrats and Republicans were only slightly differentiated on the New Politics dimension (Inglehart 1984).

The policies of the Reagan and Bush administrations stimulated a convergence of Old Politics and New Politics alignments over the 1980s and early 1990s. The tax and spending priorities of the Reagan administration sharply favored business and the more affluent sectors of society. This served to reinforce ties between business interests and the Republican Party. Furthermore, the Reagan administration pursued a conservative social agenda and developed strong political links to religious groups such as the Moral Majority and other fundamentalist organizations. To an extent atypical of modern American politics, religion was injected into partisan politics.

The Reagan and Bush administrations also clarified party positions on the New Politics agenda. Environmental protection had some roots in the Republican Party; Richard Nixon, for example, had established the Environmental Protection Agency during his first presidential term and had introduced a variety of environmental legislation. Yet Ronald Reagan openly speculated that "killer trees" were a major cause of air pollution. The policy initiatives of the Reagan administration demonstrated its hostility toward the environmental movement. Although George Bush claimed to be the environmental president in 1988, the assault on environmental protection legislation continued under his administration. Similarly, the Reagan and Bush administrations were openly antagonistic toward feminist organizations. The abortion issue became a litmus test of Republican values in the appointment of federal judges and the selection of candidates.

As the Republicans became critical of the New Politics agenda, the Democrats became advocates of these same issues. The Democrats became the partisan supporters of the environmental movement in congressional legislation. In 1984 the Democrats were the first to nominate a woman and feminist for national political office, Geraldine Ferraro. Clinton's new Democratic coalition attempted to unite the old constituency of labor unions and the new constituency of environmentalists and feminists. Similarly, the Republican party attempted to bring together its traditional middle-class and business supporters with its new voters among cultural conservatives.

We can illustrate the present social and partisan alignments with data from the 2000 American National Election Study. The survey asked respondents about their feelings toward a set of sociopolitical groups and the political parties.[7] We used a statistical analysis method to represent the interrelationship of group perceptions in graphic terms.[8] This technique maps the political space as perceived by Americans. When there is a strong similarity in how two groups are evaluated, they are located near each other in the space. When groups are evaluated in dissimilar terms, they are positioned a distance apart in the space. Thus, one can think of this figure as the map of the political space that voters use to orient themselves to social groups and political parties.

The American sociopolitical space in 2000 is depicted in figure 7.1. The traditional Left/Right cleavage of the Old Politics is quite evident as the horizontal dimension in the figure. Al Gore is located at the left of the horizontal dimension, along with Bill Clinton, and both politicians are seen as close to the labor unions. Indeed, in 2000 Gore made a more forceful appeal for the traditional class-based Democratic vote than Bill Clinton did in his two campaigns. George W. Bush is located at the opposite end of this continuum, and the nearest group is big business and the Christian Coalition.

The figure also portrays a second dimension of political cleavage. A new liberal coalition comprised of environmentalists, the women's movement, and minority groups is located at one end of the continuum. They are closer to the Democratic candidate but still distinct from the party's traditional base among the working class. The other end of this dimension is represented by Pat Buchanan, who led a conservative campaign that emphasized cultural issues in opposition to women's movements and minority groups. This conservative New Politics position in 2000 is somewhat similar to the constituency that Ross Perot mobilized for the Reform Party in the 1992 and 1996 elections. And despite the Democrats'

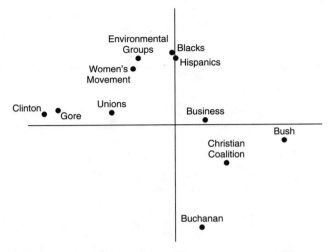

Figure 7.1   The Sociopolitical Space in the United States

Source: Multidimensional scaling of thermometer scores from the 2000 American National Election Study.

attempts to merge their Old Politics and New Politics constituencies, the distinction between these two groups is still apparent in the 2000 campaign.[9]

Comparable current data on the sociopolitical space in Britain, Germany, and France are not available, but another study uses a different method to illustrate party positions on Old Politics and New Politics issues in all four party systems. Michael Laver and W. Ben Hunt (1992) asked experts to position the parties in their respective nations on a set of policy dimensions. Figure 7.2 presents party positions on two issues: taxes versus social spending as a measure of the socioeconomic issues of the Old Politics, and the environment versus economic growth as a measure of New Politics priorities.

The top panel of the figure locates parties on the spending/taxes issue. Here we find a traditional Left/Right party alignment in each nation. The Democratic Party in the United States is located at the left end of this continuum, following the pattern found previously in mapping the sociopolitical space. At the opposite end of the Old Politics dimension is the Republican Party. From Ronald Reagan to the 1994 "Contract with America" to the George W. Bush campaign, the Republicans have developed a strong commitment to cutting public services and cutting taxes. This is now ingrained in the Republican policy image.

In Britain, the Labour Party has been the representative of the working class and the advocate for socialist policy. The party's working-class orientation is institutionalized through formal ties to the labor unions. Normally, membership in a union automatically includes a dues-paying membership in the Labour Party;

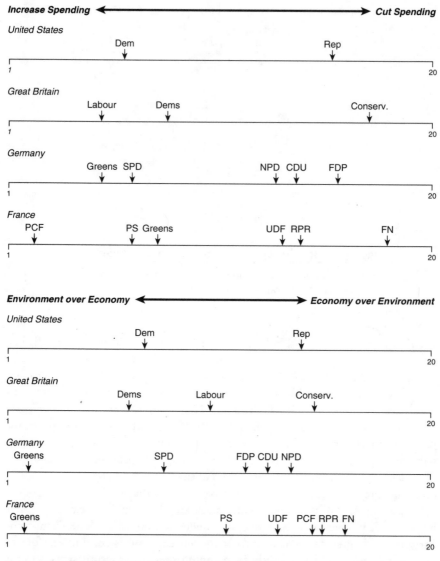

Figure 7.2   Party Positions on Two Policy Dimensions

Source: Laver and Hunt (1992, app.).

union leaders also control this large bloc of votes at Labour Party conventions. Past Labour governments have nationalized several major industrial sectors, expanded social welfare programs, and vigorously defended the interests of their working-class supporters. The Labour Party is located to the left of both the

American Democrats and the German SPD on this dimension.[10] The British Liberal Democrats are a small centrist party that occupies a midpoint on this dimension. The party was traditionally a representative of liberal, middle-class values. In recent years it has formed and reformed itself, but it still holds a centrist position on issues of the government's socioeconomic role.

Beginning with Margaret Thatcher's first election in 1979, the Conservative Party has aggressively attempted to roll back the scale of national government. Thatcher's government privatized many government-owned industries, reduced governmental social and educational programs, sold off public housing, and generally tried to lessen the scope of the government's involvement in society. These policies reinforced the Conservatives' traditional image as a party that favored business interests and that drew disproportionate support from middle-class voters. Even more than a decade after Thatcher left the party leadership, these images remain part of the Conservative Party's public image, placing it to the right on this economic dimension.

The major representative of Old Left in Germany is the Social Democratic Party (SPD). The SPD emerged from the socialist working-class movement and still consistently represents working-class interests. Although German labor unions no longer have institutional ties to the SPD, the relationship nevertheless remains close.[11] Because of these liberal traditions, the SPD is seen as favoring increased social spending—though this may have moderated a bit since the early 1990s. In the 1998 election, the SPD tried to temper this image in order to attract more moderate voters, much as the British Labour Party pursued this strategy in 1997, but the Social Democrats remain strong advocates of government social spending. The German Greens have been described as a Left-libertarian party because they combine a distinctly liberal position on many traditional issues of the social spending and the welfare state with an advocacy for New Left causes (Kitschelt 1989). Thus, political experts position the Greens to the left of the SPD on the social spending dimension in figure 7.2.[12]

The Christian Democratic Union/Christian Social Union (CDU/CSU) is the major political force on the Right in Germany. The CDU was formed after the war as a conservative-oriented catchall party (*Volkpartei*). In the state of Bavaria, the CSU runs as the party of the conservative bloc. As their names imply, both conservative parties represent religious voters on the church-state cleavage. The Union parties also advocate conservative economic policies and a free-market economy. The CDU/CSU and FDP occupy similar a conservative position on the services/taxes dimension. Indeed, during the sixteen years (1982–98) when the two parties shared control of the government, they pursued conservative economic programs that limited the size of government and stimulated economic development. The exceptional costs of German unification forced these parties to turn temporarily away from these policies, but their commitment to smaller government remains strong. The National Democratic

Party (NPD) is a small, extreme-Right party known for its nationalistic and reactionary policies, more so than for its economic agenda. Nevertheless, experts locate the NPD at the conservative end of the social services dimension.

France has two major parties that represent traditional Old Left positions: the Communist Party (PC) and the Socialists (PS). The PC strongly believes that the government is responsible for social needs and is the most leftist party in all four nations. The PC depends very heavily on working-class votes and has formal ties with the communist labor union, the CGT. Furthermore, although other communist parties have lost their Marxist ideology with the collapse of the Soviet Union, the French Communist Party remains committed to these values. The French Socialists, by comparison, have moderated their ideological image to appeal to liberal middle-class voters. Still, political experts see the PS as strongly committed to extensive governmental social programs.

France has two major conservative parties, the Rally for the Republic (RPR) and the Union for French Democracy (UDF). The RPR is the modern successor to the Gaullist forces that created the Fifth Republic and governed the republic for most of its history. The party is a representative of conservative business interests and the middle class; it favors a reduction of government social programs and taxes. The UDF is a moderate conservative party that attracts liberal elements of the middle class. The president of France, Jacques Chirac, is a leader of the RPR. At the far right of the political spectrum is the National Front (FN). The FN is an example of a New Right party, focusing its attention on cultural and social issues, such as opposition to foreigners, a nationalistic foreign policy, and traditional social values. Its identity is formed more as a backlash to the liberal themes of the New Politics than by traditional economic issues, but on issues of social spending it is perceived as sharply conservative.

If Old Politics issues such as government social spending were the only factors structuring electoral competition, then Lipset and Rokkan would still be correct in describing contemporary party systems in terms of the cleavages of the 1920s. The class-based Left/Right party alignment that historically structured partisan politics remains clearly visible on how political experts position the contemporary parties on the services/taxes dimension.

The content of the political agenda, however, now includes more than the economic and security concerns of the Old Politics. The New Politics introduce new postmaterial interests into the political debate, and this has led to a different alignment of parties. The partisan alignments along the New Politics cleavage can be seen in the bottom panel of figure 7.2, which positions parties on the environment/economy policy dimension.

In the United States, we find the same Left/Right ordering of the parties. The Democrats are seen as the advocates for environmental protection. The Republicans are perceived as more concerned with protecting the economy even at a cost to the environment. This party cleavage was aptly illustrated in the

2000 presidential election. The Democrats nominated Albert Gore, a political figure who is closely identified with environmental protection and author of a best-selling book on the environment, as their candidate. George W. Bush expressed concerns for environmental quality, but he also promised to roll back what he considered excessively strict environmental regulations and balance environmental protection against the nation's economic and energy needs. In the United States, the alignment of the two parties is now similar on both Old Politics and New Politics dimensions.

In most other party systems, the environmental issue creates a new pattern of partisan alignment. In Britain, for example, the centrist Liberal Democrats have distinguished themselves as the party most sympathetic to the environmental issue. In Germany, the Green Party is seen as a strong advocate for environmental causes and is located at the far end of this continuum. Over time the SPD has become more sympathetic to the environmental movement, but experts still position the SPD near the center of this policy scale. The Social Democrats are closer to the conservative CDU and FDP on this dimension than they are to the Greens. On the far right of this continuum is the extremist NPD, which illustrates where this party and the New Right Republikaner would be located on the New Politics dimension. As the Greens are advocates for modernization and liberal issues, the NPD (and more recently the Republikaner) are the most vocal critics of social and cultural change. Overall, the major cleavage on the environmental dimension separates the Greens from *all* the other German parties.

The ability of New Politics to transform party alignments is most clearly illustrated in the French party system. The French Greens are strong supporters of the environment, occupying an extreme New Left position. But the traditional leftist parties are neutral or critical of environmental protection. The French Socialists are at the center of this scale and have an ambivalent record on environmental matters. The French Communists, who are extremely leftist on Old Politics issues, are positioned between the conservative UDF and RPR on the environmental dimension. The Communists and the National Front hold similar positions on the environmental dimension. Overall, as we saw in the German party system, the New Politics cleavage separates the Greens from all the other French parties.

If we combine the evidence in this section, we can begin to map the sociopolitical space that voters use to orient themselves to partisan politics. In each nation there is a clear representation of political positions along the traditional socioeconomic issues that initially structured party competition in these democracies. In addition, the political controversies of advanced industrial societies are bringing new issues to the fore, and this is prompting the formation of new parties or the realignment of the established parties to represent these positions. Much of the current research on electoral politics attempts to assess the relative position of the political parties on both dimensions and the relative weight of both dimensions in structuring political choice for the electorate. The mix of these is one of the forces that fuels the current processes of electoral change in these nations.

CONTEMPORARY PARTY SYSTEMS

This chapter has described broad similarities in the ideological structure of contemporary party systems. Most political parties are still oriented to the Old Politics cleavages of class and religion. Even if these cleavages have become less salient, the political ties between social groups and political parties perpetuate these images. Parties are, after all, still turning to the same interest groups and associations for the core of their support. Contemporary publics see rightist parties as linked to business interests (and sometimes the Catholic Church), and leftist parties are allied with the labor unions.

Although major party differences exist on the Old Politics dimension, there are indications of the increasing importance of the New Politics cleavage. Earlier chapters (5 and 6) found that people are developing postmaterial values that lead to new policy interests. These new issues initially gained representation outside the established parties. The growth of citizen-action groups, for example, often reflected a mix of the new style of citizen participation and New Politics issue concerns. These interests are now gaining representation through partisan politics, which places new demands on the established parties.

Some indications of partisan change along the New Politics dimension are already evident. New parties, such as the German and French Greens, have emerged to represent New Politics concerns. These small parties draw their support from the young, the better educated, and postmaterialists—key groups defining the New Politics cleavage. A more basic change would occur if the larger established parties adopt clearer positions on New Politics issues. There is some evidence of this change in the policy and electoral strategies of the major leftist parties in several nations. These parties are attempting to combine Old Left and New Left issue appeals into a single program, though this is a difficult coalition to maintain.

The established parties have been understandably hesitant to formalize close ties to New Left or New Right groups, however, especially in Western Europe where the Old Politics ties remain strong. Parties are naturally cautious about taking clear stands on a new dimension of conflict until the costs and benefits are clear. The major European leftist parties, for example, are internally split on many Old Politics/New Politics conflicts. Whereas most industrial labor unions favor economic development projects that will strengthen the economy and produce jobs, leftist environmentalists often oppose these same projects because of their ecological consequences. Many conservative parties also face divisions between conservative business elites, new cultural conservatives, and liberal middle-class voters. Political alliances between Old Politics and New Politics groups so far have been temporary because of the conflicting values of these groups.

Added to these uncertainties are the new questions of partisan identities in the post–Cold War era. The end of communism requires a rethinking of the foreign policy stances of many parties. Many conservative parties used anticommunism as part of their political image, and this must now be replaced by other political themes. Similarly, the collapse of East European socialism has weakened the ability of social democratic parties to advocate expanding the role of government. In short, parties of the Left and the Right are rethinking some of the themes that furnished their electoral identities.

Because of the uncertainties facing the parties and the difficulties in integrating a new political cleavage into the existing party systems, future partisan change is likely to follow an uncertain course. Continuing changes in citizen values and issue interests mean that the potential for further partisan change is real.

Suggested Readings

Abramson, Paul, John Aldrich, and David Rohde. *Change and Continuity in the 1996 and 1998 Elections.* Washington, D.C.: Congressional Quarterly Press, 1999.

Budge, Ian, David Robertson, and D. Hearl. *Ideology, Strategy and Party Change.* Cambridge, U.K.: Cambridge University Press, 1987.

Dalton, Russell, ed. *Germans Divided: The 1994 Bundestagswahl and the Evolution of the German Party System.* New York and Oxford, U.K.: Berg Publishers, 1996.

Evans, Geoffrey, and Pippa Norris, eds. *Critical Elections: British Parties and Voters in Long-Term Perspective.* Thousand Oaks, Calif.: Sage Publications, 1999.

Hampton, Mary, and Christian Soe, eds. *Between Bonn and Berlin: German Politics Adrift?* Lanham, Md.: Rowman & Littlefield, 1999.

Lewis-Beck, Michael S., ed. *How France Votes.* New York: Chatham House, 1999.

Pomper, Gerald, ed. *The Election of 2000.* New York: Chatham House, 2001.

Notes

1. There are several good analytic studies of recent American elections (Pomper 2001; Abramson, Aldrich, and Rohde 1999), British elections (Evans and Norris 1999; Heath, Jowell, and Curtice 1993), German elections (Dalton 1996b; Hampton and Soe 1999; Klein et al. 2000), and French elections (Lewis-Beck, 1999; Boy and Mayer 1993).

2. Vote share is based on the most recent national election: United States (2000), Britain (2001), Germany (1998), and France (1997). Years in government is complicated by the separation of powers in the United States and France; we decided to count the number of years a party was part of the legislative majority between 1970 and 2000 as the most comparable cross-national statistic.

3. Because of the single-member district electoral system, the Liberal Democrats are routinely disadvantaged in winning seats in Parliament. In 2001, for example, the party won 18 percent of the popular vote nationwide but won only 8 percent of the seats in the House of Commons.

4. The German electoral law requires that a party win 5 percent of the national vote on the second ballot, or three district seats, in order to share in the proportional distribution of Bundestag seats. In 1998 the PDS won four district seats in East Berlin and 5 percent nationally, thus it received additional seats in Parliament based on its national share of the vote.

5. Bartolini and Mair (1989) forcefully argue that earlier historical periods were also marked by high levels of partisan volatility. But their methodology underestimates the degree of the current levels of partisan change (Dalton and Wattenberg 2000, chap. 3).

6. For instance, the 1984 Democratic primaries featured a confrontation between Old Left and New Left Democrats. Walter Mondale was identified with the traditional New Deal policies of the Democratic Party and won early endorsements from labor unions and the party establishment. Gary Hart, in contrast, explicitly claimed that he was the New Politics candidate, the representative of new ideas and a new generation. Hart's core voters were the yuppies—young, urban, upwardly mobile professionals—one of the groups linked to the New Politics cleavage.

7. These are the so-called "feeling thermometer" questions that measure positive and negative feelings toward each object. Respondents are given a thermometer-like scale to measure their "warmth" or "coldness" toward each group.

8. The feeling thermometers were analyzed using a multidimensional scaling program, and the solution was then rotated so the Clinton-Gore dimension was aligned horizontally in the scale. For earlier analyses of similar sociopolitical spaces, see Barnes, Kaase et al. (1979), Inglehart (1984), and Dalton (1996a, chap. 7).

9. Ideally what is needed is a tracking of these sociopolitical alignments over time so that we can see if there has been a systematic change in the Democrats' and Republicans' electoral alliances.

10. Other evidence suggests that the Labour Party moved dramatically to the center in the 1997 campaign in an attempt to attract moderate voters and win a parliamentary majority (Budge 1999). Even with this movement to the center, however, the Labour Party still retained its distinct orientation on class issues.

11. The German portion of the Cross National Election Project also contained a question on the partisan leanings of social groups. About three-quarters of the German public saw labor unions as leaning toward the SPD, and an equal number saw business associations and the Catholic Church as leaning toward the CDU/CSU; nearly 80 percent saw environmental groups as favoring the Greens. See Dalton (1993a, 266) and Wessels (1993).

12. A new entrant to the German party system is the Party of Democratic Socialism (PDS), a successor of the communist party of the German Democratic Republic. The PDS would be positioned on the far left of this scale.

CHAPTER 8

The Social Bases of Party Support

THERE IS A well-worn saying that people act politically as they are socially, and this has been the case for electoral politics. The preceding chapter discussed how party systems were formed to provide political representation for class, religious, and other social groups. Contemporary political parties maintain ties to their clientele groups and project images in group terms: Labour is a working-class party, the Republicans are the party of business, the Christian Democrats represent religious voters, and so forth. Although the issues and personalities of the campaign change from election to election, parties generally maintain their institutional and ideological ties to specific social groups. Most parties depend on the votes of their clientele groups to provide a stable base of electoral support.

From its beginnings, electoral research has stressed social group attachments as an important influence on voting behavior. One of the first empirical studies of American voting focused on the social bases of partisanship (Lazarsfeld, Berelson, and Gaudet 1948). This study found that an *Index of Political Predispositions* based on social class, religion, and rural/urban residence strongly influenced voting choice. Social stratification is even greater in Europe, producing even sharper group differences in voting patterns. A common cliché states that social class is the basis of British politics, and all else is just embellishment and detail. Both class and religion are strong correlates of voting in Germany and France.

This chapter begins our analysis of voting behavior by studying the group basis of voting. We highlight both the stability and change in group-based voting. On the one hand, the partisan loyalties generated by social characteristics produce stable party coalitions, since the parties routinely attract the same kinds of core voters. This constancy in the bases of party support reinforces the partisan images presented in chapter 7. On the other hand, there is strong evidence that the social bases of partisanship are changing (Franklin, Mackie, and Valen 1992). In addition, the increasing sophistication of contemporary electorates may lessen voter reliance on social cues as individuals make their own political decisions. We examine these theories by tracking group voting patterns over time and across nations.

INTERNET RESOURCE

Visit the Web sites of the American National Election
Study and the British Election Study:

US: www.umich.edu/~nes/
UK: www.essex.ac.uk/bes/

THE SOCIAL GROUP MODEL OF VOTING

Social characteristics influence a voter's choice of party in several possible ways.
First, a person's social position often indicates his or her values and political
beliefs. A French steelworker is more likely than a shopkeeper, for example, to
favor an expansion of social services or governmental regulation of business.
Opposition to liberal abortion laws is more likely among devout Catholics than
the nonreligious. Thus, social characteristics are an indirect measure of attitudinal differences between groups of voters and their perceptions of which party best
represents these policy positions.

Social characteristics also indicate some of the political cues to which an individual is exposed. A British mine worker, for example, hears about politics from
his coworkers or other working-class neighbors and friends; the mine worker also
receives political persuasion from the union representative at work and union
publications at home. This social milieu provides repeated cues on which policies
will benefit people like oneself and which party best represents one's interests—
a strong Labour Party bias in these cues is inevitable. Similarly, a Bavarian Catholic
hears about political issues at weekly church services, from Catholic social groups,
and from predominately conservative Catholic friends. This information generally encourages a favorable opinion of the Christian Social Union and its program.

In addition, social groups can be an important reference point in orienting
voters to political issues and providing information about politics. Even if an
individual is not a member of a labor union or a regular churchgoer, the knowledge that unions favor one party and the Catholic Church another can help
voters locate themselves in relation to the parties. For many citizens, the cues
provided by social networks and group party cues help to guide their political
orientations and voting behavior.

Voter reliance on social group cues is an example of the satisficing decision
making presented in chapter 2. Social cues can narrow the voter's choice to parties
that are consistent with one's social position. Voters enter an election favoring the
party (or parties) that historically supports the class or religious groups to which
they belong, while excluding parties with unsupportive records. Political parties

nurture such ties. The parties communicate their group loyalties to the voters, such as when they call themselves "Labour" or "Christian Democrats."

Voters can decide between competing parties based on the cues that social groups provide—the endorsements of labor unions, business associations, religious groups, and the like—as well as the group appeals of the parties themselves. The stable group ties of the parties mean that many voters develop standing partisan predispositions that endure across elections, simplifying the decision process still more. British industrial workers who cast their votes for Labour because the party represents people like themselves are making a reasonable electoral decision.

Reliance on social characteristics is a shortcut in making voting decisions. A citizen who is knowledgeable about all the issues and all the candidates is well prepared to make an informed voting choice and justify this decision in issue-oriented and ideological terms. Social characteristics provide a simpler, although less certain, method of choosing which party represents the voter's interests. Still, when strong social group identities are matched by clear party positions on these social cleavages, as they are in most European nations, then social characteristics can provide a very meaningful guide for voting behavior.

SOCIAL CLASS AND THE VOTE

Class politics taps the essence of what we have described as the Old Politics—an economic conflict between the haves and have-nots. The class cleavage represents the economic and material problems of industrial societies: improving standards of living, providing economic security, and ensuring a just distribution of economic rewards. Issues such as unemployment, inflation, social services, tax policies, and governmental management of the economy reinforce class divisions.

Social scientists have probably devoted more attention to the relationship between social class and voting than to any other social characteristic. Theoretically, the class cleavage involves some of the most basic questions of power and politics that evolve from Marxian and capitalist views of societal development. Empirically, one's position in the class structure is often a strong predictor of voting choice. Seymour Lipset's early cross-national study of electoral politics described the class cleavage as one of the most pervasive bases of party support:

> Even though many parties renounce the principle of class conflict or loyalty, an analysis of their appeals and their support suggests that they do represent the interests of different classes. On a world scale, the principal generalization which can be made is that parties are primarily based on either the lower classes or the middle and upper classes. (1981a, 230)

Most other early empirical studies supported these conclusions.

Research on the class cleavage normally defines social class in terms of occupation. Following Karl Marx's writings, occupations are typically classified on the basis of their relationship to the means of production. The bourgeoisie are the owners of capital and the self-employed; the proletariat are the workers who produce capital through their labor. This schema is then generalized to define two large social classes: the middle class and the working class. These class differences provided the basis for the creation of socialist and communist parties that represent the interests of the working class; conservative parties, in turn, defend the interests of the middle class.

Although this Marxian dichotomy once defined the class cleavage, the changing nature of advanced industrial societies has reshaped the class structure. The traditional bourgeoisie and proletariat have been joined by a "new" middle class, or what others have called a "salatariat." This stratum consists primarily of salaried white-collar employees and civil servants (Heath, Jowell, and Curtice 1991). Bell (1973) defined a "postindustrial" society as one in which most of the labor force holds new middle-class positions; by the 1980s nearly all Western democracies had passed the postindustrial threshold.

The new middle class is an important addition to the class structure because it lacks a clear position in the traditional class conflicts between the working class and the old middle class. The separation of management from capital ownership, the expansion of the service sector, and the growth of government (or nonprofit) employment creates a social stratum that does not conform to Marxian class analysis. The new middle class does not own capital as the old middle class did but also differs in lifestyle from the blue-collar workers of the traditional proletariat. Members of the new middle class seem less interested in the economic conflicts of the Old Politics and are more attuned to New Politics issues. Consequently, the identity of the new middle class differs from both the bourgeoisie and proletariat.

Table 8.1 presents the voting preferences of these social classes in the most recent election for which data are available.[1] Historical class alignments persist in each nation. The working class in each nation gives disproportionate support to leftist parties, ranging from 52 percent in the United States to 72 percent in Germany (the combined SPD, Green, and PDS vote). At the other extreme, the old middle class is the bastion of support for conservative parties. This traditional proletariat/bourgeoisie cleavage remains strong in each nation—but in each nation less than half of the electorate now belongs to either of these two classes.

The new middle class now constitutes the majority of voters and, more important, holds ambiguous partisan preferences. The new middle class is normally located between the working class and the old middle class in its Left/Right voting preferences. In addition, the new middle class gives disproportionate support to parties that represent a New Politics ideology, such as the German Alliance 90/Greens and the French Greens. The new middle class is a key element in the changing political alignments of advanced industrial democracies.

Before continuing, class voting in Germany deserves additional mention.

Table 8.1   Social Class and Party Support (in percentages)

	Working Class	New Middle Class	Old Middle Class
United States, 2000			
Democrat	52	53	42
Republican	48	47	58
Total	100	100	100
Great Britain, 2001			
Labour	66	40	36
Liberal Democrats	14	25	17
Conservatives	20	35	47
Total	100	100	100
France, 1996			
PC/Far left	12	8	11
Socialists	43	43	31
Greens	7	9	3
UDF	6	15	14
RPR	17	21	34
National Front	15	5	6
Total	100	101	99
Germany, 1998			
PDS	5	5	5
Alliance 90/Greens	6	8	10
SPD	61	48	24
FDP	3	6	12
CDU/CSU	25	33	49
Total	100	100	100

Sources: United States, 2000 American National Election Study (CSES); *Great Britain,* 2001 British Election Study (CSES); *Germany,* German Postelection Study 1998 (CSES); *France,* 1996 ISSP Survey.

Notes: American data are based on congressional vote; German data are for East and West electorates combined. Social class is based on the occupation of the head of the household where this information is available; otherwise, it is the occupation of the respondent.

The 1998 postelection study indicates an increase in class voting, but this largely occurred in the West. In western Germany, as in most other Western democracies, the class voting index was positive in 1998 and grew as the working class rallied around the Schröder campaign (PDI = +17). In the East, the class alignment was *actually reversed* in the two prior elections, with eastern workers supporting the CDU (Dalton and Bürklin 1996). In 1998 the "normal" class voting pattern emerged in the East, but the Left only gained 3 percent more of the working-class vote. These two differing class alignments weaken the impact of class in German electoral politics.

To place class voting in our four nations in perspective, figure 8.1 compares the strength of the class differences in partisan preferences for a dozen advanced industrial democracies.[2] The Cramer's V correlation measures the size of class voting differences. This statistic shows the greatest degree of class polarization in the Scandinavian party systems: Sweden (.26), Norway (.17). Not only are these highly fragmented party systems, which encourages the representation of social interests, but the Social Democratic Parties in these nations have a strong class identity. In addition, class voting also tends to be stronger where unions have large memberships and are politically involved; this also fits the Scandinavian case.

British class differences also rank in this upper tier, reflecting the continuing importance of class interests in British politics—and the influence of class cues on voting. Germany and France display moderate levels of class voting, slightly less than the cross-national average. Germany ranks low because of the mixed impact of East/West differences as noted previously. The United States also has weak class differences in party preferences. As many others have observed, the American party system blurs the influence of social class on voting choice (Abramson, Aldrich, and Rohde 1999, chap. 5).

Although social class remains a significant influence on voting choice in many nations, electoral research finds that class cues carry much less weight than they did a generation ago (Nieuwbeerta and De Graaf 1999). This pattern can be seen in figure 8.2, which presents the Alford index of class voting across elections in our four core nations. To maximize comparability, the analyses focus on the Left/Right voting patterns of the working class versus the combined middle class (old and new). The Alford index measures class voting as the simple difference between the percentage of the working class voting for the Left and the percentage of the middle class voting Left.[3]

The general trend in figure 8.2 is obvious; class differences are declining. The size of the class voting index in Britain has decreased by almost half during the past fifty years and in Germany by equal measure.[4] Class voting patterns follow a varied decline in American congressional elections, and in the 2000 elections the gap was virtually nonexistent (Alford index = 1). Paul Abramson and his colleagues (1999, chap. 5) show that the erosion of class voting is even more pronounced in U.S. presidential elections. In France, social class had a modest impact on voting during the French Fourth Republic. The turbulent events surrounding the formation of the Fifth Republic—including the creation of a broad-based Gaullist Party—abruptly lowered class voting in 1958. Class voting in the Fifth Republic stabilized at a level significantly below pre-1958 levels (Lewis-Beck and Skalaban 1992). There are indications, such as figure 8.2, that French class voting is also declining (also see Boy and Mayer 1993).

Despite this evidence that class voting differences are narrowing, some

Figure 8.1   The Overall Level of Class Voting

Source: 1996 International Social Survey Program.

Note: Values in parentheses are Cramer's V correlations.

researchers argue that the new class alignments of advanced industrial societies are perpetuating class voting, albeit in new forms (Evans 1999). John Goldthorpe (1987), for example, proposed a new categorization of social class incorporating notions of job autonomy and authority relationships into traditional class criteria such as income level and manual labor. Others create an expanded list of class categories that incorporate new social contexts, such as the middle-class salatariat or affluent blue-collar workers (Hout et al. 1996; Heath, Jowell, and Curtice 1991; Wright 1997). Researchers also explore criteria other than employment as potential new bases of socioeconomic cleavage. Some suggest that education might form the basis of a political cleavage separating the information-rich and technologically sophisticated from the information-poor and unskilled voter. Others maintain that conflicts between the public and private sectors are supplanting traditional class conflicts. Other innovative research defines social

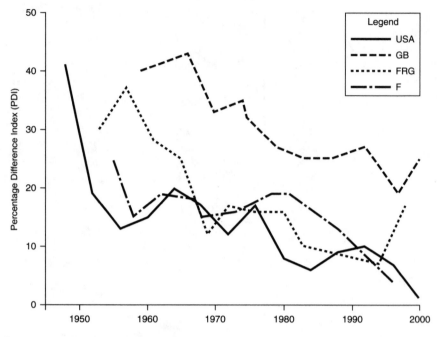

Figure 8.2 Trends in Class Voting

Sources: United States, 1948–2000, American National Election Studies; *Great Britain,* 1959, Civic Culture study; 1964–2001, British Election Studies; *Germany,* 1953–98, German Elections Studies (western Germany only 1990–98); *France,* 1955, MacRae (1967, 257); 1958, Converse and Dupeux study; 1962, IFOP survey; 1967, Converse and Pierce study; 1968, Inglehart study; 1973–88 Eurobarometer, 1996 ISSP.

Notes: Table entries are the Alford Class Voting index, that is, the percentage of the working class preferring a leftist party minus the percentage of the middle class voting for the Left. American data are based on congressional elections, except for 1948, which is the presidential vote.

position by lifestyle characteristic, distinguishing between industrial employees and yuppies, for example (Gluchowski 1987; Pew Center 1999; Delli Carpini and Sigelman 1986).

This reconceptualization of social class implies that social cues now function in more complex and differentiated ways than in the past. Yet the empirical reality remains: Even these complex new class frameworks have only a modest value in explaining how citizens vote. Richard Rose and Ian McAllister (1986, 50–51) compared several of these alternative models for British voting behavior in the 1983 election and found that they all explain a very modest share of the vote (also see Crewe 1986). Paul Nieuwbeerta (1995; Nieuwbeerta and De Graaf 1999) shows that alternative statistical measures of class voting do not change these trends. Similarly, the analyses of figure 8.1 are based on a more extensive measure of social class that includes a separate new middle-class category. Yet the average level of class differences in these nations is quite modest (Cramer's V = .15). The most persuasive evidence comes from the longitudinal comparative analyses of Franklin and his colleagues (1992, chap. 19). They combine occupation, union membership, income, education, and other class traits and find a general decline in the ability of these social characteristics to explain electoral choice in most Western democracies.

David Butler and Donald Stokes (1969, 85–87) developed a conceptual framework of group-based voting that might help identify the source of the decline in class voting. They describe the group voting as a two-step process: voters are first linked to a social group and then the group is linked to a political party. The combined strength of these two links determines the overall level of group-based voting. Using this framework, there have been changes in either (a) the relationship between voters and class groupings or (b) the relationship between class groupings and the political parties. The first explanation, for example, highlights how the changing class structure of contemporary societies may be weakening the link between individuals and class groupings. Members of the traditional social strata—industrial workers, farmers, and the self-employed—often remain integrated into class networks and remain distinct in their voting preferences. But there are simply fewer of these voters today. The growth of the new middle class lessens the percentage of the electorate for whom traditional class ties are directly relevant.[5]

The blurring of the relationship between voters and class groupings also arises from a general narrowing in the life conditions of social classes. On the one hand, the spread of affluence leads to the *embourgeoisement* of some sectors of the working class: Some workers have incomes and living standards that overlap with the middle class. On the other hand, the expanding ranks of low-paid and low-status white-collar employees and the growth of white-collar unions are producing a *proletarianization* of part of the middle class. Few individuals possess exclusively middle-class or working-class social characteristics, and the degree of class overlap is increasing over time. In sum, a convergence of life conditions contributes to the convergence of class voting patterns.

Increasing social and occupational mobility also may weaken the link between individuals and traditional social classes. All the nations in this study have had a decline in the number of farmers and an increase in middle-class employment during the late 1900s. Dramatic changes in the size of economic sectors often occurred within a few decades. High levels of social mobility mean that an individual's ultimate social position is often different from that of his or her parents. Many farmers' children moved from conservative political upbringing into unionized, leftist, working-class environments in the cities, just as many working-class children went from urban, leftist backgrounds into traditionally conservative, white-collar occupations. Some socially mobile individuals will change their adult class identity and voting behavior to conform to their new social contexts; others will not. This mix of social forces blurs traditional class and partisan alignments.

A second explanation of declining class voting involves changes in the relationship between class groups and the political parties. Over the past generation, many political parties have tried to broaden their electoral appeals, partially to attract new middle-class voters, which led to more moderate party positions on traditional class-based issues. Socialist parties in Europe shed their Marxist programs and adopted more moderate domestic and foreign policy goals. Conservative parties also tempered their views and accepted the basic social programs proposed by the Left. Socialist parties vied for the votes of the new middle class, and conservative parties sought votes from the working class. Historical analyses of party programs document a general convergence of party positions on socioeconomic issues during the last half century (Budge, Robertson, and Hearl 1987; Caul and Gray 2000). With smaller class-related differences in the parties' platforms, it seemed only natural that class cues would become less important in guiding voting behavior.

Initially, at least, this appeared to be another plausible explanation for the decline in class voting differences. However, various studies show that party positions on the class cleavage remain clearly differentiated. For example, a survey of political experts documented a clear awareness of the continuing party differences on the socioeconomic issues that underlie the class cleavage (Laver and Hunt 1992; also see chapter 7). Additional evidence from Germany shows that the partisan clarity of class cues actually has increased over the same period that class voting has diminished (Dalton 1992, 60). Furthermore, the American public still clearly perceives the partisan leanings of unions and business associations (chapter 7), and comparable data are available for Germany (Wessels 1994). In short, it does not appear that ambiguity about the class positions of the parties is the prime reason for decreased class voting—instead, these cues are less relevant to today's voters.

The decline in class voting patterns therefore seems to represent a weakening of the bonds linking voters to politically oriented class groups rather than a blurring of the political cues provided by the parties. Union members, for example, realize that labor leaders want them to vote for parties of the Left, but the union members are now more likely to make their own decisions. Thus, the nature of these changes implies that the long-term decline in class voting should continue.

RELIGION AND THE VOTE

Another major basis of social division in most Western nations is the religious cleavage in its various forms. The relationship between religion and politics arises from a centuries-old interplay of these two forces. The Reformation created divisions between Catholics and Protestants that carried over into politics. Control of the nation-building process often became intermixed with religious differences (chapter 7). In Anglican England, for example, the Protestant church supported national independence and became identified with the dominant national culture. In Germany, the tensions between Lutherans and Catholics were a continuing source of conflict and even open warfare. Gradually the political systems of Europe accommodated themselves to the changes wrought by the Reformation, and a new status quo developed. Then the French Revolution renewed religious conflicts in the nineteenth century. Religious forces—both Catholic and Protestant—defended church interests against the liberal, secular movement spawned by the events in France. Conflicts over church/state control, the legislation of mandatory state education, and disestablishment of state religions occurred across Europe.

As was true with the class cleavage, disagreements over religion structured elite conflict and defined the political alliances existing in the late nineteenth century. The political parties that formed during this period often allied themselves with specific religious interests: Catholic or Protestant, religious or secular. Thus, the party alignments that developed at the start of the twentieth century institutionalized the religious cleavage, and many features of these party systems have endured to the present (Lipset and Rokkan 1967).

Early empirical research on voting behavior underscored the continuing importance of the religious cleavage. Rose and Urwin (1969) examined the social bases of party support in sixteen Western democracies. Their oft-cited conclusion maintains that "religious divisions, not class, are the main social bases of parties in the Western world today" (p. 12). Numerous other cross-national and longitudinal studies have documented the persisting importance of the religious cleavage (Baker, Dalton, and Hildebrandt 1981, chap. 7; Wald 1983; Lewis-Beck and Skalaban 1992).

Measuring the impact of religious cues on voting behavior is more complex than for class voting. The class composition of most industrial democracies is similar, but their religious composition is more varied. Britain is largely Protestant, and nearly two-thirds of the population are nominally Anglicans. In contrast, nearly all French citizens are baptized Catholics, and the Protestant minority is very small. Germany is a mixed denominational system, with Lutheran Protestants slightly outnumbering Catholics. The United States lacks a dominant national religion; there are a significant number of Catholics, Reformation-era Protestants, Pietist Protestants, other Protestant and Christian groups, Jews, and the nonreligious.

In addition to the diverse religious composition of nations, the partisan tendencies of religious denominations also vary cross-nationally. Catholics normally support parties of the Right, and Protestants normally support parties of the Left. But historical events sometimes led to different religious alignments.

Thus, the voting cues provided by religious affiliation may differ across nations in contrast to the consistent working-class/middle-class pattern for social class.

Table 8.2 presents the relationship between religious denomination and party support in the four core nations. Religious differences in voting are often substantial; however, each nation displays its unique pattern of religious voting. The historical conflict between the Catholic Church and Liberal/Socialist parties still appears in Germany. Most Catholics support the CDU/CSU, which defends traditional values and the church's prerogatives. Among Catholics who are closely

Table 8.2   Religious Denomination and Party Support (in percentages)

United States, 2000	No religion	Jewish	Catholic	Reformation Protestant	Baptist	Other Protestant
Democrat	63	84	53	53	43	42
Republican	37	16	47	47	57	58
Total	100	100	100	100	100	100

Great Britain, 2001	No religion	Catholic	Presbyterian	Anglican
Labour	51	63	48	43
Liberal Democrats	25	14	19	19
Conservatives	24	24	33	38
Total	100	101	100	100

France, 1996	Non-Catholic	Catholic
PC/Far left	9	3
Socialists	52	35
Greens	9	7
UDF	5	16
RPR	9	30
National Front	7	9
Total	101	100

Germany, 1998	No religion	Protestant	Catholic
PDS	16	3	1
Alliance 90/Greens	10	7	8
SPD	49	52	38
FDP	4	7	8
CDU/CSU	21	30	46
Total	100	99	101

Sources: United States, 2000 American National Election Study (CSES); Great Britain, 2001 British Election Study (CSES); Germany, German Postelection Study 1998 (CSES); France, 1996 ISSP Survey.

tied to the church (those who attend church weekly), the CDU/CSU received 70 percent of their vote in 1998. In contrast, Protestants and the nonreligious give greater support to the leftist parties: SPD, Greens, and PDS.

Although more than 80 percent of the French population are baptized Catholics, sizable differences in voting behavior still separate French Catholics and non-Catholics. In 1996 only 19 percent of non-Catholics favored conservative parties, compared to 55 percent among Catholics. Because the French public is overwhelmingly Catholic, the political consequences of this imbalance on election outcomes is limited.

In Britain, the religious cleavage follows another pattern. The Anglican church historically allied itself with the political establishment; thus most Anglicans vote for the Conservative Party. Catholics lean toward the Labour Party because of their minority status and the issue of Irish independence. Presbyterians give disproportionate support to Labour and the Liberal Democrats.

Religious and moral conflicts are a recurring theme in American history (Wald 1993), yet the formal separation of church and state limits the impact of religion on partisan politics. Table 8.2 shows that the Reformation-era Protestant denominations (Anglicans, Calvinists, Lutherans, etc.) predominately supported the Democrats in 2000, whereas other Protestant groups leaned toward the Republicans. These differences are modest, however, and may reflect factors other than religion per se. Similarly, the Democratic ties of American Catholics are primarily the result of ethnic and class influences rather than explicitly religious values. Jewish Americans also gave disproportionate support to the Democrats in 2000, probably because of Joseph Lieberman's candidacy at the top of the ticket. Still, this is only 7 percent more votes for the Democratic ticket than the Jewish vote in the 1996 election.

To place these religious voting patterns into a cross-national context, the left side of figure 8.3 displays the levels of denominational-based voting in several nations. The starkest religious differences are often found in religiously divided societies, such as Germany and Canada. In France and Italy, the correlation largely results from differences between religious and nonreligious voters who are both disproportionately Catholic. Both Britain and the United States rank below the average in the size of religious differences in voting.

Another aspect of the religious cleavage is the influence of religiosity, such as church attendance or religious feelings. In predominately Catholic nations, such as France, this dimension represents a voter's integration into the Catholic culture. In mixed denominational systems, the secularization process has often stimulated an alliance between Protestants and Catholics in a joint defense of religious interests, so denominational differences are replaced by a secular/religious cleavage. In Germany, for example, the Christian Democratic Union unites active Catholics and Protestants against secular interests in society. Even in the United States, similar patterns have developed. Recent Republican Party presidential

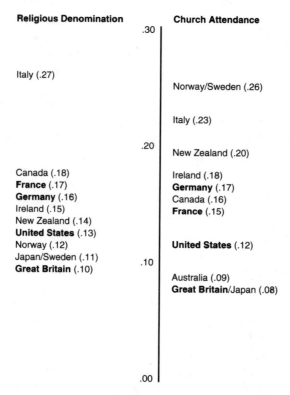

Figure 8.3   The Overall Level of Religious Voting

Source: 1996 International Social Survey Program.

Note: Values in parentheses are Cramer's V correlations.

candidates campaigned for the votes of religious conservatives from all denominations. The Republicans hoped to tap a common concern with the preservation of traditional values and opposition to abortion.

Table 8.3 presents the relationship between religious involvement, measured by the frequency of church attendance, and party preference. The voting gap between religious and nonreligious citizens is considerable in both France and Germany. For instance, only 20 percent of French citizens who attended church weekly preferred the Socialists or the Communists in 1996, compared to 63 percent among those who never went to church. Because of the Anglican church's relationship to the government, religious conflicts have not been a major factor in British electoral politics since early in the twentieth century. Similarly, religious feelings exert a limited partisan influence in America.

Table 8.3 Church Attendance and Party Support (in percentages)

	Never	Occasionally	Weekly
United States, 2000			
Democrat	60	57	42
Republican	40	43	58
Total	100	100	100
Great Britain, 1997			
Labour	56	49	46
Liberal Democrats	18	18	21
Conservatives	26	33	34
Total	100	100	100
France, 1996			
PC/Far left	14	4	1
Socialists	50	37	19
Greens	8	8	7
UDF	7	14	25
RPR	14	27	40
National Front	7	9	9
Total	100	99	101
Germany, 1998			
PDS	11	2	1
Alliance 90/Greens	11	7	6
SPD	52	48	26
FDP	3	8	10
CDU/CSU	22	35	58
Total	99	100	101

Sources: United States, 2000 American National Election Study; *Great Britain,* 1997 British Election Study (CSES); *Germany,* German Postelection Study 1998 (CSES); *France,* 1996 ISSP Survey.

The cross-national pattern of voting by church attendance is displayed on the right-hand side of figure 8.3. The religious divide (average correlation is .17) is a stronger explanation of the vote than either class or religious denomination. Despite the paucity of explicitly religious issues in most campaigns, religious attachments are often a strong predictor of party choice. In Norway and Sweden, for instance, religion reflects continuing controversies over lifestyle issues, such as temperance and moral values. In other nations, the religious/secular cleavage is related to issues such as abortion or other moral issues (chapter 6). Religion constitutes a hidden agenda of politics, tapping differences in values and moral beliefs that might not be expressed in a campaign but nevertheless influence voter choices. Indeed, there is a variety of evidence that indicates that moral or religious images continue to divide the parties in many Western democracies.[6]

Figure 8.3 also underscores the diversity of religious voting across the four core nations. Both religious denomination and church attendance are significantly related to partisan preferences in Germany. The religious cleavage in France is based on the voting differences between practicing Catholics and the nonreligious. In both the United States and Britain, there are only modest partisan differences by religious denominations or church attendance. The limited degree of religious voting in the United States illustrates the continued separation of church and state, despite the attempts by some to politicize religion.

Despite the evidence of a strong relationship between religious values and partisan preferences, we might expect the religious cleavage to follow the same pattern of decline as the class cleavage. Social modernization may disrupt religious alignments in the same manner that social class lines have blurred. Changing lifestyles and religious beliefs have decreased involvement in church activities and diminished the church as a focus of social (and political) activities. Most Western nations display a steady decline in religious involvement over the past fifty years (Franklin, Mackie, and Valen 1992, chap. 1). In the Catholic nations of Europe, for instance, frequent church attendance has decreased by nearly half since the 1950s. Predominately Protestant countries, such as the United States and the nations of northern Europe, began with lower levels of church involvement but follow the same downward trend. By definition, this secularization trend means that fewer voters are integrated into religious networks and exposed to the religious cues that can guide the vote.

The expectation about a decline in religious voting can be tested by observing the pattern of religious voting over time. Similar to the class voting index, figure 8.4 plots a religious voting index based on the difference in party preferences between religious denominations. For instance, the differences in Conservative Party support between Anglicans, nonconformist Protestants, and Catholics in Britain have changed only slightly since 1959. Similarly, the gap in leftist voting between German Catholics and Protestants averages in the 20- to 25-point range for much of the Federal Republic's existence. This gap narrowed during the 1980s, however, and the merger of a secular eastern electorate has further dampened religious voting differences since unification.

Partisan differences between American Catholics and Protestants vary across elections; the religious cleavage intensified with John Kennedy's candidacy in 1960, whereas other elections display weak religious voting. Overall, there is only a slight convergence in religious voting patterns in American congressional elections (see Abramson, Aldrich, and Rohde 1999, chap. 5, for evidence on presidential elections).

The long-term trends in voting differences between religious and nonreli-

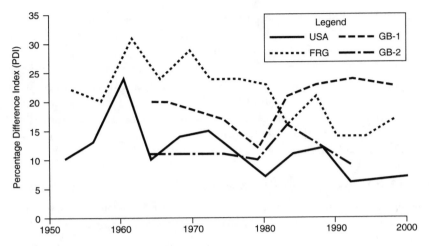

Figure 8.4   Trends in Denominational Voting

Sources: United States, 1952–2000, American National Election Studies; *Great Britain,* 1964–97, British Election Studies; *Germany,* 1953–98, German Election Studies.

Notes: Comparisons for the United States and Germany are between Protestants and Catholics. GB-1 is a comparison of the Labour Party vote of Anglicans and Catholics; GB-2 is a comparison of the Conservative Party vote of Anglicans and nonconformists.

gious citizens are also relatively stable over time (Dalton 1996a, chap. 8). Religious involvement in France has a strong and persisting impact on voting preferences, averaging more than a 40 percent difference in leftist party support. The religious cleavage in Germany was relatively strong and stable until the 1980s; it has weakened in the past two decades, especially since unification. British party differences on the religious voting index are initially quite small and display little change over time. The recent attempts of the Republican Party to court religious voters has heightened religious differences over the past three U.S. elections—but the magnitude of this gap remains limited.[7]

In summary, the trends for religious voting do not show the marked drop-off found for class voting. Despite the paucity of explicitly religious issues and the lack of religious themes in most campaigns, religious characteristics still can be a strong predictor of party choice. Weak religious voting patterns, such as those in the United States and Britain, reflect an ongoing characteristic of the party system rather than the recent erosion in religious voting. The stability of religious voting is all the more surprising because advanced industrial societies have become more secular during the past few decades. In addition, many of the societal changes that weakened the class cleavage presumably should have the same effect on religious voting.

Despite these appearances, the importance of religion as a basis of voting behavior is declining, but the pattern of decline is less obvious than for class voting. Comparisons of the voting patterns of religious denominations include only those voters with religious attachments. Individuals who attend church regularly remain well integrated into a religious network and maintain distinct voting patterns; however, there are fewer of these individuals today. By definition, the growing number of secular voters do not turn to religious cues to make their electoral choices. Thus, as the number of individuals relying on religious cues decreases, the partisan significance of religious characteristics and their overall ability to explain voting are weakened.

OTHER SOCIAL GROUP DIFFERENCES

The decline of social group–based voting is most apparent for class and religion, but a similar erosion of influence has occurred for most other social characteristics.

Regional differences occasionally flare up as a basis of political division. Britain, the United States, and now the unified Germany have seen regional interests polarize over the past generation. In other societies, such as Spain, Canada, and Italy, sharp regional differences from the past have persisted to the present (e.g., Rose 1982; Clarke, Kornberg, and Wearing 2000). Yet in most nations, region exerts only a minor influence on voting. Similarly, urban/rural residence displays only modest differences in voting patterns. Furthermore, these differences often have narrowed as the forces of modernization decrease the gap between urban and rural lifestyles.

The media have devoted considerable attention to debates about an emerging gender gap in voting. Nevertheless, the available empirical evidence points to a narrowing of male/female voting differences in most Western party systems (Studlar, McAllister, and Hayes 1998; Jelen, Thomas, and Wilcox 1994). In contemporary elections, gender is seldom a major explanation of voting patterns, normally averaging less than a 10-percentage-point gap between men and women. Significant differences begin to emerge, however, if one combines gender and life-status measures, such as employment status (Abramson, Aldrich, and Rohde 1999, chap. 5; Norris 1999a).

One possible exception to the pattern of declining social cleavages is race and ethnicity. There are sharp racial differences in partisan support within the American electorate, and these differences have widened over time (Tate 1993; Abramson, Aldrich, and Rohde 1999). For instance, 90 percent of African Americans gave their congressional votes to Democrats in 2000, compared to 63 percent among Hispanics and 46 percent among white Americans. The minority immigrant populations in Europe may produce similar differences in these party systems. Ethnicity has the potential to be a highly polarized cleavage because it may involve sharp social differences and strong feelings of group identity. Yet most societies remain relatively homogeneous in terms of ethnicity, and this limits the impact of race or ethnicity as an overall predictor of vote choice. For example, the Cramer's V correlation for race and vote is significant in the United States (.25) but quite modest in a nation such as Britain (.06) that has a smaller minority population (Saggar and Heath 1999).

This evidence leads to one of the most widely repeated findings of modern electoral research: Sociological factors have declining influence on voting behavior. Franklin and his colleagues (1992) compiled the most comprehensive evidence supporting this conclusion. They tracked the ability of a set of social characteristics (including social class, education, income, religiosity, region, and gender) to explain partisan preferences. Across fourteen democracies, they found a marked and consistent erosion in the voting impact of social structure. The rate and timing of this decline vary across nations, but the end product is the same. In party systems such as those in the United States and Canada, where social group–based voting was initially weak, the decline has occurred slowly. In other electoral systems—such as Germany, the Netherlands, and several Scandinavian nations—where sharp social divisions once structured the vote, the decline has been steady and dramatic. Franklin and his colleagues conclude with the new "conventional wisdom" of comparative electoral research:

> One thing that has by now become quite apparent is that almost all of the countries we have studied show a decline during our period in the ability of social cleavages to structure individual voting choice. (1992, 385)

NEW POLITICS AND THE VOTE

As traditional social group influences decrease in importance, the New Politics (or postmaterial) cleavage may provide the basis for a new partisan alignment. The erosion of Old Politics cleavages is at least partially the result of the increasing salience of New Politics issues (Knutsen 1987, 1995b). Environmental protection, women's rights, and other social issues are not easily related to traditional class or religious alignments. Furthermore, New Politics issues attract the attention of the same social groups that are weakly integrated into the Old Politics cleavages: the young, the new middle class, the better educated, and the nonreligious.

The development of a new basis of partisan cleavage can be a long and difficult process. Groups must organize to represent New Politics interests and mobilize voter support, but the group bases of these issues are still ill defined. The environmental and women's movements, for example, have multiple groups representing them, they seldom speak with a single voice, and the voters' bonds to specific groups are weaker than for class and religious groups. The parties also must develop clear policy images on these issues. Many established parties are hesitant to identify themselves with these issues because the stakes are still unclear and the parties are often internally divided on the issues (Rohrschneider 1993b; Dalton 1994a, chap. 9).

Despite these limiting factors, the potential impact of New Politics values on voting has increased in recent years. Small Green or New Left parties now compete in many European democracies (Richardson and Rootes 1995). In response, the established parties are gradually becoming more receptive to the political demands of New Politics groups. The entrance of Green parties into the government coalition in France (1997) and Germany (1998) and Al Gore's candidacy in the 2000 U.S. elections signal how the established parties are accepting Green issues.

People also seem willing to base their voting choices on New Politics concerns. Harvey Palmer (1995), for example, found that postmaterial values gradually became a better predictor of British party preferences than either income or occupation. Postmaterialism has also exercised a significant impact on German voting preferences, at least until unification created a new set of policy concerns (Fuchs and Rohrschneider 1998). Knutsen's research (1995b; Knutsen and Scarbrough 1995) similarly points to a growing relation between postmaterial values and party choice in most European nations. In addition, many Europeans express a willingness to vote for an environmental party—the potential electorate for a Green party rivals that of socialist and Christian democratic parties (Inglehart 1990, 266)!

Chapter 7 suggested that the initial structure of this new cleavage may focus on the conflict between New Politics and Old Politics adherents. Therefore, we used the material/postmaterial values index (chapter 5) to see if these orientations influence voting. Materialists emphasize security, stability, economic well-being, and other Old Politics objectives. Postmaterialists place greater stress on New Politics goals, such as participation, social equality, and environmental protection.

Table 8.4 displays the strong relationship between value priorities and party preferences. In every nation, postmaterialists favor the Left by a significant margin, whereas materialists lean toward the Right. The influence of changing values is especially clear for the New Left environmental parties in France and Germany. For example, 21 percent of French postmaterialists supported the Greens, compared to only 3 percent of materialists.

The overall size of these voting differences is considerable, often exceeding the Alford index scores for class or religious voting. There is a 44-percentage-point gap in Labour Party support between materialists and postmaterialists. Sizable PDI scores also appear in Germany (35) and France (33), whereas value differences are less pronounced in the United States (17).

The extent of values-based voting in advanced industrial democracies is described in figure 8.5. As other studies have noted, postmaterialism has an exceptionally strong influence in Denmark and the Netherlands (and Finland), where established political parties have responded to these new issue concerns. Values-based voting is also significant in Britain, Germany, and France; in all three nations the influence of values exceeds class voting differences (compare to figure 8.1). Repeating a pattern we have seen for other cleavages, New Politics values only weakly affect American electoral behavior.

Table 8.4   Value Priorities and Party Support (in percentages)

	Postmaterial ◄────────────► Material			
United States				
Democrat	67	59	52	50
Republican	33	42	48	50
Total	100	101	100	100
Great Britain				
Labour	70	56	47	26
Liberal Democrats	9	8	3	5
Conservatives	22	37	50	70
Total	101	101	100	101
France				
PC	6	6	5	3
Socialists	46	42	35	35
Other Left	3	1	0	2
Greens	21	17	12	3
UDF	15	20	30	29
RPR	6	8	16	19
National Front	3	6	3	10
Total	100	100	101	101
Germany				
Alliance 90/Greens	14	4	1	2
SPD	52	38	33	29
FDP	11	8	10	4
CDU/CSU	21	46	52	61
Other party	2	4	3	5
Total	100	100	99	101

Source: 1990–91 World Values Survey.

Note: Value priorities are measured with the twelve-item index (see chapter 5).

Previous electoral research found that the extent of values polarization is partially a function of the diversity of choice in a party system; with more parties, it is more likely that one will choose to represent these concerns. In addition, affluence stimulates postmaterial concerns. This is most clearly evident in the eastern/western German comparisons. Postmaterial values have a significant influence on the voting choices of many westerners (Cramer's V = .21). Eastern Germans, however, are less likely to possess postmaterial values and are preoccupied with the economic problems that accompanied German union. Thus, values play a smaller role in their voting behavior (Cramer's V = .14) even though they are voting on the same party choices. Figure 8.5 also shows that across the advanced industrial

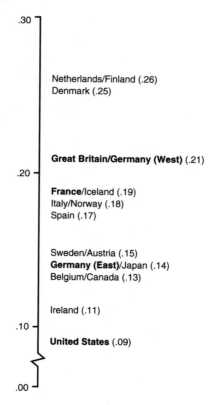

Figure 8.5   The Overall Level of Values Voting, 1990

Source: 1990–91 World Values Survey.

Note: Values in parentheses are Cramer's V correlations. Respondents without a party preference are excluded from the calculation of correlations.

democracies, the average weight of value priorities (Cramer's V = .17) now exceeds the weight of social class in determining party choice (compare to figure 8.1).

Extensive long-term trend data are not available for the twelve-item index, but we can gain some idea of these trends by comparing results from a survey in the 1970s to our current findings (figure 8.6). In contrast to class voting, which is decreasing over time, the impact of values has strengthened in most nations.[8] For example, the voting difference between materialists and postmaterialists in Germany was 22 percentage points in 1973; by 1990 this gap had increased to 35 points. Thus, the sources of partisan cleavage are changing in advanced industrial democracies—the long-standing Old Politics cleavages are being joined by a new values cleavage.

It would be a mistake to assume that New Politics differences in voting means an inexorable increase in support for leftist parties. The Old Politics cleavages will remain the major forces structuring party competition for some time. Furthermore, the partisan consequences of the New Politics depend on how parties respond to these issues. For instance, although American environmentalists normally feel closer to the Democratic Party, an early Republican president (Teddy Roosevelt) nurtured the modern environmental movement and another Republican president (Richard Nixon) created the Environmental Protection Agency. Similarly, the conservative Kohl government took more forceful action than its SPD predecessors in dealing with acid rain, pollution of the North Sea, and other environmental problems in Germany (but the new SPD government has been even more active). Environmentalism is not a Left or Right issue in the traditional Old Politics meaning of these terms; the partisan results of these issues depend on how parties respond (see Dalton 1994a, chap. 9). The real

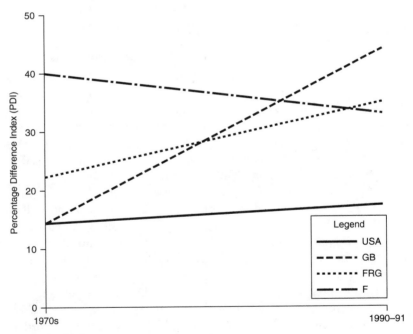

Figure 8.6   Trends in New Politics Voting

Sources: 1990–91 World Values Survey, 1973 European Communities study, and 1975 Political Action Survey.

Note: The values plotted are the Percentage Difference Index (PDI) quantities relating postmaterial value priorities to leftist party preference.

lesson is that public interests and party alignments are changing, and the party systems in advanced industrial democracies are affected by these trends.

THE TRANSFORMATION OF SOCIAL CLEAVAGES

This chapter has described a general decline in the influence of social characteristics on voting choice. Throughout much of the twentieth century, the dominant social cleavage in most democracies separated working-class and middle-class parties. But the socioeconomic transformation of these societies is weakening class alignments. Similarly, the number of churchgoers available for mobilization by confessional parties is decreasing, leading to a declining influence of religion on voting behavior. These class and religious trends are often accompanied by declines in the influence of regional, residential, and other social cleavages.

Since there is a natural logic (and political rationale) to thinking about party systems as the representation of social group differences, one response to the erosion of Old Politics group divisions has been to search for potential new social bases of alignment. Political scientists term this a *partisan realignment*. A *realignment* is defined as a significant shift in the group bases of party coalitions, usually resulting in a shift in the relative size of the parties' vote shares.

There have been many prior examples of realignment in Western party systems, in which one system of group cleavages was supplanted by another. For example, the 1930s New Deal realignment in the United States is traced to the entry of large numbers of blue-collar workers, Catholics, and blacks into the Democratic Party coalition. Realignments have been a regular feature of American electorate politics for well over a century and probably since the emergence of the first mass party coalitions around 1800 (Clubb, Flanigan, and Zingale 1980). Similar historical realignments have occurred in European party systems, such as the Labour Party's rise in the early 1900s and the Gaullist realignment at the beginning of the French Fifth Republic.

Some analysts suggest that New Politics issues—environmental protection, nuclear energy, sexual equality, consumer advocacy, and human rights—may provide the basis of a new partisan alignment. These issues are attractive to voters who are weakly integrated into Old Politics alignments. Eventually, these interests may coalesce into political movements that will realign electorates and party systems. The growing partisan polarization along the New Politics value cleavage apparently supports this realignment thesis. Value priorities have become a more important influence on voting choice, and new parties now represent these perspectives.

I am not convinced that it is accurate to think of contemporary partisan politics in the same terms as past partisan realignments. The process of partisan realignment is normally based on clearly defined and highly cohesive social groups that can develop institutional ties to the parties and provide clear voting cues to their members. A firm group base provides a framework for parties to develop institutional ties to the groups and for groups to socialize and mobilize their members.

There are few social groupings comparable to labor unions or churches that might establish the basis of a New Politics realignment. For instance, generational differences in support for New Politics parties might indicate an emerging New Politics cleavage, but age groups provide a very transitory basis for mobilizing voters. Other potential group bases of voting cues, such as education or alternative class categorizations, so far remain speculative, without firm evidence of realigning effects.

Postmaterial values are related to partisan preferences, but these values are unlikely to provide a basis for a new group-party alignment. Values define clusters of like-minded people. One cannot identify a postmaterialist in the same way that class, religion, or region provides a basis of personal identity and group mobilization. Indeed, postmaterial values are antithetical to such traditionally structured organizations as unions and churches. Instead, a vast array of single-issue groups and causes represent New Politics concerns, from the women's movement to peace organizations to environmental groups. These groups generally are loosely organized with ill-defined memberships that wax and wane.

The lack of a group basis for the New Politics cleavage highlights another aspect of the new style of citizen politics. The kinds of cleavages that divide modern electorates and the kinds of groups they define are changing. Electoral politics is moving from cleavages defined by fixed social groups to value and issue cleavages that identify communities of like-minded individuals. The growing heterogeneity, secularization, and *embourgeoisement* of society are weakening social group ties generally. Increasing levels of urbanization, social mobility, and geographic mobility work against the continued existence of exclusive, cohesive social groups. The revolutions in education and cognitive mobilization work against the dominance of disciplined, hierarchic, clientelist associations.

In summary, two kinds of changes are affecting contemporary electoral politics. First, the shift from the Old Politics toward the New Politics marks a transformation from social group cleavages to issue group cleavages. Because issue group cleavages are more difficult to institutionalize or "freeze" via social group ties to mass organizations, they may not be as stable. In addition, because many of the new issue concerns involve only a narrow sector of the public, the linkage between these issues and party support may remain unclear. Some parties may adopt vague issue stands to avoid offending specific interests; other parties may cater to special interest groups and lose their broader programmatic image.

A second change involves the weakening of social group bonds. Social groups may still represent some of the changing political interests of contemporary electorates. Nevertheless, all forms of political mobilization are subject to the atomizing influences of advanced industrial societies. Interest mobilization along any political dimension necessarily will be characterized by more complex, overlapping, and crosscutting associational networks; more fluid institutional loyalties; and looser, more egalitarian organizational structures. Thus, the question is not whether labor union leaders support leftist parties (they do) or whether labor union members perceive these cues (they do)—but whether the union rank and file will follow their leaders anymore. And the fact is that fewer individuals are following such external cues. This change affects the breadth, effectiveness, and stability of any future partisan alignment. Not only is the style of the Old Politics cleavages fading, but the prognosis for an eventual revival is not an optimistic one.

The new style of citizen politics, therefore, should include a more fluid and volatile pattern of party alignments. Political coalitions and voting patterns will lack the permanence of past class and religious cleavages. Without clear social cues, voting decisions will become a more demanding task for voters, and voting decisions will become more dependent on the individual beliefs and values of each citizen.

SUGGESTED READINGS

Anderson, Christopher J., and Carsten Zelle, eds. *Stability and Change in German Elections: How Electorates Merge, Converge, or Collide.* Westport, Conn.: Praeger, 1998.

Dalton, Russell, Scott Flanagan, and Paul Beck, eds. *Electoral Change in Advanced Industrial Democracies.* Princeton, N.J.: Princeton University Press, 1984.

Evans, Geoffrey, ed. *The End of Class Politics? Class Voting in Comparative Context.* New York: Oxford University Press, 1999.

Franklin, Mark, Tom Mackie, and Henry Valen, eds. *Electoral Change.* New York: Cambridge University Press, 1992.

Norris, Pippa. *Electoral Change in Britain since 1945.* Cambridge, Mass.: Blackwell, 1997.

NOTES

1. Most American voting studies analyze presidential elections. Because of the importance of candidate image, presidential elections reflect a different set of electoral forces than normally found in European parliamentary elections. To assure comparability of American and European results, the American data in this chapter are based on voting patterns in congressional elections.
2. We measured social class by the occupation of the respondent coded into the following categories: (1) government, (2) professional/managerial, (3) technical/clerk, (4) service/sales, (5) farming, (6) workers, and (7) other occupations.
3. In the United States, this is the percentage voting Democratic in congressional elections; in Britain, the percentage voting Labour; in Germany, the percentage voting SPD of the two-party vote (SPD and CDU/CSU) before 1980 and leftist percentage (SPD, Greens, and PDS) in later elections; in France, the percentage voting for leftist parties (PC, Socialist, and other Left).
4. Generational patterns in class voting also reinforce the argument of the long-term erosion in this cleavage (Franklin, Mackie, and Valen 1992, chap. 19). Research generally finds strong relationships between class and vote among older generations. Among younger generations, these relationships are weak and decreasing.
5. In support of this interpretation, new middle-class voters have been a major source of electoral volatility in the United States (Hout et al. 1996; Abramson, Aldrich, and Rohde 1999) and Germany (Dalton 1996b). The following table shows that the French new middle class has also shifted its vote preferences for the Left over time:

1962	1967	1968	1973	1978	1981	1988	1996
42	40	42	54	51	57	56	60

6. Laver and Hunt (1992) show that political elites in most Western democracies still perceive significant party differences on dimensions such as pro- and anticlerical and the permissiveness of social policy. There is evidence that Germans can clearly differentiate the parties in their religious leanings, and these perceptions have grown more distinct over time (Dalton 1993a, 60; Wessels 1994). Finally, chapter 7 found that the American public perceives conservative religious groups as closer to the Republican Party.

7. In 2000 there was an 18 percent gap in party support between those who never attend church and those who attend on a weekly basis. This is about double the level of religious polarization in elections of the 1950s and 1960s, but it is still half the level of religious differences in nations such as Germany and France.

8. Value polarization in France decreased between 1973 and 1990. This may be coincidental to these two surveys or may reflect the initial polarization over postmaterial issues that occurred as a result of the May Revolts. The French case deserves additional research.

CHAPTER 9

Partisanship and Electoral Behavior

SOCIAL CLEAVAGES MAY provide the foundation of modern party systems, as seen in the two previous chapters, but this represents only the beginnings of electoral decision making. Each election presents voters with choices over policy proposals and the candidates for office. Although social characteristics and group cues might be a basis for making decisions, citizens also hold a variety of political beliefs and values that affect their electoral calculus. Often these considerations go beyond group ties or the perceptions derived from group cues.

Consequently, contemporary electoral research emphasizes the attitudes and values of voters as key factors in understanding electoral choice. Most elections are not presented as conflicts over historical cleavage alignments but deal with more contemporary problems (which may reflect long-term conflicts). Citizens make judgments about which party best represents their interests, and these perceptions guide voting behavior. Attitudes toward the issues and candidates of an election are thus a necessary element in any realistic model of voting. Attitudes are also changeable, and their incorporation into a voting model helps explain variation in party results across elections.

A Sociopsychological Model of Voting

Faced by the limitations of a purely sociological approach to voting, early electoral researchers developed voting models to include psychological factors, such as attitudes and values, as influences on voting decisions and other political behavior. A team of researchers at the University of Michigan first formalized a model integrating both sociological and psychological influences on voting (Campbell et al. 1960, 1966). This sociopsychological model describes the voting process in terms of a *funnel of causality* (figure 9.1). At the wide mouth of the funnel are the socioeconomic conditions that generate the broad political divisions of society: the economic structure, social divisions such as race or religion, and historical alignments such as the North–South division in the United States. These factors influence the structure of the party system (see chapter 7) but are far removed from the voting decisions of individual citizens.

As we move through the causal funnel, socioeconomic conditions influence
group loyalties and basic value orientations. For instance, economic conditions
may bond an individual to a social class, or regional identities may form in reaction to social and political inequalities. Thus, social conditions are translated
into attitudes that can directly influence the individual's political behavior.

The causal funnel narrows further as group loyalties and value priorities are
linked to more explicitly political attitudes. Campbell and his colleagues explained
individual voting decisions primarily in terms of three attitudes: partisanship,
issue opinions, and candidate images. These beliefs are most proximate to the
voting decision and therefore have a direct and very strong impact on the vote.

Although the funnel of causality appears simple by contemporary standards
of social science, it represented a major conceptual breakthrough for voting

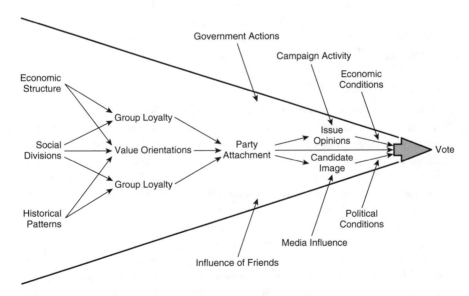

Figure 9.1   The Funnel of Causality Predicting Vote Choice

research. This model provides a useful device for organizing the factors that potentially influence voting behavior. To understand voting decisions, one has to recognize the causal relationship between the many factors involved. The wide end of the funnel represents broad social conditions that structure political conflict but are temporally and psychologically far removed from the actual voting decision. As we move through the funnel, attention shifts to factors that are explicitly political, involve individual beliefs, and are more proximate to voting choice. Social characteristics are therefore seen as an important aspect of the voting process, but their primary influence is in forming broad political orientations and group loyalties; most of the direct impact of social characteristics on voting is mediated by attitudinal dispositions. Attitudes, in turn, depend on the group loyalties and value orientations of the individual, as well as external stimuli such as friends, media, government actions, and the activities of the campaign. There is a place in the funnel of causality for each element of the voting process, and we can understand each element in relation to the others.

In addition to the descriptive value of the model, the sociopsychological approach is also very successful in predicting voting choices. Attitudes toward the parties, issues, and candidates of an election are psychologically very close to the actual voting decision and therefore are strongly related to voting choices. In fact, the model can predict voting decisions more accurately than individuals can predict their own behavior (Campbell et al. 1960, 74)!

The sociopsychological model has defined a paradigm of voting behavior that structures how we think about elections and how researchers analyze the voting process. Researchers have tested and applied the basic elements of the model in a variety of nations. This chapter examines partisan attachments as a central concept in the sociopsychological model of voting. Then chapter 10 examines how specific issue opinions provide another element in this model.

Partisan Attitudes

The sociopsychological model focuses on the specific issue opinions and candidate evaluations that determine voting behavior. Yet it soon became clear that partisan loyalties strongly influenced many of the specific political beliefs and behaviors of the citizenry. As one elderly Tallahassee voter once commented to me while waiting to vote, "I vote for the candidate and not the party. It just seems like the Democrats always choose the best candidate." Many voters begin each electoral season with already formed partisan predispositions. These partisan loyalties are a central element in an individual's belief system, serving as a source of political cues for other attitudes and behaviors.

The Michigan researchers described these party attachments as a sense of *party identification*, similar to identifications with a social class, religious denomination, or other social group. Party identification is a long-term, affective, psychological identification with one's preferred political party (Campbell et al.

1960, chap. 6; Miller 1991).[1] These party attachments are distinct from voting preferences, which explains why some Americans vote for the presidential candidate of one party while expressing loyalty to another party. Indeed, it is the conceptual independence of voting and party identification that initially gives the latter its theoretical significance.[2]

The discovery of party identification is one of the most significant findings of public opinion research. Partisanship is like a "super attitude." It provides a starting point for individual belief systems, as discussed in chapter 2. Partisanship is also the ultimate heuristic, because it provides a reference structure for evaluating many new political stimuli—what position does "my" party take on this issue—and making political choices. As seen in chapter 3, partisanship is also a stimulus for engagement in campaigns and elections. The functional importance of partisanship was emphasized by the developers of the concept:

> The present analysis of party identification is based on the assumption that the . . . parties serve as standard-setting groups for a significant proportion of the people in this country. In other words, it is assumed that many people associate themselves psychologically with one or the other of the parties, and that this identification has predictable relationships with their perceptions, evaluations, and actions. (Campbell, Gurin, and Miller 1954, 90)

Thus, the concept has become a key to understanding citizen political behavior.

After the description of party identification in the United States, the concept was exported to other democratic nations. In several cases, researchers had problems finding an equivalent measure of partisanship in multiparty systems or in nations where the term *partisanship* holds different connotations for the voters (Budge, Crewe, and Farlie 1976). The concept of a partisan "independent" is not as common in other electoral systems as it is in the United States. Thus, researchers could not simply translate the American party identification question into French or German; they had to find a functional equivalent for partisan attachments.[3] Still, most public opinion specialists agree that voters hold some party allegiances that endure over time and strongly influence other opinions and political behavior. Equivalent measures of party identifications are now included in the election studies of virtually all contemporary democracies.

The Learning of Partisanship

The importance of party identification for understanding political behavior partially results from the early origins of these attachments. Socialization studies find that children develop basic partisan orientations at a very early age, often during the primary school years (Hess and Torney 1967, 90). Children learn party loyalties before they can understand what the party labels stand for, a process similar to the development of many other group ties. These early party attachments then provide a reference structure for future political learning (which often reinforces early partisan biases).

The early-life formation of party identities means that parents play a central role in the socialization of these values. The transmission of partisanship within the family can be seen by comparing the party identifications of parents and their children. A cross-national socialization study interviewed parents and their children to compare their opinions directly (table 9.1). This research found relatively high levels of partisan agreement within American, British, and German families.[4] In the United States, for example, 70 percent of the 16–20-year-old children of Democratic parents are themselves Democrats, and 55 percent of Republican parents have Republican children. Less than 10 percent of the children actually favor the party in opposition to their parents. These levels of partisan agreements are similar to those found in a larger and more representative study of American adolescents (Jennings and Niemi 1973). The British and German surveys also show that the party attachments of these parents are frequently re-created in the values of their offspring. Parents apparently have a strong formative influence on the partisan values of their children, even before most children become active in the political process.

There are many reasons why parents are so successful in transmitting their partisanship to their children. Partisan loyalties are formed when parents are the dominate influence in a child's life, and the exposure to partisan cues from the parent is common. Parties are very visible and important institutions in the political process, and virtually all political discussion includes some partisan content: We identify candidates and judge them by their party affiliation, and we evaluate policies by their party sponsor. It does not take long for a child to identify the parents' partisan leanings from their reactions to television news and statements in family discussions. Furthermore, most parents have party attachments that endure across elections; children are thus exposed to relatively consistent and continuous cues on which party their parents prefer. For example, one of my university colleagues was proud that he had conditioned his preschool child to groan each time a specific former president appeared on television. Either through explicit reinforcement or subconscious internalization of parental values, many children learn of their parents' partisan preferences and take them as their own.

Once individuals establish party ties, later partisan experiences often follow these early predispositions. Democrats tend to vote for Democratic candidates; Republicans vote for Republicans. Thus, electoral experience normally reinforces these partisan tendencies because most citizens cast ballots for their preferred party.[5] The accumulated experience of voting for the same party and the political agreement that leads to such partisan regularity both tend to strengthen partisan ties. Consequently, researchers generally find that partisan loyalties strengthen with age or, more precisely, with continued electoral support of the same party (Converse 1969, 1976).[6]

Table 9.1   The Transmission of Parental Partisanship (in percentages)

United States

	PARENTAL PARTY PREFERENCE		
	Democrat	Republican	Independent
Child's party preference			
Democrat	70	25	40
Republican	10	54	20
Independent	20	21	40
Total	100	100	100
N	128	77	30

Great Britain

	PARENTAL PARTY PREFERENCE			
	Labour	Liberal	Conservative	None
Child's party preference				
Labour	51	17	6	29
Liberal	8	39	11	6
Conservative	1	11	50	6
None	40	33	33	59
Total	100	100	100	100
N	83	18	54	17

West Germany

	PARENTAL PARTY PREFERENCE			
	SPD	FDP	CDU/CSU	None
Child's party preference				
SPD	53	8	14	19
FDP	4	59	1	3
CDU/CSU	9	—	32	12
None	34	33	53	66
Total	100	100	100	100
N	68	12	78	67

Source: Political Action Survey.

Figure 9.2 displays this increasing percentage of those with a party identification by age.[7] Regardless of which party one supports, party bonds are stronger among older age groups. Most people in the United States and Britain develop a strong sense of party identity by middle age, which continues to strengthen through the rest of the life cycle. For example, only 46 percent of the youngest French age group say they are partisans, compared to 65 percent among the old

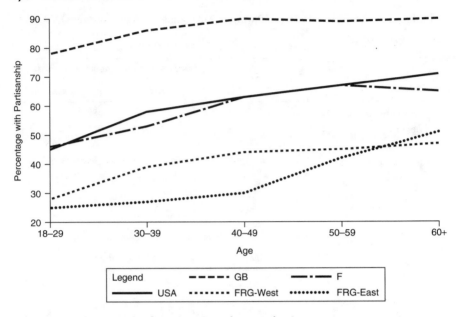

Figure 9.2   The Growth of Partisan Attachments by Age

Sources: United States, 2000 American National Election Study; *Britain,* 1997 British Election Study; *Germany,* 1998 German Election Study; *France,* 1995 French Election Study.

Note: Each nation uses a differently worded question on partisanship, so direct comparisons of the level of partisan attachments cross-nationally are not appropriate.

age group. The same general age pattern is evident for British and American electors. Measures of the strength of partisanship depict a similar pattern of party bonds intensifying with age (or more precisely, with accumulated experience of supporting the same party in successive elections).

In the last edition of this book, the Federal Republic of Germany was an exception to this general pattern. Residents of communist East Germany obviously did not have the same opportunity over the past several decades to develop attachments to the democratic parties of the West. Their experience with the current party system dates only to 1990. Thus, the overall level of partisan attachments was significantly weaker in the East. In addition, there was relatively little difference in the strength of partisan ties between young easterners and those over age 50.

As we predicted, as eastern Germans are accumulating more experience with democratic electoral politics, the life-cycle pattern of partisan learning is becoming more apparent. This learning process probably has been accelerated by the conscious attempt by the PDS to appeal to easterners; this has apparently served to integrate these citizens into the new electoral system of the Federal Republic.

The East/West gap in partisanship consequently has narrowed substantially from the pattern of the early 1990s, and the pattern of greater partisanship among the old now applies to both halves of Germany.

Thus, partisan attachments are normally learned early in life, become deeply embedded in a child's belief system, and then are reinforced by later partisan experiences. Partisanship may change in reaction to later life experiences, but these attachments are not easily altered once they have formed. For example, party identification is one of the most stable political attitudes, far exceeding the stability of opinions on several long-standing national issues: race relations, economic programs, and foreign policy (Converse and Markus 1979). Additional evidence of long-term partisan stability comes from a panel study of high school seniors and their parents. M. Kent Jennings and Greg Markus (1984) found that 78 percent of American adults and 58 percent of adolescents did not change their partisan ties across one of the most turbulent political periods in recent American history (1965–73).

Evidence from other nations mirrors this pattern. British party attachments are significantly more stable than other political beliefs (Schickler and Green 1997). On the average, between 80 and 90 percent of the British public retain constant party ties from one election to the next. Hilde Himmelweit and her colleagues (1981) interviewed a sample of British middle-class males over a twelve-year period. They found that most voters supported the same party in 1959 and 1974 (a fifteen-year time span); conversions between Labour and Conservative partisans were exceedingly rare. Longitudinal studies in Germany find that partisanship is a very stable political attitude (Baker, Dalton, and Hildebrandt 1981). The limited evidence for France shows that below the surface of substantial turbulence in the actions of party leaders, there is considerable continuity in the partisan orientations of the French public (Converse and Pierce 1986, chap. 3).

Important evidence on the relative constancy of partisan attachments comes from comparing the stability of partisanship and voting preferences (table 9.2). For instance, reinterviews with the same American voters in 1972 and 1976 found that 93 percent had stable party identifications, whereas only 75 percent had stable congressional voting preferences. Moreover, when there was some variability, more voters maintain a stable party identification while changing their vote (22 percent) than the other way around (4 percent). Party preferences are also more stable than voting preferences in Britain and Germany, but this difference is more modest than in the United States (LeDuc 1981; cf. Heath and Pierce 1992). In Europe there is a greater tendency for partisanship and vote to travel together; when one changes, so does the other (Holmberg 1994). Because of their limited amount of electing, Europeans are less likely to distinguish between long-term partisanship and current voting preferences. Still, partisanship generally is a political orientation that continues over time, even in the face of vote defections.

In sum, electoral research stresses the importance of partisanship in shaping

Table 9.2   The Relative Stability of Party Attachments
and Vote (in percentages)

Party identification	United States, 1972–76	
	VOTE	
	Stable	Variable
Stable	71	22
Variable	4	3
N = 539		

Party identification	Great Britain, 1970–74	
	VOTE	
	Stable	Variable
Stable	75	10
Variable	5	10
N = 795		

Party identification	West Germany, 1976	
	VOTE	
	Stable	Variable
Stable	71	22
Variable	4	3
N = 707		

Sources: LeDuc (1981, 261); Berger (504).

Note: The tables present percentages of the total *N* based on those who were voters and identified with a political party at each time point. American and British results are based on changes between two elections; West German data are based on changes during a three-wave 1976 election panel.

the political orientations of the public. Partisanship is a central element in an individual's belief system and a basis of political identity. These orientations are formed early in life and thus may condition later life learning. Thus, it is easy to see why researchers give it a central role in a sociopsychological model of voting choice.

THE IMPACT OF PARTISANSHIP

In sports, loyalty to a specific team helps one know whom to root for and which players to admire, and it motivates individuals to participate in support of their team. People often develop such ties early in life, and they endure through the ups and downs of the franchise. Moreover, one's attachment to the Dodgers (in my case) strengthens with repeated trips to root for one's team, even if they lose.

It is the same with feelings of partisan attachment. Political parties help to make politics "user-friendly" for citizens. When the political parties take clear and consistent policy positions, the party label provides a key informational short-cut on how "people like me" should decide. Once voters decide which party generally represents their interests, this single piece of information can act as a perceptual screen—guiding how they view events, issues, and candidates. A policy advocated by one's party is more likely to meet with favor than one advocated by the other team.

Moreover, in comparison to social group cues such as class and religion, party attachments are a much more valuable heuristic. Party cues are relevant to a much broader range of political phenomena because parties are so central to politics. Issues and events frequently are presented to the public in partisan terms, as the parties take positions on the political questions of the day or react to the statements of other political actors. Thus, reliance on partisanship may be the ultimate example of the satisficing model of politics.

The *Washington Post* performed an interesting experiment that illustrates the power of partisanship as a political cue (Morris 1995). The paper included a question on a fictitious government act on one of its opinion surveys. One form of the question included reference to either Clinton's or the Republicans' position on the issue, and another form discussed the act without any partisan cues. They found that the number of people expressing an opinion on this act increased when a partisan cue was given. Moreover, there were dramatic partisan effects. Democrats were far more likely to oppose the fictitious act when told Clinton wanted repeal; Republicans disproportionately opposed the act when told the Republicans in Congress wanted repeal.

An example from the 1992 American National Election Study demonstrates the power of partisanship to shape even nonpartisan opinions. Before the 1992 U.S. elections, the survey asked the public to judge whether the national economy would improve or worsen over the next twelve months. With George Bush in the White House, Republicans were more optimistic about the nation's future than Democrats by a 15 percent margin. After the election, with Clinton entering the presidency, Republican optimism waned and Democrats now became much more positive about the economy, by a 29 percent margin.

This reversal of the relationship between preelection and postelection surveys illustrates the power of partisanship to shape citizen perceptions of the political world. Partisanship has an even stronger influence on opinions that are more closely linked to the parties, such as evaluations of governmental performance and candidate images (Abramson, Aldrich, and Rohde 1999, chap. 8; Miller and Shanks 1996). Partisans root for the players (candidates) on their team and save their catcalls for the opponents.

Party ties also mobilize individuals to become politically active. Just like sports loyalties, attachment to a political party encourages an individual to become active in the political process to support his or her side. Voting turnout and participation in campaign activities are generally higher among strong party identifiers (chapter 3). The 2000 American National Election Study, for example, finds that turnout was 23 percent higher among strong partisans compared to independents. In addition, strong partisans are more likely to try to influence others, to display campaign paraphernalia, to attend a rally, or to give money to a candidate during the campaign. Partisanship functions in a similar way in Britain. Strong partisans voted at a slightly higher rate in the 1997 House of Commons election and were more likely to attend a campaign meeting or read the party brochures on the election. Although 95 percent of strong British partisans cared which party (team) won the election, only 63 percent of weak partisans and 26 percent of nonpartisans shared their concerns.

The cue-giving function of partisanship is strongest for voting behavior. Partisanship means that voters enter an election with a predisposition to support their preferred party. Philip Converse (1966) described partisanship as the basis for a "normal vote"—the vote expected when other factors in the election are evenly balanced. If additional factors come into play, such as issue positions or candidate images, their influence can be measured by their ability to cause defections from standing partisan commitments. For the unsophisticated voter, a long-term partisan loyalty and repeated experience with one's preferred party provide a clear and low-cost cue for voting. Even for the sophisticated citizen, a candidate's party affiliation normally signifies a policy program that serves as the basis for reasonable electoral choice.

A close relationship generally exists between partisanship and voting in parliamentary elections (Holmberg 1994). Even with multiple parties to choose from and a large swing to Labour in 1997, only 14 percent of British partisans defected from their preferred party in the election. Defection is also low in Germany, since one of the votes that citizens cast is directly for a party list. In 1994, 11 percent of partisans in western Germany defected. The limited voting opportunities in most European nations tend to lessen the separation between partisanship and vote.

The American elector, on the other hand, "has to cope simultaneously with a vast collection of partisan candidates seeking a variety of offices at federal, state, and local levels; it is small wonder that he becomes conscious of a generalized belief about his ties to a party" (Butler and Stokes 1969, 43). Thus, the separation between attitudes and behavior is most noticeable in American elections, especially when voters are asked to make a series of choices for local, state, and federal offices (Beck et al. 1992). In highly visible and politicized presidential elections, candidate images and issue appeals have the potential to counteract partisan preferences, and thus party defections are common in these elections. The success of Republican presidential candidates from Reagan to George W. Bush occurred because they attracted defectors from the Democratic majority. Even in the two-party contest of 1988, for instance, more than 12 percent of American partisans cast presidential votes contrary to their party identification.

A similar situation exists in France. The two-candidate runoff in French presidential elections is decided by the size of the vote the candidates can attract from parties other than their own (Boy and Mayer 1993). In French parliamentary elections, however, voting choice more closely conforms to standing partisan preferences.

In summary, it is easy to see why partisanship is the ultimate heuristic, because it performs a variety of functions for the partisan:

- Creates a basis of political identity
- Provides cues for evaluating political events, candidates, and issues
- Mobilizes participation in campaigns and election turnout
- Provides cues on voting preferences
- Stabilizes voting patterns, for the individual and the party system

Thus, partisan attachments became the cornerstone to our understanding of how citizens manage the complexities of politics and make reasonable decisions on the questions they face at election time.

Partisan Dealignment

Because partisanship is a central variable in the study of many different aspects of citizen political behavior, it came as some surprise when researchers first noted that party ties were eroding in many advanced industrial democracies. The initial signs of partisan decline appeared in the rising fluctuations of party outcomes from election to election (Crewe and Denver 1985). The erosion of the social group basis of party support contributed to this trend of increasing party volatility; the frozen group alignments that Lipset and Rokkan had described were beginning to thaw (chapter 8). In addition, election surveys in several nations found that partisan identifications were weakening (Dalton, Flanagan, and Beck 1984).

At first it was difficult to be certain that party bonds were eroding when this trend was intermixed with the normal patterns of partisan change between elections. Partisan change is a regular element of the electoral process, and periods of heightened partisan volatility and fragmentation dot the electoral histories of most democracies. As we argued previously, relatively few voters change their partisan preferences between adjacent elections. Some scholars thus were quite vocal in expressing their doubts that partisan ties were systematically changing across the advanced industrial democracies. For example, Peter Mair claimed that "The electoral balance now is not substantially different from that 30 years ago, and, in general electorates are not more volatile than once they were" (1993, 132; also see Klingemann and Fuchs 1995; Bartolini and Mair 1989; Keith et al. 1992; Zelle 1995).

But as our evidence has grown, adding more nations and more elections, it is now clear that a general pattern of partisan decline is affecting most Western democracies. Voters are not simply defecting from their preferred party in one or two elections. Instead, there is a continuing erosion in partisan loyalties—the same loyalties that electoral research emphasized as a core element in explaining citizen political behavior.

The weakening of party ties first became apparent in the United States (figure 9.3). American partisanship was extremely stable from the 1950s to the early 1960s; the percentage of party identifiers remained within the 70 to 75 percent range, and less than a quarter of the public claimed to be "independents" without standing partisan ties. Partisan loyalties began to weaken after the 1964 election. By the 1980s more than a third of the electorate were nonpartisans and Perot's candidacy pushed the percentage of independents still further (Wattenberg 1998; Abramson, Aldrich, and Rohde 1999, chap. 8). At the turn of the century the percentage of independents was at a new high in the 2000 election survey (41 percent).

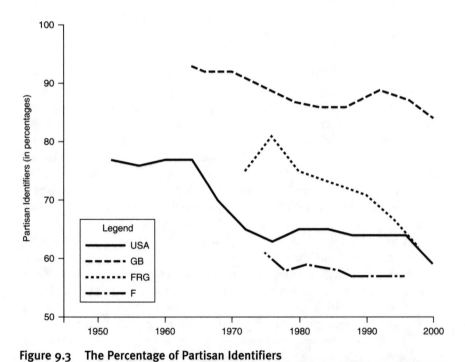

Figure 9.3   The Percentage of Partisan Identifiers

Sources: United States, 1952–2000, American National Election Studies; *Great Britain*, 1964–2001, British Election Studies; *Germany*, 1972–98, German Elections Studies (western Germany only 1990–98); *France*, Eurobarometer Surveys (1975, 1978, 1981, 1986, 1988, 1993, and 1996).

An almost identical pattern of declining party ties occurred in Britain. Because of the traditions of the British party system and the format of the British partisanship questionnaire, fewer Britons claim to be nonpartisans. In the 1964 British election study, only 4 percent claimed to lack a standing partisan preference. By the 1980s the number of nonpartisans had trebled to roughly 14 percent. Questions asking about the strength of attachments among partisans display a similar pattern. More than 40 percent of the British public were strong partisans during the late 1960s. Less than 20 percent of Britons claim to be strong partisans in the most recent elections.

Germany initially deviated from the pattern of partisanship found in other advanced industrial democracies. There was a large increase in partisanship between 1961 and 1976, as West Germans developed initial commitments to the postwar party system (Baker, Dalton, and Hildebrandt 1981, chap. 8). But at some point in the late 1970s the trend began moving in the opposite direction. Nonpartisans numbered only 16 percent of the public in 1976; by 1998 they accounted for more than 38 percent among westerners. Partisanship is even lower among easterners, since they lack prior partisan experience and are just beginning to develop party attachments.

The series of comparable French survey data is much shorter. Because of the volatility of the French party system, a relatively large number of people claim to lack any standing partisan commitment. Since the 1970s the number of partisans may have increased further, although the evidence is less certain than for the other three nations (e.g., Haegel 1993).

This weakening of party ties in our four core nations typifies a pattern that affects almost all advanced industrial democracies. An analysis of the nineteen advanced industrial democracies for which long-term survey data exist shows that the percentage of partisans has decreased in seventeen cases (Dalton 2000a). Furthermore, if we focus on the strength of partisanship, it has decreased in all nineteen nations. In nations as diverse as Austria, Canada, Japan, and New Zealand, the pattern is the same: The partisan attachments of the public weakened during the latter half of the twentieth century.

Other evidence points to growing public doubts about parties as political institutions. Surveys in Germany find that public confidence in political parties rates at the bottom of a list of diverse social and political institutions (IPOS 1995). Similarly, the British public has become significantly less trusting of political parties (Webb 1996). Indeed, the ebb of public attachment to political parties is broadly evident in most contemporary democracies.

These trends suggest that advanced industrial democracies are experiencing a new period of *partisan dealignment*. *Dealignment* means that a significant proportion of the public fails to develop party attachments or becomes openly critical of political parties as institutions of government. Electoral analysts first thought that partisan dealignment was a temporary phenomenon, as parties and politicians struggled with problems that temporarily weakened their support among the public (like a sports team on a losing streak), but it now appears to be a continuing feature of contemporary politics. After more than thirty years, for example, American partisanship remains below its high points in the 1950s and early 1960s. More important, if party identification is the most important attitude in electoral behavior research, then the breadth of these dealignment patterns should have major implications for these nations.

THE CONSEQUENCES OF DEALIGNMENT

Because partisan ties are seen as so central to the workings of electoral politics and political behavior, the erosion of these ties should have obvious and predictable effects on citizen politics. Indeed, the evidence of partisan dealignment is visible in a range of different aspects of electoral behavior.

For instance, partisanship binds individual voters to a preferred party. Thus, as these ties weaken, so should patterns of partisan-centered voting choice. Weakened party attachments lead fewer American voters to cast straight-party ballots, and split-ticket voting has risen in recent elections (figure 9.4). In the 1960s less

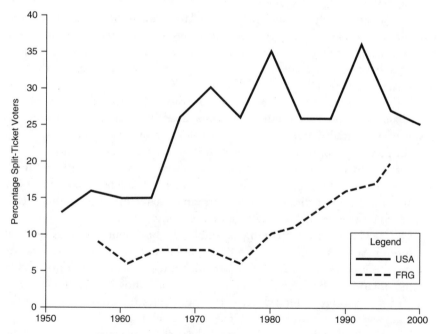

Figure 9.4   The Growth of Split-Ticket Voting

Sources: United States, 1952–92, American National Election Studies (third-party presidential candidates are counted as split voting); *Germany,* Statistiches Bundesamt (various years) and Schoen (2000) for 1994 and 1998. German data for 1990–98 are from western Germany.

than a sixth of Americans split their ballots between a presidential candidate of one party and a congressional candidate of another party. By the 1980s this had risen to a quarter of the electorate. With Perot's third-party candidacy in 1992, 36 percent of Americans split their ballots. Even without Perot, split-ticket voting remained relatively high in the 2000 election. Split-ticket voting between House and Senate votes has also increased dramatically (Stanley and Niemi 1994, 146). There is similar evidence of split-ticket voting in other Western democracies that allows the voters to divide their party choices (Dalton and Wattenberg 2000, chap. 3). This appears to be a general consequence of the dealignment trend.

Weakened partisanship is also increasing the fluidity of voting patterns. For instance, there is evidence that the number of political parties and the shift in vote shares between elections are generally increasing in advanced industrial democracies—including the four we are studying here (Dalton and Wattenberg 2000, chap. 3). Similarly, David Butler illustrated this pattern for Britain; the average fluctuation in Gallup polls measuring Conservative Party support was 7.5 percent for the 1955–64 period and 20.6 percent for the 1985–92 period (Butler 1995, 71). Although most voters continue to support the same party over time, the number of floating voters is increasing in these party systems. Partisanship was once a stable guidepost for citizen political behavior, and now fewer individuals are following its guidance.

Since partisanship also mobilizes individuals to participate in the politics, it is no surprise that dealignment has been accompanied by the decline in electoral participation (see chapter 3). Election turnout has decreased in most advanced industrial democracies. In addition, participation in campaigns—going to meetings, working for candidates, and displaying party support—has also atrophied (Dalton and Wattenberg 2000, chap. 3). If politics is like sports, then when there are fewer habitual fans, there will be fewer to attend each game and participate in the sport.

Finally, when citizens do turn out to vote, the nature of the voting process should change. If long-term party and social group cues are decreasing in importance, this should shift the decision-making process toward the issues and candidates of specific campaigns. As one indicator of this shift, trend data show a systematic tendency for voters to make their decisions later in the campaign (Dalton and Wattenberg 2000, chap. 3); campaigns are now more likely to matter because fewer voters base their choice on standing partisan predispositions. Voters are beginning to choose.

THE CAUSES OF DEALIGNMENT

There are several explanations for the spreading pattern of partisan dealignment. At least initially, the decline of partisanship was linked to political events and political crises. In the United States, the dramatic events of the 1970s initially turned many young people away from political parties. The antipartisan sentiments stirred by the Vietnam War, Watergate, and similar crises kept new voters from developing the early-life partisan attachments that could build over time. The student protests in Europe and a seemingly growing number of party scandals may have had a similar effect in other nations.

The cross-national breadth of dealignment trends, however, suggests that more than a series of coincidental political crises lie behind these trends. The sources of partisan dealignment more likely reflect broader patterns of social and political change in advanced industrial democracies. The declining role of parties as political institutions seems to play a key role in this process. Many of the parties' traditional political functions have been taken over by other institutions. A myriad of special interest groups and single-issue lobbies have developed in recent years, and political parties have little hope of representing all these groups. Instead, these groups press their interests without relying on partisan channels. Party leaders are even losing some control over the selection of elected party representatives. The most advanced example is the United States, where the expansion of open primaries and nonpartisan elections has undermined the parties' hold on recruitment. The British Labour Party has experienced a similar shift in nomination power away from the party in Parliament to party conventions and local constituency groups. In 1994 the German SPD selected its chancellor candidate through a mail ballot of its members. These and other developments lessen the importance of parties in the political process and therefore weaken the significance of parties as political reference points.

Changes in the mass media also contribute to dealignment trends. The mass media are assuming many of the information functions that political parties once controlled. Instead of learning about an election at a campaign rally or from party canvassers, television and newspapers have become the primary sources of campaign information (see chapter 2). Furthermore, the content of the mass media has changed to downplay the importance of political parties. The American media have shifted their campaign focus away from the political parties toward the candidates, and a weaker parallel trend is evident in several parliamentary democracies (Dalton and Wattenberg 2000, chap. 3).

Partisan dealignment is also encouraged by the failure of parties to deal successfully with contemporary political issues (Lawson and Merkl 1988; Zelle 1995). On the one hand, contemporary parties are struggling with problems of maintaining social services in the face of governmental budget limits. Some of the economic and welfare issues traditionally associated with the class cleavage have not been fully resolved. On the other hand, the new issues of advanced industrial societies often appear unsuited for mass political parties. Many of these issues, such as nuclear energy, minority rights, or local environmental problems, are too narrow to affect mass partisan alignments on their own. The rise of single-issue interests does not translate well into partisan attachments because of the uncertain electoral impact of these issues and the difficulty of accommodating these issues within large political coalitions. In the United States, this has led to a proliferation of citizen interest groups and direct-action politics; in Europe this has spawned similar groups as well as a variety of small parties on the Left and Right (Müller-Rommel and Pridham 1991). Analysts thus maintain that political parties have lessened their critical programmatic function of aggregating and articulating political interests.

Although these systematic factors are important, their ability to explain the dealignment trend has limitations. For instance, although it is true that some failures in party performance may have initially stimulated a dealignment trend, this trend did not reverse when a new party won control of the government or policy failure was replaced by policy success. Furthermore, each nation points to a unique set of policy failures, but the dealignment trend is a common feature across these diverse experiences. Thus, one looks for general changes affecting advanced industrial societies. Even the emphasis on the changing role of the media overlooks the diverse roles the media play across these nations, because of their different public/private ownership and different journalist norms. Thus, another factor to consider involves changes in the citizenry, which may have contributed to partisan dealignment.

Cognitive Mobilization and Apartisans

Part of the dealignment literature holds that the process of cognitive mobilization is increasing voters' political sophistication and thereby their ability to deal with the complexities of politics without reliance on external cues or heuristics (chapter 2). In addition, the growing availability of political information through the media reduces the costs of making informed decisions.

The process of cognitive mobilization thus lessens the need for citizens to develop party identifications as a shortcut to help them handle difficult and often confusing political decisions (Shiveley 1979; Borre and Katz 1973). In other words, the need to develop a habitual partisan attachment may be decreasing for certain groups of citizens, and thus they are less likely to develop party ties. Indeed, the self-defined political interests of the cognitively mobilized may drive them away from habitual party cues that provide less room for individual choice.

The cognitive mobilization theory also implies that the recent increase in independents will be concentrated among a distinct group of citizens: the better educated, the better informed, and those who are cognitively mobilized. In contrast, the early literature on partisanship held that nonpartisans were at the margins of the electoral process; they were uninvolved in elections and unsophisticated about politics (Campbell et al. 1960). If the growth of independents is concentrated among the politically unsophisticated, which is possible in some explanations of dealignment, then it would contradict the cognitive mobilization theory (and potentially represent a negative development for the contemporary democracies).

Research on the dealignment trends in advanced industrial societies tends to support the cognitive mobilization theory (Dalton 2000a). The greatest decline in partisanship occurs among the better educated and the cognitively mobilized. In addition, in most nations dealignment is concentrated among younger generations, who are now less likely to be socialized into a partisan identity. At the same time, there is less evidence that policy dissatisfaction is driving dealignment, which suggests that it is the pubic's changing norms rather than party performance that is stimulating dealignment.

These empirical findings lead us to think of party mobilization and cognitive mobilization as two alternative ways that citizens can connect themselves to the political process (Dalton 1984). Some voters remain oriented to politics based on their partisan attachments—and this is a potent source of political cues. In addition, cognitive mobilization produces another group of politically interested and well-educated voters who orient themselves to politics on their own. The combination of both traits defines a typology of four types of citizens (figure 9.5). Apoliticals are neither attached to a political party nor cognitively mobilized; this group conforms to the independents originally described by Campbell and his colleagues (1960, 143–45). Ritual partisans are mobilized into politics primarily by their strong party attachments and are not cognitively mobilized. Cognitive partisans are highly ranked on both mobilization dimensions. They have strong party attachments, and they are psychologically involved in politics even when party cues are lacking.

Apartisans are the "new independents." It is essential to distinguish apartisans from traditional independents (apoliticals). Apartisans are cognitively mobilized, which implies high levels of political involvement and sophistication, though these citizens remain unattached to any political party. Apartisans also are concentrated among the young, the better educated, and postmaterialists (Dalton 1984). Other research shows that the development of advanced indus-

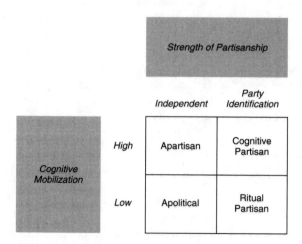

Figure 9.5   Patterns of Political Mobilization

trial societies is increasing the proportion of apartisans within contemporary publics as well as shifting the ratio of ritual and cognitive partisans. For instance, data from the American National Election Studies find that the number of apartisans more than doubled over the past forty years—to a quarter of the electorate.[8] In addition, the number of cognitive partisans has grown slightly, whereas the proportion of ritual partisans has decreased by more than half. Inglehart (1990, 366) found that the percentage of apartisans in Europe increased significantly over a single decade (1976–87). Furthermore, Inglehart found sharp differences in the percentage of apartisans across European generations, which suggests that the number of apartisans will continue to grow. Sören Holmberg's (1994) longitudinal analyses of Swedish partisanship yield similar findings.

The recognition of apartisans has several implications for contemporary political behavior. Apartisans have the political resources to follow the complexities of politics and they are free of affective party ties. Thus, these new independents are less consistent in their voting patterns because voting behavior is not dependent on long-standing party predispositions. This group also should inject more issue voting into elections and demand that candidates are more responsive to public opinion.

Apartisans should press for an expansion of citizen input beyond the narrow channel of elections and other party-related activities. The political skills of apartisans enable them to organize effective citizen action groups, citizen lobbies, protest demonstrations, and other unconventional political activities. The nonpartisan and issue-oriented characteristics of these activities make them ideal participation modes for apartisans.

Finally, ongoing processes of socioeconomic change gradually should increase the number of apartisans. The actions of parties in specific elections may hasten or retard this process in the short term. Nevertheless, the evidence suggests a long-term trend toward partisan dealignment in advanced industrial societies.

POLITICS IN A DEALIGNED ERA

Most elections involve a choice between parties or their representatives, and parties remain the central actors in the political process of most contemporary democracies. This chapter has argued that most citizens develop a psychological identification with a preferred political party, and these attachments are a potent guide for political behavior.

And yet the extent of these party ties is eroding in virtually all the advanced industrial democracies—producing a new characteristic of partisan dealignment. In addition, the decline has been more pronounced among the better educated and the politically engaged. It is as if the most sophisticated fans of the sport of politics are becoming disengaged with the partisan players they see on the field.

Furthermore, as with the weakening of the sociological model, the relative simultaneity of dealignment trends across various nations is striking. Long-term sources of partisan preferences—social characteristics and partisanship—are weakening in most advanced industrial societies. In a single nation, such developments might be explained by the specific trials and tribulations of the parties. When a pattern appears across a wide variety of nations, however, it suggests that the causes are common to advanced industrial societies. Indeed, in linking the process of cognitive mobilization to partisan dealignment, this seems to represent yet another feature of the new style of citizen politics. Cognitively mobilized citizens are better able to make, and more interested in making, their own political decisions without relying on heuristics or external cues. These new apartisans are producing the dealignment trend.

Weakening party bonds have real consequences for the operation of the political process. For instance, partisan dealignment is part of a general process of political change that is transforming the relationship between voters and parties (Dalton and Wattenberg 2000). The personal connection between parties and their members and voters is being replaced by professionalized organizations that rely on the media and direct mailing to connect to voters. Instead of depending on party members to staff election campaigns, these become professionalized activities by hired specialists. Instead of relying on party members' dues to fund party activities, many party systems are turning to public funding sources. As citizens' connections to the parties have weakened, the parties have sought alternative sources of support. Such changes in organizational style may exacerbate dealignment trends by further distancing parties from the voters.

Weakened party-line voting also may contribute to the unprecedented level of split-party control of both the federal and state governments in the United States (Brody et al. 1994). In 1988 only 40 percent of the states had one party in control of both legislative houses and the governor's office. Not since the formation of the Republican Party in the 1850s can one find any comparable split in the history of state party politics. Similarly, between 1981 and 1986 different parties controlled the House and Senate for the first time since 1916. Most visible, of course, is the division in partisan control of the presidency and Congress since 1952. From 1952 to 2000 the same party controlled the presidency and the House for just sixteen out of forty-four years. The culmination of these trends was the dramatic shift in partisan control of the U.S. Congress following the 1994 elections. After more than forty years of Democratic domination, the House fell to the Republicans without a corresponding realignment in partisan attachments.

The Federal Republic of Germany also has a federal system, and the same pattern is found there. For the first twenty years of the FRG's history, the same party coalition controlled the Bundestag (the directly elected lower house of Parliament) and the Bundesrat (which represents the majority of state governments). From 1976 until 2000 federal and state control has been divided for about one-third of this period. In Britain, one sees a growing regionalization of voting patterns, as local electoral results are less closely tied to national patterns.

Of course, one of the best signs of dealigned politics is the rise of new political parties that can draw on independents for their initial support. The number of political parties grew during the latter half of the twentieth century in most parliamentary democracies (Dalton and Wattenberg 2000, chap. 3). Even in the United States, Perot's candidacy in the 1992 and 1996 elections illustrates the potential to appeal to the growing number of nonpartisans. A candidate without prior political experience and without the support of a party apparatus garnered 19 percent of the U.S. presidential vote in 1992.[9] The rise of "flash parties," such as the success of Berlusconi's *Forza Italia!* or Jorg Haider's Freedom Party in Austria, and the general rise of New Left and New Right parties in Europe are additional indicators of the volatility now present in contemporary party systems.

Finally, the erosion of the influence of long-term sources of partisanship suggests that factors further along the funnel of causality can play a larger role in voter choice. Citizens are still voting, even if they are not relying on party cues or early-learned partisanship to the degree they once did. On the one hand, this might encourage the public to judge candidates and parties on their policies and governmental performance—producing a deliberative public that more closely proximates the classic democratic ideal. On the other hand, the lack of long-standing partisan loyalties may also make electorates more vulnerable to manipulation and demagogic appeals (Holmberg 1994, 113–14). Dealignment has the potential to yield both positive and negative consequences for electoral politics, depending on how party systems and voters react in this new context. The following chapters consider how the changing roles of issues and candidate images are affecting the calculus of elections.

SUGGESTED READINGS

Dalton, Russell, and Martin Wattenberg, eds. *Parties without Partisans: Political Change in Advanced Industrial Democracies.* New York: Oxford University Press, 2001.

Jennings, M. Kent, and Thomas Mann, eds. *Elections at Home and Abroad.* Ann Arbor: University of Michigan Press, 1994.

Rose, Richard, and Ian McAllister. *The Loyalties of Voters: A Lifetime Learning Model.* Newbury Park, Calif.: Sage Publications, 1990.

Wattenberg, Martin. *The Decline of American Political Parties.* Cambridge, Mass.: Harvard University Press, 1998.

NOTES

1. The standard party identification question is one of the most frequently asked questions in U.S. public opinion surveys. It measures both the direction of partisanship and the strength of party attachments: "Generally speaking, do you think of yourself as a Republican, a Democrat, an independent, or what?" For those expressing a party preference: "Would you call yourself a strong Republican/Democrat or a not very strong Republican/Democrat?" For independents: "Do you think of yourself as closer to the Republican or Democratic Party?"

   The question yields a seven-point measure of partisanship ranging from strong Democrat identifiers to strong Republican identifiers.

2. One of the current debates in the American voting literature is the question of how closely aggregate levels of partisanship track current voting preferences. For the contrasting sides of this debate, see MacKuen, Erikson, and Stimson (1989) and Abramson and Ostrom (1991, 1994).

3. For instance, the German version of the party identification question specifically cues the respondent that it is asking about long-term partisan leanings: "Many people in the Federal Republic lean toward a particular party for a long time, although they may occasionally vote for a different party. How about you?"

4. These data are drawn from the Political Action Survey. The study supplemented its national sample of adults with additional parent–child interviews in families in which a 16–20-year-old was still living in the parent's home. For additional analyses, see Jennings et al. (1979).

5. Fiorina (1981) describes partisanship as a "running tally" of an individual's accumulated electoral experience. If early partisan leanings are reinforced by later voting experience, party ties strengthen over time. If voting experiences counteract partisanship, then these party loyalties may gradually erode. Also see Niemi and Jennings (1991).

6. Researchers have debated whether age differences in American partisanship represent generational or life-cycle effects (Converse 1976; Abramson 1979). We emphasize the life-cycle (partisan learning) model because the cross-national pattern of age differences seems more consistent with this explanation.

7. Part of these relationships are due to patterns of accumulated partisanship over the life cycle. In addition, the lower levels of partisanship among the young can be traced partially to decreasing attachments among younger generations.

8. We define cognitively mobilized citizens as having a combination of interests and skills, that is, "very interested" in the election and/or having at least some college education. The following table presents the distribution of types using data from the American National Election Studies (also see Dalton 1984, 282):

	1952	1980	1992
Apartisans	10%	18%	24%
Cognitive partisans	32%	35%	41%
Ritual partisans	42%	28%	20%
Apoliticals	16%	19%	16%

9. The 1992 American National Election Study found that Perot garnered 10 percent of the vote among Democrat identifiers, 17 percent among Republican identifiers, and 36 percent among pure independents. This pattern continued in the 1996 election, and in 2000 both Buchanan and Nader gained the greatest percentage of their votes from independents.

CHAPTER 10

Attitudes and Electoral Behavior

PARTY CONFLICT MAY begin as the competition between rival social groups or party camps, but elections inevitably revolve around the issues and candidates of the campaign.[1] The issues and candidates are important because they give political meaning to the partisan attachments and social divisions we have discussed in earlier chapters. The electoral significance of partisanship (or class attachments) is expressed in the cluster of issue positions and candidate preferences that evolve from long-term partisan ties. Labour supporters, for example, do not just support the party out of blind loyalty, but because they share a belief in policies that the party normally advocates.

Issue beliefs and candidate images are also important because they represent the dynamic aspect of electoral politics. The distribution of partisanship may define the broad parameters of electoral competition. However, specific campaigns are fought over the policies the contenders advocate, the images of the candidates, or the government's policy performance. The mix of these factors almost always varies across elections, and thus issue beliefs and candidate images explain the ebb and flow of voting outcomes. This is why the funnel of causality (figure 9.1 on p. 173) locates issue beliefs and candidate images as proximate to voting choice. Although partisanship may partially determine these attitudes, the content of a campaign also shapes these attitudes and thus the ultimate voting decision.

Finally, as the electoral impact of long-term partisan attachments and social cues is decreasing, many political scientists maintain that there is a corresponding increase in the influence of issue opinions on voting choice (e.g., Franklin, Mackie, and Valen 1992). Martin Wattenberg (1991) has written provocatively about the rise of candidate-centered choices by American voters, and the role of candidate images is now more widely debated in European party systems (Kaase 1994; McAllister 1996).

This chapter examines the role of issues and candidate images in electoral choice. We consider both the conditions that determine the potential influence of these attitudes on the vote and their actual impact in contemporary party systems. This evidence enables us to complete our model of voter choice and discuss the implications of our findings for the democratic process.

INTERNET RESOURCE

Visit the Comparative Study of Electoral Systems Web site; the project conducted a parallel survey of voters in more than a dozen nations:

www.umich.edu/~nes/cses/cses.htm

PRINCIPLES OF ISSUE VOTING

The study of issue voting has been closely intertwined with the scholarly debate on the political sophistication of the citizenry. In theoretical terms, issue voting is presented as the defining feature of a sophisticated, rational electorate; voters evaluate the government and opposition and then thoughtfully cast a ballot for their preferred party. To the skeptics of mass democracy, this theoretical ideal seldom exists in reality. Instead, they see voters as lacking knowledge of the party's or their positions and often voting on the basis of ill-formed or even incorrect beliefs (see chapter 2).

The early empirical voting studies were often critical of the electorate's ability to make informed choices. The authors of *The American Voter* maintained that meaningful issue voting is based on three requirements: citizens should be interested in the issue, they should hold an opinion on the issue, and they should know the party or candidate positions on the issue (Campbell et al. 1960, chap. 8). *The American Voter* maintained that on most policy issues, most voters fail to meet these criteria. These researchers classified a third or less of the public as possible issue voters on each of a long list of policy topics. Moreover, Campbell and his colleagues at the University of Michigan believed that these small percentages reflected the conceptual and motivational limits of the electorate; the lack of issue voting was presumably an intrinsic aspect of mass politics (Converse 1990). These political scientists therefore rejected the notion that election results represent the policy choices of the public.

Even from the beginning of empirical voting research, there were critics of this negative image of issue voting. V.O. Key was one of the first to present survey evidence showing that citizens were "moved by concern about the central and relevant questions of public policy, of government performance, and of executive personality" (Key 1966, 7–8). In short, Key's unorthodox argument stated "voters are not fools." Key's position gradually has become less unorthodox as our understanding of citizen voting behavior has grown.

Because only a minority of the public may fulfill the criteria of rational issue voting for each specific issue, this does not mean that only a third of the total public are capable for any and all issues. Contemporary electorates are comprised of overlapping *issue publics*, groups of people interested in specific issues (see chapter 2). These issue publics vary in size and composition. A large and heterogeneous group of citizens may be interested in basic political issues such as taxes, inflation rates, budget deficits, and the threat of war. On more specific issues—agricultural policy, nuclear energy, transportation policy, foreign aid—the issue publics normally are smaller and politically distinct. Most voters are politically attentive on at least one issue, and many voters may belong to several issue publics. When citizens define their own issue interests, they can fulfill the issue-voting criteria for their issues of interest. For example, David RePass (1971) found that only 5 percent of Americans were interested in medical programs for the elderly, but more than 80 percent of this group could be classified as potential issue voters. Adopting a more diversified view of the electorate—not all citizens must be interested in all issues—greatly strengthens the evidence of issue voting.

The conflicting claims about the nature of issue voting also may arise because researchers think of issue voting in different terms or use contrasting empirical examples to support their claims. Indeed, the literature is full of descriptions of how various types of issues function within the electoral process, and why we must differentiate between issues.[2] Issue voting may be more likely for some sorts of issues than for others, and the implications of issue voting also may vary depending on the type of issue.

Figure 10.1 introduces a framework for thinking about issue voting. One important characteristic is the type of issue. *Position issues* involve conflicts over policy goals (Stokes 1963). A typical position issue might concern debates on whether or not the U.S. Congress should support the Kyoto agreement on global warming or whether or not Britain should privatize government-owned industries. Discussions of issue voting often focus on position issues that define the current political debate.

In contrast to position issues, *performance issues* involve judgments on how effectively the candidates or parties pursue widely accepted goals.[3] For instance, most voters favor a strong economy, but they may differ in how they evaluate a government's job in accomplishing this goal. Conflicting claims about performance judgments often lie at the heart of electoral campaigns. Finally, voters might judge the *attributes* of the parties or candidates; do they possess desired traits or characteristics? For example, a party must be considered trustworthy if its campaign promises are to be believed. These different issue characteristics reflect on the types of decisions being made and the implications of these decisions for judging voters and electoral outcomes.

Types of issue voting also can be characterized by the time frame of the voters' judgments (Fiorina 1981; Miller and Borrelli 1992; Abramson, Aldrich, and Rohde 1999, chap. 7). *Retrospective* judgments occur when citizens rate political actors primarily on their past performance. Evaluating Al Gore in 2000 based

Type of Issue

Time Frame	Position	Performance	Attribute
Retrospective	Policy Appraisal	Performance Evaluation	Attribute Voting
Prospective	Policy Mandate	Anticipatory Judgment	

Figure 10.1   A Classification of Issues

on the performance of the Clinton-Gore administration would be an example of retrospective voting. *Prospective* judgments are based on expectations of future performance. A voter judging Gore based on what his administration would do differently in the future would be an example of prospective voting.

Retrospective and prospective judgments hold different implications for the nature of citizen decision making. Retrospective judgments should have a firmer empirical base, since they arise from past experience. Retrospective political evaluations can be a relatively simple decision-making strategy: Praise the incumbents if times have been good, criticize them if times have been bad. A pure reliance on retrospective judgments limits the scope of citizen evaluations, however. Elections enable voters to select a government for the future, and these decisions should include evaluations of a party's promises and its prospects for success. Therefore, voting decisions should consider prospective judgments about a government's likely behavior in the future. Prospective judgments are based on a speculative and complex decision-making process. Individuals have to make their own forecasts and link these projections to the expected performance of political actors—a task that imposes a considerable information burden on the voter. How citizens balance retrospective and prospective judgments thus reflects directly on the nature of electoral decision making.

The combination of both sets of characteristics provides a typology of the different types of issue calculations that voters may use in elections. Some issue voting involves a *policy appraisal* that assesses a party's (or candidate's) past position on a policy controversy. For instance, when some voters supported Gore in 2000 because they favored strong measures to protect the environment, they were making a judgment about the past policies of the Clinton-Gore administration. Alternatively, voters may consider what a party or candidate promises in policy terms as the basis of their voting decision. When George W. Bush wanted voters to support him in 2000 in order to reduce taxes, he was asking for a *policy mandate* from the electorate.

Policy appraisal and policy mandates represent a sophisticated form of issue voting: Citizens are making choices between alternative policy goals for their government. This places high requirements on the voters: They must be informed, have a preferred policy, and see meaningful choices between the contenders. Sometimes this information is acquired directly by the voter, sometimes by using surrogate information sources (Popkin 1991; Lupia 1994).

In comparison, *performance evaluations* involve more general judgments about how a political actor (party or candidate) has been doing its job in the past. If the government has been successful, then voters support its return to office; if the government has struggled, then voters cast their ballots for an acceptable challenger to the incumbents. For example, in 1980 Ronald Reagan asked Americans to make a performance evaluation of Carter's presidency when he asked: "Are you better off than you were four years ago?" In other instances, voters might make *anticipatory judgments* about the future performance of government. For instance, some analysts claim that the Labour Party lost in 1992 because some voters doubted the party's ability to function effectively as a governing party, although they favored many of Labour's policy proposals.

Finally, some aspects of "issue voting" may involve candidate or party attributes as a basis of choice. This type of voting is less often conditioned by a time frame. Voters judge candidates on their personal characteristics, which although not immediately political in their content, are legitimate factors to consider in selecting a candidate (Kinder et al. 1980). As Carter's moral integrity helped him in 1976, Clinton's "slick Willie" image hurt him at the polls—and both images were politically relevant although they did not involve explicit policy or performance calculations. Similar stylistic considerations can influence voter choices for a political party. Tony Blair's 1997 victory in Britain and Gerhard Schröder's 1998 victory in Germany are at least partially attributed to their ability to project a dynamic, forward-looking image compared to their electoral opponents.

Electoral researchers consider attribute voting as a low level of political sophistication because this does not involve explicit policy criteria. As we will discuss later, however, many attributes involve traits that are directly relevant to the task of governing or to providing national leadership. Thus, we should consider attribute voting as a potentially meaningful basis of electoral choice.

The typology of figure 10.1 provides a framework for thinking about different aspects of issue voting. For example, Martin Wattenberg's (1991, chap. 6) analysis of support for Ronald Reagan provides an especially insightful example of how policy positions and performance evaluations are theoretically and empirically distinct aspects of issue voting. Some candidates can win because of their policy promises; some win despite their program. There is evidence that a similar interplay of factors was at work in the 2000 U.S. presidential election.

We will not explicitly examine each type of issue voting in this chapter. Still, we will highlight how various types of issues can influence contemporary electoral outcomes and the implications of each type for the nature of democratic politics.

POSITION ISSUES AND THE VOTE

Nearly a generation ago, some social scientists speculated about the imminent end of political conflict. They thought that advanced industrial societies would resolve the political controversies that have historically divided their populations (the controversies of the Old Politics), leading to the end of meaningful policy disagreements. We have witnessed just the opposite.

Contemporary electoral research documents the increased levels of policy-based voting in modern party systems. Real changes in the nature of electorates (and politics itself) have facilitated issue voting. The process of cognitive mobilization increases the number of voters who have the conceptual ability and political skills necessary to fulfill the issue-voting criteria. The growth of citizen action groups, new issue-oriented parties, and the general renaissance of ideological debate at election time are obvious signs of the public's greater issue awareness. Political elites have become more conscious of the public's preferences and more sensitive to the results of public opinion polls.

Advanced industrialism obviously has not meant the end of policy differences within these societies. Contemporary issue voting still involves many long-standing policy debates. Economic cycles inevitably stimulate shifting concerns about the economic role of government and the nature of the modern welfare system. Indeed, the 1980s saw a revival of economic controversy, spawned initially by economic recession and then by the "free market" programs of Reagan, Thatcher, Kohl, and other neoconservatives. Similarly, political events can often revive latent conflicts, such as the current debate over affirmative action in the United States, or renewed regional tensions in many democratic societies.

Issue controversies also are born from the changing nature of politics. This is most clear for foreign policy. The United States and other Western democracies are grappling with a new post–Cold War international system, in which international terrorists may become the major threat to peace. Germany is preoccupied with the problems of unification, and Europe is debating the future role of NATO and the European Union.

Another recent set of political controversies involves New Politics issues such as nuclear energy, women's rights, environmental protection, and related issues. These issues entered the political agenda of most advanced industrial democracies over the past few decades, introducing new political controversies and a heightened degree of policy polarization. Furthermore, these issues have played a special role in providing a political base for many new parties and reorienting the voting patterns of the young.

Faced with a diversity of issues across elections and electoral systems, it is difficult to provide a summary assessment of the impact of issues across time or nations. Indeed, the impact of issues should ebb and flow across time since they represent a dynamic part of elections. We can provide a general measure of the impact of policy preferences on voting behavior by examining the relationship between Left/Right attitudes and vote, however. Chapter 6 described Left/Right attitudes as a sort of "super issue," a statement of positions on the issues that are currently most important to each voter. For some voters, their Left/Right, position may be derived from positions on traditional economic conflicts; for others, Left/Right position may reflect positions on New Politics controversies—or Left/Right can signify a mix of different types of issues. The specific issues therefore might vary across individuals or across nations, but Left/Right attitudes can provide a single measure of each citizen's overall policy views.[4]

Most citizens can position themselves along a Left/Right scale, and these attitudes are linked to specific policy views, fulfilling the first two criteria of policy voting (Inglehart 1990). Figure 10.2 shows that citizens in each nation can also fulfill the third requirement: positioning the major political parties on this Left/Right scale. The figure presents the voters' average self-placement and the average score they assign to political parties in their respective nations.

American voters perceive fairly modest political differences between the Democrats and Republicans, a reflection of the diversity within these two large parties and the resulting policy overlap in the issue positions their candidates stress. And although specific presidential candidates might be perceived as relatively more or less ideological, the perceived positions of the parties themselves change relatively little from election to election.

The perceived party differences are much greater in the three European party systems. In France, for example, the political spectrum runs from the Communist Party at the leftist extreme to the National Front on the far right. By crude estimate, the French voter sees a range of party choices that extends more than twice as far across the political landscape in comparison to the differences among American political parties. Similarly, the German partisan landscape ranges from the PDS, the reformed communist party on the far Left, to the extremist Republikaner on the far Right. In Britain, the Labour and Conservative Parties assume distinct positions on the Left/Right scale, opening a void in the center that the Liberal Democrats occupy.[5] Most political observers would agree that these party placements are fairly accurate portrayals of actual party positions (e.g., Laver and Hunt 1992, chap. 7). Therefore, in overall terms citizens fulfill the third issue voting criterion: knowing party positions.

These Left/Right attitudes are strongly related to voting choice in every nation (table 10.1). The impact of Left/Right attitudes is greatest when a large number of parties offer clear policy options, as in France. A full 92 percent of self-identified French leftists favored a leftist party (Communists, Socialists, or Greens) in 1993, compared to only 5 percent among self-identified rightists. Even in the United States, there is a 46-percentage-point gap in the Democrats' share of the vote as a function of Left/Right attitudes. These voting differences are much larger than the effects of social characteristics noted in chapter 8. The

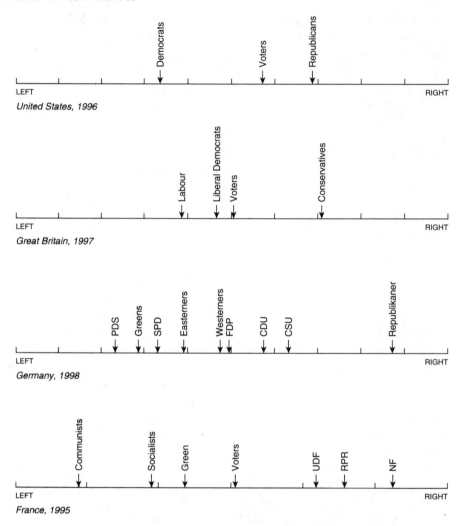

Figure 10.2   Left/Right Placement of the Parties and Voter Self-Placement

Sources: Comparative Study of Electoral Systems data for the United States, Britain, and Germany; the 1995 Presidential Election Study for France.

Notes: Figure entries are mean scores. An 11-point Left/Right scale was used in the CSES and a 7-point Left/Right scale was used in the French survey. The placement of the U.S. parties is estimated from other questions in the 1996 American National Election Study.

substantial influence of Left/Right attitudes exists because policy evaluations are located closer to the end of the funnel of causality.

The patterns of Left/Right voting also show the relative positions of the parties along this continuum. For instance, as the most extreme leftist party in

Table 10.1 Left/Right Attitudes and Party Support (in percentages)

Country	Left		Center		Right
United States, 1996					
Democrat	76	72	54	28	30
Republican	24	28	46	72	70
Total	100	100	100	100	100
Great Britain, 1997					
Labour	83	74	46	17	22
Liberal Democrats	7	15	22	12	7
Conservatives	3	4	23	66	64
Other parties	7	7	9	5	7
Total	100	100	100	100	100
Germany, 1998					
PDS	27	8	2	0	0
Greens	13	18	5	2	0
SPD	49	60	44	24	19
FDP	4	3	9	6	7
CDU/CSU	4	11	39	57	57
Rep/DVU	0	1	0	8	16
Other parties	2	0	1	3	1
Total	99	101	100	100	100
France, 1995					
PCF, extreme Left	30	12	5	2	1
Socialists	56	72	33	4	3
Greens	6	7	8	2	1
UDF	3	4	25	41	34
RPR	3	3	22	44	42
NF, other Right	2	3	7	7	19
Total	100	101	100	100	100

Source: Comparative Study of Electoral Systems, 1995 French Presidential Election Study.

France, the PC attracts the greatest share of its vote among the most extreme leftists; the Socialists do best among more moderate leftists. This pattern is mirrored in support for the UDF and RPR on the Right. Another significant contrast occurs between the Greens in Germany and France. The German Greens' disproportionate support from leftists shows their position along this continuum, whereas the French Greens are more likely to draw support from the Center, reflecting their relative positions in figure 10.2.

We can add more detail to how issue positions affect votes by studying the relationship between specific policy attitudes and party preferences. Several surveys from the International Social Survey Program include different issue positions across several policy domains (see chapter 6 for additional discussion of these items). Table 10.2 describes the relationship between these issue positions and party choices in our four nations.[6] We should be cautious about overinterpreting these data. The strength of each relationship reflects both the varying size of the relevant issue public and the clarity of party positions. The dynamic, short-term nature of issue beliefs means that either of these factors, and thus the impact of an issue, may change greatly between elections. These data, therefore, are only a snapshot

Table 10.2   The Correlation between Issue Opinions and Party Preferences

Issue	United States	Great Britain	Germany	France
Left/Right attitudes	.27	.27	.25	.57
Socioeconomic issues				
Social services over taxes	.35	.22	.21	.37
Less government regulation	.17	.14	.09	.21
Government redistributes wealth	.19	.30	.13	.30
Government controls wages	.16	.17	.14	.20
Government controls prices	.15	.14	.14	.17
Environmental issues				
Spend more on environment	.19	.16	.15	.22
Government responsible for environmental laws	.14	.12	.12	.16
Environment over economy	.07	.11	.12	—
Nuclear power a threat	.11	.14	.12	—
Gender issues				
Husband works/wife at home	.11	.15	.17	.18
Family suffers if wife works	.11	.12	.13	.16
Abortion justified if birth defect	.10	.16	.08	.14
Abortion justified if family poor	.12	.14	.13	.15
Foreign policy issues				
Spend more on defense	.14	.15	.15	.26

Sources: 1993, 1996, 1998 International Social Survey Program; Left/Right correlation from the Comparative Study of Electoral Systems and 1995 French Presidential Election Survey.

Note: Table entries are Cramer's V coefficients.

description of the relationship between issue opinions and party preferences, and not an explanation. Still, snapshots provide a valuable picture of reality.

The traditional economic issues of the Old Politics—such as support for social services and governmental measures to lessen income inequality and manage the economy—display strong relationships with party preferences in all four nations. The impact of these issues is greatest in France, where the Communist Party and the Right vie over distinctly different economic programs. In each nation, however, the strongest correlation involves an economic issue. This pattern is perpetuated across most elections because economic topics have large issue publics and most political parties have clear policies on issues of the government's role in the economic and related economic policies (see figure 7.2 on p. 138). These issues were even significantly related to partisan preferences in the 1993 American survey because Newt Gingrich and the Republicans were renewing their challenges against Clinton's social spending programs.

New Politics issues dealing with the environment have a modest impact on party choice. In Britain, for instance, the average correlation for socioeconomic issues is .19; for environmental issues the average is .13. Although many people are interested in issues such as environmental protection, the translation of policy attitudes into party preferences is still limited. Partially this is because materialist, economic issues still attract greater attention. In addition, the established parties often offer less distinct policy choices on environmental and other New Politics issues. For instance, although the German Greens have a distinct profile on environmental issues, the positions of the CDU/CSU, SPD, and FDP are less clear-cut (figure 7.2, p. 138). This same pattern applies to many gender-related issues. This reflects the tendency of New Politics issues to cut across traditional party lines. New Politics issues are significant more for their potential impact than for their present influence on electoral outcomes.

Foreign policy issues normally are weakly related to party preferences. France is the one nation where foreign policy issues often impact on partisanship; this reflects continuing conflicts over France's role in the international system ranging from its relation to NATO to the policies of European unification. Foreign policy can sometimes influence partisan choice (Aldrich, Sullivan, and Bordida 1989), but its impact is normally secondary to domestic issues. Foreign policy issues attract the primary attention of only a small share of the public, except at times of international crisis. Party differences on most foreign issues are also modest in comparison to party polarization on many other topics.

A much richer compendium of information on issue voting exists for each nation separately (Abramson, Aldrich, and Rohde 1999; Evans and Norris 1999; Boy and Mayer 1993). This literature indicates that many position issues potentially influence the partisan preferences of contemporary electorates. The impact of any one issue for the entire public is often modest because not all issues are salient to all voters. A more refined analysis of specific issue publics would find that individual voting decisions are heavily influenced by each voter's specific issue interests. When these findings are combined with evidence of increasing issue voting overall, Key's (1966) positive assessments of the public's voting decisions no longer appear so unorthodox.

PERFORMANCE ISSUES AND THE VOTE

Another element of issue voting involves performance as a basis for electoral choice. Many voters say they turn to performance criteria, judging the success of the incumbents or their prospects for the future, as part of their voting decision. Fiorina put it best when he stated that citizens "typically have one comparatively hard bit of data: they know what life has been like during the incumbent's administration. They do not need to know the precise economic or foreign policies of the incumbent administration in order to judge the results of those policies" (1981, 5). In other words, performance-based voting offers people a reasonable shortcut for ensuring that unsuccessful policies are dropped and successful policies continued.

This literature argues that it is only important that voters dispense electoral rewards and punishments—regardless of whether or not the policies and the outcomes are connected. Benjamin Page (1978, 222), for example, writes that "even if the Great Depression and lack of recovery were not at all Hoover's fault . . . it could make sense to punish him in order to sharpen the incentives to maintain prosperity in the future." He acknowledged that blame may be placed unfairly, yet "to err on the side of forgiveness would leave voters vulnerable to tricky explanations and rationalizations; but to err on the draconian side would only spur politicians on to greater energy and imagination in problem solving." Therefore, performance voting requires that voters have a target for their blame when the government falters in some respect. Typically, this target is poor economic performance, although voters can consider foreign policy performance or other policy areas.

The literature on performance-based economic voting has burgeoned in recent years. Considerable evidence documents the importance of macroeconomics on micropolitics, both in the United States (MacKuen, Erikson, and Stimson 1992) and Europe (Lewis-Beck 1988; Lewis-Beck and Paldam 2000; Anderson 1995; Norpoth 1992). Even a simple measure of performance evaluation—overall judgments about the performance of the national economy over the past twelve months—displays a significant relationship with party preferences. Figure 10.3 displays the relationship between perceptions that the economy is improving/worsening and support for the incumbent party. In each case there is a clear tendency for negative economic perceptions to hurt the incumbents and positive perceptions to benefit the party in power. In the 1997 British election, for example, John Major's Conservatives won 48 percent among those who thought the economy was improving versus only 5 percent among those who thought the economy was deteriorating.

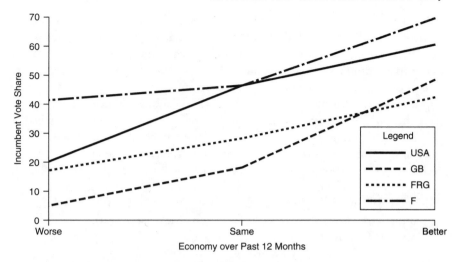

Figure 10.3   The Relationship between Economic Perceptions and Support for the Incumbent Party

Sources: Comparative Study of Electoral Systems data for the United States, Britain, and Germany; the 1995 Presidential Election Study for France.

Note: Figure entries are the percentage of the vote share given to the incumbent party.

One might ask, however, whether or not these relationships are really evidence of causality. As we noted in chapter 9, some people adjust their economic expectations to reflect their other images of the government (see p. 206). If voters like the incumbent, they are more likely to put a favorable spin on economic conditions; if voters are critical of government for one aspect of policy, they may generalize this dissatisfaction to their economic judgments. Such projections are a normal part of incumbent images (Page and Jones 1979). These projections likely magnify the relationship between economic perceptions and party preferences, but the underlying relationship is still important. A rising economic tide benefits the incumbents, and a failing economy often spells defeat at the next election.

Another factor involves the exact scope and nature of economic influences. One point of debate concerns whether voters base their political evaluations on their own personal economic situation (pocketbook voting) or the performance of the broader national economy (sociotropic voting). Most of the evidence suggests that voters follow the sociotropic model, which implies that policy outcomes rather than narrow self-interest are the driving force behind performance voting (Kinder and Kiewiet 1981; Lewis-Beck 1988). Researchers also disagree on whether voters evaluate performance retrospectively or base their judgments on prospective expectations (see Fiorina 1981; Miller and Wattenberg 1985; Mac-Kuen, Erikson, and Stimson 1992).

The state of the economy can be so important in some elections that it overrides other policy considerations. Many election analysts claim that incumbent parties are virtually unbeatable during strong economic upturns and extremely vulnerable during recessionary periods (this was before Gore's loss in 2000). For example, researchers argue that Americans and Britons elected conservative governments in 1979 and 1980 not for ideological reasons but merely because they were the only instruments available for defeating incumbents who had failed to deliver the economic goods (Crewe and Searing 1988; Wattenberg 1991). Four years after coming to power, both Margaret Thatcher and Ronald Reagan won reelection on the basis of improved economic performance (and the Falklands War in the case of Thatcher)—in spite of continuing policy differences with most of their country's voters (Norpoth 1992). Others have documented the role of economic performance in German elections (Anderson 1995).

Although narrow performance voting does not conform to democratic theory's emphasis on policy evaluation, researchers defend performance voting as entirely rational. Does it make sense, they ask, to pay much attention to the positions of an ineffective administration that seemingly cannot make good on its promises and program? Retrospective voting theorists emphasize that the only really effective weapon of popular control in a democratic regime is the electorate's capacity to throw a party from power.

CANDIDATE IMAGES AND THE VOTE

Democratic theorists describe issue voting in positive terms, but they view candidate-based voting decisions less positively. Some voting researchers have described voting on the basis of personality characteristics as "irrational" (cf. Converse 1964; Page 1978). They view candidate images as commodities packaged by image makers who manipulate the public by emphasizing traits with special appeal to the voters. People's judgments about alternative candidates are, in this view, based on superficial criteria such as the candidate's style or looks (e.g., Sullivan and Masters 1988). Indeed, there is much experimental evidence indicating that it is possible to manipulate a candidate's personal appearance to affect voters' choices.

Recently the voting literature has stressed a different approach to candidate assessments. This emerging view holds that candidate evaluations are not necessarily superficial, emotional, or purely short-term. Voters may focus on the personal qualities of a candidate to gain important information about characteristics relevant to assessing how the individual will perform in office (Kinder 1986; Miller, Wattenberg, and Malanchuk 1986; Rahn et al. 1990). This approach presumes that individuals organize their thoughts about other people into broad preexisting categories. These category "prototypes" are used in making judgments when limited factual information is available. Donald Kinder and his colleagues

(1980), for example, explored the features that citizens use to define an ideal president. They showed that people can choose attributes they believe would make for an ideal president, but these prototypic conceptions are only related to ratings of the incumbent president.

Arthur Miller, Martin Wattenberg, and Oksana Malanchuk presented data to support a rational voter interpretation of candidate evaluations. They argued that "candidate assessments actually concentrate on instrumental concerns about how a candidate would conduct governmental affairs" (1986, 536). Analyzing candidate image data from the American National Election Studies, they found that the three most important dimensions of candidate image for Americans are integrity, reliability, and competence. Such criteria are hardly irrational, for if a candidate is too incompetent to carry out policy promises or too dishonest for those promises to be trusted, it makes perfect sense for a voter to pay attention to personality as well as policies. Interestingly, both David Glass (1985) and Miller, Wattenberg, and Malanchuk (1986) found that college-educated voters are the most likely to judge the candidates by their personal attributes.

The United States is certainly in the lead in developing a pattern of candidate-centered electoral politics (Wattenberg 1991). Presidents are the focal point of the quadrennial elections, and the large shifts in vote shares between presidential elections has often been traced to the effects of candidate images (Stokes 1963). Presidents (and executives in state and local governments) are elected independently of their legislatures and largely run on personal platforms rather than as representatives of a fixed party position. Thus, candidate image is one of their major electoral resources. To an extent, a similar personalization of politics occurs in France, where the president functions separately from the legislative majority and even his own party within the legislature.

Electoral research on parliamentary systems initially suggested that popular images of party leaders had a minor impact on voting choice because these electorates did not directly vote for the chief executive. Recent research, however, finds significant effects. Clive Bean and Anthony Mughan (1989) showed that the perceived effectiveness of party leaders was moderately important in the British election of 1983 and possibly decisive in the Australian election of 1987. Analyses of German parliamentary elections similarly emphasized the growing role of candidate images (Ohr 2000). French politics has long valued the importance of a strong political leader, institutionalized in its directly elected presidency. Thus, evidence from elections and from internal party politics points to the growing importance of candidate images even in parliamentary systems (Pryce 1997; McAllister 1996; Ansell and Fish 1999). Anyone who has watched modern parliamentary campaigns, with candidates staging walkabouts for television and hosting discussion sessions with voters (in front of the cameras), must recognize that candidate images have become a growing part of contemporary electoral campaigns in virtually all advanced industrial democracies.

THE END OF THE CAUSAL FUNNEL

When we reach the end of the causal funnel and individuals are ready to vote, it is difficult to come to a precise assessment of the influence of partisanship, issues, and candidate images on voting choices. Since candidate images are at the very end of the funnel of causality, they have a strong relationship to voting preferences, at least in systems in which voters cast a ballot for a specific candidate. But at the same time, candidate images are themselves the cumulation of prior influences. Long-term partisanship can have a potent effect in cuing voters on which politicians to like and to dislike, just as voters' issue preferences can lead them toward specific candidates. Thus, it is often difficult to determine the separate causal influences when there is such overlap. In the 1994 German election, for instance, among those who voted for the CDU/CSU, 92 percent preferred Helmut Kohl as chancellor; among SPD voters, 84 percent favored Rudolf Scharping.

Furthermore, in parliamentary systems partisan and candidate preferences are often closely intertwined because parliamentary candidates normally are chosen merely for the party they represent, and in some nations citizens vote directly for parties. In very few party systems do voters directly cast ballots for the governmental leaders; British voters did not elect Blair and German voters did not elect Schröder; both were selected by the partisan majority of Parliament. Only in a system of direct election of candidates who can exercise autonomy from their party—such as the U.S. and French presidents—are we likely to see much separation between party preferences and candidate preferences.

So in the nexus of overlapping candidate, party, and issue preferences, it is difficult to separate the independent influence of each. But an illustration of the mix of factors at play can be drawn from comparing the weight of several core variables discussed in this chapter across our set of nations. Figure 10.4 combines Left/Right attitudes, economic perceptions, and candidate image to explain voting choices. (Of course, there are other factors that should be considered, such as party identification and social group cues, but the figure summarizes the key variables at the end of the causal funnel.) Each of these factors is significantly related to voting preferences, but perhaps the most interesting feature is the relative pattern across nations. The effect of candidate image—in this case, feelings toward Bill Clinton—were strongest in the American survey, even though we were predicting congressional voting preferences in 1996.[7] Although the 1997 British elections and the 1998 German elections were widely interpreted as personal triumphs for Tony Blair and Gerhard Schröder, images of the incumbent party leader exerted less weight in these two elections. This is strong evidence of the personalization of American party politics, in which candidate images sometimes overwhelm partisan images (Wattenberg 1991).

Issues—represented here by Left/Right attitudes or economic perceptions—generally carry more weight in European parliamentary elections, and this is seen in the patterns for Britain and Germany. Since European parties offer clearer

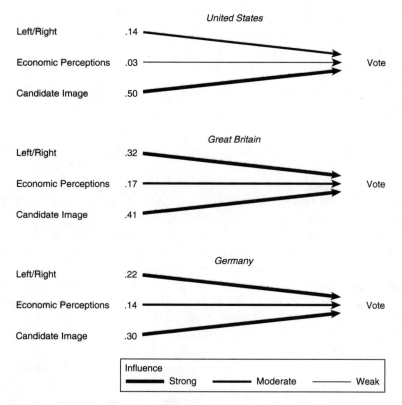

Figure 10.4   The Influence of Issues and Candidate Images on Vote

Source: Comparative Study of Electoral Systems.

Note: Figure entries are standardized regression coefficients.

party choices than American parties, and people vote for a party more so than for a candidate, it is not surprising that the policy images of the parties are a stronger basis of voting in European elections. The specific mix of issue and candidate influences will be highly variable across elections because these are short-term elements of the vote, but these trans-Atlantic differences reflect institutional structures that are likely to endure over time.[8]

CITIZEN POLITICS AND VOTING BEHAVIOR

The last several chapters have described the changing patterns of voting behavior in advanced industrial democracies. One major change is a general decline in the long-term determinants of voting choice. The influence of social class on voting preferences has decreased in virtually all Western democracies, as has the impact of religion, residence, and other social characteristics (chapter 8). Similarly, dealignment trends signal a decrease in the impact of enduring party attachments on voting decisions (chapter 9). Fewer voters now approach elections with standing party predispositions based either on social characteristics or early-learned partisan ties.

As the long-term determinants of party choice have decreased in influence, there has been a counterbalancing growth in the importance of short-term attitudes such as issue opinions (and possibly candidate image) (see Miller and Borrelli 1992; Franklin 1985; Rose and McAllister 1986). The most persuasive cross-national evidence comes from a study of voting behavior in seventeen Western democracies. In reviewing their findings, Franklin and his colleagues (1992, 400) conclude: "If all the issues of importance to voters had been measured and given their due weight, then the rise of issue voting would have compensated more or less precisely for the decline in cleavage politics."

This trend toward greater issue voting (and possibly candidate voting) in most Western nations is a self-reinforcing process. Issue voting contributes to, and benefits from, the concomitant decline in party voting patterns. The weakening of party ties increases the potential for issue opinions to influence voting choice. In addition, the increasing importance to the voter of policy preferences encourages some party defection and erodes the voter's party attachments.[9] Thus, the rise of issue voting and the decline of partisanship are interrelated trends.

This shifting balance of long-term and short-term voting influences represents another aspect of the new style of citizen politics. As modern electorates have become more sophisticated and politically interested, and as the availability of political information has expanded, many citizens can now reach their own voting decisions without relying on broad external cues such as social class or family partisanship. In short, more citizens now have the political resources to follow the complexities of politics; they have the potential to act as the independent issue voters described in classic democratic theory but seldom seen in practice.

Additional evidence in support of this interpretation comes from the work on cognitive sophistication by Sniderman, Brody, and Tetlock (1991). These researchers find that the better educated and the politically sophisticated place more weight on issues as a basis of their electoral decision making; less sophisticated voters rely more on partisanship and social cues. These findings conform to evidence from chapter 9 that locates sophisticated apartisans within the better educated, especially among the young (also see Dalton 2000a). Taking these two developments together, social change is shifting the basis of electoral choice by transforming the skills and resources of contemporary electorates.

We can illustrate the changing styles of citizen voting behavior by the changing impact of economics on the vote. Traditionally, economic conflicts were structured by social divisions: the working class versus the middle class, industrial versus agrarian interests. In this situation, one's social position was often a meaningful guide to voting decisions. As social divisions have narrowed and the group bases of political interests have blurred, social class has decreased as a source of voting cues. This does not mean that economic issues are unimportant. Quite the opposite. Contemporary evidence of economic voting is widespread, but now issue positions are individually based rather than group derived. The political cues of a union leader or business association must compete with the voter's own opinions on economic policy and party programs. That a partial return to the old issues of economic growth and security has not revived traditional class divisions provides compelling evidence that a new style of citizen politics now affects voting patterns.

This new style of individually based voting decisions may signify a boon or a curse for contemporary democracies. On the positive side, sophisticated voters should inject more issue voting into elections, increasing the policy implications of electoral results. In the long term, greater issue voting may make candidates and parties more responsive to public opinion. Thus, the democratic process may move closer to the democratic ideal.

On the negative side, many political scientists have expressed concerns that the growth of issue voting and single-issue groups may place excessive demands on contemporary democracies (see chapter 12). Without the issue-aggregating functions performed by party leaders and electoral coalitions, democratic governments may face conflicting issue demands from their voters. Governments may find it increasingly difficult to satisfy unrestrained popular demands.

Another concern involves the citizens who lack the political skills to meet the requirements of sophisticated issue voting. These people may become atomized voters if traditional political cues (party and social groups) decline in usefulness. Lacking firm political predispositions and a clear understanding of politics, these individuals may be easily mobilized by charismatic elites or fraudulent party programs. Many political analysts see the rise of New Right parties in Europe, especially those headed by a dynamic party leader, as negative consequence of a dealigned electorate. Indeed, the development of television facilitates unmediated one-on-one contacts between political elites and voters. Despite its potential for encouraging more sophisticated citizen involvement, television also offers the possibility of trivialized electoral politics in which video style outweighs substance in campaigning.

In summary, the trends discussed here do not lend themselves to a single prediction of the future of democratic party systems. But the future is within our control, depending on how political systems respond to these new challenges. The new style of citizen politics will be characterized by a greater diversity of voting patterns. A system of frozen social cleavages and stable party alignments is less likely in advanced industrial societies in which voters are sophisticated, power is decentralized, and individual choice is given greater latitude. The diversity and individualism of the new style of citizen politics are major departures from the structured partisan politics of the past.

SUGGESTED READINGS

Anderson, Christopher. *Blaming the Government: Citizens and the Economy in Five European Democracies.* Armonk, N.Y.: M.E. Sharpe, 1995.

LeDuc, Lawrence, Richard Niemi, and Pippa Norris, eds. *Comparing Democracies: Elections and Voting in Global Perspective,* 2d ed. Thousand Oaks, Calif.: Sage Publications, 2002.

Miller, Warren, and J. Merrill Shanks. *The New American Voter.* Cambridge, Mass.: Harvard University Press, 1996.

Niemi, Richard, and Herbert Weisberg, eds. *Controversies in Voting,* 4th ed. Washington, D.C.: Congressional Quarterly Press, 2001.

Wattenberg, Martin. *The Rise of Candidate-centered Politics.* Cambridge, Mass.: Harvard University Press, 1991.

NOTES

1. I want to acknowledge my collaboration with Martin Wattenberg (Dalton and Wattenberg 1993), which helped to develop my thinking on many of these issues.

2. For example, Carmines and Stimson (1980) make a distinction between "hard" issues, which are complex and difficult to evaluate, and "easy" issues, which present clear and simple choices. Kinder and Kiewit (1981) stress the distinction between personal issues of self-interest, such as voting on the basis of narrow economic self-interest, and issues that reflect national policy choices, such as voting on the basis of what will benefit most Americans.

3. Berelson, Lazarsfeld, and McPhee (1954) described these as *style issues*; Stokes (1963) used the term *valence issue.* Later research made the further distinction between performance and attributes that we present here (Miller and Wattenberg 1985; Shanks and Miller 1990).

4. Downs conceived of Left/Right labels as a way to reduce information costs rather than as fully informed ideological orientations. As he explained (Downs 1957, 98): "With this short-cut a voter can save himself the cost of being informed upon a wide range of issues."

5. Several pieces of evidence point to a conscious effort by the Labour Party to moderate its leftist image in 1997 (Evans and Norris 1999, chaps. 1 and 2). Moving closer to the voters was a key factor in propelling the party to victory.

6. The relationship is described by a Cramer's V correlation statistic. A value of .00 means that issue opinions are unrelated to party preference. A Cramer's V of .20 is normally interpreted as a moderate relationship, and .30 is considered a strong relationship.

7. Understandably, the relationship between candidate preference and vote is even higher in American presidential elections. In the 1996 election, about 95 percent of those who rated Clinton or Dole as their most favorable candidate followed by voting for the preferred candidate.

8. One productive new area of research examines how institutional context systematically affects the correlates of voting. For instance, candidate effects are predictably stronger in a candidate-based system than in party-based proportional representation. In addition, the ability of the electorate to identify party responsibility also affects the potential for issue voting. See, for example, Powell (2000), Anderson (2000), Miller and Niemi (2002), Whitten and Palmer (1999).

9. The conventional wisdom holds that partisanship is often a strong influence on issue opinions, whereas the reverse causal flow is minimal (figure 9.1, p. 173). As issue voting has increased, researchers have found that issues can remold basic party attachments. Recent studies show that the causal influence of issues in changing partisanship can be quite large (Niemi and Jennings 1991; Fiorina 1981).

CHAPTER 11

Political Representation

CONTEMPORARY DEMOCRACIES OWE their existence to a relatively modern invention: representative government. From the ancient Greeks up through the time of Rousseau, democracy was equated with the direct participation of the citizenry in the affairs of government. Political theorists believed that democracies must limit the definition of citizenship or the size of the polity so the entire public could assemble in a single body to make political decisions. The Greek city-state, the self-governing Swiss canton, and the New England town meeting exemplify this democratic ideal.

The invention of representative government freed democracies from these constraints. Instead of directly participating in political decision making, groups of citizens selected legislators to represent them in governmental deliberations. The functioning of the democratic process depended on the relationship between the representative and the represented.

The case for representative government is largely one of necessity. Democracy requires citizen control over the political process, but in a large nation-state the town meeting model is no longer feasible.[1] Proponents of representative government also stress the limited political skills of the average citizen and the need for professional politicians. Citizen control over government is routinized through periodic, competitive elections to select these elites. Elections should ensure that elites remain responsive and accountable to the public. By accepting this electoral process, the public gives its consent to be governed by the elites selected.

Many early democratic theorists criticized the concept of representative government and believed that it undermined the very tenets of democracy. Representative government transferred political power from the people to a small group of designated elites. Voters had political power only on the day their ballots were cast and then waited in political servitude until the next election—four or five years hence. Under representative government, the citizens may control, but elites rule. Jean Jacques Rousseau warned that "the instant a people allows itself to be represented it loses its freedom."

Recent proponents of direct democracy are equally critical of representative government. European Green parties, for example, criticize the structure of repre-

INTERNET RESOURCE

Visit the Eurobarometer Web site of the European Union with information on its latest citizen and elite surveys:

europa.eu/int/comm/dg10/epo/

sentative government while calling for increased citizen influence through referendums, citizen action groups, and other forms of "basic" democracy. Populist groups in the United States display a similar skepticism of electoral politics in favor of direct action. Benjamin Barber articulated these concerns:

> The representative government principle steals from individuals the ultimate responsibility for their values, beliefs, and actions. . . . Representation is incompatible with freedom because it delegates and thus alienates political will at the cost of genuine self-government and autonomy. (1984, 145)

These critics worry that the democratic principle of popular control of the government has been replaced by a commitment to routinized electoral procedures; democracy is defined by its means, not its ends. Thus, other opportunities for increasing public influence and control are not developed because elections provide the accepted standard of citizen influence. These critics are not intrinsically opposed to representative government, but they oppose a political system that stops at representation and limits or excludes other (and perhaps more influential) methods of citizen influence.

The linkage between the public and political decision makers is one of the essential questions for the study of democratic political systems. The commitment to popular rule is what sets democracies apart from other political systems. Although we cannot resolve the debate on the merits of representative government, this chapter asks how well the representation process functions in Western democracies today.

COLLECTIVE CORRESPONDENCE

In the broadest sense of the term, the representativeness of elite attitudes is measured by their similarity to the overall attitudes of the public. Robert Weissberg (1978) referred to this comparison as *collective correspondence*. When the distribution of public preferences is matched by the distribution of elite views, the citizenry as a collective is well represented by elites as a collective.

The complexity of the representation process obviously goes beyond a definition based simply on citizen–elite agreement. Some political elites may stress their role in educating the public instead of merely reflecting current public preferences. In other instances, voters may hold contradictory opinions, and the policymaking role of elites may lead them to adopt more consistent but less representative opinions. Policy preferences also are not necessarily equivalent to policy outcomes. We could add other qualifiers to this list. Still, citizen–elite agreement is the normal standard for judging the representativeness of a democratic system. This is a meaningful test of representation because it determines whether or not political decision makers enter the policy process with the same policy preferences as the public. This is a basic goal of representative democracy.

Data comparing the beliefs of top-level political elites and the public for our set of nations are extremely rare. More common are studies that focus on public–elite comparisons in a single nation (Miller and Jennings 1986; Miller 1987; Bürklin et al. 1990; Herzog and Wessels 1990; Converse and Pierce 1986; Esaiasson and Holmberg 1996; McAllister 1991). Therefore, our comparative analyses must rely on an early study of European voters and candidates to the European Parliament (EP) (Dalton 1985). Where possible, we update these results with findings from more recent studies.

Table 11.1 presents the distribution of citizen and elite opinions in Britain, Germany, and France. The broadest measure of political orientations is the Left/Right self-placement scale discussed in chapter 6. The first row in the table shows that EP elites in each nation are significantly more likely than the public to identify themselves as leftists. This liberal tendency among political elites is a common finding; a survey of voters and EP candidates in the 1994 election found a similar pattern (Thomassen and Schmitt 1997). Political elites apparently consider themselves to be more progressive than their constituencies.

Collective correspondence on specific issues varies across these three nations. The British elites are more liberal than the public on most issues. This elite bias is strongest for foreign aid and security issues, probably because they are candidates for the European Parliament. Abortion policy is the only area in which the British public is much more liberal than elites.

More recent data have been collected by the 1992 British Candidates Survey and the 1997 British Representation Study (Norris 1999d). In 1997 the average British citizen and member of the British Parliament positioned themselves at virtually the same position on the Left/Right scale. On traditional economic issues—taxes versus services, privatization and jobs versus prices—the MPs are slightly to the Right of the British public. On the two noneconomic issues of European integration and the role of women, the MPs are to the Left of the public.

Table 11.1 suggests that the German public is slightly more liberal than political elites on the Old Politics issue conflicts of economics and abortion. Conversely, elites are significantly more liberal on foreign aid, dealing with terrorists, and the free speech issue. Recent German citizen–elite studies find similar patterns of agreement. Bernhard Wessels (1993) compared the issue opinions of

Table 11.1 The Distribution of Opinions for the European Public and Elites (in percentages)

	GREAT BRITAIN		WEST GERMANY		FRANCE	
	Public	Elites	Public	Elites	Public	Elites
Leftist self-placement	42	46	42	57	47	68
Old Politics						
Public ownership of industry	30	35	34	27	41	48
Government manages economy	44	38	45	32	56	44
Codetermination	52	54	69	60	73	52
Control multinationals	50	66	66	75	72	86
Reduce income inequality	65	64	76	88	93	93
Liberalize abortion	77	58	75	65	77	74
Foreign aid						
Aid EC regions	45	90	47	98	71	90
Aid Third World	35	85	40	93	52	82
Security						
Strengthen defense	18	25	30	22	34	32
Action against terrorists	5	29	12	30	8	15
New Politics						
Nuclear energy	21	23	34	19	34	15
Protest environment	94	92	88	97	94	92
Free expression	72	78	76	79	74	86
Average liberal issue response	46	57	53	60	60	62

Sources: 1979 Eurocandidate Survey, Eurobarometer 11; both studies have been weighted to produce representative national samples.

Note: Table entries are the percentages of respondents expressing a liberal opinion on each item.

Bundestag deputies and the German public. He found close agreement on Old Politics issues such as economic growth and public order, and somewhat lower levels of agreement on New Politics goals (also see Herzog and Wessels 1990, chap. 3; Hoffmann-Lange 1992).

The closest overall match between citizen and EP elite opinions occurs in the French data. French citizens and elites generally favor liberal policies on Old Politics issues, and there are no consistent differences between political strata on these issues. The pattern on New Politics and security issues is equally mixed. Only on foreign aid issues are EP elites clearly more liberal than the French public (also see Converse and Pierce 1986, 597).

Similar data describing the views of American voters and political elites are also rare. The top panel in Table 11.2 compares the national electorate to members of Congress in 1987 (Herrera, Herrera, and Smith 1992), and the lower panel presents limited evidence from a 1998 study.[2] Although the public and elites differed somewhat in their policy views, there was no systematic bias in the direction of these differences. The public was more conservative than elites on the issue of minority aid (−.83), for example, but the public is more liberal than elites on the government providing services (+.57). On overall liberal/conservative position, the match between the public and elites is quite close (−.21), which is appropriate since this measure summarizes political positions on many policy matters. And as we noted in other nations, members of Congress were slightly more liberal than the public overall in 1986–87.

In 1998 the Pew Center (1998b) surveyed members of Congress, but this study included only a few items that were comparable to questions in public opinion surveys. Only 44 percent of members of Congress said that federal governmental programs should be maintained to deal with important problems, but 57 percent of the American public shared these opinions—similar to the

Table 11.2   The Distribution of Opinions for the American Public and Elites

	Citizens	Members of Congress	Difference
Liberal/conservative position	4.26	4.05	−.21
Government provide services	3.57	4.14	.57*
Government guarantee living standard	4.47	4.01	−.46*
Government should aid minorities	4.17	3.34	−.83*
Attitudes toward abortion	2.13	1.69	−.44*
Spend more on defense	3.82	3.58	−.24
Cooperate more with Russia	4.35	3.58	−.77*
Intervene in Central America	3.31	2.98	−.33
Maintain government programs[a]	57%	45%	
Liberal/conservative position[a]			
Conservative	37	47	
Moderate	40	31	
Liberal	19	7	

Sources: 1987 House of Representatives Survey (Herrera, Herrera, and Smith 1992) and 1986 ANES.

Notes: Entries are mean scores on a 7-point scale with 1 equal to the liberal position (abortion is a 4-point scale). Differences marked by an asterisk are significant at .01 level. Items marked with a superscript "a" in the table are from the 1998 Pew Center Survey of Members of Congress, Clinton Appointees, and Senior Civil Servants done in association with the *National Journal.*

earlier survey. On the standard liberal/conservative scale, Congress now had more self-identified conservatives than the public at large, and fewer liberals, but the percentage differences were modest on each response. These findings suggest that the Republican majority in the 1996–98 Congress shifted the balance of elite opinions away from the liberal tendencies of the 1986–88 Democratic Congress, which is what should have occurred.

In summary, if we judge collective correspondence by substantive criteria— for example, a 10 percent difference or less in issue opinions—then citizen–elite agreement is fairly common.³ Most economic, security, and New Politics issues fall within the 10 percent range for the British, German, and French comparisons to the European Parliament elites. Only foreign policy issues display sizable opinion differences between citizens and EP candidates. The samples of German and French elites appear most representative of their respective publics. Overall, an average of 53 percent of the German public give liberal responses on the thirteen issue questions, compared to 60 percent of elites. The match of citizen and elite opinions is even closer in France (60 percent versus 62 percent). The voter–elite gap is harder to compare in the United States because 7-point scales were used, but there appears to be a mix of agreement and disagreement in mass–elite comparisons.

DYADIC CORRESPONDENCE

Collective correspondence between the issue opinions of the public and the political elites does not occur as a collective process. Some degree of popular control is necessary to ensure the responsiveness of elites. Citizen–elite agreement without popular control is representation by chance, not democracy. One method of popular control makes political elites electorally dependent on a specific constituency. Weissberg (1978) defined the pairing of constituency opinion and elites as *dyadic correspondence*. In simple terms, liberal constituencies presumably select liberal representatives and conservative constituencies select conservative representatives.

In studying the connection between citizens and elites, researchers initially treated the individual legislator as the primary means of dyadic linkage. One explanation for this approach lies in the historical development of political theory on representation. Edmund Burke's classic "Speech to the Electors of Bristol" in 1774 defined a paradigm of representation that still influences modern political science. Traditionally, a *delegate* model stated the legislator's role in a deterministic fashion. Representative government required that delegates be sent to Parliament and that voters instruct the delegate on constituency preferences. The legislator was obliged to follow the constituency's mandate. Burke proposed a more independent *trustee* role for legislators. He argued that once elected, legislators should be allowed to follow their own beliefs about what they thought was best for their constituency and the nation.

This theoretical emphasis on the individual legislator was reinforced by the development of modern empirical research on political representation. Repre-

sentation research, especially from the American perspective, treated the legislator as the basis of political linkage (Miller and Stokes 1963). In part, this reflected
the weakness of American parties and the open structure of the American political process. Many American legislators can and do act as individual entrepreneurs. Research focused on whether or not individual legislators followed the
delegate or trustee model in representing their constituencies (Kuklinski 1978).

Warren Miller and Donald Stokes (1963) conducted the seminal study of
political representation in America to incorporate these theoretical models of
representation. They designed a complex study of the relationship between public
opinion and elite actions. They interviewed a small sample of the public in each
of 116 congressional districts across the nation after the 1958 congressional elections, as well as members of the House of Representatives from these same
districts. Finally, they assembled the voting records of the members of Congress
for the next legislative session.

Miller and Stokes used this information to build a model of the representation process (figure 11.1). Broadly speaking, these researchers envisioned two
pathways by which a constituency could influence the voting behavior of its
representative (Miller and Stokes 1963). One pathway defined the trustee model
of representation; the constituency could select a legislator who shares its views
(path a), so that in following his or her own convictions (path b) the legislator
represents the constituency's will. In this case, the constituency's opinion and
the legislator's actions are connected through the legislator's own policy attitudes.
A second pathway follows the delegate model. A legislator turns to his or her
district for cues on its policy preferences (path c) and then follows these cues in
making voting choices (path d). In this case, the legislator's perception of
constituency attitudes provides the linkage between actual constituency opinion
and the legislator's voting behavior.

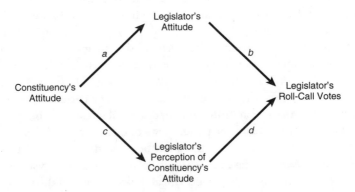

Figure 11.1 **Constituency Influence in Congress**

Miller and Stokes applied the model to three policy areas: civil rights, social welfare, and foreign policy. They found a strong relationship between constituency opinion and the legislator's voting record for civil rights and social welfare issues and a weaker connection for foreign policy. In addition, the path of constituency influence varied between policy domains. Civil rights issues primarily functioned by a delegate model; the delegate path was at least twice as important as the trustee path. For social welfare issues, the trustee path through the legislator's own attitude was the most important means of constituency influence.

This study provided hard empirical evidence of the representation process at work. Moreover, the process seemed to work fairly well. Most liberal constituencies were represented by liberal legislators, and most conservative constituencies were represented by conservative legislators. Although many have criticized the methodology of this study, its essential conclusions are still supported by most political scientists (for further discussion, see Erikson and Tedin 2001, chap. 10; Miller et al. 1999). Miller continued to work within this paradigm, exploring the relationship between party activists and the public, and how representational roles affect these relationships (Miller and Jennings 1986; Miller 1987).

Cheryl Lyn Herrera, Richard Herrera, and Eric Smith (1992) partially replicated the Miller-Stokes analyses with data from the 1986–88 Congress. They compared the opinions of members of Congress from thirty-three districts to the opinions of their constituents who were surveyed as part of the 1986 American National Election Study. Employing a variety of statistical measures, they found that the fit between constituencies and their representatives is fairly high on most issues, especially issues that are likely to have large issue publics and polarized public opinion, such as abortion, minority aid, and governmental services. Moreover, they concluded that "dyadic representation is better today than was true 30 years ago" (Herrera, Herrera, and Smith 1992, 201), implying that the democratic process in the United States was working even better than during the Miller-Stokes study in the late 1950s.

The Miller-Stokes model also was extended to representation studies in nearly a dozen other Western democracies (Holmberg 1989; Barnes 1977; Farah 1980; Converse and Pierce 1986; Higley et al. 1979). These studies often found little evidence of policy agreement between constituencies and their legislators, however. For instance, Samuel Barnes compared the issue opinions of Italian deputies to public opinion in their respective districts. He found virtually no correspondence between citizen and elite views (average correlation across eight issues was .04). Barbara Farah documented a similar lack of correspondence between district opinions and the policy views of district-elected deputies in the German Bundestag. The average correlation between district and deputy opinions was actually negative (average correlation across six issues was −.03). The French representation study also found a weak linkage between district and legislator opinions on specific policy issues (Converse and Pierce 1986, chaps. 22–23).[4]

It appeared that political representation did not occur in most democracies, or that it worked through other means.

THE PARTY GOVERNMENT MODEL

Research on political representation in non-American political systems gradually turned away from a theoretical model based on individual legislators to one based on the actions of political parties as collectives. This model of representation through parties—responsible party government—is built on several principles. Elections should provide competition between two or more parties contending for political power. Parties must offer distinct policy options so voters have meaningful electoral choices. Moreover, voters should recognize these policy differences among the parties. At the least, voters should be sufficiently informed to award or punish the incumbent parties based on their performance. National elections therefore serve as evaluations of the political parties and their activities.

Most descriptions of responsible party government also presume that members of a party's parliamentary delegation act in unison. Parties should vote as a bloc in Parliament, although there may be internal debate before the party position is decided. Parties exercise control over the government and the policy-making process through party control of the national legislature. In sum, the choice of parties provides the electorate with indirect control over the actions of individual legislators and the affairs of government.

Although the representation process may be based on individual legislators in the United States, political representation in Western Europe largely follows the party government model. In comparison to the United States, the party systems of most European democracies offer the voters greater diversity in party programs, which gives more meaning to party labels (chapter 7). Most democracies are parliamentary systems, in which unified legislative parties play a crucial role in determining control of the executive branch. The available evidence shows that party cohesion in European legislatures is considerably higher than in the American Congress (Thomassen 1994, 246). When a party votes as a united bloc, it makes little sense to discuss the voting patterns of individual legislators. Furthermore, public recognition of which party controls the government is more widespread in Western Europe than in the United States, probably as a result of the European parliamentary form of government. Giovanni Sartori maintains that "citizens in Western democracies are represented *through* and *by* parties. This is inevitable" (1968, 471; italics in original).

The party government model thus directs the voters' attention to parties as political representatives, rather than to individual deputies (Miller et al. 1999). Indeed, many Europeans (including Germans) vote directly for party lists. Dyadic correspondence is based more on a voter–party model than a district–legislator model. The voter half of the dyad is composed of all party supporters in a nation (even if there are geographic electoral districts); the elite half is composed of party officials as a collective. If the party government model holds, we should expect a close match between the policy views of voters and party elites taken as collectives.

We should stress one other point in comparing dyadic correspondence. We occasionally speak in causal terms—voter opinions presumably influence party positions—but the causal flow works in both directions. Voters influence parties, as parties try to persuade voters. This is why researchers have adopted the causally neutral term *correspondence.* The essence of the democratic marketplace is that like-minded voters and parties search out each other and ally forces. Even if one cannot determine the direction of causal flow, the similarity of opinions between voters and party elites is a meaningful measure of the representativeness of parties.

Some of the best evidence of the correspondence between voters and their parties comes from the 1994 European Parliament Election Study. This study interviewed parliamentary candidates from at least fifty political parties spread across Europe; they also interviewed the voters for these same parties. Figure 11.2 compares the Left/Right self-placement of voters and elites in each party. The horizontal axis in each figure plots the average position of party supporters; the vertical axis plots the average opinion of the party's elites. These two coordinates define a party's

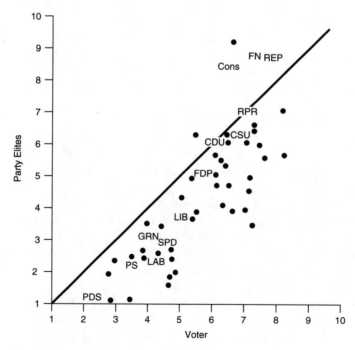

Figure 11.2   Voter and Party Elite Opinions on the Left/Right Scale

Source: 1994 European Parliament Election Study (Thomassen and Schmitt 1997, 177).

location in the figure. The 45-degree line represents perfect intraparty agreement: when the opinions of party elites exactly match those of their supporters.

Two important patterns can be gleaned from this figure. First, there is a strong relationship between voter and elite opinions within parties (r = .83). Voters with leftist preferences and elites who share these views come together in the traditional leftist parties, such as the German SPD, the British Labour Party, and the French Socialists, and there is a similar congruence on the Right. This is the evidence of party differences that underlie the party government model of representation. Second, there is a systematic tendency for party elites to say they are more leftist than their own voters (since most parties lie below the diagonal line).

Unfortunately, the 1994 EP Election Study contained very few issues, so to examine more detailed patterns of issue agreement we must turn to the 1979 EP study. In addition, to examine these data in more depth, we focus our analyses on the fourteen major parties that existed in our European core nations at the time of the study (Dalton 1985).

Figures 11.3 and 11.4 display party patterns on two Old Politics issues: the economic issue of expanding governmental ownership of industry and the religious/moral issue of abortion. Party positions on these issues follow traditional

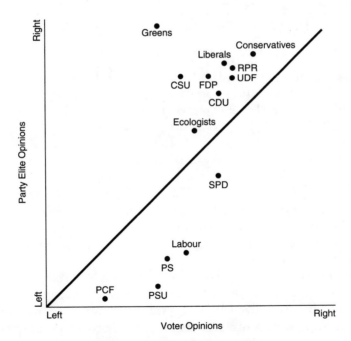

**Figure 11.3   Voter and Party Elite Opinions on Further
Nationalization of Industry**

Source: 1979 Europarliament Study.

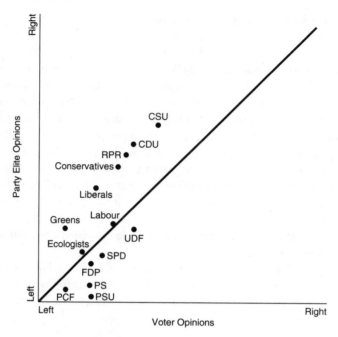

Figure 11.4   Voter and Party Elite Opinions on Abortion

Source: 1979 Europarliament Study.

Left/Right alignments. The Socialist and Communist Parties tended toward the lower-left quadrant; both their voters and party elites held liberal opinions on these Old Politics issues. For example, in 1979 supporters of the French Communist Party (PCF) were very liberal on the nationalization issues (average score = 1.78), as were PCF elites (score = 1.08). Conversely, the voters and elites of the traditional rightist parties generally shared conservative opinions on these issues. Averaged across all parties, the opinions of party elites are less than one scale point (.85 on a five-point scale) from the voter opinions on the nationalization issue, and less than half a point (.45) on the abortion issue. Because economic and religious issues are so important in structuring political conflict, a variety of more recent studies suggest that congruence on these issues remains high (Laver and Hunt 1992; Miller et al. 1999).

Attitudes toward nuclear power exemplify a salient New Politics issue. Figure 11.5 shows a basic correspondence between party voters and party elites on this issue. A voter bloc that favored (or opposed) nuclear energy is represented by party elites who generally shared these opinions. The average difference (.74) between voter and elite opinions is modest.

The pattern of party alignment on the nuclear power issue is also significant. The major established Left and Right parties did not have clear positions on

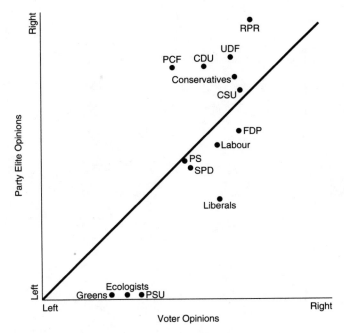

Figure 11.5 Voter and Party Elite Opinions on Nuclear Energy

Source: 1979 Europarliament Study.

this issue in 1979. The major Left parties—the German SPD, British Labour, and the French PS—all held centrist positions on this issue that were not much different from their conservative party rivals. In fact, the voters and party elites of the French Communist Party favored nuclear power more than many conservative party groups. Opposition to nuclear power was represented by a set of new parties: the German Greens, the French Ecologists, and French PSU. Although these data are aging, more recent studies of the public's environmental attitudes and their party images suggest the pattern described here has not changed fundamentally (chapter 7). Party alignments on nuclear power (and New Politics issues) cut across the traditional Left/Right party lines defined by Old Politics issues.

The issue of aid for Third World nations presents an example of the lack of voter–party agreement (figure 11.6). Party elites are consistently more liberal than their voters. Only a single party is within one scale point of its supporters, and the average voter–party difference is great (1.33). In this area, West European party elites display considerable independence from the policy opinions of their voters. This result is reminiscent of Miller and Stokes's (1963) finding that foreign policy exhibits the least evidence of dyadic correspondence for their sample of American legislators.

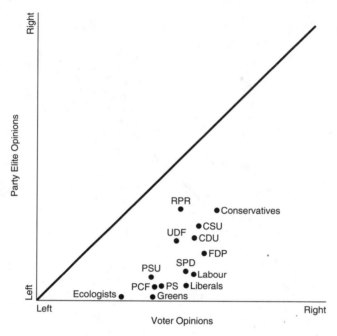

Figure 11.6   Voter and Party Elite Opinions on Aid to Third World Nations

Source: 1979 Europarliament Study.

Except for foreign policy, party elites appear fairly responsive to the views of their voters. Yet there is also a systematic tendency for party elites to exaggerate the issue differences that exist among their supporters. The intensity and ideological commitment of political elites normally generates greater issue differences among elites than among party supporters (Miller and Jennings 1986; Dalton 1985). On the nationalization of industry issue, for example, EP elites of the German SPD were significantly to the left of their voters, whereas CDU elites were to the right of their constituency. The 45-degree line in the figures represents perfect intraparty agreement, and party elites were more polarized than their supporters on the issues of nationalization, abortion, and nuclear energy.

A pattern of accentuated elite polarization also occurs in voter–elite comparisons in the United States (figure 11.7). Democratic and Republican voters in 1986 displayed only modest differences on many of their issue opinions, but party elites accentuated these differences. On six of the seven issues in the figure, Democratic elites are more liberal than their voters, and Republican elites are more conservative than their voters on six issues as well. In other words, party elites tended to *overrepresent* the opinions of their constituency by maintaining more extreme issue positions. Warren Miller (1987, chap. 3) found similar patterns when he compared the American public to delegates to national party conventions in 1980 and 1984. This general pattern explains the greater clarity of party positions at the elite level and the greater intensity of party conflict among elites.

Just as important as the overall level of dyadic correspondence are the factors affecting voter–party agreement. Some parties consistently achieve a close match between the opinions of voters and party elites, whereas other parties display less correspondence. These variations in party representation determine the efficiency of the party linkage process.

A study of voter–party agreement for forty party groups across nine nations found that the clarity of party positions is an important influence on the representation process (Dalton 1985). Characteristics that clarify party positions make it easier for voters to select a party compatible with their issue beliefs. Most policy areas display a strong and consistent tendency for centrally organized parties to be more representative of their supporters. Centralized parties may be less open to innovation and allow less internal democracy, as critics suggest, but centralized parties display greater dyadic correspondence. In addition, voter–party agreement is higher among ideological parties (of either the Left or Right). Apparently these characteristics clarify party positions and make it easier for voters to select a party consistent with their issue beliefs. A centralized party is

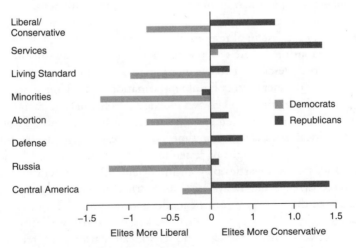

Figure 11.7 Difference between Party Voters and Party Representatives in the United States

Sources: 1987 Members of Congress Study and 1986 American National Election Study.

Note: Table entries are the mean differences between voters and elites on each issue scale.

more likely to project clear party cues, and an ideological image helps voters identify a party's general political orientation.

At the system level, Wessels (1999) has assembled evidence from several representation studies to examine the relationship between institutional structures and voter–party correspondence. He found that majoritarian systems, like the United States and Britain, place a greater emphasis on elites representing the modal voter in society, which normally pulls elites toward the center of the political spectrum. In contrast, in proportional representation systems, elites are more closely tied to representing their party voters. This is facilitated by the greater degree of party choice in most PR electoral systems and reinforces the conclusion drawn from our previous evidence that the style of representation is affected by the institutional structures of the democratic process.

PATTERNS OF POLITICAL REPRESENTATION

It is regrettable that more recent data on the representation process are not available. After all, we have claimed that the representation process is an important measure of the success of modern democracy. Furthermore, the new style of citizen politics that we have described in previous chapters might affect the representation process, though the nature of these effects is uncertain (see Thomassen 1994). On the one hand, a more sophisticated, issue-oriented public might encourage candidates and parties to be more attentive to public interests. On the other hand, partisan dealignment and candidate-centered politics may weaken representation built on a system of responsible party government. Still, there are broad conclusions about the nature of representation that flow from our findings.

This chapter describes two distinct patterns of representative government among Western democracies. Political representation in the United States is more dependent on the relationship between individual legislators and their constituencies. Citizens in most other democracies are primarily represented through their choice of political parties at election time. Some research suggests that this American–European contrast might be lessening. For instance, Warren Miller (1987, chap. 4) discusses how parties play an important role in American representation (also see Erikson and Tedin 2001, chap. 11). Our own analyses suggest that the strength of the party government model is weakening in Europe (e.g., chapter 9; Dalton and Wattenberg 2000). Still, it is probably the case that the contrasts between the American and European patterns of representation continue to hold.

Both models can provide an effective means of citizen–elite linkage, but they emphasize different aspects of representation. The American system of representative government based on individual legislators allows for greater responsiveness to the interests of each legislative district. The political process is more open to new political interests and the representation of minority groups because electoral control at the constituency level is more easily accomplished than control of an entire party. The flexibility of the American style of representation also involves some costs. An entrepreneurial style of representation makes it more difficult for the public to monitor and control the actions of their representatives between elections. This representation pattern also encourages campaigns to focus on personalities and district service rather than policy and ideological orientations. Indeed, studies of congressional elections suggest that personality and constituency service are important influences on voting patterns.

A growing body of empirical research shows that policy outcomes in America generally reflect the preferences of the public—although obviously this is, and probably should be, an imperfect linkage. Alan Monroe (1979) found a broad agreement between American policy preferences and policy outcomes for the several hundred specific cases he examined. Benjamin Page and Robert Shapiro (1983) similarly documented a significant correspondence between public preferences for policy change and actual changes in public policy.[5] Sophisticated empirical analyses by Stimson and his colleagues (1995) are providing new insights into the total impact of public opinion on the policy process, and how this influence interacts with the institutional structure of American politics.

A party government model yields a different pattern of political representation. The choice of parties provides the electorate with indirect institutional control over the actions of individual legislators through party discipline. When a party votes as a united bloc, political responsibility is more clearly established. If the public is satisfied (or dissatisfied) with the party's performance, the next election offers the opportunity to act on these evaluations. Although the party model strengthens the policy linkage between citizens and elites, this may produce rigidity and resistance to change. The highly cohesive European parliamentary parties place a necessary premium on party unity and disciplined voting. This hardly provides a fertile ground for experimentation and political change. Parties may be very responsive to their established clientele, but new social groups and internal party minorities may have difficulty gaining representation in the party government framework.

Research projects working within the party government framework also find that party choices have meaningful policy consequences. For example, Klingemann and his colleagues (1994) analyzed whether or not the programs that parties offer to the voters are translated into policy after the election. They found that parties are a meaningful vehicle for policy control in most democracies.

Many roadblocks and pitfalls stand in the way of representation through parties. In these times of change and political turmoil, the evidence of party failures is often obvious. Yet parties remain the dominant institution in the area of political representation. Citizen preferences on Old Politics issues are well represented among the top stratum of political elites. When the established parties have avoided taking clear policy stances on New Politics issues, new parties have formed to represent these views. In general terms, therefore, parties continue to perform their role as representatives of voter interests.

In summary, even close citizen–elite policy agreement is not proof that public opinion is efficiently and effectively represented in modern democracies. A large part of the correspondence that does exist must be attributed to an interactive process. Voters migrate to the party (candidate) that best represents their views, and the party convinces supporters to adopt its policies. Congruence does not prove that the public can control government. Beyond the general patterns described here, one can think of a host of specific policies in which the impact of public preferences was uncertain. Yet congruence indicates an agreement between public preferences and public policy that is expected under a democratic system. Moreover, it underscores our belief that there is a rationality of public action that elitist theories of democracy doubt exists.

SUGGESTED READINGS

Converse, Philip, and Roy Pierce. *Representation in France*. Cambridge, Mass.: Harvard University Press, 1986.

Erikson, Robert, Gerald Wright, and John McIver. *State House Democracy: Public Opinion and Public Policy in the American States*. New York: Cambridge University Press, 1994.

Esaiasson, Peter, and Sören Holmberg. *Representation from Above: Members of Parliament and Representative Democracy in Sweden*. Aldershot: Dartmouth, 1996.

Matthews, Donald, and Henry Valen. *Parliamentary Representation: The Case of the Norwegian Storting*. Columbus: Ohio State University Press, 1999.

Miller, Warren, et al. *Policy Representation in Western Democracies*. Oxford, U.K.: Oxford University Press, 1999.

Page, Benjamin, and Robert Shapiro. *The Rational Public: Fifty Years of Trends in Americans' Policy Preferences*. Chicago: University of Chicago Press, 1992.

NOTES

1. The development of two-way cable television, teleconferencing, and other communication advances may lead us to reconsider the physical limits on direct citizen participation in large collectives. Indeed, the technology exists for instantaneous national referendums and national town meetings (Poole 1983).

2. Previous comparisons of public opinion and opinions of members of Congress in 1978 and 1982 found that the two groups differed by only a few percentage points (Bishop and Frankovic 1981; Erikson and Tedin 2001, 267).

3. In purely statistical terms, almost half of the citizen–elite issue comparisons in these tables yield statistically significant differences (.01 level). This, in part, is because of the large size of the public opinion samples.

4. The power of Converse and Pierce's (1986, chaps. 22–23) analysis was to specify the conditions that strengthen or retard the representation process. They found that citizen–elite congruence varied by policy domain, competitiveness of the district, and the legislator's role conceptions.

5. State-level comparisons provide another opportunity to study the congruence between public opinion and public policy. A recent study by Robert Erikson and his colleagues shows a strong policy correspondence (Erikson, Wright, and McIver 1994).

PART FOUR

Democracy and the Future

CHAPTER 12

Citizens and the Democratic Process

WE SEEMINGLY LIVE in the best of times . . . and the worst of times for the democratic process. In the last decade of the twentieth century, a wave of democratization swept across the globe. The citizens of Eastern Europe, South Africa, and several East Asian nations rose up against their authoritarian governments. The Soviet empire collapsed, and millions of citizens were enjoying their new democratic freedoms. This led a noted political analyst, Frances Fukuyama (1992), to claim that we were witnessing the end of history. Humankind's historical evolution was converging on a single form of government—democracy—as the culmination of human development. Even some who had recently proclaimed the end of democracy's international expansion now trumpeted this third wave of democratization.[1]

In the United States, this decade also brought unprecedented affluence and economic well-being. The United States experienced its longest period of sustained economic growth in peacetime. Crime rates dropped, and progress was made on many policy fronts. To a lesser degree, our allies in Western Europe also enjoyed a peace dividend of economic stability, peace, and a new era of international security. This was, it seemed, a positive time for Western democracy. The Cold War was over, and we had won.

Despite these signs of progress, there are growing indications that the citizens of these established democracies have become increasingly critical of the politicians, political parties, and political institutions that form the basis of the democratic process (Norris 1999b; Pharr and Putnam 2000). The malaise is perhaps most visible and surprising in the United States. Beginning with the crises and political scandals of the 1960s and 1970s—Vietnam, urban unrest, and Watergate—Americans' trust in their politicians sank steadily lower. Jimmy Carter returned from Camp David in 1979 and warned Americans that declining public confidence "was a fundamental threat to American democracy." Trust in government partially rebounded during the first Reagan administration, as the president tried to reinstill a new sense of political purpose and renew the political spirit with uplifting references to a "new morning in America" and America as the "shining city on the hill." By the end of the Reagan/Bush admin-

INTERNET RESOURCE

Visit the Freedom House Web site for information on
the extent to democracy around the globe:

www.freedomhouse.org

istrations, however, public skepticism had reasserted itself, fueled by new crises and new scandals. In the mid-1990s the public's trust in politicians and various political institutions reached historic low points (Nye, Zelikow, and King 1997).

A single example illustrates the transformation in American public opinion: In April 1966, with the Vietnam War raging and race riots in Cleveland, Chicago, and Atlanta, a Harris poll found that 66 percent of Americans *rejected* the view that "the people running the country don't really care what happens to you." In December 1997, in the midst of the longest period of peace and prosperity in more than two generations, 57 percent of Americans *endorsed* that same view: In the opinion of many Americans, this is the worst of times for our democratic process.

These problems are not unique to the United States, although they may be most visible and most highly debated among Americans. Doubts about democratic politics now seem to be a common theme in advanced industrial societies. As scandals strained Britons' faith in their democratic institutions, a parliamentary committee was formed in the mid-1990s on "Standards in Public Life" (the Nolan Committee). In testifying during the committee's initial study of ethics in government, Ivor Crewe stated: "There is no doubt that distrust and alienation have risen to a higher level than ever before. It was always fairly prevalent; it is now in many regards almost universal" (Crewe 1995). During the 1990s Germany achieved a historic ambition: to unify itself as a free and democratic nation. And yet, political trust sank among the German public. Indeed, as Germany accomplished this national goal, the president, Richard von Weizsäcker, chastised Germany's political elites, claiming that politicians and political parties were "power-crazed for electoral victory and powerless when it comes to understanding the content and ideas required of political leadership" (von Weizsäcker 1992, 164). Scandals and a growing feeling of political mistrust also became more prominent issues in French politics during the 1990s.

Admittedly, anxiety about the health of democracy or partisan politics is a regular feature of political science and political punditry. Over the past quarter century there have been a plethora of books, articles, and pamphlets on the topic. There was an important debate about the nation's postwar goals during the Eisenhower administration, and John Kennedy asked Americans to renew their commitment to state and nation (see Mueller 1999, chap. 7). Perhaps the most prominent academic study is *The Crisis of Democracy*, in which Michel Crozier, Samuel Huntington, and Joji Watanuki (1975) nearly forecasted democracy's demise. The introduction to their book includes an ominous quote from Willy Brandt, who supposedly predicted: "Western Europe has only 20 or 30 more years of democracy left in it; after that it will slide, engineless and rudderless, under the surrounding sea of dictatorship" (quoted in Crozier, Huntington, and Watanuki 1975, 2).[2]

Fortunately, the passage of time has shown that the predictions of Crozier (and Brandt) were wrong, but now it appears that there are new and real causes for concern among those who value democracy. In the past the lack of support for the democratic process was one of the faults that led to the collapse of the Weimar Republic. A supportive political culture is often considered a requirement for a stable, effective democracy (Almond and Verba 1963). In other cases, the rejection of democratic norms and procedures by political extremists has led to violent attacks on the political system. Even though we see a fundamentally different pattern in present feelings of political malaise, the potential implications for democracy are still very significant.

This chapter determines how citizens judge the democratic process today. How is it that as democracy celebrates its success at the dawning of the new millennium, its citizens are apparently expressing increasing doubts about the political system? In addition, we consider how the new style of citizen politics might contribute to these developments, and what the implications are for the future functioning of the democratic process.

THE MEANING OF POLITICAL SUPPORT

Political support is a term with many possible meanings. Several political scientists have tried to identify the essential aspects of this concept and link these attitudes to their consequences.

Gabriel Almond and Sidney Verba (1963) referred to attitudes toward politics and the political system as the *political culture* of a nation. Political culture encompasses everything from beliefs about the legitimacy of the system itself to beliefs about the adequacy and appropriateness of political input structures, governmental policies, and the role of the individual in the political process. The most important of these attitudes is a generalized feeling toward the political system, or *system affect*. Feelings of system affect are presumably socialized early in life (Easton and Dennis 1969), representing a positive attitude toward the political system that is relatively independent of the actions of the current government. Almond and Verba believed that affective feelings toward the political system assure the legitimacy of democratic governments and limit expressions of discontent with the political system.

David Easton (1965, 1975) extended these ideas into a theoretical framework describing the various elements of political support. Easton distinguished between support for three levels of political objects: political authorities, the regime, and the political community. *Political authorities* are the incumbents of political office, or in a broader sense the pool of political elites from which governmental leaders are drawn. Support for political authorities focuses on specific individuals or groups of individuals. *Regime support* refers to public attitudes toward the institutions and offices of government rather than the present officeholders, attitudes toward the office of president of the United States rather than the present chief executive. This level of support also involves public attitudes toward the procedures of government and political institutions, such as the principles of pluralist democracy and support for parliamentary government. Finally, support for the *political community* implies a basic attachment to the nation and political system beyond the present institutions of government. A sense of being "English" (or "Scottish") exemplifies these attachments.

The distinction between levels of support is essential. Discontent with political authorities normally has limited political implications. Citizens often become dissatisfied with political officeholders and act on these feelings by selecting new leaders at the next election. Dissatisfaction with authorities, within a democratic system, is not usually a signal for basic political change. Negative attitudes toward political officials often exist with little loss in support for the office itself or the institutional structure encompassing this office. As the object of dissatisfaction becomes more general—the regime or political community—the political implications increase. A decline in regime support might provoke a basic challenge to constitutional structures or calls for reform in the procedures of government. Weakening ties to the political community in a democratic system might foretell eventual revolution, civil war, or the loss of democracy. Therefore, "not all expressions of unfavorable orientations have the same degree of gravity for a political system. Some may be consistent with its maintenance; others may lead to fundamental change" (Easton 1975, 437).

In addition to the objects of political support, Easton distinguished between two kinds of support: diffuse and specific (also see Muller and Jukam 1977). According to Easton, diffuse support is a state of mind—a deep-seated set of attitudes toward politics and the operation of the political system that is relatively impervious to change. For example, the sentiment "America, right or wrong" reflects diffuse support, a commitment to the political system that transcends the actual behavior of the government. In contrast, specific support is closely related to the actions and performance of the government or political elites. This kind of support is object-specific in two senses. First, specific support normally applies to evaluations of political authorities; it is less relevant to support for the regime and political community. Second, specific support is based on the actual policies and general style of political authorities.

The distinction between diffuse and specific support is important in understanding the significance of public attitudes toward the political process. Democratic political systems must keep the support of their citizens if they are to remain viable. Yet, since all governments occasionally fail to meet public expectations, short-term failures to satisfy public demands must not directly erode generalized support for the regime or political community. In other words, a democratic political system requires a reservoir of diffuse support independent of immediate policy outputs (specific support) if it is to weather periods of public disaffection and dissatisfaction.

The history of German democracy illustrates the significance of diffuse support. The Weimar Republic was built on an unstable foundation. Many Germans thought that the creation of the republic at the end of World War I contributed to Germany's wartime defeat; from the outset, the regime was stigmatized as a traitor to the nation. Important sectors of the political establishment—the military, the civil service, and the judiciary—and many citizens questioned the legitimacy of the new regime and retained attachments to the political system of the former German empire. The fledgling democratic state then faced a series of major crises: postwar economic hardships, attempted Right-wing and Left-wing coups, explosive inflation in the early 1920s, and French occupation of the Ruhr. The political system was never able to build up a pool of diffuse support for the republic. Consequently, the dissatisfaction created by the Great Depression in the 1930s easily eroded popular support for political authorities and the democratic regime. Communists and Nazis argued that the democratic political system was at fault, and the Weimar Republic succumbed to these attacks.[3]

The democratic transition in the German Democratic Republic also illustrates the importance of cultural and institutional congruence. Surveys of East German youth found a marked decrease in support for the communist principles of the GDR during the 1980s (Friedrich and Griese 1990). These youths led the populist revolution in the East that weakened the regime in the fall of 1989. Moreover, revelations in early 1990 about the communists' abuses of power eroded the regime's popular base still further and created a race toward unification with the West.

Early cross-national opinion studies provided empirical support for the proposition that popular support was a requisite of stable democracy. Almond and Verba (1963) found that system affect in the late 1950s was most widespread in the long-established democracies of the United States and Great Britain. For example, 85 percent of Americans and 46 percent of Britons spontaneously mentioned their political system as a source of national pride. This system affect indicated the diffuse support that had developed in these nations over their long democratic histories. Satisfaction with the policy outputs of government was also common in both nations. In contrast, system support was more limited in the newly formed democracies of West Germany and Italy; only 7 percent of West Germans and 3 percent of Italians mentioned their political system as a source of national pride. These findings suggested that diffuse political support was underdeveloped in these systems, raising fears that democracy was still fragile in these two formerly fascist states. The early years of the Federal Republic were closely watched by those who worried that the Bonn Republic would follow the same course as the Weimar.

Another cross-national study, by Hadley Cantril (1965), found a similar pattern in public opinions. Cantril showed that positive national self-images were more common among the stable, well-run democracies. More recent research by Inglehart (1990, chap. 1; 1997, chap. 6) finds that a democratic political culture is strongly correlated with the stability of democratic institutions. Although one can never be certain whether stable government produces popular support or whether popular support produces stable government, these two phenomena are interrelated.

Authoritarian states may endure without the support of their publics, but popular support is essential for democracies to survive. Therefore, we need to assess the breadth and depth of popular support for democracy as a crucial element in diagnosing democracy's future.

DECLINING CONFIDENCE IN AUTHORITIES

Public concerns about the democratic process normally begin with questions about the holders of power. Americans might not doubt the institutions of governance, but they might criticize Richard Nixon's actions during Watergate, George Bush's involvement in the Iran-*contra* negotiations, or Bill Clinton's multiple indiscretions.

Rather than focus on individual incumbents, we examine citizen images of political leaders in general. Indeed, a variety of evidence points to Americans' growing skepticism of their leaders. The American National Election Study has measured feelings toward political officials and the government over time (figure 12.1). The early readings described a largely supportive public. Most Americans believed that one can trust the government to do what is right (71 percent), that there are few dishonest people in government (68 percent), and that officials care what people think (71 percent). These positive feelings remained relatively unchanged until the mid-1960s and then declined precipitously. Conflict over civil rights and Vietnam divided Americans and apparently eroded public confidence in their leaders; Watergate and a seemingly endless stream of political scandals pushed support even lower over the next decade.

Distrust of governmental officials reached a low point in 1980, and then the upbeat presidency of Ronald Reagan temporarily reversed these trends. Reagan stressed the positive aspects of American society and politics—and opinions rebounded in 1984. However, the trendline turned down again during Reagan's second term and Bush's administration. At the end of the Reagan-Bush era, public trust in government was as low as it had been in 1980.

The Clinton administration had a mixed record. By 1994 these indicators had hit historic lows, partially fueling the Republicans' victory in the midterm elections. But steady economic growth and relative international stability seemed to shore up public confidence in government. Trust in government then grew from 1994 until the end of the decade. Even Clinton's personal failings did not seem to affect the public's general images of government. Yet even with the

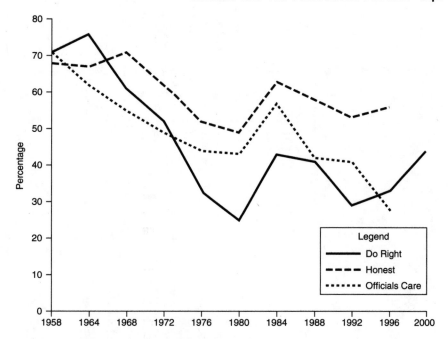

Figure 12.1   American Trust in Government (in percentages)

Source: American National Election Studies, 1958–2000.

unprecedented economic growth of the 1990s and the consolidation of democracy around the globe, Americans' trust of government rebounded only to the levels of Reagan's first administration.[4]

Other survey evidence shows that Americans' dissatisfaction with national leadership has spread beyond politics. A series of questions tap public confidence in the people running major social, economic, and political organizations (table 12.1). Confidence in the leadership of virtually all institutions has tumbled downward over the past two decades. For instance, in 1966 many Americans expressed a great deal of confidence in the executive branch (41 percent) and Congress (42 percent); these positive evaluations dropped substantially over the next two decades. Confidence in business, labor, higher education, organized religion, the military, and the medical profession underwent a similar decline.

Virtually all other long-term public opinion series replicate these downward trends (Nye, Zelikow, and King 1997; Lipset and Schneider 1987). Since 1966 the Harris poll has tracked sentiments on two measures of political alienation: "The people running the country don't really care what happens to you" and "Most people with power try to take advantage of people like yourself." Both items display the public's growing cynicism over time. Similarly, another series from the General Social Survey asked Americans if they agree with the statement "Most public officials are not really interested in the problems of the average man." The

Table 12.1 Confidence in Leadership of American Institutions

	1966	1971	1973	1976	1980	1984	1988	1993	1998	2000
Medicine	72	61	54	54	52	52	51	39	45	44
Higher education	61	37	37	38	30	29	30	22	27	27
Military	62	27	32	39	28	37	34	42	37	40
Organized religion	41	27	35	31	35	32	20	23	28	29
Supreme Court	50	23	32	35	25	35	35	30	33	34
Major corporations	55	27	29	22	27	32	25	21	28	29
Press	29	18	23	28	22	17	18	11	10	10
Executive branch	41	23	29	14	12	19	16	12	14	14
Congress	42	19	24	14	9	13	15	7	11	13
Organized labor	22	14	16	12	15	9	10	8	12	14
Average	48	28	31	29	26	28	25	22	25	25

Source: 1966 and 1971 from Harris Poll; 1973–2000, NORC General Social Surveys.

Note: Table entries are the percentage of respondents expressing a great deal of confidence in the people running each institution.

number of cynical Americans increases from 60 percent in 1973 to 76 percent in 1993. The Pew Center for Media and the Press (1998a) extended an earlier trend on evaluations of the ethical and moral practices of federal government officials; 34 percent of Americans were critical in 1964, rising to 68 percent in 1997.

When one looks back on this span of American history, it is easy to see the reasons for the public's doubts about their leaders. Over any four-year electoral cycle, one can repeatedly identify actions that have diminished the reputations of Congress and the executive branch: Watergate, Iran-*contra*, the savings-and-loan scandal, *ad infinitum*. Candidates promise one thing at election time but regularly fail to deliver on these promises or even to treat them as serious promises after they are elected (e.g., Bush's promise "Read my lips, no new taxes"). And as some of the most distinguished members of Congress have resigned their office, they have left with stinging indictments of the institution. As one former representative said upon leaving office, "May your mother never find out where you work."

Although such explanations of decreasing trust focus on the peculiar history of American politics, mounting evidence exists that these same trends also are occurring in Britain, France, and Germany. Figure 12.2 compares public feelings

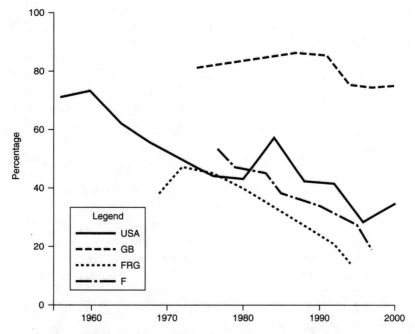

Figure 12.2   Feelings That Politicians Care What People Think

Sources: United States, American National Election Studies, 1956–2000; *Britain*, 1974 Political Action Survey and British Social Attitudes Surveys, 1987–97; *Germany*, German Election Studies, 1969–94; *France*, SOFRES Polls.

that politicians care what people think in our set of our nations.[5] Public trust in politicians has generally decreased over time. In 1977, 53 percent of the French public believed politicians cared what they thought; by 1997 only 19 percent shared this opinion. Other trends from these four nations generally display the same pattern of decreasing trust in elected officials (Curtice and Jowell 1997; Kepplinger 1996; Mayer 2000).

Even more significantly, growing public skepticism of politicians and governmental officials is apparent in virtually all the advanced industrial democracies (Dalton 1999; Norris 1999b; Pharr and Putnam 2000). A long series of Swedish opinion trends tracks a similar decline in political trust, even though Sweden's political history did not contain any of the political events that are used to explain decreasing trust in the United States (Holmberg 1999). The same pattern can be seen in nations ranging from Austria to New Zealand (Dalton 1999). It appears that a common feature of contemporary democracies is that their citizens are increasingly skeptical of their elected officials.

ORIENTATIONS TOWARD THE REGIME

Increasing public skepticism of political elites appears to be a common development in many advanced industrial democracies, but political scientists disagree on whether these opinions reflect doubts about political authorities or more fundamental questions about the regime and democratic process.

The debate was first taken up by Arthur Miller (1974a, 1974b) and Jack Citrin (1974). Miller argued that popular dissatisfaction with the repeated policy failures and political scandals of governmental officials was being generalized into broader criticism of the political process as a whole. Miller spelled out the potentially grave consequences the loss of regime support could have for the American political process.

Citrin believed that Miller overstated the problem. He interpreted the declines in political support as a sign of popular disenchantment with the incumbents of government or political authorities in general, not distrust in the system of American government. Citrin claimed that "Political systems, like baseball teams, have slumps and winning seasons. Having recently endured a succession of losing seasons, Americans boo the home team when it takes the field" (1974, 987). Citrin maintained that these boos do not show opposition to the process of democratic government, only for the players in the lineup and their recent performance on the field. Hence, a few new stars or a few winning streaks, and the decline in public confidence might be reversed; the trends of distrust thus had limited significance for Citrin.

Citrin's caution was warranted in 1974, but now almost three more decades have passed and public disenchantment continues. In addition, accumulating evidence suggests that the decline in public confidence is broader than just dissatisfaction with present political elites. Several questions from the American •

National Election Study examine the perceived responsiveness of government and political institutions (figure 12.3). These questions show a trend of decreasing confidence in parties, elections, and the government in general. Other survey series document increasing public doubts about Congress as a political institution (Hibbing and Theiss-Morse 1995). One observer of these trends suggested that the political creed for contemporary American politics should read "In God we trust: everyone else pays cash."

This erosion of public confidence in the institutions of the democratic regime is not unique to the United States. Ola Listhaug and Matti Wiberg (1995) found a general decline in public confidence in governmental institutions among Europeans between the 1980 and 1990 waves of the World Values Survey, and these trends generally continued into the 1990s (Klingemann 1999). Longer trends from commercial polling organizations reinforce the evidence on decreasing trust in political institutions. For instance, the Gallup poll found that 48 percent of the British public expressed quite a lot of confidence in the House of Commons in 1985, compared to only 24 percent in 1995. Germans' confidence in Parliament dropped significantly between 1984 and 1995 (IPOS 1995). Germans now speak

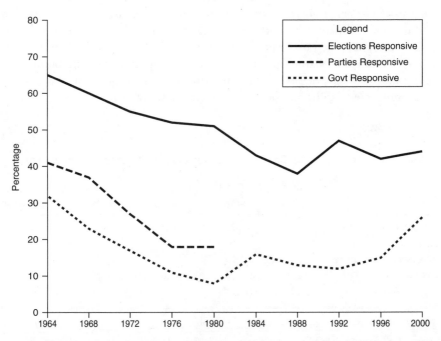

Figure 12.3   Responsiveness of American Political Institutions (in percentages)

Source: American National Election Studies, 1964–2000.

of the crisis of party government, and the German term *Politikverdrossenheit* (political vexation) has become a common part of the public's political vocabulary.

The 1998 International Social Survey Program compared confidence in institutions across our four nations (table 12.2).[6] The question wording and set of institutions differ from table 12.1, so the results are not directly comparable to that table. Still, the data present a familiar pattern. The public displays little confidence in any political institution; for instance, less than a sixth of the respondents in each nation express "complete" or "very great" confidence in the national legislature. Data from the 1995–98 World Values Survey similarly show that confidence in the legislature ranks twelfth in a list of fifteen institutions (Dalton and Wattenberg 2000, 265). Citizens express slightly more confidence in nonpolitical institutions of government, such as the legal system and the educational system. European confidence in these institutions averages lower than in the United States, despite the long-term downward American trend noted earlier.

When the signs of growing popular skepticism first appeared in American surveys during the late 1960s and early 1970s, there were reasons to link these findings to the immediate problems of American politics. And yet, the continuation of these American trends into the 1990s and parallel evidence from other advanced industrial democracies suggest that we are witnessing more than a temporary slump in politicians' performance. Contemporary publics have raised their expectations of government, and they are more demanding of politicians and their governments. Furthermore, increasingly critical media and more open public discussion of government reinforce public doubts about the political process. From the Nixon tapes to the Clinton impeachment, the public sees reasons for their skepticism. Thus, rather than a transient phenomenon, a skeptical public seems to be another feature of the new style of citizen politics.

Table 12.2   Cross-National Confidence in Societal Institutions (in percentages)

	United States	Great Britain	France	West Germany	East Germany
Educational system	34	23	23	38	30
Legal system	20	18	14	32	17
Business and industry	26	10	2	23	21
Parliament	13	6	6	15	10
Average	23	14	11	27	20

Source: 1998 International Social Survey Program.

Notes: Table entries are the percentage of respondents expressing "complete" or "a great deal" of confidence in each institution. Missing data are not included in the calculation of percentages.

THE VALUES OF A DEMOCRATIC REGIME

Many of the survey questions analyzed so far have measured support for the incumbents or institutions of the democratic process or could be interpreted in these terms. One might argue that dissatisfaction with politicians, parties, and even parliaments is a sign of the vitality of democracy (or an objective reading of politics by the public). If there is a crisis of democracy, this dissatisfaction must have been generalized to the political regime and its values.

In earlier historical periods, public dissatisfaction with politicians or the workings of the democratic process often led to (or arose from) disenchantment with the democratic process itself. This was the case with the democratic challenges of the interwar period (Linz and Stepan 1978). Even during the immediate postwar period, dissatisfaction with democracy was often focused among antidemocratic extremists on the Left or Right. If contemporary publics are losing faith in the democratic process, the implications for democracy are much more severe.

To the extent that data on support for democratic norms and procedures are available, they suggest that support for political rights and participatory norms have actually grown over the past generation. The available long-term data suggest that contemporary publics have become more politically tolerant during the postwar period (Thomassen 1995; McCloskey and Brill 1983). The expansion of democratic rights to women, racial/ethnic minorities, and homosexuals has profoundly changed the politics of advanced industrial democracies within the span of a generation (also see chapter 6). At least in principle, there is widespread public endorsement of the political values and norms that underlie the democratic process.

In addition, there is indirect evidence that perceptions of the citizens' role now emphasize a more participatory style and a greater willingness to challenge authority. Inglehart's (1990, 1997) research on postmaterial value change—with its emphasis on participatory values as a measure of postmaterialism—reinforces these points. Inglehart finds growing emphasis on political and social participation as core value priorities. Contemporary publics expect to participate in the democratic process, and interest in democratic process has increased over time (see chapter 2).

To tap regime values, opinion surveys ask whether or not democracy is considered the best form of government. Although there is no long cross-national time series for this question, the currently high degree of support suggests there has not been a major erosion in these sentiments (table 12.3).[7] On average, more than three-quarters of the public in advanced industrial democracies believe that democracy is the best form of government (also see Klingemann 1999). The two notable exceptions—Ireland and Northern Ireland—may reflect the political dissatisfaction that has accompanied the violent conflicts in the North. Another question in this survey was less evaluative, tapping public support for the ideal of democracy, which is nearly universal within Western democracies. Reviewing similar evidence, Fuchs and his colleagues (1995) concluded that democracy as a principle is positively evaluated by nearly all citizens in advanced industrial societies.

Table 12.3 Support for Democracy

Nation	Approve idea of democracy	Democracy best form of government
Australia*	—	83
Belgium	93	76
Great Britain	95	77
Denmark	98	93
Finland*	—	75
France	95	78
Germany	96	82
Greece	99	92
Ireland	93	65
Italy	93	74
Japan*	—	88
Luxembourg	98	83
Netherlands	98	85
Northern Ireland	95	65
Norway*	—	93
Sweden*	—	93
Switzerland*	—	91
United States*	—	88

Sources: Eurobarometer 31a (1989); 1994–98 World Values Survey (nations indicated by asterisks).

Other cross-national evidence on the democratic values and norms of contemporary publics reinforces these findings. A long series of German public opinion surveys, as one example, shows broad popular support for the principles of self-determination, participation, and free expression that underlie the democratic process (Dalton 1994b). Recent cross-national surveys of the advanced industrial democracies similarly display general consensus on most democratic principles, such as support for a free press or a multiparty system (e.g., Times/Mirror Center 1991). In summary, in contrast to declining support for the politicians and institutions of democracy, contemporary publics continue to display broad and even growing support for the principles and values that underlie the democratic process. We discuss this contrast in more detail in the following section.

FEELINGS OF SYSTEM SUPPORT

A final aspect of political support concerns citizen orientations toward the political system and society. System support involves the "system affect" described by Almond and Verba (1963). A strong emotional attachment to the nation presumably provides a reservoir of diffuse support that can maintain a political system through temporary periods of political stress. One measure of such feelings involves pride in one's nation. Figure 12.4 displays the percentage of respondents for a set of advanced industrial democracies who feel very proud of their nation.[8] On the whole, feelings of national pride are relatively stable across time. There are, however, marked national differences in these feelings.

National pride is exceptionally high in the United States; 97 percent of the public was "very proud" or "proud" to be an American in 1981 and 98 percent in

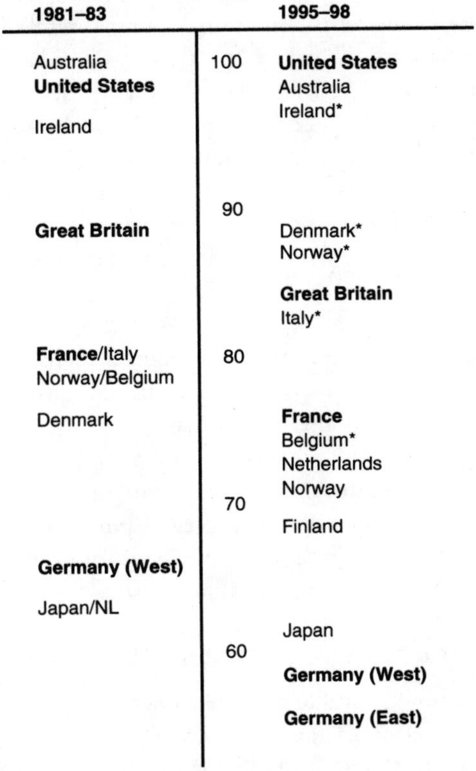

1981–83		1995–98
Australia **United States** Ireland	100	**United States** Australia Ireland*
	90	
Great Britain		Denmark* Norway*
		Great Britain Italy*
France/Italy Norway/Belgium	80	
Denmark		**France** Belgium* Netherlands Norway
	70	Finland
Germany (West)		
Japan/NL		Japan
	60	**Germany (West)**
		Germany (East)

**Figure 12.4   Feelings of National Pride
(in percentages)**

Sources: 1981–83 World Values Survey; 1995–98 World Values Survey; nations marked by an asterisk use Eurobarometer 42 (December 1994) for the most recent timepoint.

Notes: Figure presents the percentage of respondents who answered "very proud" and "proud"; missing data are not included in the calculation of percentages.

1996. The chants of "USA! USA! USA!" are not limited to Olympic competition; they signify a persisting feeling among Americans. These sentiments of national pride visibly came to the surface in the wake of the horrendous terrorist attacks on September 11, 2001—but these sentiments are long-standing in the American political culture. Most Europeans express their national pride in more moderate tones. Britons express relatively high degrees of national pride; the bifurcated division of the French political culture yields more modest rates of national pride.

Germans are especially hesitant in their statements of national pride. The trauma of the Third Reich burned a deep scar in the German psyche in both the West and the East. Especially among the young, there is a strong feeling that the nationalist excesses of the past should never be repeated. The Federal Republic, therefore, has avoided many of the emotional national symbols that are common in other industrial nations. There are few political holidays or memorials, the national anthem is seldom played, and even the anniversary of the founding of the Federal Republic attracts little public attention. Although most citizens are proud to be German, they avoid the unquestioning emotional attachment to state and nation. Moreover, the data in the figure indicate that these sentiments have carried over to the residents of eastern Germany, where national pride is also restrained.

Another element of system support involves attitudes toward society and the political system. A standard question in several recent surveys measures public support for social change through revolutionary action. Table 12.4 shows that support for revolutionary social change represents a mere trace element in each nation. Indeed, support for improving society through gradual reforms is consistently the most preferred response in each nation.

In summary, these broad measures of identification with the nation or support for the basic structure of society do not display the same downward spiral that we have found for other measures of political support. The public's doubts about the incumbents in office or the institutions of the political process have not generalized to the democratic system itself.

THE FUTURE OF DEMOCRATIC POLITICS

Citizens have grown more critical of political elites and less positive toward government. This chapter determined the present boundaries of these sentiments. The decline in political trust is most dramatic for evaluations of politicians and political elites in general. The deference to authority that once was common in many Western democracies has been replaced partially by public skepticism of elites. Closer scrutiny of governmental actions by the public and media uncovers political scandals and policy failures that further erode political trust (Pharr 2000; Della Porta 2000). The public's distrust of politicians has substantial supporting evidence.

Feelings of mistrust have gradually broadened to include evaluations of the political regime and other institutions in society. The lack of confidence in political institutions also has become widespread. Public skepticism has not signifi-

Table 12.4 Support for Social Change (in percentages)

	UNITED STATES			GREAT BRITAIN			WEST GERMANY				FRANCE		
	1981	1990	1995	1976	1983	1990	1970	1983	1990	1995	1970	1983	1990
Change society by revolutionary action	5	6	5	7	4	5	2	3	2	2	5	7	4
Improve society through reforms	66	67	75	60	59	75	70	48	59	84	78	64	70
Defend society against subversives	20	16	20	25	30	13	20	40	28	12	12	23	20
No opinion	9	11	0	8	7	8	8	9	11	2	5	6	7
Total	100	100	100	100	100	101	100	100	100	100	100	100	101

Sources: 1970 European Community Study; Eurobarometers 6 for Britain; 1981–83, 1990–91, 1995–98 World Values Surveys.

cantly affected support for the democratic regime and political community, however. As citizens are criticizing the incumbents of government, they are simultaneously expressing strong support for the democratic creed.

The consequences of declining political trust are a visible part of contemporary politics (Norris 1999b). A more skeptical public is more likely to question government policies, and this probably has contributed to the trend toward increased issue voting and growing electoral volatility. In place of the diffuse support of the past, citizens are now more likely to base their evaluations of politics on instrumental criteria. The old refrain "What have you done for me lately?" is now used more than ever. Political distrust also encourages the use of protest and other forms of unconventional political action (chapter 4). These changes often strain the democratic process, as demonstrators challenge established political elites and present governmental structures. The rise of new social movements and citizen interest groups further institutionalizes the changing nature of citizen politics.

The Democratic Elitist Perspective

Many analysts have cited these new citizen demands as evidence of a crisis of democracy (Crozier, Huntington, and Watanuki 1975; Huntington 1981). Supposedly excessive public demands were overloading the ability of governments to perform. Some conservatives used the elitist theory of democracy (chapter 2) to offer a solution to this crisis. In a crude exaggeration of the theory, they maintained that if a supportive and quiescent public ensures a smoothly functioning political system, then we must redevelop these traits in contemporary publics. The centrifugal tendencies of democratic politics (and the demands of the public) must be controlled, and political authority must be reestablished. Samuel Huntington assumed the ermine robes as spokesperson for this position:

> The problem of governance in the United States today stems from an "excess of democracy" . . . the effective operation of a democratic political system usually requires some measure of apathy and noninvolvement on the part of some individuals and groups. The vulnerability of democratic government in the United States comes . . . from the internal dynamics of democracy itself in a highly educated, mobilized, and participatory society. (1975, 37–38)

In short, these analysts maintained that the crisis of democracy developed because too many people wanted to apply the creed of democracy and egalitarian values to themselves, but democratic systems cannot meet these expectations. These analysts contended that democracy became overloaded because minorities are no longer apathetic, women are demanding equality, students are no longer docile, and the working class is no longer deferential. If these groups would only leave politics to the politicians and their expert advisers, "democracy" would again be secure.[9]

Another element of this elitist interpretation called for a reduction in the scale of government. They argued that governments had assumed too large a role in society, which contributed to the overload. This was part of the theoretical under-pinnings of Thatcher's, Reagan's, and other neoconservatives' attempts to limit the size of government. But often there were distinct biases on which programs the government should no longer address, such as social services or environmental programs, rather than programs that benefited conservative constituencies.

Taken together, the cures offered by the elitist theorists are worse than the problem they address; democracy's very goals are ignored in its defense. The crit-ics of citizen politics forget that democracy means popular control of elites, not elite control over the populace.

The New Politics Perspective

A contrasting image of the state of democracy comes from Vaclav Havel's address to a joint session of the U.S. Congress on February 8, 1990. He described the road we are traveling: "Democracy in the full sense of the word will always be no more than an ideal; one may approach it as one would a horizon, in ways that may be better or worse, but it can never be fully attained." The New Politics perspective suggests that current dissatisfaction with contemporary political systems may represent another historic step in democracy's progress toward its ideal. Just as earlier periods of dissatisfaction led to the expansion of the mass franchise, the granting of voting rights to women, and the populist reforms that strengthened the democratic process, we may be entering a new period of democratic reform.

One illustration of the present mix of orientations is seen in the relation-ship of postmaterial values with political trust and support for the democratic ideal. Figure 12.5 indicates that postmaterialists are distinctly less likely than materialists to trust politicians. Indeed, the postmaterialists' calls for political reform have partially fueled present public doubts about politicians and politi-cal institutions (Dalton 2000b). At the same time postmaterialists are much more likely to support democratic ideals. For instance, only 39 percent of the most materialist respondents in the 1995–98 World Values Survey strongly agree that democracy is the best form of government, compared to 67 percent among postmaterialists. Thus, materialists are satisfied with the present democratic state, but they have lower aspirations for democracy. Postmaterialists are less satisfied with current democratic systems, but they also have higher expectations. Post-materialists illustrate the creedal passion in support for democracy that Hunt-ington laments, but which offers the potential for democracy to move toward its theoretical ideal on the horizon.

In short, the New Politics approach offers a different diagnosis of the current situation. One key feature is the changing nature of citizen politics that we have discussed in this book. Contemporary publics are better informed and better skilled than previous electorates, and they carry different expectations about how the democratic process should function. People today are also more conscious of their political rights and more demanding in their individualism. The new style

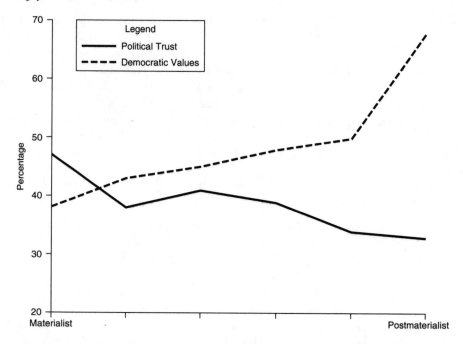

Figure 12.5   The Impact of Values on Support for Democracy and Political Trust

Source: Combined data from eight advanced industrial democracies in the 1995–98 World Values Survey.

Note: Figure plots the percentage of respondents strongly agreeing that democracy is the best form of government and the percentage of respondents who have confidence in national government.

of citizen politics encourages a diversity of political interests (issue publics), instrumental and flexible voting choices, and more direct styles of political action.

In addition, there has been an explosion of citizen interests groups, social movements, and other social groups in recent decades (Meyer and Tarrow 1998; Berry 1999). These groups represent a new style of interest representation, as citizens can focus their attention and their activity on specific policy concerns—and work through methods of direct action. These interest groups signify a new way of organizing interests and mobilizing public opinion. (One might add the creation of an omnipresent mass media to this change in the pattern of politics.) These interest groups also present a challenge to political parties and the established processes of representative government. The structures of representative democracy that were created in the late 1800s often seem ill-suited to deal with this plethora of new interests, articulated in new ways, functioning by new rules.

Democratic governments need to accommodate these changing patterns of citizen politics. For instance, the potential for citizen participation is limited by the traditional system of representative democracy, especially in Western Europe. The opportunities for electoral input are scandalously low for most Europeans. An opportunity to cast a few votes during a multiyear electoral cycle is not a record of citizen input that should be admired. Moreover, beyond elections these political systems offer their citizens few ways to participate in the decisions of government that affect their lives. Indeed, often the government has shielded itself from even basic public scrutiny, such as Britain's Official Secrets Act. The fundamental structure of contemporary democratic institutions was developed in the nineteenth century—society has changed a good deal since then.

An emphasis on new forms of citizen access and influence is not simply a call for participation for participation's sake. Expanding citizen participation opens up political systems that can become sclerosed by corporatist policymaking and bureaucratized administration. The triumvirate of business-labor-government in many advanced industrial democracies often restricts the political interests of other groups. A system that distorts access to the political process is necessarily inefficient in meeting all of society's needs. One can see elements of these problems in the recent radical changes in the Italian party system and in the pressures for political reform in Japan and other advanced industrial democracies.

Opening the political process is also a method to ensure that governments become more responsive to a broader spectrum of political demands. This does not increase the quantity of political needs—the needs of the environment, women, consumers, and other groups exist—rather, it ensures that these needs receive fair attention from the government and thereby improve the government's ability to address all societal needs.

Increased political involvement also educates citizens in the democratic process. James Wright (1976, 260) noted a basic irony in the elitists' criticisms of citizen participation. The democratic elitists believe that governments can generate more support by convincing citizens of a lie (a sense of political efficacy that is fictitious) than by encouraging citizens to participate and learn of the necessary limits to their influence. The "big lie" may work for a while, but as soon as someone points out the gap between myth and reality, the political credibility of the system falters. It happened to the Eastern European governments in 1989–91. Call it co-optation, pragmatism, or Jeffersonian idealism—involving citizens in the democratic process is one method to increase their identification with the process.

Finally, increasing citizen input improves the quality of governmental decision making. Citizen participation is not a panacea for all of society's modern ills. Even educated, informed, and politically involved citizens will still make errors in judgment. As Barber notes:

> Democracy does not place endless faith in the capacity of individuals
> to govern themselves, but it affirms with Machiavelli that the multitude

will on the whole be as wise or wiser than princes, and with Theodore Roosevelt that "the majority of plain people will day in and day out make fewer mistakes in governing themselves than another smaller body of men will make in trying to govern them." (1984, 151)

Since I presented this evaluation of contemporary democratic politics in the first edition of *Citizen Politics*, there are encouraging signs that politicians and governments are responding to these calls for reform. Calls for political reform have become the new catchphrases of politics, ranging from outsiders such as Perot to insiders such as Bill Bennett and Sam Nunn (1998). From Clinton's call for a New Covenant to the Republicans' Contract with America, politicians now claim they want to change the status quo.

Even more significantly, institutional reforms are actually changing the political process. Some citizen groups are gaining access to the formerly closed processes of policy administration. In Germany, for example, local citizen action groups have won changes in administrative law to allow for citizen participation in local administrative processes. Similar reforms in the United States provide individual citizens and citizen groups greater access to the political process (Ingram and Smith 1993).

Other forms of direct democracy are also increasing. Citizen groups in the United States and Europe are making greater use of referendums to involve the public directly in policymaking (Gallagher and Uleri 1996; Butler and Ranney 1994). The judicialization of politics is another important development (Stone Sweet 2000). Increasingly, citizens are using access to the courts to guarantee their rights of democratic access and influence. For instance, Italian environmental legislation now grants individuals legal standing in the courts when they seek to protect the environment from the actions of municipalities or governmental agencies.

There also are reforms within the structured system of party government. The formation of new parties is one sign of adaptation. In addition, even the established parties are changing internally (Scarrow, Webb, and Farrell 2000). The British Labour Party has increased the role of party members in the selection of parliamentary candidates, and the German SPD used a mail ballot of its members to select its chancellor candidate in 1994. The term limits movement is another expression of these reformist sentiments. A majority of states have now enacted some type of term limit legislation, normally through citizen initiatives. These institutional changes are difficult to accomplish, they often have unintended consequences, and they proceed at a slow pace; but once implemented they restructure the whole process of making policy that extends beyond a single issue or a single policy agenda.

Indeed, these adaptations reflect the very strength of democracy to grow and evolve—the lack of such adaptivity is what brought about the downfall of communism. As the German sociologist Ralf Dahrendorf noted during the earlier crisis of democracy debate:

What we have to do above all is to maintain that flexibility of democratic institutions which is in some ways their greatest virtue: the ability of democratic institutions to implement and effect change without revolution—the ability to react to new problems in new ways—the ability to develop institutions rather than change them all the time—the ability to keep the lines of communication open between leaders and led—and the ability to make individuals count above all. (1975, 194)

These changes in the style of representative democracy are accompanied by some risks. There may be some growing pains as the political process adjusts to increasing citizen participation, especially in the more tightly structured European political systems. One potential problem is the growing participation gap between sophisticated and unsophisticated citizens (see chapter 3). Democracies also must face the challenge of balancing greater responsiveness to specific interests against the broader interests of the nation (Bok 2001).

Participatory democracy can generate political excesses, but it also contains within it an equilibrium mechanism to encourage political balance. In America, this process has generally succeeded in retaining the benefits of new ideas while avoiding the dire predictions about the excesses of democracy. We should remember that democratic politics is not designed to maximize governmental efficiency and increase the autonomy of political elites. Just the opposite. Efficiency is partially sacrificed to ensure a more important goal: popular control of elites. Expanding participation is not a problem but an opportunity for the advanced industrial democracies to come closer to matching their democratic ideals.

In summary, the crisis of democracy is really another challenge in the ongoing history of democracy's development. Democracies need to adapt to present-day politics and the new style of citizen politics. As Dahrendorf has recently observed: "Representative government is no longer as compelling a proposition as it once was. Instead, a search for new institutional forms to express conflicts of interest has begun" (2000, 311). This process of democratic experimentation and reform may be threatening to some, and it does present a risk—but change is necessary. The challenge to democracies is whether or not they can continue to evolve, to guarantee political rights, and to increase the ability of citizens to control their lives. Can we move democracy closer to the horizon?

SUGGESTED READINGS

Bok, Derek. *The Trouble with Government.* Cambridge, Mass.: Harvard University Press, 2001.

Klingemann, Hans-Dieter, and Dieter Fuchs, eds. *Citizens and the State.* Oxford, U.K.: Oxford University Press, 1995.

Norris, Pippa, ed. *Critical Citizens: Global Support for Democratic Governance.* Oxford, U.K.: Oxford University Press, 1999.

Nye, Joseph, Philip Zelikow, and David King. *Why Americans Mistrust Government.* Cambridge, Mass.: Harvard University Press, 1997.

Pharr, Susan, and Robert Putnam, eds. *Disaffected Democracies: What's Troubling the Trilateral Democracies.* Princeton, N.J.: Princeton University Press, 2000.

Putnam, Robert. *Making Democracy Work.* Princeton, N.J.: Princeton University Press, 1993.

NOTES

1. In the mid-1980s Samuel Huntington (1984) was explaining why there would be no more democracies in the world, a theme consistent with his elitist view of democracy. By the end of the decade he was describing democratization as a wave that was transforming the international order (Huntington 1991).

2. There has been some debate over the accuracy of this quotation, since Crozier and his colleagues do not identify a source. Moreover, such a statement by Brandt was a sharp contrast to his well-known admonition that Germany actually needed to "risk more democracy." Even if Brandt did not make this statement, other prominent Europeans certainly echoed these sentiments. For instance, the French political observer Jean-Francois Revel declared that "Democracy may, after all, turn out to have been a historical accident, a brief parenthesis that is closing before our eyes" (1983, 3).

3. The argument also is made that diffuse regime support existed in most other Western democracies in the 1930s. Consequently, dissatisfaction focused on the performance of political elites in these systems. These feelings were channeled within the political process, and the basic structure of democratic government persisted in the United States, Britain, and France.

4. A flash poll taken by the *Washington Post* (September 28, 2001) immediately after the terrorist attacks on September 11, 2001, found that Americans' trust in government had doubled in the two weeks following the attacks (64 percent trustful). This is a stunning but perhaps temporary reversal of the trend in political support. Community leaders in Oklahoma City noted a similar burst in civic pride following the attacks of the federal building in 1995. But the dramatic impact of the New York City attacks may change public sentiments in more fundamental terms, especially if patterns of social behavior also change.

5. The question wording and coding categories were slightly different in each nation, so one should not directly compare the levels of support across nations in this figure. For such comparisons, see Klingemann (1999) and tables 12.2 through 12.4 in this chapter.

6. The 1998 ISSP has a relatively short list of political institutions. For a more extensive comparison of confidence in institutions, see Listhaug and Wiberg (1995) and Klingemann (1999).

7. The two questions were as follows: "Let us consider the idea of democracy, without thinking of existing democracies. In principle, are you for or against the idea of democracy?" "Which of the following opinions about different forms of government is closest to your own? (1) In any case, democracy is the best form of government, whatever the circumstance may be; (2) In certain cases, a dictatorship can be positive; (3) For someone like me, it doesn't make any difference whether we have a democracy or a dictatorship."

8. The question asked was, "How proud are you to be (nationality)?" The responses were (1) very proud, (2) quite proud, (3) not very proud, and (4) not at all proud. The figure presents the "very proud" and "proud" responses.

9. Huntington's advice on limiting political demands overlooks the possibility of constraining the input of Harvard professors, corporate executives, and the upper class. His focus solely on the participation of average citizens suggests that he has confused the definitions of plutocracy and democracy.

Major Data Sources

IN 1948 RESEARCHERS at the University of Michigan conducted one of the first national election surveys based on scientific sampling methods. The four scholars who eventually directed the early surveys—Angus Campbell, Philip Converse, Warren Miller, and Donald Stokes—wrote the landmark study of American electoral behavior, *The American Voter*. Since then the Center for Political Studies (formerly part of the Survey Research Center) has continued this election study series at each biennial national election. The University of Michigan series has become a national resource in the social sciences and is used by researchers in hundreds of universities worldwide.

A comparable series of British election studies was begun by David Butler and Donald Stokes with the 1964 election. These scholars continued the series through the 1966 and 1970 elections, and then a team of researchers at the University of Essex, led by Ivor Crewe, continued the series in 1974 and 1979. Between 1983 and 1997 the British election studies were conducted by Anthony Heath, Roger Jowell, and John Curtice of Social and Community Planning Research (SCPR) in London. A new research team at the University of Essex directed the 2001 British election study.

Academic studies of German elections trace their roots back to the 1961 study conducted by Gerhard Baumert, Erwin Scheuch, and Rudolf Wildenmann from the University of Cologne. The Cologne researchers and their students have continued this series to the present through the work of Max Kaase, Hans-Dieter Klingemann, Franz Pappi, and the Forschungsgruppe Wahlen (Manfred Berger, Wolfgang Gibowski, Dieter Roth, Mattias Jung et al.) in Mannheim. The 1998 German election study is a cooperative undertaking of the Mannheimer Zentrum für Europäische Sozialforschung (MZES), the Wissenschaftszentrum Berlin für Sozialforschung (WZB), the Zentralarchiv für empirische Sozialforschung, Cologne, and the Zentrum für Umfragen, Methoden, und Analysen (ZUMA), Mannheim.

France lacks a project of continuous academic monitoring and public dissemination of data on citizen electoral behavior. A number of individual scholars have conducted surveys of specific French elections: Roland Cayrol and his associates, Philip Converse and Roy Pierce, and Michael Lewis-Beck, Nonna Mayer, and Daniel Boy and their colleagues. The emerging series of election studies provides an opportunity to track the evolution of French political behavior during the Fifth Republic.

Most of the data analyzed in this volume were drawn from these data sources. A specific listing of these studies follows. Most of these data were acquired from the Interuniversity Consortium for Political and Social Research (ICPSR) at the University of Michigan in Ann Arbor. Additional data were made available by the ESRC Archive at the University of Essex, England, and the Zentralarchiv für empirische Sozialforschung (ZA), University of Cologne, Germany. Neither the archives nor the original collectors of the data bear responsibility for the analyses presented here.

American National Election Studies (ANES)

1948 American National Election Study (N = 622). Angus Campbell and Robert Kahn.

1952 American National Election Study (N = 1899). Angus Campbell, Gerald Gurin et al.

1956 American National Election Study (N = 1762). Angus Campbell, Philip Converse et al.

1960 American National Election Study (N = 1181). Angus Campbell, Philip Converse et al.

1964 American National Election Study (N = 1571). Political Behavior Program.

1968 American National Election Study (N = 1557). Political Behavior Program.

1972 American National Election Study (N = 2705). Warren Miller, Arthur Miller et al.

1976 American National Election Study (N = 2248). Warren Miller, Arthur Miller et al.

1980 American National Election Study (N = 1614). Warren Miller et al.

1984 American National Election Study (N = 2257). Warren Miller et al.

1988 American National Election Study (N = 2040). Warren Miller et al.

1992 American National Election Study (N = 2485). Warren Miller et al.

1996 American National Election Study (N = 1714). Steven Rosenstone et al.

2000 American National Election Study (N = 1807). Nancy Burns et al.

British Election Studies

1964 British Election Study (N = 1769). David Butler and Donald Stokes.

1966 British Election Study (N = 1874). David Butler and Donald Stokes.

1970 British Election Study (N = 1885). David Butler and Donald Stokes.

1974 British Election Study, February (N = 2462). Ivor Crewe, Bo Saarlvik, and James Alt.

1974 British Election Study, October (N = 2365). Ivor Crewe, Bo Saarlvik, and James Alt.

1979 British Election Study (N = 1893). Ivor Crewe, Bo Saarlvik, and David Robertson.

1983 British Election Study (N = 3955). Anthony Heath, Roger Jowell, and John Curtice.

1987 British Election Study (N = 3826). Anthony Heath, Roger Jowell, John Curtice, and Sharon Witherspoon.

1992 British Election Study (N = 3534). Anthony Heath, Roger Jowell, and John Curtice.

1997 British Election Study (N = 3615). Anthony Heath, Roger Jowell, John Curtice, and Pippa Norris.

2001 British Election Study (N = 3219). David Sanders, Paul Whiteley, Harold Clarke, and Marianne Stewart.

German Election Studies

1953 The Social Bases of West German Politics (N = 3246). UNESCO Institute.

1961 West German Election Study (N = 1679, 1633, 1715). Gerhart Baumert, Erwin Scheuch, and Rudolf Wildenmann.

1965 West German Election Study, October (N = 1305). DIVO Institut.

1965 West German Election Study, September (N = 1411). Rudolf Wildenmann and Max Kaase.

1969 West German Election Study (N = 1158). Hans Klingemann and Franz Pappi.

1972 West German Election Study (N = 2052). Manfred Berger, Wolfgang Gibowski, Max Kaase, Dieter Roth, Uwe Schleth, and Rudolf Wildenmann.

1976 West German Election Study (N = 2076). Forschungsgruppe Wahlen.

1980 West German Election Study (N = 1620). Forschungsgruppe Wahlen.

1983   West German Election Study (N = 1622). Forschungsgruppe Wahlen.

1987   West German Election Study (N = 1954). Forschungsgruppe Wahlen.

1990   German Election Study, November (West = 984; East = 1095). Forschungsgruppe Wahlen.

1994   German Election Study, September (West = 1013; East = 1068). Forschungsgruppe Wahlen.

1998   German Postelection Study 1998 (West = 978; East = 1041). Mannheimer Zentrum für Europäische Sozialforschung (MZES), the Wissenschaftszentrum Berlin für Sozialforschung (WZB), the Zentralarchiv für empirische Sozialforschung, and the Zentrum für Umfragen, Methoden, und Analysen (ZUMA), Mannheim.

French Election Studies

1958   French Election Study (N = 1650). Georges Dupeux.

1967   French Election Study (N = 2046). Philip Converse and Roy Pierce.

1968   French Election Study (N = 1905). Ronald Inglehart.

1978   French Election Study (N = 4507). Jacques Capdevielle, Elisabeth Dupoirier, Gerard Frunberg, Etienne Schweisguth, and Colette Ysmal.

1988   French Presidential Election Survey (N = 1013). Roy Pierce.

1995   French National Election Study (N = 4078). Michael Lewis-Beck, Nonna Mayer, Daniel Boy et al.

1997   French National Election Study (N = 3010). Centre d'Etudes de la Vie Politique Française (CEVIPOF), Centre d'Informatisation des Données Socio-Politiques (CIDSP), and Centre de Recherches Administratives, Politiques et Sociales.

Major Cross-National Studies

1959   The Civic Culture Study (USA = 970, Great Britain = 963, West Germany = 955). Gabriel Almond and Sidney Verba.

1974   Political Action Study (USA = 1719, Great Britain = 1483, West Germany = 2307). Samuel Barnes, Max Kaase et al.

1981–83   World Values Survey (USA = 1729, Great Britain = 1231, West Germany = 1305, France = 1200). Gallup Research.

1990–91   World Values Survey (USA. = 1839, Great Britain = 1484, West Germany = 2101, France = 1002, East Germany = 1336). Ronald Inglehart and the European Values Systems Study Group.

1995–98   World Values Survey (USA = 1542, Great Britain = 1093, West Germany = 1017, East Germany = 1009). Ronald Inglehart, Hans-Dieter Klingemann et al.

1996–2000   Comparative Study of Electoral Systems (USA = 1714, Great Britain = 3615, Germany = 2021).

1970–present   European Community Surveys/Eurobarometers, an ongoing series of opinion surveys conducted by the Commission of the European Union.

1972–present   International Social Survey Program, a coordinated series of public opinion surveys conducted by various sociological institutes in the United States and Europe.

International Social Survey Program Data: Role of Government Survey, 1996

ONE OF THE key sources of public opinion data in this book is the International Social Survey Program (ISSP). To assist students and instructors in understanding the causes and correlates of public opinion, we have prepared a subset of the data from the 1996 ISSP for instructors to use in connection with *Citizen Politics*. These data have been extensively recoded and reformatted for ease of student use, by means such as merging categories to ensure reasonable group sizes in cross-tabular analyses. Students can use these data for small research exercises designed by the instructor or for longer-term research projects that explore the themes in this book or other aspects of public opinion.

This appendix includes a brief description of the International Social Survey Program and an abbreviated codebook that describes the variables included in this subset. Portable files for the Statistical Package in the Social Sciences (SPSS) are downloadable from the Chatham House Web site (www.sevenbridgespress.com/chathamhouse/citizen). There is a file containing data for the four core nations of this book (the United States, Britain, Germany, and France).

THE INTERNATIONAL SOCIAL SURVEY PROGRAM

The International Social Survey Program (ISSP) is a continuing, annual program of cross-national collaboration. It brings together preexisting social science survey research projects and coordinates research goals, thereby adding a cross-national perspective to the individual national studies. On a nearly annual basis, the collaborating research institutes collect a common research module on a specific topic, such as the role of government, religion, work orientations, social inequality, or the environment.

ISSP evolved from a bilateral collaboration between the ALLBUS survey of the Zentrum für Umfragen, Methoden, und Analysen (ZUMA) in Mannheim,

Germany, and the General Social Survey (GSS) of the National Opinion Research Center, University of Chicago. In late 1983 Social and Community Planning Research, London, joined in this collaboration through the British Social Attitudes Survey (BSA), and the Research School of Social Sciences, Australian National University, organized the ISSP in 1984. Since 1984, ISSP has grown to thirty-one nations, the founding four—Germany, the United States, Great Britain, and Australia—plus Austria, Italy, Ireland, Hungary, the Netherlands, Israel, Norway, the Philippines, New Zealand, Russia, Japan, Bulgaria, Canada, the Czech Republic, Slovenia, Poland, Sweden, Spain, Cyprus, France, Portugal, Slovakia, Latvia, Chile, Bangladesh, Denmark, and South Africa. Additional information about the ISSP can be found on its Web site (www.issp.org). These surveys are available from the Interuniversity Consortium for Political and Social Research at the University of Michigan, the Zentralarchiv für empirische Sozialforschung at the University of Cologne, and other national social science data archives.

Variable List

| V01 | Country |
| V02 | Weight variable |

Political Involvement

V03	How much interested in politics
V04	Voted in last election
V05	Participation in public protest meetings
V06	Participation in demonstrations
V07	Protest scale

Partisanship

V08	Combined party affiliation: Left–Right
V09a	USA: Vote preference
V09b	Britain: Party affiliation
V09c	Germany: Party affiliation
V09d	France: Party affiliation

Tolerance

V10	Revolutionaries: hold public meetings
V11	Revolutionaries: publish books
V12	Allow public protest meetings
V13	Allow demonstrations
V14	Allow antigovernment strike

Policy Issues

V15	Worse type of judicial mistake
V16	Computers are a threat to privacy
V17	Government: redistribute wealth
V18	Government: control wages by law
V19	Government: control prices by law
V20	Government: cut spending
V21	Government: create new jobs
V22	Government: less regulation of business
V23	Government: support industry for new products
V24	Government: support declining industries
V25	Government: reduce working week

Government Spending

V26	Government should spend on environment
V27	Government should spend on health
V28	Government should spend on law enforcement
V29	Government should spend on education
V30	Government should spend on defense
V31	Government should spend on retirement
V32	Government should spend on unemployment benefits
V33	Government should spend on culture and arts

Power of Institutions

V34	Power of trade unions
V35	Power of business and industry
V36	Power of government

Role of Government

V37	Government responsible for providing jobs for all
V38	Government responsible for keeping prices under control
V39	Government responsible for health care for sick
V40	Government responsible for providing standard of living for the old
V41	Government responsible for providing industry with help to grow
V42	Government responsible for proving standard of living for unemployed
V43	Government responsible for reducing income differences rich/poor
V44	Government responsible for financial help for students
V45	Government responsible for providing decent housing
V46	Government responsible for strict environmental laws

Political Support

V47	Satisfied with democracy
V48	Obey laws without exception
V49	Politicians have not much impact
V50	Elections make government pay attention
V51	Politicians keep promises
V52	Trust in civil servants
V53	Political trust scale

Political Efficacy

V54	People like me have no influence in government
V55	Average citizen: influence in politics
V56	Good understanding of important political issues
V57	Others better informed than me
V58	Political efficacy scale

Taxes

V59	Reduce taxes or more social service
V60	Taxes for high incomes
V61	Taxes for middle incomes
V62	Taxes for low incomes

Government Control of Industry

V63	Government versus private ownership: Electricity
V64	Government versus private ownership: Hospitals
V65	Government versus private ownership: Banking
V66	Government ownership scale

Social Characteristics

V67	Respondent's gender
V68	Respondent's age
V69	Marital status
V70	Education level
V71	Respondent: Current employment status
V72	Spouse: Current employment status
V73	Respondent's occupation
V74	Spouse's occupation
V75	Respondent working for private or public sector
V76	Religious denomination
V77	Frequency of church attendance
V78	Subjective social class

V79   Trade union membership
V80   Size of household
V81   Size of community
V82a   United States: Region
V82b   Britain: Region
V82c   Germany: Region
V82d   France: Region

Codebook

V01   Country

1. United States (USA)   N = 1332
2. Great Britain (GB)   N = 989
3. France (F)   N = 1312
4. Germany (West) (D-W)   N = 2361
5. Germany (East) (D-E)   N = 1109

V02   Weighting factor

Weighting factor; this should be used to weight the cases in the British and French samples to produce representative cross sections. (See the weighting option in SPSS.)

1. Self-weighted

V03   Political interest

How interested would you say you personally are in politics?

1. Very/fairly interested
2. Somewhat interested
3. Not very/not at all
0. Missing data

V04   Voted in last election

Did the respondent vote in the last national election?

1. Voted vote
2. Did not vote
0. Missing data

V05   Active in protest meetings

In the past five years how many times have you done each of the following to protest against a government action you strongly oppose: Attended a public meeting organized to protest against the government?

1. Never

2. Once
3. More than once
0. Missing data

V06 Active in demonstrations

And in the past five years how many times have you done each of the following to protest against a government action you strongly oppose: Gone on a protest march or demonstration?

1. Never
2. Once
3. More than once
0. Missing data

V07 Protest scale

A summary index based on the combination of V05 and V06.

1. Never
2. One activity
3. Two activities
4. More than two activities
0. Missing data

V08 Party preference: Left–Right

Political party preference, combined for only Left or Right parties, derived from V09A–V09D.

1. Left party
2. Right, conservative party
0. Missing data

V09A USA: Party preference

Which party did you vote for in the last presidential election?

1. Democrat (Clinton)
2. Perot
3. Republican (Bush)
0. Missing data; other nation (Britain, France, Germany)

V09B Britain: Party preference

If there were a general election tomorrow which political party do you think you would be most likely to support?

1. Labour
2. Liberal Democrats

3. Conservatives

0. Missing data; other nation (U.S., France, Germany)

V09C   Germany: Party preference

Germany: If there were a general election next Sunday, which party would you elect with your second vote?

1. PDS
2. Greens
3. SPD
4. FDP
5. CDU/CSU
6. Republikaner
0. Missing data; other nations (U.S., Britain, France)

V09D   France: Party preference

France: Which political party did you support in the last presidential election?

1. Communist Party (Hue)
2. Socialist Party (Jospin)
3. Green (Yoynet)
4. Other parties
5. RPR/UDF (Chirac, Balladur)
6. National Front (Le Pen)
0. Missing data; other nation (U.S., Britain, Germany)

V10   Revolutionaries: hold public meetings

There are some people whose views are considered extreme by the majority. First, consider people who want to overthrow the government by revolution. Do you think such people should be allowed to . . . hold public meetings to express their views?

1. Definitely allowed
2. Probably allowed
3. Probably/definitely not allowed
0. Missing data

V11   Revolutionaries: publish books

(Should) revolutionaries should be allowed to: Publish books expressing their views?

1. Definitely allowed
2. Probably allowed
3. Probably/definitely not allowed
0. Missing data

V12   Allow protest meetings

There are many ways people or organizations can protest against a government action they strongly oppose. Please show which you think should be allowed and which should not be allowed by ticking a box on each line. Forms of protest: Organizing public meetings to protest against the government.

1. Definitely allowed
2. Probably allowed
3. Probably/definitely not allowed
0. Missing data

V13   Allow demonstrations

(Should we) allow forms of protest: Organizing protest marches and demonstrations.

1. Definitely allowed
2. Probably allowed
3. Probably/definitely not allowed
0. Missing data

V14   Allow antigovernment strike

(Should we) allow forms of protest: Organizing a nationwide strike of all workers against the government.

1. Definitely allowed
2. Probably allowed
3. Probably/definitely not allowed
0. Missing data

V15   Worse type judicial mistake

All systems of justice make mistakes, but which do you think is worse?

1. To convict an innocent person
2. To let a guilty person go free
0. Missing data

V16   Computer threat privacy

The government has a lot of different pieces of information about people that computers can bring together very quickly. Is this . . .

1. A very serious threat to individual privacy
2. A fairly serious threat
3. Not a serious threat
4. Not a threat at all to individual privacy
0. Missing data

VI7   Government: redistribute wealth

What is your opinion of the following statement: It is the responsibility of the government to reduce the differences in income between people with high incomes and those with low incomes.

1. Agree
2. Neither agree nor disagree
3. Disagree
0. Missing data

VI8   Government: control wages by law

Here are some things the government might do for the economy. Please show which actions you are in favor of and which you are against: Government action for economy: Control of wages by law.

1. In favor of
2. Neither in favor of nor against
3. Against
0. Missing data

VI9   Government: control prices by law

Government action for economy: Control of prices by law.

1. In favor of
2. Neither in favor of nor against
3. Against
0. Missing data

V20   Government: cuts in spending

Government action for economy: Cuts in government spending.

1. In favor of
2. Neither in favor of nor against
3. Against
0. Missing data

V21   Government: create new jobs

Government action for economy: Government financing of projects to create new jobs.

1. In favor of
2. Neither in favor of nor against
3. Against
0. Missing data

V22   Government: less regulation

Government action for economy: Less government regulation of business.

1. In favor of
2. Neither in favor of nor against
3. Against
0. Missing data

V23   Government: new products

Government action for economy: Support for industry to develop new products and technology.

1. In favor of
2. Neither in favor of nor against
3. Against
0. Missing data

V24   Government: declining industries

Government action for economy: Support for declining industries to protect jobs.

1. In favor of
2. Neither in favor of nor against
3. Against
0. Missing data

V25   Government: reduce working week

Government action for economy: Reducing the working week to create more jobs.

1. In favor of
2. Neither in favor of nor against
3. Against
0. Missing data

V26   Spend on environment

Listed below are various areas of government spending. Please show whether you would like to see more or less government spending in each area. Remember that if you say "much more," it might require a tax increase to pay for it. More or less government spending for: The environment.

1. Spend more
2. Spend the same as now
3. Spend less
0. Missing data

V27   Spend on health

More or less government spending for: Health.

1. Spend more
2. Spend the same as now
3. Spend less
0. Missing data

V28   Spend on law enforcement

More or less government spending for: The police and law enforcement.

1. Spend more
2. Spend the same as now
3. Spend less
0. Missing data

V29   Spend on education

More or less government spending for: Education.

1. Spend more
2. Spend the same as now
3. Spend less
0. Missing data

V30   Spend on defense

More or less government spending for: The military and defense.

1. Spend more
2. Spend the same as now
3. Spend less
0. Missing data

V31   Spend on retirement

More or less government spending for: Old age pensions.

1. Spend more
2. Spend the same as now
3. Spend less
0. Missing data

V32   Spend on unemployment

More or less government spending for: Unemployment benefits.

1. Spend more
2. Spend the same as now

3. Spend less
0. Missing data

V33   Spend on culture, arts

More or less government spending for: Culture and the arts.

1. Spend more
2. Spend the same as now
3. Spend less
0. Missing data

V34   Power of unions

Do you think that trade (USA: labor) unions in this country have too much power or too little power?

1. Too much power
2. About the right amount of power
3. Too little power
0. Missing data

V35   Power of business

How about business and industry? Do they have too much power or too little power?

1. Too much power
2. About the right amount of power
3. Too little power
0. Missing data

V36   Power of government

And what about the (USA: federal) government, does it have too much power or too little power?

1. Too much power
2. About the right amount of power
3. Too little power
0. Missing data

V37   Responsible: provide jobs

On the whole, do you think it should be or should not be the government's responsibility to: Provide a job for everyone who wants one?

1. Definitely should be
2. Probably should be

3. Probably/definitely should not be

0. Missing data

V38 Responsible: control prices

On the whole, do you think it should be or should not be the government's responsibility to: Keep prices under control?

1. Definitely should be
2. Probably should be
3. Probably/definitely should not be
0. Missing data

V39 Responsible: health care for sick

On the whole, do you think it should be or should not be the government's responsibility to: Provide health care for the sick?

1. Definitely should be
2. Probably should be
3. Probably/definitely should not be
0. Missing data

V40 Responsible: help the elderly

On the whole, do you think it should be or should not be the government's responsibility to: Provide a decent standard of living for the old?

1. Definitely should be
2. Probably should be
3. Probably/definitely should not be
0. Missing data

V41 Responsible: help industry

On the whole, do you think it should be or should not be the government's responsibility to: Provide industry with the help it needs to grow?

1. Definitely should be
2. Probably should be
3. Probably/definitely should not be
0. Missing data

V42 Responsible: help unemployed

On the whole, do you think it should be or should not be the government's responsibility to: Provide a decent standard of living for the unemployed?

1. Definitely should be
2. Probably should be
3. Probably/definitely should not be

o. Missing data

V43   Responsible: reduce income differences

On the whole, do you think it should be or should not be the government's responsibility to: Reduce income differences between the rich and poor?

1. Definitely should be
2. Probably should be
3. Probably/definitely should not be
o. Missing data

V44   Responsible: help students

On the whole, do you think it should be or should not be the government's responsibility to: Give financial help to university students from low-income families?

1. Definitely should be
2. Probably should be
3. Probably/definitely should not be
o. Missing data

V45   Responsible: provide housing

On the whole, do you think it should be or should not be the government's responsibility to: Provide decent housing for those who can't afford it?

1. Definitely should be
2. Probably should be
3. Probably/definitely should not be
o. Missing data

V46   Responsible: environmental laws

On the whole, do you think it should be or should not be the government's responsibility to: Impose strict laws to make industry do less damage to the environment?

1. Definitely should be
2. Probably should be
3. Probably/definitely should not be
o. Missing data

V47   Satisfied with democracy

All in all, how well or badly do you think the system of democracy in (respondent's country) works these days?

1. It works well and needs no changes
2. It works well but needs some changes

3. It does not work well and needs a lot of changes
4. It does not work well and needs to be completely changed
0. Missing data

V48   *Obey laws without exception*

In general, would you say that people should obey the law without exception, or are there exceptional occasions on which people should follow their consciences even if it means breaking the law?

1. Obey the law without exception
2. Follow conscience on occasions
0. Missing data

V49   *Politicians don't have impact*

How much do you agree or disagree with each of the following statements? Even the best (politician) cannot have much impact because of the way government works.

1. Agree
2. Neither agree nor disagree
3. Disagree
0. Missing data

V50   *Elections make government pay attention*

How much do you agree or disagree with each of the following statements? Elections are a good way of making governments aware of the important political issues facing our country.

1. Agree
2. Neither agree nor disagree
3. Disagree
0. Missing data

V51   *Politicians keep promises*

How much do you agree or disagree with each of the following statements? People elected as (MPs) try to keep the promises they have made during the election.

1. Agree
2. Neither agree nor disagree
3. Disagree
0. Missing data

V52   Trust civil servants

How much do you agree or disagree with each of the following statements? Most (civil servants) can be trusted to do what is best for the country.

1. Agree
2. Neither agree nor disagree
3. Disagree
0. Missing data

V53   Trust in government scale

This is a count of the number of items on political trust (V50–V52) that the respondent agrees with:

1. Low trust (no trustful responses)
2. One
3. Two
4. High trust (three trustful responses)
0. Missing data

V54   People like me have no say

How much do you agree or disagree with each of the following statements? People like me don't have any say about what the government does.

1. Agree
2. Neither agree nor disagree
3. Disagree
0. Missing data

V55   Average citizen has influence

How much do you agree or disagree with each of the following statements? The average citizen has considerable influence on politics.

1. Agree
2. Neither agree nor disagree
3. Disagree
0. Missing data

V56   Good understanding of issues

How much do you agree or disagree with each of the following statements? I feel that I have a pretty good understanding of the important political issues facing our country.

1. Agree
2. Neither agree nor disagree

3. Disagree

0. Missing data

V57 *Most people informed*

How much do you agree or disagree with each of the following statements? I think most of the people are better informed about the important political issues facing our country.

1. Agree
2. Neither agree nor disagree
3. Disagree
0. Missing data

V58 *Political efficacy scale*

This is a count of the number of efficacious responses on the political efficacy questions (V54–V57):

1. Low efficacy (no efficacious responses)
2. One
3. Two
4. High efficacy (three or four)
0. Missing data

V59 *Reduce taxes or social spending*

If the government had a choice between reducing taxes or spending more on (social services), which do you think it should do? (We mean all taxes together, including wage deductions, income tax, tax on goods and services, and all the rest.)

1. Reduce taxes, even if this means spending less on (social services)
2. Spend more on (social services), even if this means higher taxes
0. Missing data

V60 *Taxes: high incomes*

Generally, how would you describe taxes in (respondent's country) today? (Again we mean all taxes together, including wage deductions, income tax, tax on goods and services, and all the rest.) First for those with high incomes, are taxes . . .

1. Much too high
2. Too high
3. About right
4. Too low/much too low
0. Missing data

V61   Taxes: middle incomes

Generally, how would you describe taxes in (respondent's country) today? Next for those with middle incomes, are taxes . . .

1. Much too high
2. Too high
3. About right
4. Too low/much too low
0. Missing data

V62   Taxes: low incomes

Generally, how would you describe taxes in (respondent's country) today? Lastly, for those with low incomes, are taxes . . .

1. Much too high
2. Too high
3. About right
4. Too low/much too low
0. Missing data

V63   Government run: electricicity

Do you think each of the following should mainly be run by private organizations or companies or by government? Electricity (USA: electric power)

1. Mainly run by private organizations
2. Mainly run by government
0. Missing data

V64   Government run: hospitals

Do you think each of the following should mainly be run by private organizations or companies or by government? Hospitals

1. Mainly run by private organizations
2. Mainly run by government
0. Missing data

V65   Government run: banking

Do you think each of the following should mainly be run by private organizations or companies or by government? Banks

1. Mainly run by private organizations
2. Mainly run by government
0. Missing data

V66   Government ownership scale

This is a count of the number of areas in which the respondent favors government ownership (V63–V65):

1. No government ownership
2. Ownership in one area
3. Ownership in two areas
4. Ownership in three areas
0. Missing data

V67   Respondent's gender

Gender of respondent

1. Male
2. Female
0. Missing data

V68   Respondent's age

Age of respondent

1. Under age 30
2. 30–44
3. 45–59
4. 60 years or over
0. Missing data

V69   Respondent's marital status

Marital status

1. Married or living as married
2. Widowed
3. Divorced; separated
4. Never married, not married, single
0. Missing data

V70   Respondent's education

What kind of a complete general school education do you have? (USA: What is the highest degree?)

1. Primary school
2. Some secondary or completed secondary
3. Some college or completed college
0. Missing data

V71 *Respondent's current employment status*

Respondent: Current employment status—current economic position, main source of living.

1. Full-time employed
2. Part-time employed
3. Unemployed
4. Retired
5. Housework
0. Missing data

V72 *Spouse's current employment status*

Spouse: Current employment status—current economic position.

1. Full-time employed
2. Part-time employed
3. Unemployed
4. Retired
5. Housework
0. Missing data

V73 *Respondent's occupation*

Respondent's occupation: Present/past occupation, except for Germany, which included only present occupation.

1. Manager, executive
2. White collar
3. Manual workers
4. Farming
0. Missing data (not in labor force, never had a job)

V74 *Spouse/partner occupation*

Spouse occupation: Present/past occupation, except for Germany, which included only present occupation.

1. Manager, executive
2. White collar
3. Manual workers
4. Farming
0. Missing data (no spouse, spouse not in labor force, never had a job)

V75 Respondent: Working for private or public sector

Private versus public sector (If respondent works dependent): Do you work at present or did you work in the public sector before?

1. Works for government or public sector
2. Works for private firm or sector
3. Self-employed
0. Missing data

V76 Respondent's religious denomination

USA: What is your religious preference? Is it Protestant, Catholic, Jewish, some other religion, or no religion? (If Protestant) What specific denomination is that? (GB: Do you regard yourself as belonging to any particular religion? If yes, which?)

1. Catholic
2. Protestant
3. Other Christian
4. Jewish
5. Non-Christian
6. No religion
0. Missing data

V77 Attend religious services

How often do you attend religious services? (GB: Apart from such special occasions as weddings, funerals, and baptism, how often nowadays do you attend services or meetings connected with your religion?)

1. Weekly to monthly
2. Several times a year
3. Less frequently
4. Never
0. Missing data

V78 Subjective social class

Subjective social class (USA): If you were asked to use one of four names for your social class, which would you say you belong to: The lower, the working, the middle, or the upper class?

1. Lower class/working class
2. Middle class/upper class
0. NA

V79   Trade union membership

Trade (labor) union membership: Are you a member in a trade union at present? (GB: Are you now a member of a trade union or staff association?) (USA: Do you belong to a labor union?)

1. Member
2. Not a member
0. Missing data, including unemployed

V80   How many persons in household

Size of household: Total number of persons living in household.

1. 1 person
2. 2 persons
3. 3 persons
4. 4 persons
5. 5 or more persons
0. Missing data

V81   Size of community

Size of place where respondent lives.

1. Under 50,000 inhabitants
2. 50,000–100,000 inhabitants
3. 100,000–500,000 inhabitants
4. 500,000 inhabitants or more
0. Missing data; data not available for Britain

V82a   USA: Region

United States: States were recoded into regions (U.S. Bureau of Census: Regional classification).

01. New England
02. Middle Atlantic
03. East North Central
04. West North Central
05. South Atlantic
06. East South Central
07. West South Central
08. Mountain
09. Pacific
00. Missing data (other nations)

V82b   Great Britain: Region

Great Britain: Districts—The Registrar General's Standard Regions have been used.

01. Scotland
02. Northern, North West, Yorkshire, and Humberside
03. West Midlands, East Midlands
04. Wales
05. East Anglia, South West, South East
06. Greater London
00. Missing data (other nations)

V82c   Germany: Region

Germany: Federal states

01. Schleswig-Holstein
02. Hamburg
03. Niedersachsen
04. Bremen
05. Nordrhein-Westfalen
06. Hessen
07. Rheinland-Pfalz
08. Baden-Wuerttemberg
09. Bayern
10. Saarland
11. Berlin-Ost
12. Mecklenburg-Vorpommern
13. Brandenburg
14. Sachsen-Anhalt
15. Thueringen
16. Sachsen
17. Berlin-West
00. Missing data (other nations)

V82d   France: Region

France: Regions recoded from Departments

1. Northwest
2. Southwest
3. Paris Basin
4. Paris
5. East
6. Southeast
0. Missing data

References

Aberbach, Joel, and Jack Walker. 1970. Political trust and racial ideology. *American Political Science Review* 64:1199–1219.

Abramson, Paul. 1979. Developing party identification. *American Journal of Political Science* 23:79–96.

Abramson, Paul, and John Aldrich. 1982. The decline of electoral participation in America. *American Political Science Review* 76:502–21.

Abramson, Paul, John Aldrich, and David Rohde. 1999. *Change and Continuity in the 1996 and 1998 Elections.* Washington, D.C.: Congressional Quarterly Press.

Abramson, Paul, and Ronald Inglehart. 1994. Education, security and postmaterialists: A comment. *American Journal of Political Science* 38:797–814.

———. 1995. *Value Change in Global Perspective.* Ann Arbor: University of Michigan Press.

Abramson, Paul, and Charles Ostrom. 1991. Macropartisanship: An empirical reassessment. *American Political Science Review* 85:181–92.

Abramson, Paul, and Charles Ostrom. 1994. Question wording and partisanship. *Public Opinion Quarterly* 58:21–48.

Aldrich, John, John Sullivan, and E. Bordida. 1989. Foreign affairs and issue voting. *American Political Science Review* 83:123–41.

Almond, Gabriel, Russell Dalton, and G. Bingham Powell, eds. 2002. *European Politics Today,* 2d ed. New York: Addison-Wesley Longman.

Almond, Gabriel, G. Bingham Powell, Kaare Strom, and Russell Dalton, eds. 2000. *Comparative Politics Today.* 7th ed. New York: Addison-Wesley Longman.

Almond, Gabriel, G. Bingham Powell, Kaare Strom, and Russell Dalton. 2001. *Comparative Politics.* 3d ed. New York: HarperCollins.

Almond, Gabriel, and Sidney Verba. 1963. *The Civic Culture.* Princeton, N.J.: Princeton University Press.

———, eds. 1980. *The Civic Culture Revisited.* Boston: Little, Brown.

Anderson, Christopher. 1995. *Blaming the Government: Citizens and the Economy in Five European Democracies.* Armonk, N.Y.: M.E. Sharpe.

———. 2000. Economic voting and political context. *Electoral Studies* 19:151–70.

Ansell, Christopher, and Steven Fish. 1999. The art of being indispensable: Noncharismatic personalism in contemporary political parties. *Comparative Political Studies* 32:283–312.

Arnold, Douglas. 1990. *The Logic of Congressional Action.* New Haven, Conn.: Yale University Press.

Ashford, Sheena, and Noel Timms. 1992. *What Europe Thinks: A Study of Western European Values.* Brookfield, Vt.: Dartmouth.

Bagehot, Walter. 1978. *The English Constitution.* Oxford, U.K.: Oxford University Press.

Baker, Kendall, Russell Dalton, and Kai Hildebrandt. 1981. *Germany Transformed: Political Culture and the New Politics.* Cambridge, Mass.: Harvard University Press.

Barber, Benjamin. 1984. *Strong Democracy.* Berkeley: University of California Press.

Barnes, Samuel. 1977. *Representation in Italy.* Chicago: University of Chicago Press.

Barnes, Samuel, Max Kaase et al. 1979. *Political Action.* Beverly Hills, Calif.: Sage.

Bartolini, Stefano, and Peter Mair. 1989. *Identity, Competition and Electoral Availability.* New York: Cambridge University Press.

Bauer-Kaase, Petra. 1994. German unification. In D. Hancock and H. Welsh, eds. *German Unification.* Boulder, Colo.: Westview.

Bean, Clive. 1996. Partisanship and electoral behaviour in comparative perspective. In M. Simms, ed., *The Paradox of Parties: Australian Political Parties in the 1990s.* Sydney: Allen and Unwin.

Bean, Clive, and Anthony Mughan. 1989. Leadership effects in parliamentary elections in Australia and Britain. *American Political Science Review* 83:1165–79.

Beck, Paul Allen, et al. 1992. Patterns and sources of ticket-splitting in subpresidential voting. *American Political Science Review* 86:916–28.

Beedham, Brian. 1993. What next for democracy? *The Economist* (September 11); special supplement, "The Future Surveyed."

Bell, Daniel. 1960. *The End of Ideology.* New York: Free Press.

———. 1973. *The Coming of Post-industrial Society.* New York: Basic Books.

Bennet, William, and Samuel Nunn. 1998. *A Nation of Spectators.* Washington, D.C.: National Commission on Civic Renewal.

Berelson, Bernard, Paul Lazarsfeld, and William McPhee. 1954. *Voting.* Chicago: University of Chicago Press.

Berry, Jeffrey. 1989. *The Interest Group Society.* Glenview, Ill.: Scott Foresman.

———. 1999. *The New Liberalism: The Rising Power of Citizen Groups.* Washington, D.C.: Brookings Institution.

Betz, Hans-Georg. 1994. *Radical Right-wing Populism in Europe.* New York: St. Martin's Press.

Bishop, George, and Kathleen Frankovic. 1981. Ideological consensus and constraint among party leaders and followers in the 1978 election. *Micropolitics* 1:87–111.

Blais, André. 2000. *To Vote or Not to Vote: The Merits and Limits of Rational Choice Theory.* Pittsburgh: University of Pittsburgh Press.

Blais, André, and Ken Carty. 1990. Does proportional representation foster voter turnout? *European Journal of Political Research* 18:167–81.

Bok, Derek. 2001. *The Trouble with Democracy.* Cambridge, Mass.: Harvard University Press.

Borre, Ole, and Daniel Katz. 1973. Party identification and its motivational base in a multiparty system. *Scandinavian Political Studies* 8:69–111.

Borre, Ole, and Elinor Scarbrough, eds. 1995. *Beliefs about the Scope of Government.* Oxford, U.K.: Oxford University Press.

Bowler, Shaun, David Farrell, and Richard Katz, eds. 1999. *Party Discipline and Parliamentary Government.* Columbus: Ohio State University Press.

Boy, Daniel, and Nonna Mayer, eds. 1993. *The French Voter Decides.* Ann Arbor: University of Michigan Press.

Brady, Henry, Sidney Verba, and Kay Schlozman. 1995. Beyond SES: A resource model of political participation. *American Political Science Review* 89:271–94.

Braithwaite, V., T. Makkai, and Y. Pittelkow. 1996. Inglehart's materialism-postmaterialism concept: Clarifying the dimensionality debate through Rokeach's model of social values. *Journal of Applied Social Psychology* 26:1536–55.

Brody, Richard. 1978. The puzzle of political participation in America. In A. King, ed., *The New American Political System.* Washington, D.C.: American Enterprise Institute.

Brody, Richard, et al. 1994. Accounting for divided government. In M. K. Jennings and T. Mann, eds., *Elections at Home and Abroad.* Ann Arbor: University of Michigan Press.

Bromley, Catherine, John Curtice, and Ben Seyd. 2002. Confidence in government. In Roger Jowell et al., *British Social Attitude Survey.* Brookfield, Vt.: Dartmouth.

Bryce, James. 1921. *Modern Democracies,* vol. 1. New York: Macmillan.

Budge, Ian. 1999. Party policy and ideology: Reversing the 1950s. In Geoffrey Evans and Pippa Norris, eds., *Critical Elections: British Parties and Voters in Long-term Perspective.* Thousand Oaks, Calif.: Sage Publications.

Budge, Ian, Ivor Crewe, and David Farlie, eds. 1976. *Party Identification and Beyond.* New York: Wiley.

Budge, Ian, David Robertson, and D. Hearl. 1987. *Ideology, Strategy and Party Change.* Cambridge, U.K.: Cambridge University Press.

Budge, Ian, et al. 1998. *The New British Politics.* New York: Addison-Wesley Longman.

Bürklin, Wilhelm, et al. 1997. *Eliten in Deutschland: Rekrutierung und Integration.* Leverkusen: Leske + Budrich.

Burns, Nancy, Kay L. Schlozman, and Sidney Verba. 2001. *The Private Roots of Public Action.* Cambridge, Mass.: Harvard University Press.

Butler, David. 1995. *British General Elections since 1945.* Oxford, U.K.: Blackwell.

Butler, David, and Austin Ranney, eds. 1994. *Referendums around the World: The Growing Use of Democracy.* Washington, D.C.: American Enterprise Institute.

Butler, David, and Donald Stokes. 1969. *Political Change in Britain.* New York: St. Martin's Press.

———. 1974. *Political Change in Britain.* 2d ed. New York: St. Martin's Press.

Campbell, Angus, Gerald Gurin, and Warren Miller. 1954. *The Voter Decides.* Evanston, Ill.: Row, Peterson.

Campbell, Angus, et al. 1960. *The American Voter.* New York: Wiley.

———. 1966. *Elections and the Political Order.* New York: Wiley.

Cantril, Hadley. 1965. *The Patterns of Human Concerns.* New Brunswick, N.J.: Rutgers University Press.

Carmines, Edward, and James Stimson. 1980. The two faces of issue voting. *American Political Science Review* 74:78–91.

———. 1989. *Issue Evolution: Race and the Transformation of American Politics.* Princeton, N.J.: Princeton University Press.

Caul, Miki, and Mark Gray. 2000. From platform declarations to policy outcomes. In R. Dalton and M. Wattenberg, eds., *Parties without Partisans.* Oxford, U.K.: Oxford University Press.

Charlot, Monica. 1980. Women in politics in France. In H. Penniman, ed., *The French National Assembly Elections of 1978.* Washington, D.C.: American Enterprise Institute.

Citrin, Jack. 1974. Comment. *American Political Science Review* 68:973–88.

Clarke, Harold, and Nitish Dutt. 1991. Measuring value change in western industrialized societies. *American Political Science Review* 85:905–20.

Clarke, Harold, Allan Kornberg, and Peter Wearing. 2000. *A Polity on the Edge: Canada and the Politics of Fragmentation.* Toronto: Broadview Press.

Clarke, Harold, and Marianne Stewart. 1998. The decline of parties in the minds of citizens. *Annual Review of Political Science* 1:357–78.

Clarke, Harold, et al. 1999. The effect of economic priorities on the measurement of value change: New experimental evidence. *American Political Science Review,* 93:637–47.

Clubb, Jerome, William Flanigan, and Nancy Zingale. 1980. *Partisan Realignment.* Beverly Hills, Calif.: Sage Publications.

Conover, Pamela, and Stanley Feldman. 1984. How people organize the political world. *American Journal of Political Science* 28:95–126.

Conradt, David. 2001. *The German Polity.* 6th ed. New York: Longman.

Converse, Philip. 1964. The nature of belief systems in mass publics. In D. Apter, ed., *Ideology and Discontent.* New York: Free Press.

———. 1966. The normal vote. In Angus Campbell et al., eds., *Elections and the Political Order.* New York: Wiley.

———. 1969. Of time and partisan stability. *Comparative Political Studies* 2:139–71.

———. 1970. Attitudes and nonattitudes. In E. Tufte, ed., *The Quantitative Analysis of Social Problems.* Reading, Mass.: Addison Wesley.

———. 1972. Change in the American electorate. In A. Campbell and P. Converse, eds., *The Human Meaning of Social Change.* New York: Russell Sage.

———. 1975. Public opinion and voting behavior. In F. Greenstein and N. Polsby, eds., *Handbook of Political Science.* Vol. 4. Reading, Mass.: Addison Wesley.

———. 1976. *The Dynamics of Party Support.* Beverly Hills, Calif.: Sage Publications.

———. 1990. Popular representation and the distribution of information. In J. Ferejohn and J. Kuklinski, eds., *Information and Democratic Processes.* Urbana: University of Illinois Press.

Converse, Philip, and Georges Dupeux. 1962. Politicization of the electorate in France and the United States. *Public Opinion Quarterly* 26:1–23.

Converse, Philip, and Greg Markus. 1979. Plus ça change . . . The new CPS election study panel. *American Political Science Review* 73:32–49.

Converse, Philip, and Roy Pierce. 1986. *Representation in France.* Cambridge, Mass.: Harvard University Press.

Conway, Mary Margaret. 2000. *Political Participation in the United States.* 3d ed. Washington, D.C.: CQ Press.

Crepaz, Markus. 1990. The impact of party polarization and postmaterialism on voter turnout. *European Journal of Political Research* 18:183–205.

Crewe, Ivor. 1981. Electoral participation. In D. Butler et al., eds., *Democracy at the Polls.* Washington, D.C.: American Enterprise Institute.

———. 1986. On the death and resurrection of class voting. *Political Studies* 34:620–38.

———. 1995. Standards in Public Life: First Report of the Committee on Standards in Public Life. Oral evidence in *Transcripts of Evidence,* vol. II, CM 2850-II. London: HMSO.

Crewe, Ivor, and D. T. Denver, eds. 1985. *Electoral Change in Western Democracies.* New York: St. Martin's Press.

Crewe, Ivor, and Donald Searing. 1988. Mrs. Thatcher's crusade: Conservatism in Britain, 1972–1986. In B. Cooper et al., eds., *The Resurgence of Conservatism in the Anglo-American Countries.* Durham, N.C.: Duke University Press.

Cronin, Thomas. 1989. *Direct Democracy: The Politics of Initiative, Referendum and Recall.* Cambridge, Mass.: Harvard University Press.

Crozier, Michel. 1964. *The Bureaucratic Personality.* Chicago: University of Chicago Press.

———. 1982. *Strategies for Change.* Cambridge, Mass.: MIT Press.

Crozier, Michel, Samuel Huntington, and Joji Watanuki. 1975. *The Crisis of Democracy.* New York: New York University Press.

Curtice, John, and Roger Jowell. 1997. Trust in the political system. In R. Jowell et al., eds., *British Social Attitudes—The 14th Report.* Brookfield, Vt.: Dartmouth.

Cyert, Richard, and J.G. March. 1963. *A Behavioral Theory of the Firm.* Englewood Cliffs, N.J.: Prentice Hall.

Dahl, Robert. 1971. *Polyarchy.* New Haven, Conn.: Yale University Press.

———. 1989. *Democracy and its Critics.* New Haven, Conn.: Yale University Press.

Dahrendorf, Ralf. 1975. Excerpts from remarks on the ungovernability study. In. M. Crozier et al., eds., *The Crisis of Democracy.* New York: New York University Press.

———. 2000. Afterword. In S. Pharr and R. Putnam, eds., *Disaffected Democracies.* Princeton, N.J.: Princeton University Press.

Dalton, Russell. 1977. Was there a revolution? *Comparative Political Studies* 9:459–73.

———. 1984. Cognitive mobilization and partisan dealignment in advanced industrial democracies. *Journal of Politics* 46:264–84.

———. 1985. Political parties and political representation. *Comparative Political Studies* 17:267–99.

———. 1992. Two German electorates? In G. Smith et al., eds., *Developments in German Politics.* London: Macmillan.

———. 1993a. *Politics in Germany.* New York: HarperCollins.

———, ed. 1993b. *The New Germany Votes: Unification and the Creation of the New German Party System.* Oxford, U.K.: Berg Publishers.

———. 1994a. *The Green Rainbow: Environmental Groups in Western Europe.* New Haven, Conn.: Yale University Press.

———. 1994b. Communists and democrats: Democratic attitudes in the two Germanies. *British Journal of Political Science* 24(1994):469–93.

———. 1996a. *Citizen Politics: Public Opinion and Political Parties in Western Democracies.* 2d ed. Chatham, N.J.: Chatham House.

———, ed. 1996b. *Germans Divided: The 1994 Bundestagswahl and the Evolution of the German Party System.* New York and Oxford, U.K.: Berg Publishers.

———. 1999. Political support in advanced industrial democracies. In P. Norris, ed., *Critical Citizens.* Oxford, U.K.: Oxford University Press.

———. 2000a. The decline of party identification. In R. Dalton and M. Wattenberg, eds., *Parties without Partisans.* Oxford, U.K.: Oxford University Press.

———. 2000b. Value change and democracy. In S. Pharr and R. Putnam, eds., *Disaffected Democracies.* Princeton, N.J.: Princeton University Press.

———. 2002. Politics in Germany. In G. Almond, R. Dalton, and G. Powell, eds., *European Politics Today*. New York: Addison-Wesley Longman.

Dalton, Russell, and Wilhelm Bürklin. 1996. The social bases of the vote. In R. Dalton, ed., *Germans Divided*. New York and Oxford, U.K.: Berg Publishers.

Dalton, Russell, Scott Flanagan, and Paul Beck, eds. 1984. *Electoral Change in Advanced Industrial Democracies*. Princeton, N.J.: Princeton University Press.

Dalton, Russell, and Robert Rohrschneider. 1998. The greening of Europe: Environmental values and environmental behavior. In Roger Jowell et al., eds., *British—and European—Social Attitudes: The 15th Report*. Brooksfield, Vt.: Ashgate.

Dalton, Russell, and Martin Wattenberg. 1993. The not so simple act of voting. In A. Finifter, ed., *The State of the Discipline*. Washington, D.C.: American Political Science Association.

———, eds., 2000. *Parties without Partisans: Political Change in Advanced Industrial Democracies*. Oxford, U.K.: Oxford University Press.

Della Porta, Donatella. 2000. Social capital, beliefs in government and political corruption. In S. Pharr and R. Putnam, eds., *Disaffected Democracies*. Princeton, N.J.: Princeton University Press.

Delli Carpini, Michael, and Scott Keeter. 1996. *What Americans Know about Politics and Why It Matters*. New Haven, Conn.: Yale University Press.

Delli Carpini, Michael, and Lee Sigelman. 1986. Do yuppies matter? Competing explanations of their political distinctiveness. *Public Opinion Quarterly* 50:502–18.

Downs, Anthony. 1957. *An Economic Theory of Democracy*. New York: Wiley.

Duch, Raymond, and Michael Taylor. 1993. Postmaterialism and the economic condition. *American Journal of Political Science* 37:747–79.

———. 1994. A reply to Abramson and Inglehart's "Education, security and postmaterialism." *American Journal of Political Science* 38:815–24.

Dunlap, Riley, George Gallup, and Alec Gallup. 1992. *Health of the Planet*. Princeton, N.J.: Gallup International Institute.

Dye, Thomas, and Harmon Ziegler. 1970. *The Irony of Democracy*. Belmont, Calif.: Duxbury.

Easton, David. 1965. *A Systems Analysis of Political Life*. New York: Wiley.

———. 1975. A reassessment of the concept of political support. *British Journal of Political Science* 5:435–57.

Easton, David, and Jack Dennis. 1969. *Children in the Political System*. New York: McGraw-Hill.

Eckstein, Harry. 1984. Civic inclusion and its discontents. *Daedalus* 113:107–46.

Ehrmann, Henry, and Martin Schain. 1992. *Politics in France*. 5th ed. New York: HarperCollins.

Erikson, Robert. 1978. Constituency opinion and congressional behavior. *American Journal of Political Science* 22:511–35.

Erikson, Robert, and Kent Tedin. 2001. *American Public Opinion*. 6th ed. New York: Allyn & Bacon.

Erikson, Robert, Gerald Wright, and John McIver. 1994. *State House Democracy: Public Opinion and Public Policy in the American States*. New York: Cambridge University Press.

Esaiasson, Peter, and Sören Holmberg. 1996. *Representation from Above: Members of Parliament and Representative Democracy in Sweden*. Aldershot, Vt.: Dartmouth.

Evans, Geoffrey, ed. 1999. *The End of Class Politics?: Class Voting in Comparative Context*. New York: Oxford University Press.

Evans, Geoffrey, and Pippa Norris, eds. 1999. *Critical Elections: British Parties and Voters in Long-Term Perspective*. Thousand Oaks, Calif.: Sage Publications.

Farah, Barbara. 1980. *Political representation in West Germany*. Ph.D. dissertation, University of Michigan.

Feldman, Stanley. 1989. Reliability and stability of policy positions. *Political Analysis* 1:25–60.

Ferejohn, John, and James Kuklinski, eds. 1990. *Information and Democratic Processes*. Urbana: University of Illinois Press.

Fiorina, Morris. 1981. *Retrospective Voting in American National Elections*. New Haven, Conn.: Yale University Press.

———. 1990. Information and rationality in elections. In J. Ferejohn and J. Kuklinski, eds., *Information and Democratic Processes*. Urbana: University of Illinois Press.

———. 1992. *Divided Government*. New York: Macmillan.

Flanagan, Scott. 1982. Changing values in advanced industrial society. *Comparative Political Studies* 14:403–44.

———. 1987. Value change in industrial society. *American Political Science Review* 81:1303–1319.

Fleury, Christopher, and Michael Lewis-Beck. 1993. Anchoring the French voter: Ideology vs. party. *Journal of Politics* 55:1100–1109.

Franklin, Mark. 1985. *The Decline of Class Voting in Britain.* Oxford, U.K.: Oxford University Press.

———. 1996. Political participation. In L. LeDuc et al., eds., *Comparing Democracies.* Thousand Oaks, Calif.: Sage Publications.

Franklin, Mark, Tom Mackie, and Henry Valen, eds. 1992. *Electoral Change.* New York: Cambridge University Press.

Friedrich, Walter, and Hartmut Griese. 1990. *Jugend und Jugendforschung in der DDR.* Opladen: Westdeutscher Verlag.

Fuchs, Dieter, Giovanna Guidorossi, and Palle Svensson. 1995. Support for the democratic system. In H. Klingemann and D. Fuchs, eds., *Citizens and the State.* Oxford, U.K.: Oxford University Press.

Fuchs, Dieter, and Hans-Dieter Klingemann. 1989. The Left-Right schema. In M.K. Jennings and J. van Deth, eds., *Continuities in Political Action.* Berlin: deGruyter.

———. 1995. Citizens and the state. In H. Klingemann and D. Fuchs, eds., *Citizens and the State.* Oxford, U.K.: Oxford University Press.

Fuchs, Dieter, and Robert Rohrschneider. 1998. Postmaterialism and electoral choice before and after German unification. *West European Politics* 21:95–116.

Fukuyama, Francis. 1992. *The End of History and the Last Man.* New York: Free Press.

———. 1999. *The Great Disruption: Human Nature and the Reconstitution of Social Order.* New York: Free Press.

Gabel, Matthew. 1998. *Interests and Integration: Market Liberalization, Public Opinion, and European Union.* Ann Arbor: University of Michigan Press.

Gallagher, Michael, and Pier Vincenzo Uleri, eds. 1996. *The Referendum Experience in Europe.* Basinstoke: Macmillan.

Gallup, George. 1976a. *International Public Opinion Polls: Britain.* New York: Random House.

———. 1976b. *International Public Opinion Polls: France.* New York: Random House.

Glass, David. 1985. Evaluating presidential candidates: Who focuses on their personal attributes. *Public Opinion Quarterly* 49:517–34.

Gluchowski, Peter. 1987. Lebensstile und Wandel der Wählerschaft in der Bundesrepublik Deutschland. *Aus Politik und Zeitgeschichte* (March 21):18–32.

Gluchowski, Peter, and Ulrich von Wilamowitz-Moellendorff. 1998. The erosion of social cleavages in Western Germany, 1971–97. In C. Anderson and C. Zelle, eds., *Stability and Change in German Elections.* Westport, Conn.: Praeger.

Goldthorpe, John. 1987. *Social Mobility and Class Structure in Modern Britain.* Oxford, U.K.: Clarendon Press.

Gordon, Stacy, and Gary Segura. 1997. Cross-national variation in the political sophistication of individuals: Capability or choice? *Journal of Politics* 59:126–47.

Graber, Doris. 1988. *Processing the News: How People Tame the Information Tide.* 2d ed. New York: Longman.

Gray, Mark, and Miki Caul. 2000. Declining voter turnout in advanced industrial democracies 1950–97. *Comparative Political Studies* 33:1091–1122.

Gurr, T. Robert. 1970. *Why Men Rebel.* Princeton, N.J.: Princeton University Press.

Haegel, Florence. 1993. Partisan ties. In D. Boy and N. Mayer, eds., *The French Voter Decides.* Ann Arbor: University of Michigan Press.

Hall, Peter. 1999. Social capital in Britain. *British Journal of Political Science* 29:417–61.

Hampton, Mary, and Christian Soe, eds. 1999. *Between Bonn and Berlin: German Politics Adrift?* Lanham, Md.: Rowman & Littlefield.

Harding, Steve. 1986. *Contrasting Values in Western Europe.* London: Macmillan.

Harrison, Lawrence, and Samuel Huntington, eds. 2000. *Culture Matters: How Values Shape Human Progress.* New York: Basic Books.

Heath, Anthony, Roger Jowell, and John Curtice. 1991. *Understanding Political Change: The British Voter 1964–87.* New York: Pergamon Press.
———. 1994. *Labour's Last Chance: The 1992 Election and Beyond.* Brookfield, Vt.: Dartmouth Publishing.
Heath, Anthony, and Dorren McMahon. 1992. Changes in values. In R. Jowell et al., eds., *British Social Attitudes: The 9th Report.* Brookfield, Vt.: Dartmouth Publishing.
Heath, Anthony, and Roy Pierce. 1992. It was party identification all along. *Electoral Studies* 11:93–105.
Heidenheimer, Arnold, and Peter Flora, eds. 1981. *The Development of the Welfare State.* New Bruswick, N.J.: Transaction Books.
Held, David. 1987. *Models of Democracy.* Stanford, Calif.: Stanford University Press.
Herrera, Cheryl Lyn, Richard Herrera, and Eric R.A.N. Smith. 1992. Public opinion and congressional representation. *Public Opinion Quarterly* 56:185–205.
Herzog, Dietrich, and Bernhard Wessels, eds. 1990. *Abegeordnete und Bürger.* Opladen: Westdeutscher Verlag.
Hess, Robert, and Judith Torney. 1967. *The Development of Political Attitudes in Children.* Chicago: Aldine.
Hibbing, John R., and Elizabeth Theiss-Morse. 1995. *Congress as Public Enemy: Public Attitudes toward American Political Institutions.* New York: Cambridge University Press.
Higley, John, et al. 1979. *Elites in Australia.* London: Routledge & Kegan Paul.
Himmelweit, Hilda, et al. 1981. *How Voters Decide.* London: Academic Press.
Hoffmann-Lange, Ursula. 1992. *Eliten, Macht und Konflikt in der Bundesrepublik.* Opladen: Leske + Budrich.
Hollifield, James. 1993. *Immigrants, Markets and States.* Cambridge, Mass.: Harvard University Press.
Holmberg, Sören. 1989. Political representation in Sweden. *Scandinavian Political Studies* 12:1–36.
———. 1994. Party identification compared across the Atlantic. In M. K. Jennings and T. Mann, eds., *Elections at Home and Abroad.* Ann Arbor: University of Michigan Press.
———. 1999. Down and down we go: Political trust in Sweden. In P. Norris, ed., *Critical Citizens.* Oxford, U.K.: Oxford University Press.
Hout, Michael, et al. 1996. The democratic class struggle in the United States, 1948–92. *American Sociological Review* 60:805–28.
Huntington, Samuel. 1974. Postindustrial politics: How benign will it be? *Comparative Politics* 6:147–77.
———. 1975. The democratic distemper. *Public Interest* 41:9–38.
———. 1981. *American Politics: The Promise of Disharmony.* Cambridge, Mass.: Harvard University Press.
———. 1984. Will more countries become democratic? *Political Science Quarterly* 99:193–218.
———. 1991. *The Third Wave.* Norman: University of Oklahoma Press.
Hurwitz, Jon, and Mark Peffley. 1987. How are foreign policy attitudes structured? *American Political Science Review* 81:1099–120.
Ignazi, Piero. 1992. The silent counter-revolution. *European Journal of Political Research* 22:3–34.
Inglehart, Ronald. 1977. *The Silent Revolution.* Princeton, N.J.: Princeton University Press.
———. 1979. Political action. In S. Barnes, M. Kaase et al., eds., *Political Action.* Beverly Hills, Calif.: Sage Publications.
———. 1981. Post-materialism in an environment of insecurity. *American Political Science Review* 75:880–900.
———. 1984. Changing cleavage alignments in Western democracies. In R. Dalton, S. Flanagan, and P. Beck, eds., *Electoral Change in Advanced Industrial Democracies.* Princeton, N.J.: Princeton University Press.
———. 1990. *Culture Shift in Advanced Industrial Society.* Princeton, N.J.: Princeton University Press.
———. 1995. Political support for environmental protection. *PS—Political Science and Politics* 28:57–72.
———. 1997. *Modernization and Postmodernization: Cultural, Economic and Political Change in 43 Nations.* Princeton, N.J.: Princeton University Press.

Inglehart, Ronald, and W. Baker. 2000. Modernization, cultural change, and the persistence of traditional values. *American Sociological Review* 65:19–51.

Ingram, Helen, and Steven Smith, eds. 1993. *Public Policy for Democracy.* Washington, D.C.: Brookings.

Inkeles, Alex, and David Smith. 1974. *Becoming Modern: Individual Change in Six Developing Countries.* Cambridge, Mass.: Harvard University Press.

IPOS. 1995. *Einstellung zur Aktuelle Frage.* Mannheim, Germany: IPOS.

Jackman, Robert. 1972. Political elites, mass publics and support for democratic principles. *Journal of Politics* 34:753–73.

———. 1987. Political institutions and voter turnout in the industrialized democracies. *American Political Science Review* 81:405–24.

Jacoby, William. 1991. Ideological identification and issue attitudes. *American Journal of Political Science* 35:178–205.

Jelen, Ted, Sue Thomas, and Clyde Wilcox. 1994. The gender gap in comparative perspective. *European Journal of Political Research* 25:171–86.

Jennings, M. Kent. 1987. Residues of a movement: The aging of the American protest generation. *American Political Science Review* 81:367–82.

———. 1992. Ideological thinking among mass publics and political elites. *Public Opinion Quarterly* 56:419–41.

Jennings, M. Kent, and Thomas Mann, eds. 1994. *Elections at Home and Abroad.* Ann Arbor: University of Michigan Press.

Jennings, M. Kent, and Greg Markus. 1984. Partisan orientations over the long haul. *American Political Science Review* 78:1000–1018.

Jennings, M. Kent, and Richard Niemi. 1973. *The Character of Political Adolescence.* Princeton, N.J.: Princeton University Press.

———. 1981. *Generations and Politics.* Princeton, N.J.: Princeton University Press.

Jennings, M. Kent, and Jan van Deth, eds. 1989. *Continuities in Political Action.* Berlin: deGruyter.

Jennings, M. Kent, et al. 1979. Generations and families. In Samuel Barnes, Max Kaase et al., eds., *Political Action.* Beverly Hills, Calif.: Sage Publications.

Jowell, Roger, et al., eds. 1998. *British—and European—Social Attitudes: The 15th Report.* Brooksfield, Vt.: Ashgate.

Kaase, Max. 1982. Partizipative revolution: Ende der parteien? In J. Raschke, ed., *Bürger und Parteien.* Opladen: Westdeutscher Verlag.

———. 1989. Mass participation. In M.K. Jennings and J. van Deth, eds., *Continuities in Political Action.* Berlin: deGruyter.

———. 1994. Is there personalization in politics? *International Political Science Review* 15:211–30.

Kaase, Max, and Kenneth Newton. 1998. Commitment to the welfare state. In Roger Jowell et al., eds., *British—and European—Social Attitudes: The 15th Report.* Brooksfield, Vt.: Ashgate.

Katz, Richard, and Peter Mair, eds. 1994. *How Parties Organize: Change and Adaptation in Party Organizations in Western Democracies.* Thousand Oaks, Calif.: Sage Publications.

Keith, Bruce, et al. 1992. *The Myth of the Independent Voter.* Berkeley: University of California Press.

Kepplinger, Hans Mathias. 1996. Skandale und politikverdrossenheit—ein langzeitvergleich. In O. Jarren et al., eds., *Medien und Politische Prozeß.* Opladen: Westdeutscher Verlag.

Key, V.O. 1966. *The Responsible Electorate.* Cambridge, Mass.: Belknap Press.

Kinder, Donald. 1986. Presidential character revisited. In R. Lau and D. Sears, eds., *Political Cognitions.* Hillsdale, N.J.: Lawrence Erlbaum.

Kinder, Donald, and D.R. Kiewiet. 1981. Sociotropic politics. *British Journal of Political Science* 11:129–61.

Kinder, Donald, and David Sears. 1985. Public opinion and political action. In E. Aronson and G. Lindzey, eds., *The Handbook of Social Psychology.* Vol. 2. Reading, Mass.: Addison Wesley.

Kinder, Donald, et al. 1980. Presidential prototypes. *Political Behavior* 2:315–37.

Kitschelt, Herbert. 1989. *The Logics of Party Formation.* Ithaca, N.Y.: Cornell University Press.

Klein, Markus, et al., eds. 2000. *50 Jahre empirische Washlforschung in Deutschland.* Opladen: Westdeutscher Verlag.

Klingemann, Hans-Dieter. 1979. Measuring ideological conceptualizations. In S. Barnes and M. Kaase et al., eds., *Political Action.* Beverly Hills, Calif.: Sage Publications.

———. 1999. Mapping political support in the 1990s. In P. Norris, ed., *Critical Citizens.* Oxford, U.K.: Oxford University Press.

Klingemann, Hans-Dieter, and Dieter Fuchs, eds. 1995. *Citizens and the State.* Oxford, U.K.: Oxford University Press.

Klingemann, Hans-Dieter, Richard Hofferbert, and Ian Budge. 1994. *Parties, Policy and Democracy.* Boulder, Colo.: Westview Press.

Knutsen, Oddbjorn. 1987. The impact of structural and ideological cleavages on West European democracies. *British Journal of Political Science* 18:323–52.

———. 1995. Party choice. In J. Van Deth and E. Scarbrough, eds., *The Impact of Values.* New York: Oxford University Press.

Knutsen, Oddbjorn, and Elinor Scarbrough. 1995. Cleavage politics. In J. Van Deth and E. Scarbrough, eds., *The Impact of Values.* New York: Oxford University Press.

Kornhauser, William. 1959. *The Politics of Mass Society.* New York: Free Press.

Kuklinski, James. 1978. Representativeness and elections. *American Political Science Review* 72:165–77.

Kuklinski, James, Robert Luskin, and John Bolland. 1991. Where is the schema? *American Political Science Review* 85:1341–1357.

Lane, Robert. 1962. *Political Ideology.* New York: Free Press.

———. 1973. Patterns of political belief. In J. Knutson, ed., *Handbook of Political Psychology.* San Francisco: Jossey-Bass.

Lane, Jan-Erik, and Svante Errson. 1991. *Politics and Society in Western Europe.* 2d ed. Newbury Park, Calif.: Sage Publications.

Laver, Michael, and W. Ben Hunt. 1992. *Policy and Party Competition.* New York: Routledge.

Lawson, Kay, and Peter Merkl, eds. 1988. *When Parties Fail.* Princeton, N.J.: Princeton University Press.

Lazarsfeld, Paul, Bernard Berelson, and Hazel Gaudet. 1948. *The People's Choice.* New York: Columbia University Press.

LeDuc, Lawrence. 1981. The dynamic properties of party identification. *European Journal of Political Research* 9:257–68.

LeDuc, Lawrence, Richard Niemi, and Pippa Norris, eds. 2002. *Comparing Democracies.* 2d ed. Thousand Oaks, Calif.: Sage Publications.

Leege, David, Lyman Kellstedt et al. 1993. *Rediscovering the Religious Factor in American Politics.* Armonk, N.Y.: M.E. Sharpe.

Leighley, Jan. 1995. Attitudes, opportunities and incentives. *Political Research Quarterly* 48:181–209.

Lewis-Beck, Michael. 1988. *Economics and Elections.* Ann Arbor: University of Michigan Press.

———. 1999. *How France Votes.* New York: Chatham House.

Lewis-Beck, Michael, and Martin Paldam, eds. 2000. *Economics and Elections,* special issue of *Electoral Studies* 19.

Lewis-Beck, Michael, and Andrew Skalaban. 1992. France. In M. Franklin et al., eds., *Electoral Change.* New York: Cambridge University Press.

Lijphart, Arend. 1999. *Patterns of Democracy: Government Forms and Performance in Thirty-six Countries.* New Haven, Conn.: Yale University Press.

Linz, Juan, and Alfred Stepan, eds. 1978. *The Breakdown of Democratic Regimes.* Baltimore: Johns Hopkins University Press.

Lippmann, Walter. 1922. *Public Opinion.* New York: Harcourt Brace.

Lipset, Seymour Martin. 1981a. *Political Man: The Social Bases of Politics.* Baltimore: Johns Hopkins University Press.

———. 1981b. The revolt against modernity. In P. Torsvik, ed., *Mobilization, Center-Periphery Structures and Nation-building.* Bergen: Universitetsforlaget.

———, and Everett Ladd. 1980. Public opinion and public policy. In P. Duignan and A. Rabushka, eds., *The United States in the 1980s.* Stanford, Calif.: Hoover Press.

————, and Stein Rokkan, eds. 1967. *Party Systems and Voter Alignments*. New York: Free Press.

————, and William Schneider. 1983. *The Confidence Gap*. New York: Free Press.

————, and William Schneider. 1987. The confidence gap during the Reagan years, 1981–87. *Political Science Quarterly* 102:1–23.

Listhaug, Ola, and Matti Wiberg. 1995. Confidence in political and private institutions. In H. Klingemann and D. Fuchs, eds., *Citizens and the State*. Oxford, U.K.: Oxford University Press.

Lovenduski, Joni, and Pippa Norris, eds. 1996. *Women in Politics*. New York: Oxford University Press.

Lupia, Arthur. 1994. Shortcuts versus encyclopedias. *American Political Science Review* 88:63–76.

Lupia, Arthur, and Mathew McCubbins. 1998. *The Democratic Dilemma: Can Citizens Learn What They Need to Know?* Cambridge, U.K: Cambridge University Press.

Luskin, Robert. 1987. Measuring political sophistication. *American Journal of Political Science* 18:361–82.

Mackie, Thomas, and Richard Rose. 1991. *International Almanac of Electoral History*. Washington, D.C.: CQ Press.

MacKuen, Michael, Robert Erikson, and James Stimson. 1989. Macropartisanship. *American Political Science Review* 83:1125–1142.

————. 1992. Peasants or bankers? *American Political Science Review* 86:597–611.

MacRae, Duncan. 1967. *Parliament, Parties, and Society in France, 1946–58*. New York: St. Martin's Press.

Mair, Peter. 1993. Myths of electoral change and the survival of traditional parties. *European Journal of Political Research* 24:121–33.

————. 1997. *Party System Change*. Oxford, U.K.: Clarendon Press.

————. 2000. In the aggregate: Mass electoral behaviour in Western Europe, 1950–2000. In H. Keman, ed., *Comparative Politics*. London: Sage.

Mann, Thomas. 1978. *Unsafe at Any Margin*. Washington, D.C.: American Enterprise Institute.

Markus, Greg, and Philip Converse. 1979. A dynamic simultaneous equation model of electoral choice. *American Political Science Review* 73:1055–1070.

Marsh, Alan. 1974. Explorations in unorthodox political behavior. *European Journal of Political Research* 2:107–31.

————. 1977. *Protest and Political Consciousness*. Beverly Hills, Calif.: Sage Publications.

Maslow, Abraham. 1954. *Motivations and Personality*. New York: Harper & Row.

Matthews, Donald, and Henry Valen. 1999. *Parliamentary Representation: The Case of the Norwegian Storting*. Columbus: Ohio State University Press.

Mayer, Nonna. 2000. *The decline of political trust in France*. Paper presented at the meeting of the International Political Science Association, Quebec, Canada.

McAllister, Ian. 1991. Party voters, candidates and political attitudes. *Canadian Journal of Political Science* 24:237–68.

————. 1992. *Political Behaviour: Citizens, Parties and Elites in Australia*. Melbourne: Longman Cheshire.

————. 1996. Leadership. In L. LeDuc, R. Niemi, and P. Norris, eds., *Comparing Democracies*. Newbury Park, Calif.: Sage Publications.

McClosky, Herbert. 1964. Consensus and ideology in American politics. *American Political Science Review* 58:361–82.

McClosky, Herbert, and Alida Brill. 1983. *Dimensions of Tolerance: What Americans Think about Civil Liberties*. New York: Russell Sage.

McClosky, Herbert, et al. 1960. Issue conflict and consensus among party leaders and followers. *American Political Science Review* 54:406–27.

McCrone, David, and Paula Surridge. 1998. National identity and national pride. In R. Jowell et al., eds., *British—and European—Social Attitudes: The 15th Report*. Brooksfield, Vt.: Ashgate.

McIntosh, Mary, and Martha MacIver. 1994. *The structure of foreign policy attitudes in East and West Europe*. Paper presented at the annual meetings of the International Studies Association.

Meyer, David, and Sidney Tarrow, eds. 1998. *The Social Movement Society: Contentious Politics for a New Century*. Lanham, Md.: Rowman & Littlefield.

Michelat, Guy. 1993. In search of Left and Right. In D. Boy and N. Mayer, eds., *The French Voter Decides*. Ann Arbor: University of Michigan Press.

Miller, Arthur. 1974a. Political issues and trust in government. *American Political Science Review* 68:951–72.

———. 1974b. Rejoinder. *American Political Science Review* 68:989–1001.

Miller, Arthur, and Stephen Borrelli. 1991. Confidence in government during the 1980s. *American Politics Quarterly* 19:147–73.

———. 1992. Policy and performance orientations in the United States. *Electoral Studies* 11:106–21.

Miller, Arthur, and Martin Wattenberg. 1985. Throwing the rascals out. *American Political Science Review* 79:359–72.

Miller, Arthur, Martin Wattenberg, and Oksana Malanchuk. 1986. Schematic assessments of presidential candidates. *American Political Science Review* 80:521–40.

Miller, Warren. 1976. The cross-national use of party identification as a stimulus to political inquiry. In I. Budge, I. Crewe, and D. Farlie, eds., *Party Identification and Beyond.* New York: Wiley.

———. 1987. *Without Consent: Mass-Elite Linkages in Presidential Politics.* Lexington: University Press of Kentucky.

———. 1991. Party identification, realignment, and party voting: Back to the basics. *American Political Science Review* 85:557–68.

Miller, Warren, and M. Kent Jennings. 1986. *Parties in Transition: A Longitudinal Study of Party Elites and Party Supporters.* New York: Russell Sage Foundation.

Miller, Warren, and J. Merrill Shanks. 1996. *The New American Voter.* Cambridge, Mass.: Harvard University Press.

Miller, Warren, and Donald Stokes. 1963. Constituency influence in Congress. *American Political Science Review* 57:45–56.

Miller, Warren, et al. 1999. *Policy Representation in Western Democracies.* Oxford, U.K.: Oxford University Press.

Miller, William, and Richard Niemi. 2002. Voting: Choice, conditioning and constraint. In L. LeDuc, R. Niemi, and P. Norris, eds., *Comparing Democracies*. 2d ed. Thousand Oaks, Calif.: Sage Publications.

Miller, William, et al. 1990. *How Voters Change.* New York: Oxford University Press.

Moon, David. 1990. What you use depends on what you have. *American Politics Quarterly* 18:3–24.

Monroe, Alan. 1979. Consistency between public preferences and national policy decisions. *American Politics Quarterly* 7:3–21.

Morris, Richard. 1995. What informed public? *Washington Post National Weekly Edition* (April 10–16):36.

Mueller, John. 1999. *Capitalism, Democracy, and Ralph's Pretty Good Grocery.* Princeton, N.J.: Princeton University Press.

Muller, Edward. 1972. A test of a partial theory of potential for political violence. *American Political Science Review* 66:928–59.

Muller, Edward, and Thomas Jukam. 1977. On the meaning of political support. *American Political Science Review* 71:1561–1595.

Müller-Rommel, Ferdinand, and Geoffrey Pridham. 1991. *Small Parties in Western Europe.* Newbury Park, Calif.: Sage Publications.

Nevitte, Neil. 1996. *The Decline of Deference.* Petersborough, Canada: Broadview Press.

Nie, Norman, Jane Junn, and Kenneth Stehlik-Barry. 1996. *Education and Democratic Citizenship in America.* Chicago: University of Chicago Press.

Nie, Norman, Sidney Verba, and John Petrocik. 1979. *The Changing American Voter.* Cambridge, Mass.: Harvard University Press.

Niemi, Richard, and M. Kent Jennings. 1991. Issues and inheritance in the formation of party identification. *American Journal of Political Science* 35:970–88.

Niemi, Richard, and Anders Westholm. 1984. Issues, parties and attitudinal stability. *Electoral Studies* 3:65–83.

Niemi, Richard, John Mueller, and Tom Smith. 1989. *Trends in Public Opinion: A Compendium of Survey Data.* Westport, Conn.: Greenwood Press.

Niemi, Richard, and Herbert Weisberg, eds. 2001. *Controversies in Voting.* 4th ed. Washington, D.C.: Congressional Quarterly Press.

Nieuwbeerta, Paul. 1995. *The Democratic Class Struggle in Twenty Countries 1945–90.* Amsterdam: Thesis Publishers.

Nieuwbeerta, Paul, and Nan Dirk De Graaf. 1999. Traditional class voting in 20 postwar societies. In G. Evans, ed., *The End of Class Politics?* New York: Oxford University Press.

Noelle-Neumann, Elisabeth, 1981. *The Germans, 1967–80.* Westport, Conn.: Greenwood Press.

Noelle-Neumann, Elisabeth, and Renate Köcher. 1987. *Die verletzte Nation: über den Versuch der Deutschen, ihren Charakter zu ändern.* Stuttgart: Deutsche Verlags-Anstalt.

Noelle-Neumann, Elisabeth, and Edgar Piel, eds. 1984. *Allensbacher Jahrbuch der Demoskopie, 1978–83.* Munich: Saur.

Norpoth, Helmut. 1992. *Confidence Regained: Economics, Mrs. Thatcher, and the British Voter.* Ann Arbor: University of Michigan Press.

———. 1996. Economics. In L. LeDuc et al., eds., *Comparing Democracies: Elections and Voting in Global Perspective.* Thousand Oaks, Calif.: Sage Publications.

Norris, Pippa. 1999a. A gender-generation gap. In G. Evans and P. Norris, eds., *Critical Elections.* London: Sage.

———. 1999b. *Critical Citizens: Global Support for Democratic Governance.* Oxford, U.K.: Oxford University Press.

———. 1999c. Conclusions: The growth of critical citizens and its consequences. In P. Norris, ed., *Critical Citizens.* Oxford, U.K.: Oxford University Press.

———. 1999d. New politicians? Changes in party competition at Westminster. In G. Evans and P. Norris, eds., *Critical Elections.* London: Sage.

———. 2000. *Virtuous Circle: Political Communications in Postindustrial Societies.* Cambridge, Mass.: Cambridge University Press.

Norris, Pippa, and Joni Lovenduski. 1995. *Political Recruitment: Gender, Race, and Class in the British Parliament.* Cambridge, U.K.: Cambridge University Press.

Nye, Joseph, Philip Zelikow, and David King, eds. 1997. *Why Americans Mistrust Government.* Cambridge, Mass.: Harvard University Press.

Ohr, Dieter. 2000. Wird das Wählerverhalten zunehmend personalisierter, or ist jede Wahl anders? In M. Klein et al., eds., *50 Jahre empirische Wahlforschung in Deutschland.* Opladen: Westdeutscher Verlag.

Page, Benjamin. 1978. *Choices and Echoes in Presidential Elections.* Chicago: University of Chicago Press.

Page, Benjamin, and Charles Jones. 1979. Reciprocal effects of policy preferences, party loyalties and the vote. *American Political Science Review* 73:1071–1089.

Page, Benjamin, and Robert Shapiro. 1983. Effects of public opinion on public policy. *American Political Science Review* 77:175–90.

———. 1992. *The Rational Public: Fifty Years of Trends in Americans' Policy Preferences.* Chicago: University of Chicago Press.

Palmer, Harvey. 1995. Effects of authoritarian and libertarian values on Conservative and Labour party support. *European Journal of Political Research* 27:273–92.

Parry, Geraint, George Moyser, and Neil Day. 1992. *Political Participation and Democracy in Britain.* Cambridge, U.K.: Cambridge University Press.

Patterson, Thomas. 1993. *Out of Order.* New York: Knopf.

Peffley, Mark, and Jon Hurwitz. 1985. A hierarchical model of attitude constraint. *American Journal of Political Science* 29:871–90.

Pew Center for the People and the Press. 1998a. *Deconstructing Distrust: How Americans View Government* (www.people-press.org/trustrpt.htm).

———. 1998b. *Public Appetite for Government Misjudged: Washington Leaders Wary of Public Opinion* (www.people-press.org/leadrpt.htm).

———. 1999. *Retro-Politics: The Political Typology.* (www.people-press.org/typo99rpt.htm).

Pharr, Susan. 2000. Officials' misconduct and political distrust. In S. Pharr and R. Putnam, eds., *Disaffected Democracies.* Princeton, N.J.: Princeton University Press.

Pharr, Susan, and Robert Putnam, eds. 2000. *Disaffected Democracies: What's Troubling the Trilateral Democracies.* Princeton, N.J.: Princeton University Press.

Pierce, John, et al. 1992. *Citizens, Political Communication and Interest Groups*. New York: Praeger.

Pierson, Paul. 1994. *Dismantling the Welfare State?* New York: Cambridge University Press.

Piven, Frances Fox, and Richard Cloward. 2000. *Why Americans Don't Vote: And Why Politicians Want It That Way*. rev. ed. Boston: Beacon Press.

Poguntke, Thomas. 1993. *Alternative Politics*. Edinburgh: University of Edinburgh Press.

Pomper, Gerald, et al. 2001. *The Election of 2000*. New York: Chatham House.

Poole, Ithel de Sola. 1983. *Technologies of Freedom*. Cambridge, Mass.: Belknap Press.

Popkin, Samuel. 1991. *The Reasoning Voter*. Chicago: University of Chicago Press.

Powell, G. Bingham. 1982. *Contemporary Democracies*. Cambridge, Mass.: Harvard University Press.

———. 1986. American voting turnout in comparative perspective. *American Political Science Review* 80:17–44.

———. 2000. *Elections as Instruments of Democracy: Majoritarian and Proportional Visions*. New Haven, Conn.: Yale University Press.

Prothro, James, and Charles Grigg. 1960. Fundamental principles of democracy. *Journal of Politics* 22:276–94.

Pryce, Sue. 1997. *Presidentializing the Premiership*. New York: St. Martin's Press.

Putnam, Robert. 1993. *Making Democracy Work*. Princeton, N.J.: Princeton University Press.

———. 1995. Bowling alone. *Journal of Democracy* 6:65–78.

———. 2000. *Bowling Alone: The Collapse and Renewal of American Community*. New York: Simon and Schuster.

———, ed. 2002. *Politics in Flux*. Oxford, U.K.: Oxford University Press.

Rahn, Wendy M., et al. 1990. A social-cognitive model of candidate appraisal. In J. Ferejohn and J. Kuklinski, eds., *Information and Democratic Processes*. Urbana: University of Illinois Press.

Reif, Karlheinz, and Ronald Inglehart, eds. 1991. *Eurobarometer: The Dynamic of European Public Opinion*. London: Macmillan.

RePass, David. 1971. Issue saliency and party choice. *American Political Science Review* 65:389–400.

Revel, Jean-Francois. 1983. *How Democracies Perish*. New York: Harper and Row.

Richardson, Dick, and Chris Rootes, eds. 1995. *The Green Challenge: The Development of Green Parties in Europe*. London and New York: Routledge.

Riesman, David, et al. 1950. *The Lonely Crowd*. New Haven, Conn.: Yale University Press.

Robertson, David. 1976. *A Theory of Party Competition*. New York: Wiley.

Rochon, Thomas. 1998. *Culture Moves: Ideas, Activism, and Changing Values*. Princeton, N.J.: Princeton University Press.

Rohrschneider, Robert. 1993a. Environmental belief systems in Western Europe. *Comparative Political Studies* 26:3–29.

———. 1993b. New party versus old left realignments. *Journal of Politics* 55:682–701.

Rokeach, Milton. 1973. *The Nature of Human Values*. New York: Free Press.

Rokkan, Stein. 1970. *Citizens, Elections and Parties*. Oslo: Universitets Forlaget.

Roller, Edeltraud. 1995. Political agendas and beliefs about the scope of government. In O. Borre and E. Scarbrough, eds., *Beliefs about the Scope of Government*. Oxford, U.K.: Oxford University Press.

Rose, Richard. 1982. *The Territorial Dimension in Politics*. Chatham, N.J.: Chatham House.

———. 1984. *Do Parties Make a Difference?* Chatham, N.J.: Chatham House.

Rose, Richard, and Ian McAllister. 1986. *Voters Begin to Choose: From Closed-class to Open Elections in Britain*. Beverly Hills, Calif.: Sage Publications.

———. 1990. *The Loyalties of Voters: A Lifetime Learning Model*. Newbury Park, Calif.: Sage Publications.

Rose, Richard, William Mishler, and Christian Haerpfer. 1998. *Democracy and Its Alternatives: Understanding Post-communist Societies*. Cambridge, U.K.: Polity Press.

Rose, Richard, and Derek Urwin. 1969. Social cohesion, political parties and strains in regimes. *Comparative Political Studies* 2:7–67.

———. 1970. Persistence and change in Western party systems since 1945. *Political Studies* 18:287–319.

Rosenberg, Shawn, and Patrick McCafferty. 1987. The image and the vote: Manipulating voter's preferences. *Public Opinion Quarterly* 51:31–47.

Rosenstone, Steven, and John Hansen. 1993. *Mobilization, Participation and Democracy in America.* New York: Macmillan.

Rucht, Dieter. 1997. The structure and culture of collective protest in West Germany since 1950. In D. Meyer and S. Tarrow, eds., *The Social Movement Society.* Boulder, Colo.: Rowman and Littlefield.

Safran, William. 1998. *The French Polity.* New York: Longman.

Saggar, Shamit, and Anthony Heath. 1999. Race: Towards a multicultural electorate? In G. Evans and P. Norris, eds., *Critical Elections.* Thousand Oaks, Calif.: Sage.

Sartori, Giovanni. 1968. Representational systems. *International Encyclopedia of the Social Sciences* 13:470–75.

———. 1976. *Parties and Party Systems.* New York: Cambridge University Press.

Scarrow, Susan. 2000. Parties without members? In R. Dalton and M. Wattenberg, eds., *Parties without Partisans.* Oxford, U.K.: Oxford University Press.

———. 2001. Direct democracy and institutional design: A comparative investigation. *Comparative Political Studies* 34:651–65.

Scarrow, Susan, Paul Webb, and David Farrell. 2000. From social integration to electoral contestation. In R. Dalton and M. Wattenberg, eds., *Parties without Partisans.* Oxford, U.K.: Oxford University Press.

Schattschneider, E.E. 1942. *Party Government.* New York: Rinehart.

Schickler, Eric, and Donald Green. 1997. The stability of party identification in Western democracies. *Comparative Political Studies* 30:450–83.

Schlozman, Kay, Nancy Burns, and Sidney Verba. 1994. Gender and the pathways to participation. *Journal of Politics* 56:963–90.

Schoen, Harald. 2000. Stimmensplitting bei Bundestagswahlen. In Markus Klein et al., eds., *50 Jahre empirische Wahlforschung in Deutschland: Entwicklung, Befunde, Perspektiven, Daten.* Wiesbaden: Westdeutscher Verlag.

Schumpeter, Joseph. 1943. *Capitalism, Socialism and Democracy.* London: Allen & Unwin.

Schuman, Howard, and Stanley Presser. 1981. *Questions and Answers in Attitudinal Surveys.* New York: Academic Press.

Schuman, Howard, Charlotte Steeh, Lawrence Bobo, and Maria Krysan. 1997. *Racial Attitudes in America: Trends and Interpretations.* Rev. ed. Cambridge, Mass.: Harvard University Press.

Scott, Jacqueline, Michael Braun, and Duane Alwin. 1998. Partner, parent, worker: Family and gender roles. In R. Jowell et al., eds., *British—and European—Social Attitudes.* Brookfield, Vt.: Ashgate Publishing.

Semetko, Holli, and Klaus Schoenbach. 1994. *Germany's Unity Election.* Cresskill, N.J.: Hampton Press.

Semetko, Holli, et al. 1991. *The Formation of Campaign Agendas.* Hillsdale, N.J.: Lawrence Erlbaum.

Sennet, R. 1978. *The Fall of Public Man: On the Social Psychology of Capitalism.* New York: Vintage Books.

Shanks, Merrill, and Warren Miller. 1990. Policy direction and performance evaluations. *British Journal of Political Science* 20:143–235.

———. 1991. Partisanship, policy and performance. *British Journal of Political Science* 21:129–97.

Shapiro, Robert, and Lawrence Jacobs. 1989. The relationship between public opinion and public policy. In S. Long, ed., *Political Behavior Annual.* Boulder, Colo.: Westview.

Shiveley, W. Philips. 1979. The development of party identification among adults. *American Political Science Review* 73:1039-1054.

Skocpol, Theda, and Morris Fiorina, eds. 1999. *Civic Engagement in American Democracy.* Washington, D.C.: Brookings Institution Press.

Skocpol, Theda, M. Ganz, and Z. Munson. 2000. A nation of organizers: The institutional origins of civic voluntarism in the United States. *American Political Science Review* 94:527–46.

Smith, Steven, and Douglas Wertman. 1992. *U.S.-West European Relations during the Reagan Years: The Perspective of West European Publics.* New York: St. Martin's Press.

Smith, Tom, and Paul Sheatsley. 1984. American attitudes toward race relations. *Public Opinion* 7:14ff.

Sniderman, Paul, Richard Brody, and James Kuklinski. 1984. Policy reasoning and political values. *American Journal of Political Science* 28:74–94.

Sniderman, Paul, Richard Brody, and Philip Tetlock. 1991. *Reasoning and Choice.* New York: Cambridge University Press.

Sniderman, Paul, and Thomas Piazza. 1993. *The Scar of Race.* Cambridge, Mass.: Harvard University Press.

Sniderman, Paul, et al. 1991. The fallacy of democratic elitism. *British Journal of Political Science* 21:349–70.

———. 2000. *The Outsiders: Prejudice and Politics in Italy.* Princeton, N.J.: Princeton University Press.

Stanley, Harold, and Richard Niemi. 2000. *Vital Statistics of American Politics.* 7th ed. Washington, D.C.: CQ Press.

Stimson, James. 1999. *Public Opinion in America: Moods, Cycles and Swings.* 2d ed. Boulder, Colo.: Westview Press.

Stimson, James, Michael McKuen, and Robert Erikson. 1995. Dynamic representation. *American Political Science Review* 89:543–65.

Stokes, Donald. 1963. Spatial models of party competition. *American Political Science Review* 57:368–77.

———. 1966. Some dynamic elements of contests for the presidency. *American Political Science Review* 60:19–28.

Stokes, Donald, and Warren Miller. 1962. Party government and the saliency of Congress. *Public Opinion Quarterly* 26:531–46.

Stone Sweet, Alec. 2000. *Governing with Judges.* Oxford, U.K.: Oxford University Press.

Stouffer, Samuel. 1955. *Communism, Conformity and Civil Liberties.* New York: Doubleday.

Studlar, D., Ian McAllister, and B. Hayes. 1998. Explaining the gender gap in voting: A cross-national analysis. *Social Science Quarterly* 79:779–98.

Sullivan, Dennis, and Roger Masters. 1988. Happy warriors: Leaders' facial displays, viewers' emotions and political support. *American Journal of Political Science* 32:345–68.

Swanson, David, and Paolo Mancini, eds. 1996. *Politics, Media, and Modern Democracy.* Westport, Conn.: Praeger.

Taagepera, Rein, and Matthew Shugart. 1989. *Seats and Votes: The Effects and Determinants of Electoral Systems.* New Haven, Conn.: Yale University Press.

Tate, Katherine. 1993. *From Protest to Politics: The New Black Voters in American Elections.* Cambridge, Mass.: Harvard University Press.

———. 2001. *Black Faces in the Mirror.* Princeton, N.J.: Princeton University Press.

Taylor-Gooby, Peter. 1998. Commitment to the welfare state. In R. Jowell et al., eds., *British—and European—Social Attitudes.* Brooksfield, Vt.: Ashgate.

Teixeira, Ruy. 1992. *The Disappearing American Voter.* Washington, D.C.: Brookings Institution.

Thomassen, Jacques. 1994. Empirical research into political representation. In M.K. Jennings and T. Mann, eds., *Elections at Home and Abroad.* Ann Arbor: University of Michigan Press.

———. 1995. Support for democratic values. In H. Klingemann and D. Fuchs, eds., *Citizens and the State.* Oxford, U.K.: Oxford University Press.

Thomassen, Jacques, and Hermann Schmitt. 1997. Policy representation. *European Journal of Political Research* 32:165–84.

Tilly, Charles. 1969. Collective violence in European perspective. In H. Graham and T. Gurr, eds., *Violence in America.* New York: Bantam.

———. 1975. Revolutions and collective violence. In F. Greenstein and N. Polsby, eds., *Handbook of Political Science.* Vol. 3. Reading, Mass.: Addison Wesley.

———, et al. 1975. *The Rebellious Century.* Cambridge, Mass.: Harvard University Press.

Times/Mirror Center for the People and the Press. 1991. *The Pulse of Europe: A Survey of Political and Social Values and Attitudes.* Washington, D.C.: Times/Mirror Center.

Tocqueville, Alexis de. 1966. *Democracy in America.* New York: Knopf.

Toffler, Alvin. 1980. *The Third Wave*. New York: Morrow.

Topf, Richard. 1995a. Electoral participation. In H. Klingemann and D. Fuchs, eds., *Citizens and the State*. Oxford, U.K.: Oxford University Press.

———. 1995b. Beyond electoral participation. In H. Klingemann and D. Fuchs, eds., *Citizens and the State*. Oxford, U.K.: Oxford University Press.

Ühlinger, Hans-Martin. 1989. *Politische Partizipation in der Bundesrepublik*. Opladen: Westdeutscher Verlag.

Uhlaner, Carole. 1989. Rational turnout. *American Journal of Political Science* 33:390–422.

Uslaner, Eric, and Ronald Weber. 1983. Policy congruence and American state elites. *Journal of Politics* 45:186–93.

Van Deth, Jan, and Elinor Scarbrough, eds. 1995. *The Impact of Values*. New York: Oxford University Press.

Van Deth, Jan, et al., eds. 1999. *Social Capital and European Democracy*. New York: Routledge.

Verba, Sidney, and Norman Nie. 1972. *Participation in America*. New York: Harper & Row.

Verba, Sidney, Norman Nie, and J.O. Kim. 1971. *The Modes of Democratic Participation*. Beverly Hills, Calif.: Sage Professional Papers in Comparative Politics.

———. 1978. *Participation and Political Equality*. New York: Cambridge University Press.

Verba, Sidney, and Gary Orren. 1985. *Equality in America*. Cambridge, Mass.: Harvard University Press.

Verba, Sidney, Kay Schlozman, and Henry Brady. 1995. *Voice and Equality: Civic Voluntarism in American Politics*. Cambridge, Mass.: Harvard University Press.

Von Weizsäcker, Richard. 1992. *Richard von Weizsäcker im Gespräch mit Gunter Hofmann und Werner Perger*. Frankfurt: Eichborn.

Wahlke, John, et al. 1962. *The Legislative System*. New York: Wiley.

Wald, Kenneth. 1983. *Crosses on the Ballot*. Princeton, N.J.: Princeton University Press.

———. 1993. *Religion and Politics in America*. 2d ed. New York: St. Martin's Press.

Wallas, Graham. 1908. *Human Nature and Politics*. London: Constable.

Wattenberg, Martin. 1991. *The Rise of Candidate-centered Politics*. Cambridge, Mass.: Harvard University Press.

———. 1998. *The Decline of American Political Parties, 1952–96*. Cambridge, Mass.: Harvard University Press.

———. In press. *Where Have All the Voters Gone?*

Webb, Paul. 1996. Antipartisanship and anti-party sentiment in the UK: Correlates and constraints. *European Journal of Political Research* 29:365–82.

Weisberg, Herbert, and Janet Box-Steffensmeier, eds. 1999. *Reelection 1996: How Americans Voted*. New York: Chatham House.

Weisberg, Herbert, and Jerold Rusk. 1970. Dimensions of candidate evaluation. *American Political Science Review* 64:1167–1185.

Weisberg, Herbert, Jon Krosnick, and Bruce Bowen. 1996. *An Introduction to Survey Research, Polling, and Data Analysis*. 3d ed. Thousand Oaks, Calif.: Sage Publications.

Weissberg, Robert. 1978. Collective versus dyadic representation in Congress. *American Political Science Review* 72:535–47.

Wessels, Bernhard. 1993. Politische Repräsentation als Prozeß gesellschaftlich-parlamentarischer Kommunikation. In D. Herzog et al., *Parlament und Gesellschaft*. Opladen: Westdeutscher Verlag.

———. 1994. Gruppenbindung und rationale Faktoren als Determinaten der Wahlentscheidung in Ost- und West Deutschland. In H. Klingemann and M. Kaase, eds., *Wahlen und Wähler*. Opladen: Westdeutscher Verlag.

———. 1997. Organizing capacity of societies and modernity. In J. van Deth, ed., *Private Groups and Public Life*. London: Routledge.

———. 1999. System characteristics matter: Empirical evidence from ten representation studies. In W. Miller et al., *Policy Representation in Western Democracies*. Oxford, U.K.: Oxford University Press.

Westholm, Anders, and Richard Niemi. 1992. Political institutions and political socialization. *Comparative Political Studies* 25:25–41.

Westle, Bettina. 1992. Politische Partizipation. In O. Gabriel, ed., *Die EG-Staaten im Vergleich.* Opladen: Westdeutscher Verlag.

Westle, Bettina. 1999. *Kollektive Identität im vereinten Deutschland: Nation und Demokratie in der Wahrnehmung der Deutschen.* Opladen: Leske + Budrich.

Whitten, Guy, and Harvey Palmer. 1999. Cross-national analyses of economic voting. *Electoral Studies* 18:49–67.

Wilcox, Clyde. 1991. Support for gender equality in West Europe. *European Journal for Political Research* 20:127–47.

Wolfinger, Raymond, and Steven Rosenstone. 1980. *Who Votes?* New Haven, Conn.: Yale University Press.

World Bank. 2000. *World Development Report 2000.* Washington, D.C.: World Bank.

Wright, Erik. 1997. *Class Counts: Comparative Studies in Class Analysis.* Cambridge, U.K.: Cambridge University Press.

Wright, James. 1976. *The Dissent of the Governed.* New York: Academic Press.

Young, Ken. 1992. Class, race and opportunity. In R. Jowell et al., eds., *British Social Attitudes: The 9th Report.* Brookfield, Vt.: Dartmouth Publishing.

Zaller, John. 1992. *The Nature and Origins of Mass Opinion.* New York: Cambridge University Press.

Zelle, Carsten. 1995. Social dealignment vs. political frustration. *European Journal for Political Research* 27:319–45.

Ziegler, Harmon. 1993. *Political Parties in Industrial Democracy.* Itasca, Ill.: F.E. Peacock.

Zimmerman, Michael. 1990. Newspaper editors and the creation-evolution controversy. *Skeptical Inquirer* 14:182–95.

———. 1991. A survey of pseudoscientific sentiments of elected officials: A comparison of federal and state legislators. *Creation/Evolution* 29:26–45.

Zuckerman, Alan. 1982. New approaches to political cleavage. *Comparative Politics* 15:131–44.

Index

About the Author

RUSSELL J. DALTON is director of the Center for the Study of Democracy and professor of political science at the University of California, Irvine. His scholarly interests include comparative political behavior, political parties, social movements, and empirical democratic theory.

Dalton is author or coauthor of *Critical Masses: Citizens, Environmental Destruction, and Nuclear Weapons Production in Russia and the United States* (1999), *The Green Rainbow: Environmental Interest Groups in Western Europe* (1994), *Politics in Germany* (1993), and *Germany Transformed* (1981). His edited or coedited books include *European Politics Today* (2001), *Parties without Partisans* (2001), *Comparative Politics Today* (2000), *Germans Divided* (1996), *The New Germany Votes* (1993), *Challenging the Political Order* (1990), and *Electoral Change* (1984). He is now working on a comparative study of political trust and democratic institutional change in advanced industrial democracies.